D1391146

PSYCHOLOGICAL PROCESSES IN COGNITION AND PERSONALITY

THE SERIES IN CLINICAL AND COMMUNITY PSYCHOLOGY

CONSULTING EDITORS

Charles D. Spielberger and Irwin G. Sarason

Averill Patterns of Psychological Thought: Readings in Historical and Contemporary Texts
Bermant, Kelman, and Warwick The Ethics of Social Intervention
Brehm The Application of Social Psychology to Clinical Practice
Cattell and Dreger Handbook of Modern Personality Theory
Cohen and Ross Handbook of Clinical Psychobiology and Pathology, volume 1
Cohen and Ross Handbook of Clinical Psychobiology and Pathology, volume 2
Friedman and Katz The Psychology of Depression: Contemporary Theory and Research
Froehlich, Smith, Draguns, and Hentschel Psychological Processes in Cognition
     and Personality
Iscoe, Bloom, and Spielberger Community Psychology in Transition
Janisse Pupillometry: The Psychology of the Pupillary Response
Kissen From Group Dynamics to Group Psychoanalysis: Therapeutic Applications of Group
     Dynamic Understanding
Krohne and Laux Achievement, Stress, and Anxiety
London Personality: A New Look at Metatheories
Manschreck and Kleinman Renewal in Psychiatry: A Critical Rational Perspective
Morris Extraversion and Introversion: An Interactional Perspective
Olweus Aggression in the Schools: Bullies and Whipping Boys
Reitan and Davison Clinical Neuropsychology: Current Status and Applications
Smoll and Smith Psychological Perspectives in Youth Sports
Spielberger and Diaz-Guerrero Cross-Cultural Anxiety, volume 1
Spielberger and Diaz-Guerrero Cross-Cultural Anxiety, volume 2
Spielberger and Sarason Stress and Anxiety, volume 1
Sarason and Spielberger Stress and Anxiety, volume 2
Sarason and Spielberger Stress and Anxiety, volume 3
Spielberger and Sarason Stress and Anxiety, volume 4
Spielberger and Sarason Stress and Anxiety, volume 5
Sarason and Spielberger Stress and Anxiety, volume 6
Sarason and Spielberger Stress and Anxiety, volume 7
Spielberger, Sarason, and Milgram Stress and Anxiety, volume 8
Ulmer On the Development of a Token Economy Mental Hospital Treatment Program

IN PREPARATION

Burchfield Stress: Psychological and Physiological Interactions
Hobfoll Stress, Social Support, and Women
London The Modes and Morals of Psychotherapy, Second Edition
Rickel, Gerrard, and Iscoe Social and Psychological Problems of Women: Prevention and Crisis
     Intervention
Spielberger and Vagg The Assessment and Treatment of Test Anxiety
Spielberger, Sarason, and Defares Stress and Anxiety, volume 9
Spielberger and Sarason Stress and Anxiety: Sourcebook of Theory and Research, volume 10
Strelau, Farley, and Gale The Biological Bases of Personality and Behavior
Williams and Westermeyer Refugees and Mental Health

PSYCHOLOGICAL PROCESSES IN COGNITION AND PERSONALITY

Edited by
Werner D. Froehlich
University of Mainz, Federal Republic of Germany
Gudmund Smith
Lund University, Sweden
Juris G. Draguns
The Pennsylvania State University, University Park, USA
Uwe Hentschel
University of Mainz, Federal Republic of Germany

with a Foreword by
Herschel W. Leibowitz

HEMISPHERE PUBLISHING CORPORATION
Washington   New York   London

DISTRIBUTION OUTSIDE THE UNITED STATES
McGRAW-HILL INTERNATIONAL BOOK COMPANY
Auckland   Bogotá   Guatemala   Hamburg
Johannesburg   Lisbon   London   Madrid   Mexico
Montreal   New Delhi   Panama   Paris   San Juan
São Paulo   Singapore   Sydney   Tokyo   Toronto

PSYCHOLOGICAL PROCESSES IN COGNITION AND PERSONALITY

Copyright © 1984 by Hemisphere Publishing Corporation. All rights reserved. Printed in the United States of America. Except as permitted under the United States Copyright Act of 1976, no part of this publication may be reproduced or distributed in any form or by any means, or stored in a data base or retrieval system, without the prior written permission of the publisher.

1 2 3 4 5 6 7 8 9 0   E B E B   8 9 8 7 6 5 4 3

This book was set in Press Roman by Hemisphere Publishing Corporation. The editors were Valerie M. Ziobro, Brenda Munz Brienza, and Janet Mais; the production supervisor was Miriam Gonzalez; and the typesetter was Peggy M. Rote.
Edwards Brothers, Inc., was printer and binder.

Library of Congress Cataloging in Publication Data
Main entry under title:

Psychological processes in cognition and personality.

(The Series in clinical and community psychology)
Bibliography: p.
Includes index.
1. Personality and cognition—Addresses, essays,
lectures. I. Fröhlich, Werner D., date
II. Series. [DNLM: 1. Cognition—Congresses. 2. Concept
formation—Congresses. 3. Perception—Congresses.
4. Personality—Congresses. BF 311 P974]
BF698.9.C63P75   1983   150   82-21230
ISBN 0-89116-243-7
ISSN 0146-0846

Contents

V

MEANING ASSIGNMENT, RECOGNITION, AND THINKING
AS PROCESSES

VI

PSYCHOPHYSIOLOGY IN MICROGENESIS

VII

WHERE SHOULD MICROGENETIC RESEARCH
GO FROM HERE?

Foreword

This volume is a welcome and valuable contribution to the literature for a number of reasons. With the exception of Juris Draguns and his coworkers, activity within the framework of microgenesis has been almost exclusively European in origin, and the dialogue with the international community has been limited. The present volume makes available a comprehensive view of the many facets of this approach and identifies the extensive primary literature.

The opportunities for integration among diverse approaches increase as psychology matures. Historically, the subject matter of microgenesis has been of concern to investigators of sensory and perceptual phenomena, albeit at a different level of conceptualization. Identification of the contribution of the initial events in the visual system was the objective of the early career research of Nobel laureate H. K. Hartline. His classical studies of the primitive eye of the horseshoe crab have provided a valuable framework for understanding the sensory and perceptual events associated with activity during the first fraction of a second after light strikes the retina. Because the subject matter of microgenesis overlaps in time with these processes, our ultimate understanding of the role of sensory, perceptual, and cognitive variables must be based on consideration of all of these factors and mechanisms. The geographic and conceptual isolation of researchers in these fields has hindered the necessary interchange of ideas.

The potential for a fruitful multidisciplinary approach to the temporal development of perception is by no means limited to the initial events in the visual process. By using the powerful analytical tool of Fourier analysis, our understanding of the sensory basis for recognition of complex objects has been significantly advanced. With this technique, it is possible to specify the spatial frequency components of the visual stimulus subserving complex perceptual events and to relate these to psychophysical and neurological mechanisms. Identification and experimental manipulation of the optical components of complex stimuli provides a new and exciting procedure to analyze the mechanisms subserving object recognition as well as their temporal characteristics. The feasibility of meaningful investigations of individual differences in the ability to process such stimuli among normal observers as well as individuals with neurological deficits has been established.

Whether we prefer to identify our primary interest as sensory physiology, perception, information processing, cognition, or microgenesis, we are all interested in understanding the same phenomena. There is much that we can learn from one another. The present volume should serve to overcome one of the barriers to mutual effort and cooperation.

Herschel W. Leibowitz

Preface

Process-oriented approaches to psychology have proliferated over the last few decades. This book takes stock of the variety of conceptualizations and methods applied to the study of perceptual and cognitive processes as these unfold over time, the duration of which may sometimes not exceed even a fraction of one second.

The tradition of such investigation can be traced to the late 1920s, when Gemelli in Italy, Sander in Germany, and Werner in Germany and the United States published investigations of the perceptual process under the names of *microgenesis* and *Aktualgenese.* These studies were devoted to processes of percept formation in various contexts. More recently, in Sweden and Norway, these approaches were continued under the name of *percept-genetic approaches to personality.* For a long time, however, these approaches remained on the fringes of conceptual and empirical effort in the mainstream of modern psychology. The recent upsurge of interest in information processing holds promise of changing this situation.

With this hope in mind, the contributions of 19 authors have been brought together. They provide in our view a realistic and manifold cross section in content and format of currently pursued process-oriented research, not only in perception and cognition, but in a number of domains of psychology. Some of the investigators are steeped in the traditions of microgenetic investigation at its conceptual and methodological sources; others have found their way to this topic from a variety of practical concerns or proceeding from a comprehensive theoretical formulation. The aim of some writers is, therefore, the integration of perceptual responses unfolding over time with the indicators and formulations of psychophysiology. Others have applied themselves to the task of relating such responses to personality, of finding clues in them of incipient or actual personality disturbance, and of detecting commonalities between such response sequences and more global domains of individual functioning. Points of contact with, and limitations of, information theory in relation to these temporal phenomena have been established, and new tailor-made approaches have been sought to provide statistical methods for process analyses applied to the phenomena in question.

The contributors to this volume come from nine countries and represent a variety of specializations in psychology: general experimental, physiological, personality, developmental, and clinical. They were brought together under the auspices of Stiftung Volkswagenwerk at a conference at the University of Mainz (Federal Republic of Germany) in June 1977. This meeting was the first international conference concerned with the development of percepts and concepts over time. The contributions assembled in this volume represent the expanded and revised versions of their papers. The conference was made possible by a grant from the Volkswagenstiftung (Volkswagen Foundation). We, the editors, express our sincere appreciation for this generous support and for the support of the Friends of the University of Mainz (Freunde der Universität Mainz), which was used for re-typing of the revised chapter manuscripts. The participation of the third editor (J.G.D.) in the planning of this Conference was facilitated by a fellowship from the German Academic Exchange Service (Deutscher Akademischer Austauschdienst); this support is gratefully acknowledged.

It is hoped that this book will be useful as an introduction to current work in this area and that it may contribute toward integration of all of these approaches into the mainstream of the international psychology of the late 20th century.

Werner D. Froehlich
Gudmund Smith
Juris G. Draguns
Uwe Hentschel

I

AIMS AND METHODS OF PROCESS–RELATED APPROACHES

1

Microgenesis by Any Other Name . . .

Juris G. Draguns
The Pennsylvania State University,
University Park, Pennsylvania, USA

Contemporary observers of microgenetic research are confronted with a paradox. On the one hand, there are a limited number of research centers, notably at the universities of Lund, Mainz, and Oslo, at which microgenesis is being systematically and continuously investigated, in addition to a great many more episodic and scattered efforts taking place elsewhere.[1] On the other hand, there has been a general flowering of process-oriented research related to perception, cognition, motivation, and personality. The growth of such research has been variously sparked by the increased interest in mediational activity, the rising prominence of information processing as a field of investigation, the ever greater acceptance of cognitive conceptualizations in psychology, and the general shift in emphasis from the products to the processes of behavior. While differing in their conceptual antecedents and in their theoretical and empirical objectives, these approaches (e.g., Erdelyi, 1974; Haber, 1969; Kreitler & Kreitler, 1972, 1976) are broadly concerned with events that transpire between the presentation of a stimulus and the formation of a stabilized response to it and are, as such, germane to microgenesis in the classical sense of the term (Sander, 1928).

My objective in this chapter is to relate to microgenesis the methods and results of a host of process-oriented investigators, some of whom may not have heard of the word and may not care to be identified with the concept. The result of this venture may be integration of microgenesis into the mainstream of the psychological literature, a development whose time has come.

Lest important distinctions be blurred, microgenesis has, first of all, to be distinguished from a variety of other related process-oriented approaches. What

---

[1] A considerable amount of microgenetic research has been conducted over several decades in the Soviet Union. It goes back to the pioneering efforts of Lange (1892), who formulated a "law of perception" according to which all percepts traverse a series of qualitatively different and ever more definite stages of consciousness. The more recent work extends over a variety of basic and applied areas. This is not the place to provide a systematic review of this literature. A number of Soviet studies are included in the text of the chapter as they relate to specific points raised. The author is greatly indebted to Dr. Talis Bachmann of the Tartu State University Psychology Department for calling his attention to this research and for making many of these studies available to him.

are the essential features of microgenesis? Contrary to what the term implies,[2] the scope of microgenesis need not be restricted to fleeting and subtle events that unfold over brief periods of time. The essential hallmark of microgenesis is a sequence of directly observable events between the presentation of a stimulus and the formation of a stable response (Flavell & Draguns, 1957; Froehlich, 1964; Graumann, 1959b; Sander, 1928). To elaborate, microgenesis is a series of experiences that, as the accumulated empirical research shows, proceed discontinuously and in a succession of readily discernible stages. As such, it stands in contrast to other developmental progressions, notably ontogenesis and phylogenesis, that permit the influence of developmental processes over days, months, years, decades, centuries, or millennia but do not allow one to capture development in process. Similarly, microgenesis differs from a variety of information-processing (Haber, 1969) and cognitive (Neisser, 1967) approaches that are concerned with the process of perception or cognition but conceptualize it in terms of a variety of mediational activities. These activities can lend themselves to a variety of explanatory, predictive, and model-building uses; yet they are distinct from the observable phenomena that occur in microgenesis.

What is fundamental to microgenesis is a process of search that is triggered by the discrepancy between the information inherent in the stimulus and the activity, task, or solution demanded of the observer. Microgenesis, then, is necessarily a heuristic activity (Linschoten, 1959) that is triggered by the demand or challenge of going beyond the information given (Bruner, 1957) or of completing the incomplete (Arnheim, 1969). These operations typically require time and provide the opportunity for observing the alternation of stages in the formation of a percept, the attainment of a solution, or the development of a stabilized, automatized response. Thus microgenesis cuts across the domains of functioning into which psychology is so neatly divided—perception, cognition, motivation, and the rest—and may last from seconds to days, or longer, provided that it unfolds in observable time.

Much of the empirical and conceptual effort in the past was directed toward identifying parallels between microgenetic and other developmental sequences, especially ontogenesis. This chapter is written with the objective of sparking and stimulating a comparable research undertaking toward relating microgenetic and other process-related approaches that pertain roughly to the same time spans but differ in their observational versus inferential quality. At the end of the trail, one could envisage the integration of these different, yet complementary, ways of investigating psychological processes.

That this is not an idle dream is attested by Erdelyi's (1947) novel integration of microgenetic, perceptual-defense, and information-processing findings in a reformulation of response processes to anxiety-arousing and threatening, yet not optimally distinct, stimuli. On a more general scale, the Estonian psychologist Bachmann (1977) explicitly drew on microgenetic data and formulations in arriving at a model of the interacting attentional, mnemonic, informational, and other determinants of a perceptual act. Of particular interest, from the micro-

---

[2] It is evident by this time that *microgenesis* as a term has misleading connotations, as pointed out by Graumann (1959b); because it has sunk roots in English-language usage, however, it is now difficult to replace. In this chapter, it is used as a semantic equivalent of *Aktualgenese* in German and does not imply the adoption of a specific theoretical model or of an explicit stand on the issue of macro–micro correspondence.

genetic point of view, is the overlapping nature of sensory analysis, sensory-objective synthesis, concrete-image formation, and abstract image in Bachmann's model of perception over time.

APPROACHES TO THE STUDY OF MICROGENESIS

To facilitate such integration, it may be useful to introduce and categorize the major approaches to the study of microgenesis. Although a multitude of methods for the study of microgenesis have been developed (see Böhm, 1959; Flavell & Draguns, 1957; Graumann, 1959b for reviews), they fall roughly into three broad categories. The first of these, on which the bulk of explicitly microgenetic research, both classical and modern, is based, involves progressions of stimuli from maximal or pronounced information deprivation to the presentation of adequate or optimal amounts of information for the response or decision at hand. To this end, the normally continuous process of microgenesis is fractionated into a limited number of discrete presentations of gradually increasing information input. Presentation of a stimulus tachistoscopically, at gradually increasing exposures, is probably the most prominent technique of this type, although a host of others have been developed. Their common denominator is the progressive introduction of information that, in the optimal case of everyday confrontation with objects of our experience, is instantaneously available.

Related to this format, yet different from it, is the approach of facilitating an observable microgenetic progression by means of the repeated presentation of the same stimulus; the subject attains recognition here not by dint of increasing information inputs but by extracting ever more information from the suboptimally clear or intense stimuli. This mode of stimulus presentation is more closely associated in the literature with the topic of perceptual learning (e.g., Dodwell, 1971; Hershenson & Haber, 1965; Sperling, 1960) than with microgenesis. It confronts the experimenter with the problem of establishing a subtle imbalance between the information given and the task at hand. If the gap between them is too wide, no progress toward recognition occurs. If it is too narrow, recognition is instantaneous, and the opportunity for observing microgenesis is lost.

The last approach depends on the naturalistic observation of perceptual or cognitive acts in process. It is closest to the phenomenon of microgenesis as it occurs in a variety of real-life situations, yet it is the approach that poses the greatest difficulties of operationalization. The problem is one of capturing our perceptual and cognitive processes as we are confronted with a variety of sensorily impoverished, cognitively complex, or intellectually taxing stimuli. This problem is but a special case of making our covert operations overt, of externalizing our internal processes. Even if the historically important taboos against introspection are dropped, and there are signs that this is indeed happening (see Mahoney, 1974; Radford, 1974), two problems remain: (a) verbal report and subjective experience do not correspond, and (b) putting one's thoughts into words affects the progress of the task at hand in a variety of ways. These difficulties are exacerbated as these tasks become cognitively more challenging, personally more meaningful, and affectively more involving.

The scope of situations to which the concept of microgenesis can be legitimately applied is wide but not unlimited. Its outside edge is reached as we come to developmental progressions that unfold beyond one specific span of experienced time. Microgenesis, to hark back to the term by which it is known in German, is *actual genesis*—a progression that is observable from start to finish. Perhaps we need an additional term, not yet invented, for other temporally extended and segmented progressions that are not ontogenetic yet transcend the confines of a discrete and observable time span. Various slow processes of self-realization and self-knowledge, spontaneous or facilitated by psychotherapy or psychoanalysis, come to mind in this connection.

It is obvious that there is a vast range of varied microgenetic phenomena. There are also characteristic courses microgenesis can take and certain techniques for triggering it. In broadest terms, microgenesis can begin with a whole or a part. In the former case, an entire stimulus is presented, however impoverished, distorted, or obstructed it may be. In the latter instance, fragments are shown in an ever-increasing number. Werner's (1948, 1956, 1957) application of the orthogenetic principle to microgenesis is primarily derived from observations of the first variety; as in other developmental sequences, the stages of diffusion and fragmentation are traversed, only to give way to integration. By contrast, Sander (1928) proposed another succession of stages from simple reproduction of discrete detail, through confusion upon accumulation of discrepant and incongruous detail, to the formation of a preliminary gestalt and, finally, of a stabilized and complete image. These two formulations are different but not necessarily incompatible; they rest in two distinct ways of gradually introducing the stimulus.

Yet, the problem is more complicated than that. Recent microgenetic research (e.g., Lastowski, 1976; Lesswing, 1973) highlights the difficulty of eliciting diffuse whole responses at the beginning of microgenesis, even by the classical techniques of tachistoscopically presenting the complete stimulus. Individual differences come into play, perhaps akin to the cognitive style of field dependence–field independence, although empirical attempts to link established measures of this variable with characteristic modes of microgenetic progression have, so far, failed to yield conclusive results (e.g., Schiller, 1970). Apart from such enduring stylistic and other personality variables, situationally determined sets, explicitly communicated through experimental instructions or implicitly assumed by the subject, undoubtedly come into play (see Marks, 1967, 1968, for demonstrations of such effects on other aspects of microgenesis). Extricating these three strands of stimulus, person, and task characteristics as they steer the course of microgenesis toward the apprehension of the whole or the accumulation of detail remains an important task for future microgenetic research. Pending the resolution of this problem, we are faced with three types of microgenesis, each of them potentially divisible into two successions of different stages.

CONVERGENCES WITH OTHER DOMAINS OF PSYCHOLOGY

Scanning contemporary and recent approaches to psychology reveals many that are related to these three process-oriented approaches; of particular interest are studies undertaken outside of the specific domain of microgenesis. Global acts of readaptation provide maximal contrast with the traditional microgenetic approaches. Such macroscopic acts can be observed in the traditional visual inversion experiments that produce temporary disorientation and gradual adaptation to the new version of the visual world. The process of this transformation is well worth studying. Cegalis (1971) in his doctoral dissertation has brought the lens-inversion method into direct contact with microgenesis as experienced in more miniature situations and has continued research along these lines (Cegalis, 1973; Cegalis & Leen, 1977; Cegalis & Murdza, 1976; Cegalis & Young, 1974). The parallels between microgenesis and this adapting to what is first experienced as distortion and incongruity and ends up being accepted as the "natural order of things" may potentially be uncovered.

An even more dramatic adaptive challenge is associated with the postoperative recovery of sight and the gradual process of learning to make sense of and realistically apprehend a variety of stimuli. What in a normal adult results in an experience of instantaneous identification of stimuli engenders a laborious, protracted search in the newly sighted. In the famous monograph by von Senden (1960), the features of these microgenetic sequences are faintly discernible. It is not easy to derive general conclusions from a collection of case reports spanning many centuries and originating in a variety of countries. Even though von Senden's outspokenly empiricist conclusions from this compilation of evidence have been challenged (see Banissoni & Ponzo, 1968), it is evident that a newly sighted person emerges from blindness to a phenomenal world of confusion, conflict, misperception, and illusion, a world in which identification and recognition are achieved, but only by dint of effort and time.

A special and fascinating instance of real-life microgenesis is provided in a situation characterized not by deficit but by talent. Artistic and scientific creation requires time, is marked by false starts and abrupt changes in direction, is accompanied by emotional states from euphoria to dejection, and is potentially divisible into stages and phases. It is remarkable that, for all the upsurge of research in creativity, the process aspect of artistic and scientific production remains to this day neglected. Csikszentmihalyi and Getzels (1971) have had the rare opportunity of conducting a systematic study while "looking over the shoulders" of artists in the actual process of artistic creation; they distinguished several types of this observable sequence and related them to characteristics of the artists and of their products. Vicariously, Arnheim (1962) addressed himself to the same task within the confines of a single major artistic creation; he had access to Picasso's sketches and notebooks for the definitive version of Guernica. On the basis of these materials, he reconstructed the genesis of this masterpiece. It is interesting that Arnheim made explicit use of microgenetic literature in this task. The old collection of reconstructions of instances of scientific and mathematical creativity by Hadamard (1945) contains references to different stages of creative process, and some of their categorizations are not unlike the P phases observed in a variety of microgenetic experiments by the University of Lund investigators (Kragh & Smith, 1970). Cooperation between scientific and artistic creators and the investigators of this creation in process would seem a fruitful avenue of study worthy of systematic and vigorous pursuit.

But whereas only few people contribute innovatively or productively to science or the arts, all of us are involved in making unique and novel decisions in the course of our lives. These are decisions for which we have no precedent and that often involve emotional participation, vacillation, provisional commitment akin to *Vorgestalten* (Flavell & Draguns, 1957; Sander, 1928/1962), and marked reduction in a subjective sense of imbalance and tension once the judgment has been arrived at and the decision made. The practitioners of the new discipline of biographical psychology on both sides of the Atlantic have begun to contribute raw material of relevance to the microgenesis of personal decision making. The psychologist who has gone furthest in this quest is Thomae, who has both provided the results of a naturalistic exploratory study of arriving at the most difficult decisions in his subjects' lives on the basis of their retrospective accounts (Thomae, 1960) and introduced a model of personal conflict resolution and decision making (Thomae, 1974).

Going beyond individual performance, practitioners of group psychotherapy and observers of the group process (Bion, 1959; Tuckerman, 1965) have for a long time known about the gradual evolution of cognitive, affective, and interpersonal aspects of group activity. Tucker (1973), in a systematic study of group process, was struck by the similarities of the phases of these progressions to Werner's (1948) formulation of the orthogenetic principle. Specifically, he discerned a general trend from the global and diffuse character of early intragroup interaction to both greater differentiation and greater integration at the more advanced stages of the group process. These parallels between sociogenesis and microgenesis open the possibility of further study of transformations formally akin to those experienced in the classical microgenetic demonstrations in group problem solving and group decision making. Microgenesis, then, is a game that two or more people can play!

These extensions of microgenesis into a more global macroscopic arena have brought with them several advantages as well as a number of unresolved problems. For one advantage, they open the possibility of establishing formal similarities among diverse experiences extended in time regardless of their specific nature. For another, the study of these global, personal, and affectively involving progressions allows the investigation of the extent of individually characteristic styles of extracting information, resolving uncertainty, and arriving at cognitive and perceptual judgments in the presence of incomplete stimulus inputs. In this connection, it is well worth noting that, despite the noteworthy achievements of the Lund research group (Kragh & Smith, 1970; Smith & Danielsson, 1977) and certain successes in relating individually characteristic microgenetic features to anxiety (Froehlich, 1964), there have been disappointments (e.g., Lastowski, 1976; Schiller, 1970) in attempting to link microgenetic variables with global and conventional personality characteristics, such as temperament and cognitive style. On the basis of the inconclusive results obtained, a different research strategy may be indicated. Mischel's (1973, 1977) revised specificity doctrine puts a premium on a search for situations of maximal similarity in generalizing from experimental and assessment settings to behavior in real-life milieus. In microgenesis, such an approach would link some of the classical experimental techniques involving metacontrast and tachistoscopic presentation with some of the more global and naturalistic progressions already described here. Is there any discernible parallel between the style of decision making that occurs in the face of a rapidly flashed picture and that used in the course of weighing complex and ambiguous information preparatory to a far-reaching personal and subjective commitment? One of the reasons for the success of the Lund investigators' program of studies (Kragh & Smith, 1970) would seem to be the closeness in content between the experimental measures of defense employed and the criterion measures of defensive behavior outside the laboratory.

But while opportunities for extending microgenesis beyond the confines of the laboratory are tempting, the systematic study of personal decision making, global readaptation, and apprehension of meaningful complexity and novelty brings with it a number of challenging issues. The occurrence of these kinds of sequences is haphazard and unpredictable; it remains difficult to capture them systematically other than through recall and reconstruction, which, inevitably, bring distortion with them. Of course there is the expedient of trying to come up with artificial, experimental replicas of these real-life events, but the success of such simulation hinges both on the experimenters' ability to recreate lifelike and ego-involving situations and on the subjects' inclination toward, and skill in, role playing.

The research by Rimoldi (1976) and his associates, conducted over several decades in Chicago and Buenos Aires, represents a response to some of these challenges. Going beyond the naturalistic observation of problem solving as it occurs, Rimoldi devised a number of methods for objective and systematic study directed toward the solution of a variety of experimental and practical problems. In all of these methods, emphasis is placed on ascertaining the nature and sequence of steps taken by the problem solver before arriving at the final answer. This systematic approach to the study of cognition in process was developed independently, without reference to the results and methods of microgenetic investigation. Yet, the empirical study of problem-solving strategies, tactics, and styles by Rimoldi and others has produced some findings that converge with results of microgenetic research. In particular, Rimoldi documented increased levels of emotional participation in the presolution phases of problem-solving activity and indicated relationships between styles of problem solving and personality characteristics. Problem solving, then, is an activity on which a person's experiences and resources are focused in a heightened state of organismic participation.

A more modest compromise toward the study of microgenesis beyond the confines of the traditional experiment is the investigation of perception of events, a topic that, according to Gibson (1969), remains neglected in the mainstream of experimental psychology. In contrast to the usual laboratory stimuli, events involve information from several sense modalities and are complex. In the classical period of microgenetic research, Hausmann (1935) and Mörschner (1940) were able to demonstrate the occurrence of microgenetic progressions in the perception of complex object configurations and of objects in space—without the expedient of any kind of artificially induced stimulus impoverishment. These tasks require time and go through a succession of stages. Somewhat related results have been obtained in observing the apprehension of objects by means of a sense modality that, in most people, remains unpracticed and little used as an avenue for independent acquisition of knowledge about the external world—that of touch (Hippius, 1934). Exploration of an object may undergo extension in time as a person is confronted, not only with too little, but with too much information to assimilate. This state of affairs occurs at some point in the course of microgenesis as the several impressions, hypotheses, and leads, whether fragmentary or holistic, come to be mutually exclusive and incompatible. This is when, in Sander's (1928) terminology, the stage of confusion comes about; various investigators of microgenesis are in agreement that the process is riddled with apparent incongruities, discontinuities, and a degree of affective participation that appears disproportionate to the relatively innocuous character of the task at hand. Several investigators have gone beyond the description of the clash of hypotheses and expectancies that "naturally" occurs in microgenesis. Froehlich (1964) investigated the effect of perceptual incongruity (i.e., the imposition upon fairly conventional pictures of features surprising and unusual in content) on the experience of microgenesis; Graumann (1959a) contributed the humorous demonstration of what happens when a subject's expectation of hearing a polished or at least competently written poem is disappointed and gives way to the experience of a formally and substantively inferior poetic product. Pinillos and Brengelmann (1953), in the early phases of developing their picture-recognition test, discovered that pictures unusual or moderately incongruous in content, perspective, arrangement, or composition were particularly useful for diagnostic purposes. Microgenesis, then, is fostered by the amodal characteristic of incongruity as well as by the related characteristics of novelty and complexity—features that loom large in Berlyne's (1960) list of factors that provoke curiosity. Consequently, microgenesis is set off by characteristics that foster any kind of heuristic activity.

As such, microgenesis is an adaptive act that involves the various resources of the person. Traditionally, it has been studied on the basis of the person's verbal report, which, however, provides glimpses into only one of the several response systems involved. The theoretical stance of the pioneers of microgenetic investigation (Sander, 1928; Werner, 1948) helped them conceive of these progressions as instances of a self-fueled and self-propelled development with a specific direction and a predetermined outcome. By the same token, their theoretical perspective caused them to underplay the role of experience and learning in these microgenetic experiences. That learning plays an important role in microgenesis is demonstrated by the observation of a great many microgenetic investigators that the presentation of a stimulus sequence can be effectively accomplished one time per subject. Microgenetic studies lend themselves poorly to the establishment of test-retest reliability! More subtly, the subject learns the features of specific subjects presented and also learns how to learn—by establishing more efficient and effective strategies of information extraction. If the subject learns, or attempts to, then the question arises, What impels him or her to learn? Why does the person not sit passively and wait for the termination of the progression of the series from ambiguity to clarity, as indeed a few deviant subjects, mostly burdened by serious psychopathology, in fact do?[3] The behavior of obsessive compulsives investigated by Kragh (1955) comes to mind in this connection. Cooperation and the desire to comply with and please the experimenter no doubt play a part. More fundamentally, however, I am inclined to agree with Hunt (1963) and Jones (1966) that information deprivation is inherently an aversive state to experience and that subjects are motivated to put an end to it as best they can. This has been explicitly demonstrated by Nicki (1970) with traditional operant methods; subjects indicated their preference by pressing keys more frequently for clear pictures after exposure to blurred versions of the same stimuli. Imposing meaning on an object of experience, labeling it, coming up with a solution, illusory or real, all of these behaviors carry their own reward by reducing—at least momentarily or fleetingly—the burden of uncertainty.

Motivational factors have been underemphasized in traditional microgenetic investigation. Their incorporation into microgenetic research projects requires the development of new indicators to supplement and to amplify the traditional verbal descriptive response. The use of psychophysiological indicators of arousal

[3] A more extensive treatment of this topic is found in Draguns (1981).

(Froehlich, 1978; Froehlich & Laux, 1969), EEG measures (Beyn, Volkov, & Zhirmunskaya, 1968; Beyn, Zhirmunskaya, & Volkov, 1967; Zhirmunskaya & Beyn, 1974), and semantic differential scales (Black, 1975; Draguns, 1967) has yielded a number of converging findings, all pointing to an emotionally aroused experience in the early stages of confrontation with a faint, indistinct, or incomplete stimulus, even though some ambiguity remains concerning some aspects of the valence of unclear stimuli (cf. Black, 1975; Draguns, 1967).

As Poulsen (1976) has pointed out, perception has the dual character of action and experience. Traditional microgenetic research has emphasized the experiential, verbally reportable aspect of perception. The application of a variety of activity indicators, as illustrated in some of the studies just summarized, may help redress this imbalance. A special place among such indicators of microgenetic activity is occupied by eye movements (Mackworth & Bruner, 1970), which might be regarded as the external, muscular measures of microgenesis. Western as well as Soviet studies (Zinchenko, 1969; Zinchenko, Chi-Tsin, & Tarakanov, 1963) document age trends in deployment of eye movements as well as differences associated with the content, arousal value, and amount of information in the stimulus. Eye movements would seem to provide an index of the efficiency of visual operations and, as such, are capable of differentiating productive and unproductive information extractors. Kolada (1973), for example, demonstrated, outside of the microgenetic paradigm, that schizophrenics rely more on gross head movements, as opposed to subtler eye movements, in responding to simple stimuli.

From the use of nonverbal indicators as additional avenues of information, it is but a step to relying on them as the primary source of data about microgenesis. Research on subliminal perception (Dixon, 1971), perceptual defense, and microgenesis, as integrated in the recent theoretical formulation by Erdelyi (1974), suggests that (a) we respond to stimuli with a variety of verbal and nonverbal systems, and (b) the responses of these systems are not fully synchronized, in time or otherwise. Even in the supraliminal, verbally reportable segment of contact with the stimulus, there may be two distinct response systems, those of recognition and differentiation (Francès, 1962). Somewhat similarly, Kaswan (1958) and Kaswan and Young (1963), in the course of their microgenetic studies, identified the two response systems of detection and discrimination, the former concerned with the presence or absence of stimuli, the latter geared to relating stimuli to each other. Russian psychologists Varskii and Guzeva (1962) identified four thresholds in the course of microgenesis: (a) the appearance of flickering form, (b) the detection of angular features, (c) generally adequate perception of form, and (d) optimal perception of the figure and all its features. The lack of synchrony between various modes of response in the course of the microgenetic sequence is illustrated in another Russian study by Petrenko and Vasilenko (1977). These investigators found that the shift in semantic differential ratings preceded the recognition of the object to which these ratings corresponded. Connotative meaning thus was ahead of denotative meaning.

The experience of microgenesis may be thought of as spanning the distance between these various points of reference, or thresholds of reactivity. Extending this reasoning, subliminal perception may be conceived of as a downward extension of the traditional span of microgenesis and perceptual defense. In this segment of our experience, we are mute, yet responsive; our organisms communicate what we are as yet unable or unwilling to put into words. Lieberman (1974) made a preliminary attempt to apply this rationale in a combined study of subliminal and supraliminal perception of verbal stimuli, in an explicit attempt to draw together subliminal perception, microgenesis, and perceptual defense and to integrate them within a psychoanalytic explanatory framework. His pattern of results is complex and cannot readily be summarized here. Suffice it to say that links emerged between characterological orientations toward aggression and passivity, as established on the Holtzman Inkblot Test, and the response to stimuli at or below the thresholds of visibility; defensive style, on the other hand, was best expressed in the supraliminal segment of stimulus presentation. This complicated and not-quite-conclusive study may point the way toward further integration of several independently pursued traditions of perceptual research.

There remains the question of the adaptive significance of microgenesis, which subsumes individual differences in the process, and of their personality-related and psychopathological correlates. Taking a bird's-eye view of this area, I would venture to say that differences in the speed and efficiency of microgenetic operations have been rather solidly established and that this speed and efficiency has repeatedly been shown to increase with age through childhood and adolescence (Costa Molinari, Rom Font, Malga Montserrat, & Penzo, 1964; Draguns & Multari, 1961; Droz-Georget, 1965; Mackworth & Bruner, 1970; Potter, 1966; Zucchi, 1960) and to decrease with major psychopathology, especially within the range of psychosis (Alvarez Villar & Narros Martin, 1958; Brengelmann, 1953; Cashdan, 1966; Draguns, 1961, 1963; Ebner & Ritzler, 1969; Hauss, 1970). But the obverse question, on the variables associated with optimally efficient information extraction in microgenesis, remains unanswered. Partial leads toward such an answer are provided in the research by Westcott (1967), who concerned himself with intuition, operationally defined, among other things, on the basis of the early and veridical recognition of weak or ambiguous stimuli.

Beyond these findings, we have the results of the studies at Lund and Oslo, extending over more than two decades, that point to parallels between defenses in front of a rapidly flashed picture on the screen and in the face of real-life threatening stimuli (Kragh & Smith, 1970). Similar correspondences have been established by the Scandinavian investigators between the time course of responding to conflictual stimulus inputs (e.g., on the Stroop color-word test) and the time course of, generally, expanding and managing effort in response to challenging tasks. But the efforts to link events during microgenesis with more global personality attributes have, as I have pointed out, not been uniformly or consistently successful. The trouble lies, I suspect, with the imperfect measures used and also with the complexities of personality organization that allow for a greater degree of specificity in behaving at a time and place than has until recently been realized.

CAUTIONS

So far, my general purpose in this chapter has been expansionist, in attempting to bring under the umbrella of microgenesis a variety of process-oriented approaches. To heighten incongruity, I would like at this late stage to urge caution and to counsel restraint against another kind of expansion of microgenesis: that is, in the direction of a general theoretical model applicable to events that phenomenally occur at a moment in time. Two principles are repeatedly voiced yet appear questionable: (a) that every perceptual and cognitive act is subject to microgenesis and (b) that a variety of perceptual and cognitive deficits can be explained on the basis of arrests at an early, or at least other-than-final, stage of microgenesis. The first assertion is unprovable for the myriad immediately available conceptual and perceptual responses emitted by human beings. I accept the formulation of the Lund group (Kragh & Smith, 1970) that the temporally extended, nonautomatized response is ontogenetically primary and that the host of responses that we momentarily emit come about through practice and learning in an increasingly habituated and familiar environment.

The second statement has given rise to a variety of thought-provoking formulations (Arieti, 1962; Kantor & Herron, 1965; see Flavell & Draguns, 1957, for earlier ones) pointing to similarities and parallels between the productions of schizophrenics, aphasics, and other functionally or organically incapacitated groups on the one hand and the responses during microgenesis by psychiatrically unimpaired and normal people on the other. But similarity is often in the eye of the beholder and is, in any case, something other than identity. While Werner's (1948, 1956) statements on the macro–micro correspondence (cf. Graumann, 1959b; Linschoten, 1959) may have merit, they remain to be restricted and operationalized so that such similarities can be predicted and not inferred post hoc. It is not to be denied that the cognitive state of some, though not all, psychotic patients may contribute another source of stimulus impoverishment or information deprivation. To borrow the title of one of Ingmar Bergman's films—which Bergman borrowed from the Gospel—such a patient sees the world "through a glass darkly." The result of it is perceptual and cognitive inefficiency, difficulty of concept attainment, and, occasionally, perseveration at a stage that normal people may experience fleetingly while confronting the stimulation. Moreover, this state of affairs does not extend to all the instances of impaired perceptual and cognitive functioning. All told, the fixation principle would appear to have only limited explanatory utility, a point on which I am in agreement with a searching and thorough critic of this formulation (deKoningh, 1967).

I have arrived at the end of the trail. To summarize: The number of explicitly microgenetic investigations in a variety of areas is greatly exceeded by the number of studies of perceptual, cognitive, motivational, and personal processes. The results of this work are, despite differences in theoretical orientation and research tradition, more often convergent than contradictory and are typically compatible. Microgenesis may serve, then, as the point of reference for the investigation of a variety of phenomena, all of which require an extended search in time. It is fruitful and meaningful to look for commonalities in all of these explorations and searches regardless of domain and modality. It is premature, however, to invoke microgenesis as an explanatory principle for deviations, distortions, and deficits of response in the absence of an observable temporal progression.

REFERENCES

Alvarez Villar, A., & Narros Martin, G. La percepción visual en las diversas entidades nosológicas psiquiátricas. *Revista de Psicología General y Aplicada*, 1958, *13*, 739–766.

Arieti, S. The microgeny of thought and perception. *Archives of General Psychiatry*, 1962, *6*, 454–468.

Arnheim, R. *Picasso's Guernica: The genesis of a painting*. Berkeley and Los Angeles: University of California Press, 1962.

Arnheim, R. *Visual thinking*. London: Faber & Faber, 1969.

Bachmann, T. Sovremennaya psikhofizika, fenomenogiya eksperimenta i pererabotka zritel'noi informatsii (Contemporary psychophysics, phenomenology of the experiment, and visual information processing). *Tartu Riikliku Ülikooli Toimetised, 1977, 429,* 11–33.

Banissoni, M., & Ponzo, E. Percezione strutturata e trasposizione di forme nelle prime experienze visive di tre cieche della nascità operate di osteo-odonto-cheratoprotesi di Strampelli. *Rivista di Psicologia, 1968, 62,* 515–535.

Berlyne, D. E. *Conflict, arousal, curiosity.* New York: McGraw-Hill, 1960.

Beyn, E. S., Volkov, V. N., & Zhirmunskaya, E. A. Elektrofiziologicheskiye issledovaniya v protsesse uznavaniya predmetnikh izobrazhenii pri ikh pred'yavlenii (Electrophysiological investigations of the process of recognizing images of objects in the course of their presentation). *Voprosy Psikhologii,* 1968, No. 3, pp. 36–46.

Beyn, E. S., Zhirmunskaya, E. A., & Volkov, V. N. Electroencephalographic investigations in the process of recognizing images of objects during their tachistoscopic presentation: I. *Neuropsychologia, 1967, 5,* 203–217.

Bion, W. R. *Experiences in groups.* New York: Basic Books, 1959.

Black, H. K. Semantic differential ratings of impoverished stimuli: A replication. *Bulletin of the Psychonomic Society, 1975, 5,* 81–83.

Böhm, W. Methodische Möglichkeiten der experimentellen Wahrnehmungserschwerung bei der auditiven Aktualgenese. *Zeitschrift für experimentelle und angewandte Psychologie, 1959, 1,* 422–452.

Brengelmann, J. C. Der visuelle Objekterkennungstest. *Zeitschrift für experimentelle und angewandte Psychologie, 1953, 6,* 422–452.

Bruner, J. S. Going beyond the information given. In J. S. Bruner, E. Brunswik, L. Festinger, F. Heider, K. F. Münzinger, C. E. Osgood, & D. Rapaport, *Contemporary approaches to cognition.* New York: Ronald, 1957.

Cashdan, S. Delusional thinking and the induction process in schizophrenia. *Journal of Consulting Psychology, 1966, 30,* 207–212.

Cegalis, J. A. *Perceptual adaptation: An analysis of conflict.* Unpublished doctoral dissertation, Pennsylvania State University, 1971.

Cegalis, J. A. Prism distortion and accommodative change. *Perception and Psychophysics, 1973, 13,* 494–498.

Cegalis, J. A., & Leen, D. Individual differences in responses to induced perceptual conflict. *Perceptual and Motor Skills, 1977, 44,* 991–998.

Cegalis, J. A., & Murdza, S. Changes of auditory work discrimination induced by inversion of the visual field. *Journal of Abnormal Psychology, 1976, 85,* 318–323.

Cegalis, J. A., & Young, R. The effect of inversion-induced conflict on field-dependence. *Journal of Abnormal Psychology, 1974, 83,* 373–379.

Costa Molinari, J. M., Rom Font, J., Malga Montserrat, A., & Penzo, W. Tipificación de nuestra técnica taquistoscópica. *Revista de Psicología General y Aplicada, 1964, 19,* 577–585.

Csikszentmihalyi, M., & Getzels, J. W. Discovery-oriented behavior and the originality of creative products: A study with artists. *Journal of Personality and Social Psychology, 1971, 19,* 47–52.

deKoningh, H. L. Over de Vorgestalt theorie van Conrad: Een psychologische evaluatie. *Nederlands Tijdschrift voor de Psychologie, 1967, 22,* 98–129.

Dixon, N. F. *Subliminal perception: The nature of a controversy.* London: McGraw-Hill, 1971.

Dodwell, P. C. On perceptual clarity. *Psychological Review, 1971, 78,* 275–295.

Draguns, J. G. Investment of meaning in schizophrenics and in children: Studies of one aspect of microgenesis. *Psychological Research Bulletin* (Lund University, Sweden), 1961, *1*(Whole No. 5).

Draguns, J. G. Responses to cognitive and perceptual ambiguity in chronic and acute schizophrenia. *Journal of Abnormal and Social Psychology, 1963, 66,* 24–30.

Draguns, J. G. Affective meaning of reduced stimulus input: A study by means of the semantic differential. *Canadian Journal of Psychology, 1967, 21,* 231–241.

Draguns, J. G. Why microgenesis? An inquiry into the motivational sources of going beyond the information given. *Psychological Research Bulletin* (Lund University, Sweden), 1981, *21*(4).

Draguns, J. G., & Multari, G. Recognition of perceptually ambiguous stimuli in grade school children. *Child Development, 1961, 32,* 541–550.

Droz-Georget, R. L. Contribution à l'étude des dévaluations et sousestimations d'excitants visuels en présentation tachistoscopique brève. *Archives de Psychologie*, 1965, *40*(158), 1–90.

Ebner, E., & Ritzler, B. Perceptual recognition in chronic and acute schizophrenics. *Journal of Consulting and Clinical Psychology*, 1969, *33*, 200–206.

Erdelyi, M. H. A new look at the New Look: Perceptual defense and vigilance. *Psychological Review*, 1974, *81*, 1–25.

Flavell, J. H., & Draguns, J. G. A microgenetic approach to perception and thought. *Psychological Bulletin*, 1957, *54*, 197–217.

Francès, R. *Le développement perceptif*. Paris: Presses universitaires de France, 1962.

Froehlich, W. D. *Unstimmigkeit, Erwartung und Kompromiss*. Unpublished professorial dissertation (Habilitationsschrift), University of Bonn, 1964.

Froehlich, W. D. Stress, anxiety, and the control of attention: A psychophysiological approach. In C. D. Spielberger & I. G. Sarason (Eds.), *Stress and anxiety* (Vol. 5). Washington: Hemisphere, 1978.

Froehlich, W. D., & Laux, L. Serielles Wahrnehmen, Aktualgenese, Informationsintegration und Orientierungsreaktion: I. Aktualgenetisches Modell und Orientierungsreaktion. *Zeitschrift für experimentelle und angewandte Psychologie*, 1969, *16*, 250–277.

Gibson, E. J. *Principles of perceptual learning and development*. New York: Appleton, 1969.

Graumann, C. F. Zur Psychologie des kritischen Verhaltens. *Studium generale*, 1959, 694–716. (a)

Graumann, C. F. Aktualgenese: Die deskriptiven Grundlagen und theoretischen Wandlungen des aktualgenetischen Forschungsansatzes. *Zeitschrift für experimentelle und angewandte Psychologie*, 1959, *6*, 410–448. (b)

Haber, R. N. (Ed.), *Information-processing approaches to visual perception*. New York: Holt, 1969.

Hadamard, J. S. *An essay on the psychology of invention in the mathematical field*. Princeton, N.J.: Princeton University Press, 1945.

Hausmann, G. Zur Aktualgenese räumlicher Gestalten. *Archiv für die gesamte Psychologie*, 1935, *93*, 289–334.

Hauss, K. *Emotionalität und Wahrnehmung*. Göttingen: Verlag für Psychologie, 1970.

Hershenson, M., & Haber, R. N. The role of meaning in the perception of briefly exposed words. *Canadian Journal of Psychology*, 1965, *19*, 42–46.

Hippius, R. Erkennendes Tasten als Wahrnehmung und als Erkenntnisvorgang. *Neue psychologische Studien*, 1934, *10*, 1–163.

Hunt, J. McV. Motivation inherent in information processing and action. In O. J. Harvey (Ed.), *Motivation and social interaction: Cognitive determinants*. New York: Ronald, 1963.

Jones, A. Information deprivation in humans. *Progress in Experimental Personality Research*, 1966, *2*, 241–307.

Kantor, R. E., & Herron, W. G. Perceptual learning in the reactive-process schizophrenia. *Journal of Projective Techniques and Personality Assessment*, 1965, *29*, 58–70.

Kaswan, J. W. Tachistoscopic exposure time and spatial proximity in the organization of visual perception. *British Journal of Psychology*, 1958, *49*, 131–138.

Kaswan, J. W., & Young, S. Stimulus exposure time, brightness and spatial factors as determinants of visual perception. *Journal of Experimental Psychology*, 1963, *65*, 113–123.

Kolada, S. J. *Attention in schizophrenia: Visual search, selectivity, and selective strategy in the functional visual field of schizophrenics*. Unpublished doctoral dissertation, Pennsylvania State University, 1973.

Kragh, U. *The actual-genetic model of perception-personality*. Lund: Gleerup, 1955.

Kragh, U., & Smith, G. J. W. (Eds.). *Percept-genetic analysis*, Lund: Gleerup, 1970.

Kreitler, H., & Kreitler, S. Cognitive orientation: A model of human behaviors. *British Journal of Psychology*, 1972, *63*, 9–30.

Kreitler, H., & Kreitler, S. *Cognitive orientation and behavior*. New York: Springer, 1976.

Lange, N. N. Zakon pertseptsii (The law of perception). *Voprosy Filosofii i Psikhologii*, 1892, *3*(13), 18–54; (15), 53–68; *4*(16), 25–38.

Lastowski, F. A. *Individual differences in microgenesis of perception*. Unpublished doctoral dissertation, Pennsylvania State University, 1976.

Lesswing, N. J. *Perceptual microgenesis: A descriptive inquiry*. Unpublished master's thesis, Pennsylvania State University, 1973.

Lieberman, H. J. *A study of the relationship between developmentally determined personality and associated thought styles and tachistoscopic exposure time as reflected in conflict resolution.* Unpublished doctoral dissertation, Pennsylvania State University, 1974.

Linschoten, J. Aktualgenese und heuristisches Prinzip. *Zeitschrift für experimentelle und angewandte Psychologie,* 1959, *6,* 449–473.

Mackworth, N. H., & Bruner, J. S. How adults and children search and recognize pictures. *Human Development,* 1970, *13,* 149–177.

Mahoney, M. J. *Cognition and behavior modification.* Cambridge, Mass.: Ballinger, 1974.

Marks, E. Some situational correlates of recognition-response level. *Journal of Personality and Social Psychology,* 1967, *6,* 102–106.

Marks, E. Personality factors in the performance of a perceptual recognition task under competing incentives. *Journal of Personality and Social Psychology,* 1968, *8,* 69–74.

Mischel, W. Toward a cognitive social learning reconceptualization of personality. *Psychological Review,* 1973, *80,* 252–283.

Mischel, W. On the future of psychological measurement. *American Psychologist,* 1977, *32,* 246–254.

Mörschner, W. Beiträge zur Aktualgenese des Gegenstanderlebens. *Archiv für die gesamte Psychologie,* 1940, *107,* 125–149.

Neisser, U. *Cognitive psychology.* New York: Appleton, 1967.

Nicki, R. M. The reinforcing effect of uncertainty reduction on a human operant. *Canadian Journal of Psychology,* 1970, *24,* 389–400.

Petrenko, V. F., & Vasilenko, S. V. O pertseptsivnoi kategorizatsii (On perceptual categorization). *Vestnik Moskovskogo Universiteta, Seriya Psikhologiya,* 1977, *14*(1), 26–34.

Pinillos, J. L., & Brengelmann, J. C. Bilderkennung als Persönlichkeitstest. *Zeitschrift für experimentelle und angewandte Psychologie,* 1953, *1,* 480–500.

Potter, M. C. On perceptual recognition. In J. S. Bruner, R. R. Olver, & P. M. Greenfield (Eds.), *Studies in cognitive growth.* New York: Wiley, 1966.

Poulsen, A. Perceptual projects: A theory of veridicality and distortion in perception. *Scandinavian Journal of Psychology,* 1976, *17,* 1–9.

Radford, J. Reflections on introspection. *American Psychologist,* 1974, *29,* 245–261.

Rimoldi, H. J. A. Solución de problemas y procesos cognoscitivos. *Revista de Psicología General y Aplicada,* 1976, *31,* 391–419.

Sander, C. F. Experimentelle Ergebnisse der Gestaltpsychologie. In *Bericht über den 10. Kongress für experimentelle Psychologie.* Jena, 1928. (Reprinted in C. F. Sander & H. Volkelt (Eds.), *Ganzheitspsychologie.* Munich: Beck, 1962.)

Schiller, M. *Feldabhängigkeit: Unstimmigkeit und Kompromiss,* Unpublished thesis (Diplomarbeit), University of Bonn, 1970.

Senden, M. von. *Space and sight: The perception of space in the congenitally blind before and after operation* (P. Heath, trans.). Glencoe, Ill.: Free Press, 1960.

Smith, G. J. W., & Danielsson, A. From open flight to symbolic and perceptual tactics: A study of defense in preschool children. *Scripta Minora, Regiae Societatis Humaniorum Litterarum Lundensis,* 1977, No. 3.

Sperling, G. The information available in brief visual presentations. *Psychological Monographs,* 1960, *74* (11, Whole No. 498).

Thomae, H. *Der Mensch in der Entscheidung.* Munich: Barth, 1960.

Thomae, H. *Konflikt, Entscheidung, Verantwortung: Ein Beitrag zur Psychologie der Entscheidung.* Stuttgart: Kohlhammer, 1974.

Tucker, D. M. Some relationships between individual and group development. *Human Development,* 1973, *16,* 249–272.

Tuckerman, B. W. Developmental sequence in small groups. *Psychological Bulletin,* 1965, *63,* 384–399.

Varskii, B. V., & Guzeva, M. A. O zavisimosti prostranstvennikh porogov zreniya ot kharaktera vosprinimayemogo kontura (On the relationship of spatial visual thresholds to the nature of perceptible contour). *Voprosy Psikhologii,* 1962, *8,* 101–114.

Werner, H. *Comparative psychology of mental development.* New York: International Universities, 1948.

Werner, H. Microgenesis and aphasia. *Journal of Abnormal and Social Psychology,* 1956, *52,* 347–353.

Werner, H. The concept of development from a comparative and organismic point of view. In D. B. Harris (Ed.), *The concept of development.* Minneapolis: University of Minnesota Press, 1957.

Westcott, M. *Toward a psychology of intuition.* New York: Academic, 1967.

Zhirmunskaya, E. A., & Beyn, E. S. (Eds.). *Neyrodynamika mozga pri optikognosticheskoi deyatel'nosti* (Neurodynamics of the brain in the course of opticognostic activity). Moscow: Meditsina, 1974.

Zinchenko, V. P. *Formirovanye zritel'nogo obraza* (Formation of the visual image). Moscow: Moscow State University Press, 1969.

Zinchenko, V., Chi-Tsin, & Tarakanov, V. V. The formation and development of perceptual activity. *Soviet Psychology and Psychiatry,* 1963, *2,* 3.

Zucchi, M. Ricerche tachistoscopiche sulla percezione ambigua del bambino. *Archivio di Psicologia, Neurologia e Psichiatria,* 1960, *21,* 183-208.

2

Microgenesis as a Functional Approach to Information Processing Through Search

Werner D. Froehlich
University of Mainz, Federal Republic of Germany

The meaning of microgenesis (in German, *Aktualgenese*) seems to be manifold (cf. Chap. 1). On the one hand, microgenesis encompasses a variety of experimental and quasi-experimental procedures; they share, however, a common meaning and a general functional aim. Microgenetic as well as percept-genetic methods were introduced by Gemelli, Sander, and Werner independently in order to make observable steps or stages in microprocesses that direct early and preliminary awareness of "something" in the external world toward an assignment of its figural or cognitive meaning, that is, toward a stabilized percept related to its distal position and validity. This general instrumental aim signals the kinds of situation to which main references are made. Microgenesis is a search that leads to orientation, overcoming on its course uncertainties and ambiguities by a stepwise process that links reconstructions of the external world with most private assumptions. It takes place in a psychophysiological system that possesses readiness for it. As an explanatory construct, on the other hand, microgenesis confronts its student with some ambiguity and surplus of meaning.

When asked about microgenesis, the late proponent of Gestaltism, Professor Wolfgang Metzger, in a private conversation, made a rather sarcastic statement. He compared microgenesis with an empty tube of toothpaste that, surprisingly enough, provides paste time and again whenever it is squeezed in the right way. Actually, the explanatory meaning of microgenesis is based on three groups of theoretical assumptions. The first of them concerns the heritage of Gestalt psychology and psychophysics; the second deals with parallels between microgenesis and everyday perception; the third group of assumptions refers to multiconditional

I am deeply indebted to the late Professor Friedrich Sander, one of my academic teachers, who was a most friendly and patient guide into both microgenesis and academic life. I further want to express my thanks to my distinguished colleagues and friends, J. Draguns and G. Smith, who helped me by editing this chapter and several other chapters in this volume. Last, not least, U. Hentschel was another friendly and patient guide in helping overcome delays and organizational problems in a most efficient way.

The projects on microgenesis and related issues were supported by grants Fr 132, 1, 3, 6, 7, 8, and 13 to the author by Deutsche Forschungs-Gemeinschaft (German National Research Foundation).

Russian names are transcribed according to English usage; when referring to publications in German, the German transcription of the name is retained (V. Zinchenko = W. Sintschenko).

developmental principles that provide eventually for some parallel between microgenesis, ontogeny, and phylogenesis.

I would like to venture the assumption, however, that the tube is not as empty
as the late Dr. Metzger thought. Microgenesis as a research instrument in the functional framework just described dates back to the late 1920s. In the ensuing
decades, in a manner very similar to the history of attention research, on one hand,
there was a remarkable abstinence from theorizing about processes; on the other
hand, the impact of the experimental procedure led to some further developments
in applied fields such as personnel selection, diagnostics, and clinical psychology.
One of the reasons for this theoretical abstinence might have been the barrier of
risk looking into the "black box," established by Ockhamian-minded behaviorists,
whereas in the applied fields the *horror vacui* motivated more risky efforts, as
exemplified by projective techniques and their impact on applied microgenetic procedures (cf., Kragh, 1955). Obviously, the risk level came to be lowered in general
and theoretical psychology, too, when mediating cognitive processes and so-called
cognitive controls became prominent. Most recently, the increasing amount of
attention attracted by all kinds of cognitive happenings and their derivations
suggests that a little "mentalistic" touch, anathematized to some extent in the
1930s through the 1950s, now fits our modern society, appearing as it does in its
new disguise as "cognitive" approaches. The increasing sophistication in research
technology, data assessment, and experimental design as well as the development
of a more differentiated vocabulary have resulted in microgenetic approaches being
frequently hidden in such concepts as "information processing" (Haber, 1969),
"search through sequential stimulus presentation" (Neisser, 1967), "visual thinking" (Arnheim, 1969; Zinchenko, 1971), or "intolerance of ambiguity" (Smock,
1955). Besides their common reference to serial procedures of picture presentation, these approaches share the general assumption that cognitive efforts are
organized sequentially in compensating for deficiencies of information presented.

There are therefore good reasons why our impression of microgenetic approaches remains blurred, even after a careful inspection of outstanding reviews
(Flavell & Draguns, 1957; Graumann, 1959; Chap. 1 in this volume), of monographs (Kragh, 1955; Kragh & Smith, 1970), and of various recent studies in microgenesis and perceptgenesis. It seems hard to understand how microgenesis can
serve as a universal umbrella for approaches in general, differential, and clinical
psychology, in biology, and in developmental psychology and psychiatry. The
situation of the reviewer and student of this field reminds me of a philosopher
looking in a completely darkened room for a black cat that eventually is found to
be in the room. It is also reminiscent of the six actors holding their own most
personal concepts of truth and looking to their common author to overcome the
relativity of the six "truths" in Pirandello's famous absurd comedy *Six Characters in Search of an Author*.

My purpose in this chapter is neither to redo Draguns' analysis nor to put the
black cat back into the dark room. Rather, it is to satisfy the six actors. I have
written the chapter to pinpoint the basic functional features underlying microgenetic approaches in terms of their procedural and theoretical implications. I
make special reference to the problem of assessing clues that concern adaptive,
emotional, and precognitive impact at stages corresponding to various functional
levels. My aim is to show by means of recent studies and some of our own data
that microgenesis seems to hold a rather privileged position in the family of process

analyses; because of my special fields of experience, I make selected references to microgenesis in general psychology and psychophysiology.

A FUNCTIONAL FRAME OF REFERENCE

General Descriptive Aims

Microgenetic approaches are designed to assess various aspects of multidimensional processes that lead from awareness through assumptions to an assessment of the particulars of a given phenomenon, event, or object. These aspects are defined as developments over time under concrete task and stimulus conditions. In classical approaches, reference is mainly to perceptual judgments at a cognitive level of experience, whereas recent research includes also the different levels of peripheral and central modulation that characterize information processing in terms of the perceptual and conceptual system. Microprocesses to be assessed are conceptualized as ordered sequences of events that occur in the temporal period between the presentation of a series of stimuli and the formation of a single and stabilized cognitive response, a *percept*. The subject is asked to find out, from trial after trial, what the final stimulus pattern will look like, in other words, what it might become through search and guesses and what it will signify or mean in the given situation to an observer.

The modes of microgenetic stimulus presentation are guided by this functional aim. To some extent, they are similar to serial or sequential tasks. They differ, however, in the aspect of the "growth" of the stimulus from an incomplete, impoverished, or fragmentary stimulus presentation into a complete and complex as well as meaningful representation of figures, objects, or events. This provides for the serial or sequential input's conditional property with regard to the short or transient episode of a meaning assessment during a stepwise increase in clarity and distinctiveness, from trial to trial.

Microgenetic Procedures

As already indicated, there is a typical mode of stimulus presentation in microgenetic experiments. The standard condition holds that a patterned stimulus be presented in a way that would provide for a stepwise increase of clarity, complexity, distinctiveness, or some combination of these. Exceptions are those special techniques that Smith and his colleagues use to assess general stabilization patterns in afterimages or aftereffects (see Chap. 10).

Using visual patterns, the increase of stimulus accessibility develops in standard cases over 15 trials. From trial to trial the amount of complexity or clarity of the stimulus increases. This general description holds for most of the classic investigations in the fields of visual, auditory, and haptic information processing carried out by Sander (1926, 1927, 1928) and his collaborators (for review, see Graumann, 1959). Another microgenetic procedure was suggested by Smith and Henriksson (1955). It consists of the supraliminal presentation of a visual frame of reference (e.g., a living room) where details, additional cues, or nonfitting elements are introduced tachistoscopically, starting at a subliminal level of presentation time. Because, under given conditions during this procedure, the subliminal frame of reference phenomenologically changes its meaning to the observer to some extent, the technique was labeled "metacontrast." A third group of procedures refers most explicitly to visual thinking. Sintschenko, Munipow, and Gordon (1973) asked subjects familiar with reading a compass card to find out via "visualization" the exact position of a compass needle that is presented in an unfamiliar and incomplete card scheme (e.g., an inclined needle on a card that offers only one cue, southeast, placed in the upper left section of the incomplete card scheme). The task, therefore, demands, in the place of reasoning, a comparison of the visually presented information with a revisualized familiar framework. In this case, the steps in meaning assessment and response formation take place through contact with a supraliminally presented incomplete visual framework and through knowledge of the complete scheme as part of the representational repertoire.

In terms of the instructions used with regard to different task conditions, the motivational base of these microdevelopments can be characterized as "effort after meaning" or "effort after coping with ambiguity" (Froehlich, 1978). At the end of a microgenetically induced process, there is something like veridical identi- fication or meaning assessment in terms of subjective evidence, that is, in terms of a most probable outcome of search. What happens between the trial sequences is to some extent reminiscent of the so-called guessing games used in information theory. An observer is asked to cope with blurred, uncertain, or hidden informa- tion in microgenesis. What he or she sees, hears, or senses does not instantaneously provide the signal values, cues, or hints necessary for immediate meaning assess- ment. Thus, pattern recognition, categorization, and formation of a stable cogni- tive response are delayed. In a microgenetic task, the observer obviously depends for a given time on her or his subjective guesses and assumptions until she or he finally gets the "message" on the basis of some evidence. "Heuristic principles" are invoked that guide and direct the search at peripheral and central levels of perceptual behavior to find out what there is with which to deal with a given situation in the most "effective" way (cf. Linschoten, 1959).

Response Levels and Stages

Most writers on microgenesis agree that information processing under these conditions develops over several qualitatively different stages. A definition of stages, however, depends on procedural impacts (i.e., stimulus presentation) as well as on response levels. Most challenging is, for several reasons, a concentra- tion on those stages that refer to interactions between outside-input processing and internal processes that guide perception, reasoning, visual thinking, and mem- ory. These interactions produce impact at a conceptual or representational level, where imagination and fantasy play a prominent role. The questions are, there- fore, how a combination of fragmentary inputs is put together with these in- gredients of the most personal world in order to provide a base for preliminary meaning assessment (i.e., for perceptual hypotheses) and what the main stages or phases look like that motivate further search, guide combinatory activities, and lead to an assessment of a final outcome?

At the level of stimulus properties, microgenetic processes develop between the poles of blurred impressions of stimulus fragments and of pattern assessment leading to recognition of a distal event. In terms of experiential qualities, the devel- opments seem to take place between the poles of ambiguity or uncertainty and of subjective evidence about the stimulus event's nature and meaning. Interpretations provided by Sander (1928) in particular lead to the further expectation that during the process there is a decrease of emotionally tuned feelings, some sort of tension release. Within the given limits of an appropriate assessment of these experienced qualities, both arguments—the orientation toward stimulus properties and that toward experiential qualities, respectively—could provide a further hint in the direction of probabilistic features paralleled by changes in emotional arousal and activation. In terms of the assumed impact of cognitive organization, microgenetic processes seem to develop between the poles of indifference or instability and of differentiation or stability. This position can be derived especially from Werner's interpretations (Werner, 1926, 1927) and seems to be fundamental to the view held by Kragh and Smith (1970).

In the classic descriptive attempts provided by Gemelli (1928), Sander (1926, 1927, 1928), and Werner (1926, 1927), the main findings, as summarized above, were drawn from free verbal reports and drawings. Stages varying between poles of figural and experienced moments seem to be no monotonous function of stimulus impact; they most probably represent, as Sander (1928) concluded, qualitatively different steps showing some discontinuities like the jumps of particles in microphysics. A further elaboration of the mere phenomenological features within the framework of Husserl's philosophy was provided most explicitly by Graumann (1959). It should be noted that in more recent studies experiential data are typically reduced to ratings of stimulus dimensions (e.g., complexity) and subjective qualities (e.g., certainty; see Froehlich & Laux, 1969). To assess connotative meaning aspects, the semantic differential was used by Draguns (1967) and Black (1975). Another solution to the problem of handling experiential data in some appropriate way was proposed by Kragh and Smith (1970). The information assessed in terms of stimulus properties, experiential qualities, and cognitive organization toward stability could be reduced into two main phases, a preparatory P phase and a concluding C phase, in order to denote two different transitory conditions that develop in the process.

Last, not least, a psychophysiological approach to the problem of stages should be mentioned. Zinchenko (1971), Zinchenko and Virgiles (1972), and Sintschenko, Munipow, and Gordon (1973) proposed a *hierarchic stage model* that refers to different functional levels of the nervous system involved at a given state of affairs in a microgenetic task. Based on research in subvocalization (Aarons, 1971) and studies of short-term memory and visual thinking, there is some evidence of the impact of peripheral and central functions in an ordered sequence: (a) fixation duration and eye movements, representing the peripheral motor part of the system, denote search activity and scanning; (b) the duration of alpha inhibition and similar signs of cortical activation in EEG represent the impact of central activities; while (c) changes in EMG at the laryngeal position represent a peripheral aspect of speech motor readiness, that is, response formation. The proportions of time during which these different activities dominate seem to be related to such factors as task difficulty, task familiarity, and the investment of central activities in a given task. In this case, the quality of stages refers in a most direct way to the different functional levels involved during a given time. The descriptive levels of peripheral and central arousal, however, do not provide in my view for an integration of cognitive and physiological data. To interpret findings of the Zinchenko type, emphasis must be placed on task properties. A very similar restriction holds for most descriptive approaches in physiological psychology (for discussion, see Froehlich, 1978).

A more elaborate psychophysiological approach to the problem of stages seems to be deducible from a model proposed by Pribram and McGuinness (1975). There is a body of evidence for a central mechanism of *effort control* that balances and evaluates onsets and offsets of orienting (intake) and preparatory subsystems (rejection and stabilization). This leads to the hypothesis of dominance of orienting responses, neuronal model establishment, and comparison directed toward habituation during the stage of intake and stimulus selection; during the stage of reasoning, on the other hand, the system is mainly involved in developing preparatory tonic changes while the outside reference is more or less inhibited owing to the balance mechanism. While the first stage mainly shows its impact in phasic changes as experienced through orienting responses, the second stage implies preparatory activation as demonstrated through contingent negative variations in EEG (for references, see Froehlich, 1978; Chap. 18 in this volume).

For theoretical as well as practical reasons (e.g., the application of microgenesis in diagnostic and clinical work), it appears desirable to combine data obtained at the "cognitive" (e.g., introspective) level with those gathered at the psychophysiological level. The impact of precognitive segregational activities followed by those belonging to the reasoning type was demonstrated at the level of verbal statements as early as 1928 by Sander, when he described stages of *schlichte Wiedergabe* (simple reproduction of some fragments) as forerunners of *Vorgestalten* (assessment of meaning spheres, leading to perceptual hypotheses). The ground seems to be prepared for a multivariate definition of stages. Although the impact of qualitatively different stages on a single dependent variable can be assessed with the help of so-called process factor analyses (cf. Froehlich, 1978; Pawlik, 1965), some recent models are available for conducting multivariate regression analyses to trace process patterns at different levels (e.g., Einhorn, Kleinmuntz, & Kleinmuntz, 1979).

There is no doubt that data obtained at the descriptive level of experiential qualities have served as guidelines for developing microgenetic models to assess cognitive progresses and developments and that they will continue to do so. Experiential data, however, refer to judgments in the form of overt verbal expressions of "cognitive responses" offered during a given trial. The critical event that most probably takes place during stimulus contact, stimulus offset, and overt response formation nevertheless remains shrouded in darkness. As long as we refer in microgenetic investigations mainly to overt judgments (verbal reports), we actually refer to something like an intellectualized interpretation of what has been seen, experienced, felt, and remembered on a given occasion; the logical basis for a definition of stages seems to be a secondhand ex post facto conclusion. By virtue of a multilevel and multivariate view, it would seem to be possible to get additional information that refers more directly to event-related process patterns in the "internal milieu"; moreover, these patterns would show some of the ways the brain controls its own input at various instances of meaning assessment. But again it should be noted that the inclusion of these levels makes sense only if the task properties are chosen in such a way as to reflect and represent the functional principle we are dealing with: meaning assessment through search. This more extensive view of stages, as demonstrated in my later section on the recapitulation hypothesis, seems to provide a golden bridge between adaptive, effort-related, precognitive, and cognitive views that contribute to a theoretical framework for microgenesis.

EXPLANATORY AND THEORETICAL IMPLICATIONS

The explanatory and theoretical meaning of microgenesis goes to a remarkable extent beyond its functional scope and its descriptive properties. In the following sections I deal with three different groups of assumptions that do not represent some triune structure at all. They do eventually represent a reversal of microgenesis because one can start with some researchable facts and, through a series of steps, arrive at a stage where blurred or fused impressions are dominant.

Merogenetic and Hologenetic Approaches

Despite differences in the experimental procedures through which they were realized, early microgenetic models (Gemelli, 1928; Sander, 1926, 1927, 1928; Werner, 1926, 1927) are explicitly grounded in Gestalt psychology and its extensions into a general theory of cognitive growth and ontogenetic development. In this context, figural or thought fragments get their meaning from embeddedness, belongingness, and insight in accordance with gestalt laws, for example, those of figure–ground segregation or symmetry. Another implication is more camouflaged and less easily detected. It is the fact that segregation of figural detail and pattern texture depends on psychophysical properties at intake. Starting at the beginning of this century, evidence began to accumulate about how segregation of stimulus properties depended on energy level (for a review see Forgus & Malamed, 1976). The lower this level at a given trial, the fewer details are available and the less they can probably serve as clues for meaning assessment.

To label the two kinds of procedures derived from these two different sets of theoretical implications, Sander in the late 1950s (personal communication) introduced two technical terms:

1. If the stimulus presentation starts with figural fragments, for instance, dots, lines, or angles, and continues in a way that offers, trial by trial, more and more figural details by way of cumulation, parts of the finally presented whole constitute the bases for guesses, assumptions, and hypotheses. Preliminary or final statements about figural and object meaning are, in my view, attributions with regard to a distal stimulus event, which appears with increasing complexity and completeness. The technique of stimulus presentation, therefore, is named *merogenetic* (Greek *meros*, "part").

2. If, on the other hand, the energy level of stimulus presentation is increased from trial to trial—as in tachistoscopic threshold experiments or using a polarization device to control the level of luminance—or if the amount of clarity and distinctiveness increases as a result of a refocusing procedure, these techniques are labeled *hologenetic* (Greek *holon*, "whole"). Hologenetic procedures thus refer to presentations of a complete stimulus pattern that start at some combination of low time, luminosity, and area ratios or at the low edge of the detectability range. All these procedures provide for an impoverishing effect in terms of energy and therefore aggravate figure–ground discrimination in early microgenetic stages. In my view, they exercise a strong pull toward proximal cue utilization.

The differences of information processing in these two conditions are identifiable. Merogenetic tasks demand a collection of distinguishable elements and their integration into chunks, categories, or schemes. The process is based on sequential comparison, and it is supported by perceptually mediated ideas, thoughts, and conclusions and by the impact of memory. Thus there is some similarity to processes involved in search through sequentially presented visual displays in memory tasks; but this similarity holds only at a given trial level because, in microgenetic experiments, stimulus complexity and completeness vary. Hologenetic tasks refer to a psychophysical model at the energetic level. The stimulus pattern to be assessed and evaluated appears initially in a dimmed, blurred, or unaccentuated way. Stages of meaning assessment start in this case at a subliminal level of processing, or in more general terms, they start with difficulties in detecting the edges of a shape, which are necessary to segregate a figure from the background. In his or her progression toward meaning assessment, the observer passes through stages that show, at the experiential level, marked interactions between proximal cue evaluation and various contributions of the "internal world" of earlier experience and imagination; in other words, interindividual variance increases both in content and in themes. In this critical stage, cognitive controls or cognitive styles may, therefore, direct to some extent information processing as well as response formation. These latter impacts suggest the usefulness of hologenetic procedures as diagnostic instruments in obtaining information about the individual modes of stabilizing percepts through controls and defenses (cf. Kragh, 1955; Kragh & Smith, 1970; Chaps. 10 and 12 in this volume). Some further implications are discussed in my later section on micro–macro correspondences.

Taking into consideration these differences between merogenetic and hologenetic approaches, the predication of differences in terms of results obtained seems to be no big surprise. Merogenetic and hologenetic results in fact differ with regard to the functional meaning of stages or steps obtained as well as with regard to the number, contents, and complexity of stages at the level of experiential data (cf. Graumann, 1959). Both approaches, however, obviously share some functional properties:

1. Merogenetic and hologenetic tasks both refer to the way an observer tries to assess and stabilize figural or realistic meaning through perception.

2. In both approaches, the amount of information increases through interactions among intake iconic representations, imagery, and hypotheses.

3. At the level of intake, increases in complexity or clarity are critical; at the level of internal factors, there is a decrease in the impact of processes that provide the bases for guesses and assumptions in ambiguous or uncertain perceptual situations.

4. An additional shared impact concerns checking procedures that lead to corrections, suspensions, or compromises if the observer is unable to integrate new inputs into the framework of her or his earlier assumptions.

Recapitulation Hypothesis: Representative Design, Levels, and Stages

Sander (1928) speculated quite cautiously that there might be some similarity between everyday perception and microgenetic perception in basic features of stages that remain hidden in everyday perception because of the speed of such perceptual events and their automatized nature. Microgenetic experiments, with their special mode of stimulus presentation, could, he thought, eventually make these stages observable. If this recapitulation hypothesis is upheld, it would demonstrate the virtually unique position of microgenesis as a representative design as well as a process construct. Dealing with recapitulation, however, is like a risky walk into unknown territory. There is an implicit agreement that stages in microgenesis develop with nonmonotonous increases of clarity and distinctiveness of stimulus; stages represent qualitative steps. Recapitulation is in this case simply an invitation to look at similar qualitative changes in various situations, the everyday case included. In microgenetic research, however, change patterns are assessed in most cases via ex post facto conclusions from verbal statements, that is, from the judgments of an observer. At this cognitive level, some of the pattern's features, for example, the impact of mediating processes, remain "hidden" per se. Recapitulation hypothesis, in my view, provides an excellent pretext for reconsidering the problems of levels and stages at great length and from different angles. To begin this job properly, let me guide a tour through a series of everyday situations and representative fields of activities, providing for a common descriptive framework.

Representative Design

External stimuli or events in a more or less neutral or familiar situation convey the impression of immediacy. Stimulus contact, meaning assessment, and internal response (e.g., identification) appear as unity. At the experiential level, there is something like instantaneity of the whole act. For a biologically minded interpreter, these evidences are both trivial and irrelevant. Perception, no doubt, is mediated by a series of internal microprocesses at various levels. At the sensory-motor level, there is the impact of microsaccades and macrosaccades, eye movements, eye blinks, and head movements that provide for multiple or intermittent stimulus contact. A central mechanism of receptive fields, orienting responses, and set formation together with the cortical impact of imagery, visualization, and memory intervene and lead to changes in the perceptual system, related systems, and peripheral consequences. Experienced instantaneity, therefore, is based on noninstantaneous microprocesses, at different levels of the complex system involved, that mediate, direct, and energize or inhibit perceptual integration at a given moment. In microgenetic procedures, the time an observer spends in contact with an external event per trial is predetermined and kept unusually brief. One therefore has to look for those internal processes that are traversed in extremely short time intervals to provide for comparison with the everyday case. On the other hand, the observer in microgenetic experiments has some freedom of choice as to the time between stimulus offset and response and judgment formation. This leads to the question of interchangeability, or functional equivalence, between lower level and higher level activities showing their impact during and after stimulus contact, both with regard to intended response formation and the percept's stabilization.

When an everyday observer deals with ambiguous, impoverished, or unfamiliar intake, he or she most probably experiences a degree of effort after meaning through search. As a result of various feedbacks, he or she might be able to talk about these feelings, provided there is enough time and need to do so. In more complex situations that provide for some challenge and risk, transient stages (e.g., preliminary assumptions) may play an imminent functional role, but their impact, again, remains covert. A radar or sonar operator, for example, finds himself in a quasi-hologenetic situation. A spot or an acoustic cue, mostly covered by back-ground clutter or noise at first appearance, at a subliminal level, could become a critical signal a little later. Therefore the observer tries to localize and identify the signal value through further effort; he seems to be guided and directed by pre-liminary assumptions based on task experience. A merogenetic type of a task con-sists, for example, of observing a large visual display that extends over the visual field. In this case, the observer obtains information from a collection of cues through scanning and following up cue or sign patterns. The observer's behavior seems to be guided by critical clues that, through hypotheses, lead to further scan-ning and assignment of meaning as an integrated outcome. To evaluate microgenesis as a representative design in these two cases, two arguments seem to provide for limitations:

1. An operator knows about means–end relationships that guide her or his further search activities; this knowledge makes the operator cautious and attentive. A microgenetic observer neither knows to what extent another trial's input will provide information nor, in the critical stages of an experiment, what the final stimulus pattern will mean exactly. The operator fills the gap between unstructured awareness and the final outcome's meaning in terms of his or her experience, whereas the subject in a microgenetic experiment is guided mainly by her or his intention to categorize something in a probabilistic frame of reference. Moreover, the latter framework in the early stages is, for the most part, a highly personal construction about what there is in the external world.

2. Although the operator as well as the everyday observer acts on the risks of false alarms or missed signals, the microgenetic observer cannot expect to suffer consequences of wrong decisions except for a little blame when getting a final trial's information from the experimenter.

With regard to these descriptively derived limitations, a comparison among everyday search, an operator's behavior, and a subject's behavior in microgenetic tasks seems to be provided only at the abstract level of a hypothesis's functions. Stages of hypothesis formation provide for some redundancy (values) at the price of having missed in a given trial episode some potential entropy (risks; costs). Very similar ideas were developed by Brunswik (1957) and led to the famous lens model of perception; another step toward formalization was taken with the development of signal detection theory (Swets, Tanner, & Birsdall, 1961) as an attempt at grasp-ing basic features of decisional impact on perception. The hypothesis view, on the other hand, provides for a somewhat holistic kind of analysis, being mainly dependent on judgments in microgenetic experiments; in signal-detection experi-ments, stimulus conditions are relatively simple so that there is no problem in assessing discrimination and criteria measures as main parameters in a most direct way at the response level. Because of changes of stimulus pattern in microgenetic experiments, microprocesses at a single trial level may well provide for a better understanding of hypothesis formation through changes at a precognitive and predecisional level.

Parallel Processing

In microgenetic studies, the time between stimulus onset and offset defines the stimulus contact for a given trial. In merogenetic tasks this time interval is chosen at a psychophysically determined supraliminal level; in standard paradigms it is about 100 to 250 msec and constant over the whole series. In hologenetic studies, time is critical because it increases trial after trial, starting at a subliminal energy level (lower than 50 msec). As mentioned earlier, microgenesis refers to what happens *between* stimulus presentation and response formation per trial. Another critical interval is that between internal response formation and overt response. Owing to the motivational impact of the given task, between overt response, readiness signal, and next stimulus presentation, the organism prepares for next intake; but it also reconsiders hypotheses developed earlier, the kind of information segregated before, and last but not least, the loads of values and costs. After stimulus offset, the organism has the choice of time to develop an appropriate overt judgment (for more details on the temporal frame, see Froehlich & Laux, 1969). An intertrial interval is chosen in most cases in such a way as to provide for a slowing down of arousal specific to stimulus and response as well as for a stabilization of recent intake and further hypothesis formations.

In reaction-time experiments, *operation time* depends on the discriminatory impact of the stimulus. If there is one simple signal and one response, reaction time is about 200 to 300 msec (1 bit). As the number of bits increases, there is a monotonous relationship between bits and operation time (Froehlich & Koszik, 1971). If the stimulus is complex and operations are of a more or less indefinite nature, as is the case in microgenesis, microprocesses do not principally impinge on perceptual-motor activities at lower levels as in a simple recognition task, but they include higher level activities in order to overcome the imperfect information assessed during shortened stimulus contact or impoverished intake. Thus, in microgenetic tasks, the impact of higher level activities in the visual system is critical. There are, however, some arguments in favor of another view of the speed-processing problem:

1. Looking at *processing times* at the bioelectric level (the level of evoked potentials in EEG), intensity decoding, and to some extent complexity decoding, are done within extremely short intervals (early in the microgenetic progression), whereas the decisional impact seems to be processed at the well-known latency level of about 300 msec (P_{300}; for references see Chap. 18). Operation time, on the other hand, seems to be much more influenced by slow changes at the tonic level that develop after processing is terminated. Both components, however, depend to some extent on activational background, for example, in cases of intake readiness or preparatory settings.

2. Recent investigations in the field of subliminal perception show that the brain can deal with low-energy or fragmentary input in a quasi-cognitive or decisional way. Once an optimal level of activation is provided, the cortex can detect and analyze fragmentary or fused cues at extremely low stimulus-contact levels. Eventually, these "preliminary" cues direct further internal activities toward operation (cf. Dixon, 1971; Chap. 16 in this volume). These internally mediated pushes are not necessarily registered, but they tune to some extent both operation characteristics and the cognitive content in overt responses.

3. Generally, visual search and recognition at a single trial level can be performed in at speed-per-item rate much lower than we would predict from our traditional knowledge about processing time and operation time. Recent research on visual search through sequentially presented displays provides some strong

arguments against an additive relationship between the two components (cf. Colgate, Hoffman, & Eriksen, 1973; Schneider & Shiffrin, 1977; Shiffrin & Schneider, 1977; Sternberg, 1966). Naturally, this holds within the limits of the search paradigm, presentation times used, and several other factors (cf. Erikson & Spencer, 1969; Nickerson, 1966).

A first theoretical attempt to deal with the problem of shortened speed-per-item rates was provided by Neisser (1967). He proposed a two-stage model based on the assumption that a "preattentive stage" precedes and guides a stage of "focal attention." While preattentive activities at extremely high speed provide for some probabilistic and preliminary segmentation, the discrimination process, operating normally at a much lower speed, is economized owing to its concentration on those segments where relevant cues are expected to appear. In a series of experiments and computer simulations, Hoffman (1978) demonstrated the value of another, more advanced model. The main assumption holds that the two stages can interact most effectively. The high speed of search relative to operation time seems to be based on a *parallel evaluation.* This evaluation leads to a quick rejection of elements presumably bearing no information (Hoffman, 1978, p. 8). It thus seems to be logical that parallel evaluation also serves as a guide toward faster intake of those elements that are presumed to bear the greatest amount of information in helping overcome ignorance or uncertainty at a given trial. There is no empirical basis yet for dealing with a generalization of parallel evaluation to subliminal perception or processing of fragmentary input. Eventually, it is reasonable to assume that a momentarily relevant expectancy or perceptual hypothesis could replace the high-speed segmentation process on an "internal" screen in response-formation processes. A helpful set of assumptions and findings is provided by recent research on imagery and perception.

Functional Equivalences in Perception

One of the classical assumptions in research on perception holds that, at so-called low visual levels, the manner in which information is processed is not influenced by expectations or knowledge as cognitive ingredients; but it is very much influenced by structural and functional properties of those mechanisms involved in the low-level processing itself (Marr, 1976). Do we actually capture at lowest levels (e.g., in the initial stage of a microgenetic experiment or at a first glance at outside events) mainly the impact of mechanism like receptive fields, energy distributions, and so on? The question seems to be insoluble because of the functional impact that leads us to cognitive statements in terms of subvocal or overt "judgments" where influence of higher level activities is manifest. At these higher levels, the ways in which information is processed are more dependent on a person's expectancies and knowledge (Bruner, 1957; Neisser, 1967). In microgenetic experiments as well as in everyday perception through search, we thus have some good reason to assume that fragmentary or fused inputs are completed by earlier experience, memory, ideas, chunks, imagery, and to some extent fantasy. Naturally, the language of responses itself exhibits the impact of a higher level of functioning. The field on which modulations and integrations take place is embedded in a dynamic modulation system that is based at lower levels on multistable controls and at higher levels on adaptive controls that relate internal representations to external events. There is little chance to grasp the impacts of lower and higher level activities in terms of overt verbal responses. A preliminary hint, however, is provided by studies on afterimages and aftereffects. Besides the fact that their phenomenological appearance leads to some insight about the ways a person stabilizes images resulting from stimulus contact at a low level (cf. Chap. 10), there is another most interesting feature to be observed: Mental images seem to provide for some functional equivalents of stimuli, objects, and events under given task conditions. Mental imagery seems to result, furthermore, in an activation or reactivation of information-processing mechanisms at both levels, the lower and the higher one (Shepard, 1979; Shepard & Podgorny, 1978). These influences, as demonstrated in recent experiments (Finke, 1980), seem to act on those lower mechanisms whose operating conditions were thought to be not influenced at all by *how* stimuli, objects, or events might be conceptualized; a crucial variable in this context, besides task conditions and stimulus material, seems to be a given person's vividness of imagination (Sheehan & Neisser, 1969), a somewhat neglected characteristic in perceptual research in general and in microgenesis in particular.

Mental imagery seems to interfere with visually mediated impacts most probably also in cases of subliminal or fragmentary visual-intake conditions. Interferences of this kind seem to occur whenever images and external stimuli activate the same visual mechanisms at the same time (Finke, 1980). This holds especially for those cases in which ambiguous or blurred impressions lead to combined efforts at various levels and in which precognitive and predecisional moments become the basis for equivalencing activities. In this way we get a preliminary answer to the question why subjects in microgenetic experiments are telling more than they actually could "know" at a given trial (cf. Nisbett & Wilson, 1977).

Intuitive Appraisal and the Orienting Response

One can assume that interactions such as parallel processing and functional equivalences combine preattentive, precognitive, and predecisional efforts toward response formation at relatively high speed. But my task is not to defend the recapitulation hypothesis at a most theoretical level with some dashes of speculation; rather, it is to define some measures that could be used in addition to verbal reports in order to find the way back into a process analysis at various functional levels. At the same time, this presupposes some readiness to say goodbye to the assumption that all we can get, we must get via ex post facto avenues, that is, via overt judgments.

Interestingly enough, the history of microgenesis provides some help in opening locked doors again. The Italian philosopher, psychologist, and theologian Gemelli used a hologenetic task to support an epistemological position that can be traced to the writings of Saint Augustine and Saint Thomas Aquinas. In this view, perception starts with some "intuitive knowledge" that is converted stepwise into an "experience of meaning" (Gemelli, 1928). Because of the emotional impact of intuitive knowledge, Gemelli (1949a, 1949b) extended his view into a phenomenological theory of emotion as a prerequisite of perception. The functional role of *intuitive appraisal* was extensively analyzed by Arnold (1960), with special regard to parallels between phenomenological evidence and physiological processes. In Arnold's view, intuitive appraisal precedes cognitive evaluations (i.e., reflexive appraisal), emotional feelings, and overt behavior, the latter occurring because of the impact of action tendencies. Intuitive appraisal operates at relatively low levels as far as its embeddedness in the multistable parts of the limbic forebrain is concerned; interconnections with cortical and noncortical parts of the brain and the pathways to perceptual and motor memory systems provide for its general functional properties in guiding subsequent activities into biologically and psychologically meaningful avenues. It was mainly Lazarus who, starting in the 1960s (Lazarus, 1966), gave rise to the idea that *cognitive appraisal* (the reflexive derivation of intuitive appraisal in Arnold's view) governs perception-emotion relationships in challenging coping situations. Although the story of appraisal started and ended in "mentalistic" regions, Arnold referred to precognitive and predecisional events taking place involuntarily and at high speed whenever an organism was confronted with some "new" stimuli, objects, events, or situations.

A first and lowest level consequence of intuitive appraisal seems to be the so-called what-is-it reflex in animals and humans, originally described by Sechenov and Pavlov. This reflex became prominent again in the elaborate analyses of Sokolov and his students. They described functional aims and neurophysiological mechanisms of the *orienting response* (OR) and its various components (for a review see Sokolov & Vinogradova, 1975). An OR is aroused by new, unfamiliar, or incompatible stimuli. It directs the organism toward intake readiness and prepares it for activities as long as the neuronal model of the stimulus is not stabilized. With stabilization or restabilization, the OR fades away (becomes habituated) or combines with instrumental activities leading to the establishment of conditioned responses. There is good reason to assume that OR is an unlearned component that leads to the development of selective attention, investigatory behavior, and such higher level cognitive efforts as expectancies and interests (Floru & Froehlich, 1982).

In my view, what happens at a so-called low visual level could be represented by *phasic* and *tonic* components of OR in terms of evoked potentials, readiness potentials in EEG, and changes in peripheral motor effectors that are functionally involved (cf. Zinchenko, 1972). Visceral components of OR like heart rate changes or GSR also can be used, once a temporal framework for their observation is provided (cf. Froehlich & Laux, 1969). Another psychophysiological reference seems to be provided by baseline-related controls of general activation at the cortical level (i.e., EEG desynchronization or alpha blocking). There is some evidence that OR measures together with some control of evoked potentials are helpful in assessing those changes that refer to impacts of lower and higher level activities in the visual system, whereas verbal responses might be helpful in assessing their relationship to functionally equivalent parallel processing.

Functional Equivalents in Higher Processes

This step can also be based on historical milestones in the history of microgenesis. Werner (1926, 1927) interpreted his experiments on micromelodies and microharmonies as a microdevelopment that grows from blurred and unstructured impressions via concrete clues toward accentuated, differentiated, and relatively stable patterns. He emphasized in his early writings a formal principle that some years later became prominent in Werner's comparative studies on development (Werner, 1940): An unstructured territory gains more and more texture and accents. It finally represents a *structured field* where complex patterns get their meaning via integration. Also, the development of meaning assignment in a microgenetic episode tends toward articulation, differentiation, and integration of structural patterns. The mediating microprocesses are provided in this view by "dynamic forces" that seem to be general characteristics of how the "field" works.

Sander (1926, 1927, 1928) and his student Ipsen (1925) in their classic investigations on figural and thought development assumed that preliminary, vague, and amorphous images combine with assumptions about final outcome by virtue of an integrative process. This process leads to judgments that represent something between a distal object's presumed shape and most subjective guesses about its meaning. Whereas the denotative meaning of verbalized impressions during these transient stages refers to so-called meaning-spheres (German: *Vorgestalten*; the English term was proposed by Werner, 1956), their connotations refer to an impact of emotional feelings and dynamic urges on the final assignment of meaning. These two views are based on very similar assumptions derived from gestalt theory, especially as far as dynamic qualities are concerned.

Another very similar position is held within the framework of *hypothesis theory* (Bruner, 1951, 1957; Postman, 1951), which, however, pertains to higher level activities in perception. This position underlines the Tolmanian view that the organism neither looks at external events nor acts as a tabula rasa; it is always tuned and directed by expectancies. These expectancies can be based on momentary experience, earlier experience, habits, sets, or attitudes. They are directed toward selectivity by means of a dynamic filter in perception, and they direct activities on the basis of known or assumed cue contingencies. In experimental investigations it was demonstrated that hypotheses in ambiguous perceptual situations can dominate over facts and that they can direct further checking of reality and lead to perceptual compromises as long as factual evidence is missed. Miller, Galanter, and Pribram (1960) described in their cybernetic model the important role of hypotheses that seem to gear microsubroutines, the so-called test-operation-test-exit (TOTE) loops.

These three groups of approaches have in common a reference to organismic processes that bring together externally mediated input and internal processing's outcomes in order to overcome some momentarily dominating instability in the cognitive system when it is oriented toward veridical assessment of external events. At a theoretical metalevel this includes the further assumption that there is, in terms of the process aims, some functional equivalence between different precognitive input elements and anticipated meaning stemming from internal processes that provide for imagery.

In their well-known sensory-tonic field theory of perception, Werner and Wapner (1952) built another golden bridge. In several experiments of the rod-and-frame type, Werner and his students demonstrated a convincing way that exteroceptive (sensory) and proprioceptive (tonic) inputs interact and direct responses toward a balanced compromise. Werner and Wapner (1952) further assumed that an "internal field" provides, *before* stimulus influences, for dynamic integration at the sensory-tonic processing level. Another assumption deals with the embeddedness of field processes in an organism's conditions at a given time. Because of this embeddedness, the *releasing modalities* of field tensions encompass not only perceptual-motor responses but sets, attitudes, and motives, the latter being mediated by "viscerotonic" changes. Furthermore, Werner and Wapner assumed some conversions and reversions in the energy flow between these avenues so that, for example, the impact of sets, motives, and attitudes can influence overt perceptual responses, and intake properties can also lead to changes in symbolic processes. This chain of assumptions, naturally, earned some severe criticism (cf. Allport, 1955) concerning where to localize the "internal dynamic field" and how to deal experimentally with its assumed properties.

There is, however, some evidence about stabilizing, balancing, and release properties of the "internal field" in neuropsychological models based on a variety of findings. Pribram (Pribram, 1979a, 1979b; Pribram & McGuinness, 1975) in particular took the risk of developing a general model of the brain that deals with mechanisms providing for the system's control over its own input. At precognitive and cognitive levels, processes of arousal and stabilization seem to eventuate in intake or rejection of external input processing as a result of effort controls and evaluation impacts, the latter owing to cognitive styles in hemispheres and self-versus other-directed impacts on fissural and perifissural mechanisms. The cortical control seems to be provided by feeler gauges, feedbacks, and interconnections that relate sensory, motor, and associative impacts to central and peripheral processes under conditions of a dynamic stable-state control. To assess some of these "field" properties, baseline information at different physiological levels (e.g., EEG, heart rate, and GSR under "neutral" conditions) can be compared with signs of arousal (phasic stabilization) and activation (tonic stabilization) during the process of meaning assignment. As developed elsewhere (Froehlich, 1978), intake and rejection of input in terms of functional shifts from OR into preparatory activation seem to be model cases for understanding the role of functional equivalents in hypothesis formation and the latter's overt consequences as a dynamic property of a system that tends toward restabilization through effort-control mechanisms.

An empirical argument, in my view, underlines the importance of psychophysiological approaches when dealing with equivalence problems at the so-called higher level. On the basis of findings in the field of imagery and perception, as well as in the field of parallel processing in short-term memory mentioned earlier, subjects in microgenetic experiments may be expected not only to tell more than they actually could know but in some cases to *do* much better than the adaptive functional state of stabilization in the inner milieu is momentarily prepared for. In a very simple discrimination task of the go–no-go type, one can observe that the level of sensory-tonic preparedness seems to have little influence on the speed and efficiency of a motor response. In a microgenetic analysis of effort control, however, the finding is very different. If an observer is requested to push a button when an imperative stimulus (flash) is preceded by a high-pitched tone as a warning signal, and if the same observer is requested to omit motor responses when the same imperative stimulus is preceded by a low-pitched tone, he or she understands the task immediately and does the job most appropriately. Obviously and trivially, this is due to a mental set induced by verbal instructions; there is little doubt that this set operates at the "higher level." The signs of adaptive stabilization—assessed in terms of the contingent negative variation (CNV) (slow negativity in EEG) during interstimulus interval per trial blocks averaged in a serial order—show some interesting developments signifying the different functional stages involved. The early component of CNV (latency between 600 and 1,500 msec after a warning signal) decreases over trials under go conditions, whereas it changes gradually from positive to negative under no-go conditions. These changes can in my view be interpreted as indicating a shift in the functional properties, from anticipation of delivery of information by the imperative signal, to an OR to the warning stimulus (for details see Froehlich, Floru, Glanzmann, Juris, Knoblauch zu Hatzbach, & Nist, 1980). This finding eventually leads to some methodological consequences in microgenetic experiments. To catch some of the properties in covert processes of stabilization and functional shifts, and to interpret these results in terms of the denotative and connotative aspects in overt responses, a multilevel definition of stages is a necessary prerequisite. Although a close view of qualitative differences in changes over trials per level-measure is provided by process-factor analyses (cf. Froehlich, 1978; Pawlik, 1965), a multilevel definition of stages can be done with the help of so-called process-tracing models that are based on multiple regression analysis (cf. Einhorn, Kleinmuntz, & Kleinmuntz, 1979).

Synopsis. Microgenetic experiments turn out to be most helpful instruments for analyzing stages of meaning assignment at the various levels of visual and cognitive functions and their functional equivalents as long as visual search and a need or intention toward percept stabilization provide for passing through an internally established, more or less probabilistic frame of cognitive reference (hypothesis). Although some basic features of recapitulation are dependent on this limitation as well as on the temporal frame provided in experimental procedures—the importance of warning signals included—the recapitulation hypothesis leads to the conclusion that microgenesis still lacks an appropriate theoretical network for dealing with its explanatory meaning at a less introspective and phenomenological level than over its first five decades. What happens at a given trial should be further scrutinized with special regard to the microstructure of processes taking place immediately before stimulus contact (expectancy), during stimulus contact, and after stimulus offset and during response formation. At the same time, at a macroprocess level, it will be necessary to deal with functional shifts and equivalence problems with regard to both the pattern changes in "internal" processes and those becoming externalized by means of overt responses. The information in this section, despite its rather speculative nature, is intended as an invitation to use the microgenetic paradigm as a representative design in general psychology of perception to the same extent as it is used as a tool in differential and clinical psychology.

A Critical Note on Micro–Macro Correspondence

A third theoretical pillar of microgenesis as a process construct was brought into discussion by Werner (1940, 1956) and Conrad (1947, 1948) for two different reasons:

1. Early stages in microgenesis as well as in the ontogenesis of cognitive functions seem to have two common features. They start in an undifferentiated state and end up in accentuated, differentiated, and integrated field patterns. Both are directed toward a qualitatively and quantitatively improved state of affairs in terms of biologic and psychological plans.
2. Looking at basic features of clinical symptoms, as in aphasia, gives rise to the impression that these symptoms reflect to some extent an earlier stage of factual or potential ontogenetic development.

Although the first assumption takes into account the concept of stages as a common element for generalization, as well as the teleological aspect in microgrowth

and macrodevelopment, the second is confined to formal isomorphism (see Graumann, 1959). In the latter case, the framework of common elements seems to be
reduced to some formal similarity of stage patterns. Although there seems to be
a good reason for Werner's formal ontomicrogenetic isomorphism (see the next
paragraph), its extension into the view of clinical symptoms as regression seems
to go beyond the realm of researchability; it seems thus to be an allegory. A very
similar argument holds, in my view, for Brown's recent attempt to extend the
range of parallels again in order to make statements about a quasi-triadic process
feature in phylogenesis, ontogenesis, and microgenesis. In this view, the phyletic,
Jacksonian concept of "levels" refers to rudimentary structural formations. The
ontogenetic concept helps to recognize psychological levels as intimately related
patterns in motor, perceptual, affective, and linguistic components of behavior.
The microgenetic approach, last not least, brings together structural and psychological aspects that are more or less instantaneously traversed (Brown, 1977).
Brown, furthermore, derives from this general assumption another theory of clinical
symptoms in the psychiatric field, one that illustrates par excellence the logical
difficulties in this kind of general process view: "The levels that are recaptured in
pathological change are also stages through which cognitive formation must pass.
Cognition involves an incessant recapitulation of these evolutionary (phylogenetic)
and developmental (ontogenetic) stages. Accordingly, this process is referred to as
microgenesis" (Brown, 1977, p. 7).

The less allegorical view of perceptual development in a maturing organism being
recapitulated in the development of stages of perceptual processes in normal adults,
as held most explicitly by Framo (1952), leads to other consequences that should
be labeled "thematic (or material) ontomicrogenetic isomorphism" (Graumann,
1959, p. 435). This view of micro–macro correspondence fits perfectly into the
scene of the early 1950s when "personality through perception" and "cognitive
controls" came to govern the minds of cognitively inclined differential psychologists. Thematically centered approaches, naturally, make main reference to *content*
and *meaning* in observers' verbal judgments. Kragh (1955) took a first systematic
step in this direction. Using TAT pictures and similar displays and presenting
them in a hologenetic way, Kragh analyzed contents of his subjects' verbal statements. He assumed that life events (e.g., the loss of a beloved person) have an
impact on facilitation or delay of responses as well as on connotative contents.
In his later work (see Chap. 12 in this volume), Kragh developed the so-called
DMT (Defense Mechanism Test), which turned out to be a rather successful instrument in personal selection and clinical psychology. For his early studies, Kragh
was rather severely criticized for his method and aim (cf. Klein, 1957; Smith,
1956). Despite some progress in method and main assumptions (cf., e.g., Bjerstedt,
1956; Kragh & Smith, 1970; Smith & Kragh, 1955; Smith & Klein, 1953), the
problem of thematic correspondences and recapitulation of ontogenetically relevant
events in microgenesis seems to be insoluble in terms of experimental procedures
and operational definitions. The issue and impact of thematic micro–macro correspondences seem to remain a source for projective assumptions and psychodynamic
interpretations at this level of generalization.

Interestingly enough, however, there are results that could eventually offer a
new look at the micro–macro scene at a formal level of explanation. Smith and
Danielsson (1980) most recently demonstrated by a metacontrast procedure how
open flight responses in children evolve into symbolic and perceptual avenues in

the course of development. This seems to be a most promising hint toward some reformulations of emotional control and the micro–macro correspondences stemming from functional equivalents at higher levels of cognition. In her theory of emotion, Arnold (1960) assumed that *felt action tendencies* follow directly from intuitive appraisal. In my view, Smith & Danielsson (1980) have demonstrated how intuitive appraisal in microgenesis, that is, the hologenetically mediated awareness of a threatening face or event in a neutral visual context, is processed at a person's different developmental stages. While direct flight seems to be the most "intuitive" response in children, symbolic flights or a perceptual-interpretative kind of defense reflect the ways a differentiated system can deal with action tendencies. In other terms, functional equivalence in response formation seems to depend on phylogenetic and ontogenetic factors as its modus operandi.

Summary

The process of microgenesis is conceptualized in this chapter in a restricted way that takes into account classic features of this approach as they were independently provided by Gemelli, Sander, and Werner. Microgenesis denotes a sequence of events that occurs in the temporal period between the presentation of a series of stimulus patterns (in most cases visual stimuli) and the formation of a single, relatively stabilized cognitive response to this stimulus pattern. The subject is asked to find out, trial after trial, what the final picture might become. He or she is thus involved in search. In both cases, the merogenetic and the hologenetic, the stimulus pattern begins to be accessible only at a low level of complexity, clarity, and distinctiveness. A progressive increase in these dimensions captures stages of information processing through search. The definition of stages seems to be a central problem in microgenetic research. On the one hand, overt responses (as, e.g., verbal judgments or descriptions in terms of self-ratings) provide some information at a cognitive level. On the other hand, what happens in the time period between trials seems to provide the information needed to deal with the recapitulation hypothesis and representative design problems at different functional levels. The role of preattentive, preemotional, and precognitive impacts as well as the role of hypotheses seem to be embedded in the general assumption of functional equivalents at different levels. The "hidden" nature of these mediating processes and stages provides for some challenge in following them up in multilevel analyses. Assumptions about micro–macro correspondence seem to be based on analogies, allegories, and—to a remarkable extent—secondary interpretations of ex post facto judgments, their "realistic" impact remaining, with a few exceptions, shrouded in darkness. The general problem of micro–macro correspondence, however, seems to be a permanent challenge for interdisciplinary research in the biologic, clinical, psychological, and cross-cultural fields; it might be that these "united" efforts will lead to a scientific answer within the next decade.

DISTAL AND PROXIMAL AIMS IN MICROGENESIS

In this final section of the chapter, I illustrate with some more recent findings the positions I have already developed. We assume that merogenetic and hologenetic procedures differ to some extent in their functional aims and results. As I have stated, microgenetic paradigms deal in a representative way with aspects of perceptual segregation and differentiation, perceptual thinking, and effort after meaning or effort after coping with ambiguity. Whereas merogenesis was born under the auspices of later configurationism and thus deals mainly with the assessment of the distal aim, hologenesis is based on psychophysics and has recently become an adjunct of approaches to subliminal perception and social perception. In the latter case, most obviously, looking at the way observers deal with proximal cues and impacts of their personal worlds and imagery has become a major research perspective. A scrutiny of both microgeneses, the merogenetic and the hologenetic, should, in my view, help overcome some confusion. As a preliminary list of criteria, the points developed in the section on recapitulation hypothesis seem useful: (a) representative levels, (b) parallel processing, (c) functional equivalents at lower and higher levels of the perceptual system, and (d) psychophysiological levels of instability (OR) and stabilization.

Distal Aims in Merogenetic Approaches

In one of his classical investigations, Sander asked adolescent subjects to combine two L-shaped and two vertical line fragments in subjectively meaningful ways by drawing. While a few subjects ended up with abstract ornaments, most of them produced drawings that represented realistic and social meaning. The figural fragments became, to cite some examples, a picturesque street in a village, a man watching an airplane, or two people involved in a discussion. Both solutions, the geometric as well as the realistic, were in Sander's view (Sander, 1926, 1928) influenced by some plans that most immediately and more or less automatically came into the subjects' minds when confronted with the stimulus charts. From these findings and experiments on accentuation in auditive functioning (see Graumann, 1959, for review), Sander drew the conclusion that the _transition_ and _integration_ of merely figural components into _meaning spheres_ seem to be the most crucial "stages" in information processing that is directed toward identification and localization of what an outside event could mean. These transient stages, however, can only be investigated in those cases where an impoverished stimulus pattern has to be completed by stepwise approaches to its very nature of meaning in terms of internally mediated compensations.

In a next step toward representative design, Sander parceled out from a meaningful ink drawing ("farmer's wife") simple figural components that do not by themselves provide for meaningful clues toward the complete pattern. The components (dots, lines, angles) then were accumulated in a random procedure so that there resulted a series of 15 pictures showing a stepwise increase in complexity and completeness. The series was presented, in an ordered sequence starting with the lowest pattern complexity, to subjects who did not know the final pattern's meaning. After inspecting the stimulus chart, subjects were asked to draw what they had just seen and to make verbal comments. As Figure 2.1 (B3 and C3) shows, the subjects started with relatively simple, but to some extent idealized, reproductions of geometric-figural components, for example, lines, angles, and curves. With increasing complexity of the stimulus pattern (Fig. 2.1, A10), the pattern seems to lose its self-sufficient figural-geometric impact; some subjects described this loss as a "chaotic impression," for Sander (1928) a strong argument to assume that a breakdown of "pregnant signification" (German _Prägnanzprinzip_) leads automatically to felt tension and to emotional experiences. Tensions of the latter kind,

Figure 2.1 A: Stimuli 3, 10, and 15 of a merogenetic task
used by Sander. B and C: Drawings provided by
two of the subjects after stimulus inspection.
(From "Experimentelle Ergebnisse der Gestaltpsychologie" by F. Sander, in *Bericht über den
10. Kongress für Experimentelle Psychologie,*
Jena, 1928. Courtesy of Dr. Sander's family
holding copyrights).

however, seem to be released immediately when the subject becomes aware of some
internally mediated assumptions that direct her or his further steps toward meanin-
ful reinterpretations and expectancies. Additional figural components that become
visible during the following trials are now incorporated into the established framework if they fit; if they do not fit, either their interpretation or the hypothetical
framework is changed until final recognition takes place.

What this descriptive feature to some extent illustrates is the lower level impact
of dynamic field properties and the higher level impact of functional equivalents
in interaction between hypotheses and intake information. Two main assumptions
were derived from these early experiments:

1. The process of picking up fragments that increase in complexity and completeness is not geared solely to the external changes in a monotonic relationship.
There are qualitatively different stages, in reference to which, it can be demonstrated how an observer combines proximal cues and hints with regard to a distal
aim. The process develops in a dialectic and dynamic network; one pole is provided
by outside evidence and the other by internal productions and re-productions. In

Sander's description, the process starts with (a) *simple reproduction* and geometric-ornamental schematization owing to gestalt laws; it then passes through (b) some *chaotic experience* caused by the breakdown of pure figural efforts to (c) a stage where *meaning spheres* (i.e., hypotheses) temporarily dominate and stabilize the experienced impact and direct further ways of meaning assignment; finally, there is (d) *recognition*, that is, covert and overt attribution of realistic meaning.

2. The role of meaning spheres and assumptions is stressed in a way that is reminiscent of Machian epistemology to some extent and combines, in my view, aspects of "intuitive appraisal" and of the hypothesis theory of the Bruner-Postman type: The human mind "instinctively and involuntarily" deals with the "material of observation" in such a way that assumptions about missing details, about conditions and consequences, help overcome "natural deficits" in perception, cognition, and action in a "biologically meaningful" way (Mach, 1917, p. 235).

It was mainly Brunswik who applauded Sander for his effort to look at *eidotropic* (form-oriented) and *ontotropic* (reality-oriented) *impacts* in an integrated way. In this view, processes of visual integration are guided by a typical rivalry between geometric-ornamental and realistically meaningful potentialities in perceptual and cognitive organization. Whereas Gestalt psychology traditionally underlined figural components and the laws under which they are brought together, projective tests like Rorschach inkblots mainly look for meaning contents and form levels. "One way out of this dilemma would be the sum of stimulus materials posing a clearcut and balanced rivalry between geometrical-ornamental and realistically meaningful possibilities of organization. . . . Some of Sander's series of decreasingly fragmentary line-drawings . . . may well lend themselves for adaptation to tests of rivalry between *formalism* and *realism*" (Brunswik, 1957, pp. 134–135).

This rivalry together with its dynamic characteristics can be demonstrated in reversed merogenetic and hologenetic procedures, labeled by Sander as "*Gestaltzerfall*" (gestalt disintegration), that also seem to provide an experimental base for dealing with the regressional aspects in micro–macro correspondences (cf. Hardick, 1933; Knab-Barwell, 1950; Rathmann, 1932; Richters, 1955; Sander & Iinuma, 1928). In my view, these disintegration experiments provide strong evidence for the *functional plasticity* of the perceptual and conceptual systems involved. In one of my own investigations (Froehlich, 1964), responses to increasing fragmentation were compared, using geometric patterns and the "farmer's wife" drawing as stimuli. Disruption was provided by increasing the interval between projection of two randomly selected parts on the same screen in a multichannel mirror tachistoscope. In the case of a geometric pattern (a composition of lines, angles, and triangles), subjects mainly reported an increasing *instability* as far as the composition of figural parts was concerned; they ended up reporting two different part compositions. The fragmentation of a meaningful picture, however, led to somewhat more dramatic responses in the transient stages as well as to some unexpected signs of meaning dominance at the end of the serial disruption. Most subjects did not refer to fragmentation of figural components. They described changes in *meaning*. Typical examples are, for instance, references to changed facial expressions, to bodily position, and to bodily movements (to some extent, ultimately due to gamma phenomenon and backward masking). In a few cases, the main references were made to presumed technical problems in the tachistoscope.

It should be noted that the nature of the change was not announced by the experimenter; the task was simply to describe what happened on the screen. In both cases, however, instability seemed to be the proximal cue that directed the person toward formalistic or realistic solutions when interpreting the "facts" given.

At the level of experience (i.e., self-reports) Sander made special reference to emotionally tuned responses. In later investigations, however, these hints turned out to be more or less related to basic features of relatively mild *tensions* and their *release*. Only when using stimulus materials, such as threatening pictures, that provide for emotional impacts does the reference to emotional feelings find its expression. At the level of psychophysiological assumptions (developed in earlier sections more extensively; for references see also Froehlich, 1978), it would be expected that the impact of effort control would parallel different stages in selective attention and hypothesis formation in the form of functional shifts. From a theoretical point of view, this seems to be important in defining the functional meaning of stages in the framework of functionally equivalent processes that increase in complexity during microgenesis. The interpretation of *intensity changes* related to functional shifts in effort control (cf. Pribram & McGuinness, 1975) should, to be meaningful, be undertaken at the psychophysiological level. What this means is that the basic features of the process at both levels, the psychological and the physiological, have to be related in terms of the functional principle involved.

A first attempt at a solution could start at the level of the OR. For Sokolov (1967), perception as a process is based on information processing in the "analytic mechanisms" of the CNS. The OR seems to be the most important agent of information-related regulation in these mechanisms. It is turned on when an organism is confronted with new or unexpected events. In this case, an input's *entropy* is directed toward finding out "what" there is. Sokolov (1966) further assumed that stimulus novelty is the result of a discrepancy between stabilized neuronal models and recent input. Thus, a cortical mechanism seems to control elicitation and inhibition of the OR because of internal states at the neuronal model level. The OR, moreover, seems to reflect within given limits the internal efforts toward model establishment provided by repeated stimulus contact. If the effort is successful, that is, if model establishment or reestablishment is terminated, the OR becomes habituated. To deal with this *orientation dimension* properly in microgenetic studies, a very important restriction should be introduced. An OR keeps its functional properties as long as there is no further influence or cue available that would make the OR a *conditioned response*. Classic habituation experiments, for example, consist of presenting an identical stimulus (e.g., a 100-Hz sinus tone) repeatedly. After about 10 to 15 trials, the OR terminates because of redundancy at the central level. In microgenetic experiments, stimulus contact *and* response formation are embedded in a task that relates input registration, information processing, and response formation to the purpose of assigning a final meaning. Moreover, the patterns presented in a microgenetic order will vary in the amount of information carried from trial to trial. In other words, only in the first trial can we conceivably grasp a "pure" unconditioned OR that also reflects to some extent an organism's readiness to deal with an input of initial hints in a task with which the subject is dealing in a manner that is "set" by means of instructions. The following responses are, therefore, loaded with complex *conditioned relationships* that are provided as a result of the task (that is, directing the subject to search for meaning), of earlier input and information processing, and of assumptions (i.e., hypotheses). At this level of scrutiny it should be necessary to talk about a conditioned OR or about *orientation-related phasic arousal*. In this frame of reference one can assume that the ORs assessed over microgenetic trials could reflect functional shifts during model establishment or hypothesis formation, the former referring to lower level processes in the system, the latter to a higher level kind of process that includes functional equivalences.

In one study (Froehlich & Laux, 1969), a series of 15 pictures was used that increased stepwise in complexity owing to a random procedure. The final picture showed a line drawing of a girl in a bathtub. The stimulus material was developed by Smock (1955) and adjusted to the microgenetic task. The choice of stimulus material was determined by the need to keep male subjects interested through the whole task, which was lengthy because of the necessity for extensive time controls. Pictures were presented tachistoscopically in a merogenetic order at a supraliminal time (100 msec) that was kept constant over task, as were area and illumination. GSR measures were taken before and after trials for baseline assessment; they were taken during the trial (i.e., beginning with stimulus onset and terminating 12 sec later) to get phasic and tonic components of specific changes. At 12 sec after the stimulus offset, a buzzer signaled to the subjects to begin their verbal reports (Group 1) or to provide optionally their ideas of what the final picture might be (Group 2). The 12-sec interval was chosen to provide for a slowdown of specific GSR components to the base line. After 20 sec, another signal terminated the response-time interval, which was followed after another 20 sec by the presentation of the next picture. This time order was derived from a series of pilot studies. Group 1 ($n = 16$ male students) were asked to make verbal statements about what they would guess the picture would finally become; Group 2 ($n = 20$ male students) were also instructed to make guesses but at a subvocal level, in other words, just to think about the final picture's meaning. The reason for these two task conditions is obvious: to discover (a) whether the preparation for an open-speech motor response influences the GSR component of the OR and (b) to what extent the course of GSR–OR over trials is influenced by reasoning versus overt speech in input integration at the cognitive level.

The main results of this study were: (a) The trends of phasic OR did not differ substantially under conditions of overt and covert response preparation as far as their course was concerned. There was, however, a heightened level of basic arousal under conditions of overt speech preparation. (b) The difference between phasic changes and basic conductance level corresponded to some extent to the level of pattern integration in Group 1; the measure of pattern integration was based on ratings of verbal contents (for details see Froehlich & Laux, 1969). (c) The order of trends in OR measures (corrected for basic conductance) turned out to be quadratic at a .99 level of probability superimposed upon some linear components. The shape of the trend was reminiscent of a U curve.

At first glance, the last result especially seems to demonstrate development over functionally and qualitatively different stages. A slowing down of OR over the first few trials seems to reflect a kind of stabilization in terms of model establishment; the turning point could reflect some functional shift; and the increase of phasic arousal toward the end could be traced to the impact of functionally equivalent processes of higher order (i.e., hypotheses). To avoid premature overinterpretations, these assumptions were checked in terms of two different kinds of additional analyses:

1. An analysis of *elementary process functions* based on a special version of primary-component factor analysis (courtesy of F. Kahlau) revealed—in addition to a constant load over process owing to brightness and in addition to another factor that reflects onset and offset over trials—a component that loads mainly on those trials that, at the experiential level, seem to be critical for hypothesis formation or hypothesis impact. On the one hand, this result supports the constancy of levels of energy over trials and the representation of stimulus onset and offset in the OR; on the other hand, it reflects some kind of a functional shift that is event related in a logical way.

2. In his doctoral thesis Velden (1974) demonstrated that there is a relationship between *information content* (entropy) in printed language and OR developments in a merogenetic task. The OR in this case reflected to a remarkable extent the amount of information carried by the stimulus events trial by trial. On a theoretical level, this should lead to some modifications of Sokolov's entropy model (Sokolov, 1963, 1966, 1967). In terms of our own studies, this could mean that the information carried by the stimulus pattern could have led to the main effect in the merogenetic visual task as well. The pictures were composed by means of a random procedure, that is, dot patterns were added, using the same number of dots per target but distributing them in a random order over the field. All subjects received the same kind of information because the picture patterns were constant over all subjects. An information-content analysis (see Chap. 6) led to the surprising result that the beautiful quadratic trend in OR followed in a significant way the amount of information carried in terms of increasing *density* (distance measures) combined with *angles*.

Another study done in the same way using the same stimuli (girl in a bathtub) produced another result in a larger sample ($n = 89$ "silent" observers as in Group 2). The trends assessed in terms of OR-GSR showed a quadratic trend (.99) as well as a *cubic trend* (.99), that is, a most marked second- and third-order contrast. The stimulus dimension contributed to trend variance at a .95 level, whereas interindividual differences were assessed at a .99 level. Froehlich, de Ridder, and Wallau (1973) interpreted these findings as evidence of increasing complexity in the process stages that could be assessed only in larger samples because of marked interindividual differences. OR, considered as an index of the impact of the arousal system, seems to appear on the first trial at "pure" OR level, then decreases owing to figural redundancy, increases again owing to novelty or hypothesis formation, but then begins a decrease before task completion and pattern completeness (Fig. 2.2, solid line). This could mean that a subject in this task shifts from *orienting efforts* and *intake proneness* to another kind of activity that is based on his or her subjectively good position from which to *conceptualize* and *predict* further outcomes. While the first turning point (Trials 4 through 6) seems to refer to the shift from formalism toward hypothesis formation, it might be that the second turning point (Trials 10 through 12) has to do with completed reasoning and input rejection.

Taking into account the results of Gilsdorf and Froehlich (Chap. 6), a little more speculation may be useful in formulating further hypotheses about microgenesis. If the information carried by stimulus patterns predicts the up-and-down feature of the quadratic trend, main influences of the higher order (i.e., cognitive) processes should be expected where these two trends do not overlap. This is the

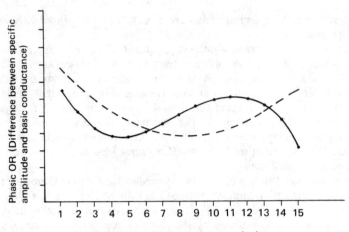

Figure 2.2   Idealized cubic (solid line) and quadratic trend (dotted line)
over 15 trials, using stimuli with increasing complexity. The
cubic trend is based on $n = 86$ subjects, the quadratic on
$n = 20$. (Data from Froehlich, de Ridder, & Wallau, 1973,
and Froehlich & Laux, 1969, respectively.)

case especially between Trials 5 and 11, where hypothesis formation plays a prominent role as a developing functional equivalent. This interpretation gets some
indirect support from a twin study (Froehlich, de Ridder, & Wallau, 1973). Mono-
zygotic twins (subsample $n = 35$; age about 30; hematologic control) in a paired-
comparison analysis of variance showed more marked similarities with regard to
the quadratic trend than with regard to the cubic trend, whereas this similarity
could not be shown in dizygotic twins. Assuming that the strength of genetic impact is more likely to be demonstrated in basic visual functions than in socially
tuned cognitive functions, this result supports the hypothesis about the meaning
of the trends and the "cognitive" interpretation of the third-order component's
changes. One expects to have more stringent details in terms of effort controls
after including measures of tonic readiness that can be derived from EEG's CNV.

To sum up and draw some conclusions, a psychophysiological view of merogenesis stresses the importance of its basic features as a representative design in
dealing with the rivalry between figuralism and realism. Combining data from the
experience level with those available at the level of functional state control seems,
within the limits of a first attempt in this direction, to complete naturally and
meaningfully the explanatory network of microgenesis. The definition of stages
in terms of functional shifts at the experiential level and at the level of effort
control seems to be particularly helpful. I further assume that there is a neglected
field of application that now is open to microgenetic investigations of the
figuralism–realism type. Pribram and McGuinness (1975) gave rise to the idea that
severe states of psychological stress or emotional arousal impair effort control with
consequences on (a) appropriate shifts from arousal-mediated intake to activation-
mediated preparatory tonification as well as on (b) coupling and decoupling of
stimulus and response contingencies (cf. Froehlich, 1978). Eventual deficits of
this kind resulting from chronic or transient stress and emotional attitudes could

be assessed in terms of microgenesis with special regard to their impact on cognitive processing where search leads to meaning assignment. Another advantage consists, in my view, in comparing microgenetic processing in neutral and in ego-involving tasks as well as with neutral and stress-related stimulus symbols. The problem of functional equivalents in merogenetic approaches seems to be soluble in terms of early (figural) and later (higher level) processes and in terms of the functional shifts discussed extensively in this section. It should be noted, however, that the assessment of content-related features that play an imminent role in hypothesis formation as "meaning spheres" still provides the framework for any kind of interpretation. At the same time, the physiological measures proposed in this chapter tell us something about how adaptive processes at the intensity level contribute to making an observer think and tell more than she or he could "know."

Proximal Cues and Distal Aims in Hologenetic Approaches

As stated earlier, hologenetic approaches, being similar to threshold models, eventually lead us to insights about what happens beyond the level of the assessment of figural components, that is, about the dynamic conditions of figure–ground segregation under subliminal conditions of stimulus presentation. The level of complexity, as far as the figural intake conditions are concerned, is the lowest; on the other hand, subjects in hologenetic tasks are motivated to search in the same way as subjects in a merogenetic task. In most general terms, this provides for a very marked impact of higher level activities in order to overcome the low-level kind of segregated stimulus information. What is eventually labeled as a "meaning sphere" develops extremely early in the process and is at the same time extremely unstable. In other terms, the span of functionally equivalent elements is wider, and at the same time, the two probabilistic features overlap and interact. Two observations provide rather self-evident illustrations of these principles: (a) in hologenetic tasks, there are more response omissions to be expected than in merogenetic tasks; (b) subjects are more suggestible, so that a "click" in the apparatus not followed by another stimulus presentation can lead to a response that refers to something that from the subject's point of view has happened on the screen (cf. Kuhn, 1958). The latter observation can be interpreted as the "power of expectancy"; it can also be interpreted as an activating event that eventuates in arousal of all parts of the system involved. The importance of proximal cues and personal reminiscences is obvious and leads to diagnostic and clinical uses of hologenetic approaches.

From a technical point of view, there are some severe problems to overcome. The stimulus material, for example, should not be too complex to provide for figure–ground segregation; color prints should be avoided as stimulus material because color detection is dependent on energy level in the well-known Purkinje shift; when starting with subliminal energy levels, subjects need some time for darkness adaptation; the increase at the energy level in tachistoscopic procedures has side effects (e.g., gamma movements, activation, etc.) that interfere with figural segregation; and so forth. Using noncomplex stimuli makes the hologenetic task a recognition task that is most useful for the purpose of predicting visual acuity in very general terms (e.g., Chap. 18). Using complex stimuli with a touch of emotional impact makes the task to some extent a combination of acuity and projective ability, but the functional shifts from "intuitive appraisal" to subjective evidence are hard to assess.

In the so-called metacontrast experiments, there are some obvious advantages. In the early 1930s Werner could demonstrate that a figure (a ring) presented immediately after another visual stimulus (a circle) at the same position leads to the impression that the first figure, the circle, has been blurred and fused. An established visualized stimulus pattern seems to lose some of its figural stability when another figure arouses some of the neighboring "field" segments after a very short period of time. Quite obviously, this time has to do with the working mechanisms of iconic storage and short-term memory. Smith (cf., e.g., Smith & Henriksson, 1955) took the first steps toward the use of a very similar backward masking procedure in microgenetic research. In a hologenetic procedure (Step 1) the subject is familiarized with a visually presented frame of future reference. When this frame is stabilized (i.e., correctly recognized), another hologenetic procedure (Step 2) provides for an introduction of an additional stimulus pattern. When interpreting what happened on the screen, the subject makes reference to what he or she "knows," that is, to the stable frame of reference established earlier. In this case, hypothesis formation is to some extent guided by comparing new input information with the established figural or realistic framework. Hypothesis formation, in these cases, shows its impact with reference to something known and evidenced. The proximally mediated cues seem to be used in terms of a localized distal aim.

The impact of proximal cues is most articulated in those cases where the realistic framework (Step 1) is successively unbalanced by introducing in Step 2 some objectively meaningful detail that does not fit the embedding framework. In this case, the observer's task is to deal with ambiguity as she or he becomes aware of increasing evidence. An observer's situation is to some extent similar to that of somebody whose established insight fails in the face of factual information. On a theoretical level, this is obviously a problem of how and to what extent a subject uses functionally equivalent techniques in overcoming the lack of belongingness between two visually induced messages, how he or she modifies and corrects earlier frames of reference under the impact of new evidence, and what hypotheses fill the gap. Mainly because of this phenomenological impact, what should be emphasized is the importance of *directional changes in expectancies* that develop between the poles of the given visual frame of reference and proximal cues.

One set of experiments on ambiguity used a metacontrast paradigm (for details see Froehlich, 1964). In a series of pretests, stimulus materials were selected. Several pictures, showing a dog with a human head, a living room with a big car or big animal in it, a captain who sees in the bull's-eye the sea level in a vertical position, an office with a big traffic sign, and so on, were rated by 40 subjects to assess the experienced level of incongruity when confronted with these pictures. The final selection was based on paired comparisons. Three patterns got the highest ranking and were administered in another pilot experiment to check the number of trials and the illumination-time rates and to get some preliminary information on response dimensions. It finally turned out that a photographic picture of an office was recognized after about 12 trials, at a presentation time of 150 msec, starting at Trial 1 with .55 msec, the time progression being $t_2 = t_1 \sqrt{2}$; $t_3 = t_2 \times 2$, and so forth. Recognition criteria were items like table, chair, typewriter, picture on the wall, window, radiator. These criteria were used in the main experiment to define operationally the recognition of frame of reference in Step 1 of the procedure. The critical pattern that turned out to be most ambiguity-inducing was a traffic sign in the left corner that could also signify in the early stages of holo-genetic awareness some kind of a hat-and-coat stand. The critical stimulus was introduced in Step 2 of the procedure at projection times starting with .35 msec and progressing over 19 potential trials to 2,000 msec. Illumination was held constant over all trials in Steps 1 and 2 of the procedure.

Figure 2.3 shows the complete stimulus pattern as it appeared in Step 2 with increasing clarity, whereas in Step 1 the office was to be seen without the traffic sign. The task was to inspect most carefully what there was to be seen on the screen of a mirror tachistoscope. Each trial was preceded by a buzzer. Subjects were asked to make verbal statements about what they had seen or guess what the final picture would become. There was no special announcement made that strange things could appear. The subjects, furthermore, had the choice of terminating the task during Step 2 of the procedure whenever they "found out" on the basis of subjective evidence what the pattern meant to them. Motivation for a further search, however, was stimulated by telling subjects after the recognition of the criterion items in the room that they had missed some important details. In different experimental sessions 68 male and female students participated. For obvious reasons, they were selected out of a larger sample of about 300 because of their extreme scores on tests of interference, intolerance of ambiguity, and manifest anxiety.

An overall result was the fact that, at the beginning of Step 2, subjects started to report some instability in the frame pattern. This instability was related to the

Figure 2.3 Incongruent picture used in a hologenetic task. (From *Unstimmig-keit, Erwartung und Kompromiss* by W. D. Froehlich, Unpublished professorial dissertation, University of Bonn, 1964.)

whole frame pattern (changing its size, for example) or to some critical details in it (e.g., additional chairs or pictures on the wall). At the next stage, disorder, movement, and also the shadowlike appearance of big objects or people were reported. This transient stage seems to reflect the subjects' ways of dealing with increasing instability of the visual perception by means of higher order associations projected on the formerly stable frame. The final stage was most heterogeneous. About one-third of the subjects ended their search by *subdividing* the impressions into two categories, stating that there was an office room *and* there was a traffic sign, too. The rest of the subjects, however, arrived at *compromises* or *homogenizations.* A typical example of compromise was the statement that there was an office with a big towel on a kind of hat-and-coat stand. Homogenization refers to a change or a redefinition of meaning, exemplified in such statements as "This is a magazine room in a warehouse where somebody has brought together several objects from offices and traffic departments" or "This is an office of a travel agent." In other words, a search that takes place under conditions of ambiguity in an established framework with freedom to end the search upon development of a subjective certainty of meaning, is not necessarily terminated in veridical assignment of meaning. Subjective ways of looking at things, styles, and attitudes toward the task, together with the kind of risk involved, seem to determine proximally what distal events should look like and when to finish the task. In these complex hologenetic tasks, the impact is not that of some rivalry between figural and realistic features but between the turns an observer performs when interpreting how things look.

The formal features of this process were assessed through the number of trials and through ratings of the level of differentiation versus homogenization, which were done by trained raters based on tape-recorded protocols. Subjects with high color-word interference, for example, generally ended the search much earlier than those lower in interference. Subjects scoring high in intolerance of ambiguity on a questionnaire also ended very early with extremely low differentiations in their responses, whereas high-anxious subjects differentiated much more in their final statements. Owing to sample size and a general lack of interactions between the screening variables, these latter results should not be overinterpreted (for details see Froehlich, 1964, pp. 99 ff.).

Synoptically relevant is a borderline situation between a distal and proximal kind of orientation, represented most strikingly in experiments on *visual thinking.* When Sintschenko et al. (1973) asked their subjects to find their way in a visually presented maze, to deal with embedded figures, and to localize a compass needle's position presented on an incomplete compass card, subjects made reference to some visualized schemes. The solution of these problems developed stepwise and under quite different functional impacts (assessed in terms of peripheral and central physiological processes). But the way a subject made use of functionally equivalent elements was a matter of personal strategy, just as, for example, a chess player who acquires her information in a lopsidedly hologenetic way may—after a short glance at the board—fail to observe an individual figure's position and thus miss a castling of the white party. Finding the way through a visually presented maze could be done by means of trials and errors (similar to merogenetic processing) but also and most effectively by building up some cognitive map of left and right turns; in the latter case, proximal cue processing dominated to some extent. Visual thinking, in my view a neglected field in microgenetic research, builds a golden bridge between the two kinds of task conditions. Responses to visual-thinking tasks offer hints to how visually mediated reasoning is related to localized effects when the observer or subject has the freedom to choose between hologenetic or merogenetic preferences.

Hologenetic tasks provide challenges and problems. They obviously have impact at all levels mentioned: parallel processing, functional equivalents at lower and higher visual system's levels, and all kinds of intuitive and reflexive appraisals that Lazarus would dream about. But verbal response contents, when interpreted ex post facto by an experimenter or a clinical psychologist or by means of sophisticated analytical schemes of content, pose some difficulties in generalizing efforts toward definitions of stages. Psychophysiological approaches with the exception of those proposed by Sintschenko et al. (1973) cannot be applied because of the impact of increasing energy that overlaps with cognitively relevant measures at this level. Only in a few cases does this problem seem to be soluble (see Chap. 18). For descriptive issues, however, metacontrast experiments seem to have a promising future in general psychology. Smith and his students (cf. Smith & Danielsson, 1980) in particular have demonstrated the usefulness of this descriptive tool in developmental and clinical psychology. While merogenesis seems to be on the way to developing a theory of its own at both levels—the phenomenological and the psychophysiological—hologenesis continues to be in search of an explanatory general frame of reference. Pending the formulation of such a theory, the existence of hologenesis provides an open invitation for theorizing, from hypothesis theory and subliminal perception, through perceptual controls and defenses, up (or down) to psychodynamics. Let it therefore remain for the time being a descriptive instrument with a challenging appeal that, in most cases, tells us more than we know about. It might be that we may eventually do much better with hologenetic approaches than we know.

REFERENCES

Aarons, L. Subvocalization: Aural and EMG feedback in reading. *Perceptual and Motor Skills,* 1971, *33,* 271–306.

Allport, F. H. *Theories of perception and the concept of structure.* New York: Wiley, 1955.

Arnheim, R. *Visual thinking.* New York: Holt, 1969.

Arnold, M. B. *Emotion and personality* (2 vols.). New York: Columbia University Press, 1960.

Bjerstedt, A. Levels of strictness with respect to micro-macro-correspondences: A note on the "actual-genetic" model. *Theoria,* 1956, *22,* 199–203.

Black, H. K. Semantic differential ratings of impoverished stimuli: A replication. *Bulletin of the Psychonomic Society,* 1975, *5,* 81–83.

Brown, J. *Mind, brain, and consciousness: The neuropsychology of cognition.* New York: Academic, 1977.

Bruner, J. S. Personality dynamics and the process of perceiving. In R. R. Blake & G. Ramsey (Eds.), *Perception: An approach to personality.* New York: McGraw-Hill, 1951.

Bruner, J. S. On perceptual readiness. *Psychological Review,* 1957, *64,* 123–152.

Brunswik, E. *Systematic and representative design of psychological experiments, with results in physical and social perception.* Berkeley and Los Angeles: University of California Press, 1957.

Colgate, R. L., Hoffman, J. E., & Eriksen, C. W. Selective encoding from multielement visual displays. *Perception and Psychophysics,* 1973, *14,* 217–224.

Conrad, K. Über den Begriff der Vorgestalt und seine Bedeutung für die Hirnpathologie. *Nervenartz,* 1947, *18,* 189–193.

Conrad, K. Strukturanalyse hirnpathologischer Fälle. Über Gestalt- und Funktionswandel bei einem Fall von transcortikaler motorischer Aphasie. *Deutsche Zeitschrift für Nervenheilkunde,* 1948, *158,* 372–434.

Dixon, N. F. *Subliminal perception: The nature of a controversy.* London: McGraw-Hill, 1971.

Draguns, J. G. Affective meaning of reduced stimulus input: A study by means of the semantic differential. *Canadian Journal of Psychology,* 1967, *21,* 231–241.

Einhorn, H. J., Kleinmuntz, D. N., & Kleinmuntz, B. Linear regression and process tracing models of judgment. *Psychological Review,* 1979, *86,* 465–485.

Eriksen, C. W., & Spencer, T. Rate of information processing in visual perception: Some results and methodological considerations. *Journal of Experimental Psychology,* 1969, *79*(2, Pt. 2).

Finke, R. A. Levels of equivalence in imagery and perception. *Psychological Review,* 1980, *87,* 113–132.

Flavell, J. H., & Draguns, J. G. A microgenetic approach to perception and thought. *Psychological Bulletin,* 1957, *54,* 197–217.

Floru, R., & Froehlich, W. D. *Psychophysiologie der Aufmerksamkeit.* Bern: Huber, 1982.

Forgus, R. H., & Malamed, L. E. *Perception: A cognitive-stage approach.* New York: McGraw-Hill, 1976.

Framo, J. L. *Structural aspects of perceptual development in normal adults: A tachistoscopic study with the Rorschach technique.* Unpublished doctoral dissertation, University of Texas, 1952.

Froehlich, W. D. *Unstimmigkeit, Erwartung und Kompromiss.* Unpublished professorial dissertation (Habilitationsschrift), University of Bonn, 1964.

Froehlich, W. D. Stress, anxiety, and the control of attention: A psychophysiological approach. In C. D. Spielberger & I. G. Sarason (Eds.), *Stress and Anxiety* (Vol. 5). Washington: Hemisphere, 1978.

Froehlich, W. D., de Ridder, E., & Wallau, K. *Genetische Bedingungen der OR* (Research Rep. Fr. 132/8). Bonn and Bad Godesberg: Deutsche Forschungsgemeinschaft, 1973.

Froehlich, W. D., Floru, R., Glanzmann, P., Juris, M., von Knoblauch zu Hatzbach, L., & Nist, W. The temporal development of early and late CNV in a simple discrimination paradigm: The effect of motor preparation and average reaction time. In H. H. Kornhuber & L. Deecke (Eds.), *Motivation, motor and sensory processes of the brain: Electrical potentials, behavior and clinical use* (Progress in Brain Research Series). Amsterdam: Elsevier, 1980.

Froehlich, W. D., & Koszik, K. *Die Macht der Signale.* Hamburg: Rowohlt, 1971.

Froehlich, W. D., & Laux, L. Serielles Wahrnehmen, Aktualgenese, Informationsintegration und Orientierungsreaktion: I. Aktualgenetisches Modell und Orientierungsreaktion. *Zeitschrift für experimentelle und angewandte Psychologie,* 1969, *16,* 250–277.

Gemelli, A. Über das Entstehen von Gestalten. *Archiv für die gesamte Psychologie,* 1928, *65,* 205–268.

Gemelli, A. Orienting concepts in the study of affective states: I. *Journal of Nervous and Mental Disorders,* 1949, *110,* 198–214. (a)

Gemelli, A. Orienting concepts in the study of affective states: II. *Journal of Nervous and Mental Disorders,* 1949, *110,* 299–314. (b)

Graumann, C. F. Aktualgenese: Die deskriptiven Grundlagen und theoretischen Wandlungen des aktualgenetischen Forschungsansatzes. *Zeitschrift für experimentelle und angewandte Psychologie,* 1959, *6,* 410–448.

Haber, R. N. (Ed.). *Information-processing approaches to visual perception.* New York: Holt, 1969.

Hardick, L. Über den Umschlag von Einstellungen unter dem Einfluss kritischen Erfahrungen. *Archiv für die gesamte Psychologie,* 1933, *87,* 321–350.

Hoffman, J. E. Search through a sequentially presented visual display. *Perception and Psychophysics,* 1978, *23,* 1–11.

Ipsen, G. Zur Theorie des Erkennens. *Neue psychologische Studien,* 1925, *1,* 279–472.

Klein, G. S. Review of U. Kragh's "The actual-genetic model of perception personality." *Contemporary Psychology,* 1957, *2,* 64–66.

Knab-Barwell, A. H. *Die Aktualgenese der Wahrnehmung im Film.* Unpublished doctoral dissertation, University of Heidelberg, 1950.

Kragh, U. *The actual-genetic model of perception-personality.* Lund: Gleerup, and Copenhagen: Munksgaard, 1955.

Kragh, U., & Smith, G. J. W. (Eds.). *Percept-genetic analysis.* Lund: Gleerup, 1970.

Kuhn, W. F. *Aktualgenetische Untersuchungen an Schizophrenen.* Unpublished doctoral dissertation, University of Bonn, 1958.

Lazarus, R. S. *Psychological stress and the coping process.* New York: McGraw-Hill, 1966.

Linschoten, J. Aktualgenese und heuristisches Prinzip. *Zeitschrift für experimentelle und angewandte Psychologie*, 1959, *6*, 449–473.

Mach, E. *Erkenntnis und Irrtum*. Leipzig: Barth, 1917.

Marr, D. Early processing of visual information. *Philosophical Transactions of the Royal Society of London*, 1976, *275*, 483–524.

Miller, G. A., Galanter, E., & Pribram, K. H. *Plans and the structure of behavior*. New York: Holt/Dryden, 1960.

Neisser, U. *Cognitive psychology*. New York: Appleton, 1967.

Nickerson, R. S. Response times with a memory dependent decision task. *Journal of Experimental Psychology*, 1966, *72*, 761–769.

Nisbett, R. E., & Wilson, T. D. Telling more than we can know: Verbal reports on mental processes. *Psychological Review*, 1977, *84*, 231–259.

Pawlik, K. Elementarfunktionen ("Faktoren") einfacher Lernvorgänge. In H. Heckhausen (Ed.), *Bericht über den 24. Kongress der Deutschen Gesellschaft für Psychologie*. Göttingen: Hogrefe, 1965.

Postman, L. Towards a general theory of cognition. In M. Sherif & J. H. Rohrer (Eds.), *Social psychology at the cross-roads*. New York: Harper, 1951.

Pribram, K. H. The biology of emotions and other feelings. In R. Plutchik & H. Kellerman (Eds.), *Theories of emotion*. New York: Academic, 1979. (a)

Pribram, K. H. Emotions. In S. B. Filskov & T. J. Boll (Eds.), *Handbook of clinical neuropsychology*, 1979. (b)

Pribram, K. H., & McGuinness, D. Arousal, activation, and effort in the control of attention. *Psychological Review*, 1975, *82*, 116–149.

Rathmann, S. *Über den Zerfall auditiv-motorischer Gestalten*. Unpublished doctoral dissertation, University of Jena, 1932.

Richters, G. *Untersuchungen über den Zerfall einer sinnvollen optischen Gestalt*. Unpublished B.A. thesis, University of Bonn, 1955.

Sander, F. Über räumliche Rhythmik. *Neue psychologische Studien*, 1926, *1*, 123–158.

Sander, F. Über Gestaltqualitäten. In *Bericht über den 8. internationalen Kongress für Psychologie*. Groningen, 1927.

Sander, F. Experimentelle Ergebnisse der Gestaltpsychologie. In *Bericht über den 10. Kongress für experimentelle Psychologie*. Jena, 1928.

Sander, F., & Iinuma, R. Beiträge zur Psychologie des stereoskopischen Sehens: I. *Archiv für die gesamte Psychologie*, 1928, *65*, 191–207.

Schneider, W., & Shiffrin, R. M. Controlled and automatic human information processing: I. Detection, search, and attention. *Psychological Review*, 1977, *84*, 1–66.

Sheehan, P. W., & Neisser, U. Some variables affecting vividness of imagery in recall. *British Journal of Psychology*, 1969, *60*, 71–80.

Shepard, R. N. Psychophysiological complementarity. In M. Kubovy & J. R. Pomerantz (Eds.), *Perceptual organization*. Hillsdale, N.J.: Erlbaum, 1979.

Shepard, R. N., & Podgorny, P. Cognitive processes that resemble perceptual processes. In W. K. Estes (Ed.), *Handbook of learning and cognitive processes* (Vol. 5). Hillsdale, N.J.: Erlbaum, 1978.

Shiffrin, R. M., & Schneider, W. Controlled and automatic human information processing: II. Perceptual learning, automatic attending and a general theory. *Psychological Review*, 1977, *84*, 127–190.

Sintschenko, W., Munipow, W., & Gordon, V. Visuelles Denken. *Ideen des Exakten Wissens*, 1973, *5*, 297–305.

Smith, G. J. W. Review of U. Kragh's "The actual-genetic model of perception-personality." *Theoria*, 1956, *22*, 61–69.

Smith, G. J. W., & Danielsson, A. Von offen gezeigten Fluchttendenzen zu symbolischen und wahrnehmungsmässigen Strategien. In U. Hentschel & G. J. W. Smith (Eds.), *Experimentelle Persönlichkeitspsychologie: Die Wahrnehmung als Zugang zu diagnostischen Problemen*. Wiesbaden: Akademische Verlagsgesellschaft, 1980.

Smith, G. J. W., & Henriksson, M. The effect on an established percept of a perceptual process beyond awareness. *Acta Psychologica*, 1955, *11*, 346–355.

Smith, G. J. W., & Klein, G. S. Cognitive controls in serial behavior patterns. *Journal of Personality*, 1953, *22*, 188–213.

Smith, G. J. W., & Kragh, U. Do microgenetic sequences reflect life-history? *Acta Psychologica*, 1955, *11*, 504–512.

Smock, C. D. The influence of psychological stress on the "intolerance of ambiguity." *Journal of Abnormal and Social Psychology,* 1955, *50,* 177–182.

Sokolov, E. N. Perception and the conditioned reflex. London: Oxford University Press, 1963.

Sokolov, E. N. Orientation reflex as information regulator. In A. Leontyev, A. Lurya, & A. Smirnov (Eds.), *Psychological research in the USSR* (Vol. 1). Moscow: Progress, 1966.

Sokolov, E. N. Die reflektorischen Grundlagen der Wahrnehmung. In H. Hiebsch (Ed.), *Ergebnisse der russischen Psychologie.* Berlin: Akademie Verlag, 1967.

Sokolov, E. N., & Vinogradova, O. S. (Eds.). *Neuronal mechanisms of the orienting reflex.* Hillsdale, N.J.: Erlbaum, 1975.

Sternberg, S. High-speed scanning in human memory. *Science,* 1966, *153,* 652–654.

Swets, J. A., Tanner, W. P., & Birsdall, T. G. Decision processes in perception. *Psychological Review,* 1961, *68,* 301–340.

Velden, M. An empirical test of Sokolov's entropy model of the orienting response. *Psychophysiology,* 1974, *11,* 682–691.

Werner, H. Über Mikromelodik und Mikroharmonik. *Zeitschrift für Psychologie,* 1926, *98,* 74–89.

Werner, H. Über die Ausprägung von Tongestalten. *Zeitschrift für Psychologie,* 1927, *101,* 159–181.

Werner, H. *Comparative psychology of mental development.* New York: Harper, 1940.

Werner, H. Microgenesis and aphasia. *Journal of Abnormal and Social Psychology,* 1956, *52,* 347–353.

Werner, H., & Wapner, S. Toward a general theory of perception. *Psychological Review,* 1952, *59,* 324–338.

Zinchenko, V. Productive perception. *Voprosy Psikhologii,* 1971, *17*(6), 27–42.

Zinchenko, V. On micro-structural methods in cognitive research. *Ergonomics: Research from the Institute of Technical Esthetics* (Pt. 3). Moscow: All-Union Scientific Institute of Technical Esthetics, 1972.

Zinchenko, V., & Virgiles, N. *Formation of visual image.* New York: Plenum, 1972.

MICROGENETIC STAGES AND THE PROBLEM OF EQUIFINALITY

ast critical remark pertains to the lockstep fashion in which microgenetic eem to unfold. In most cases, the last step of a microgenetic sequence is fined as a full-blown, distinct percept or concept. The question I would Are all preceding steps (or phases, or stages) in such a sequence ordered ng to a definite relation? In other words, is only Step N the necessary and nt condition for the occurrence of Step $N + 1$? A statistical solution to this problem could be found by using an appropriate model of Mokken analysis. e is reason to suspect that in microgenesis, like in developmental processes ral, there is some branching off. The final stage in perceptgenesis can prob-reached on more than one path on partly convergent or divergent lines. nffy (1968) discussed this problem of developing systems under the heading *finality*; several steps in a developmental sequence can be equivalent for the e of reaching a final stage of development. I admit that the concept of equi-is not foreign to microgenesis under other headings, but I think more re-on this topic would be extremely helpful in defining and comparing seem-daptive behaviors originating at the same level of microgenesis. Microgenesis, opinion, could be a typical case for combining a general model of subordi-stages with an analysis of coordinated equivalent "substages" and knots of gent and divergent lines of microgenesis in the individual.

MICROGENESIS AS A PARADIGM OF AN EXPERIMENTAL DEVELOPMENTAL PSYCHOLOGY

torically, microgenesis has been among the first and most powerful research gies in the experimental analysis of developmental processes. In contrast traditional descriptive approach to an understanding of development, micro-s tries to single out the relevant structures and functions of developmental e. The analysis of developmental processes through experiments with adults ieved by a time-compressed experimental modification of age-related func-for example, exposing objects tachistoscopically or blurring them. As just examples of this approach, lenses have been used to reduce the magnitude me types of optical illusions, leaving unaltered other types not dependent hanges of percepts (Sjostrom & Pollack, 1971); the same result has been uced by hypnotic age regression (Parrish, Lundy, & Leibowitz, 1968); and eneralization of regular past-tense endings to irregular verbs has been simu-in the learning of an artificial language by college students (Palermo & Howe,).

sofar as microgenesis is part of the mainstream of developmental research aims at an explanation of developmental change, the special research strategy his approach could be called the "simulation of developmental processes" es, Reese, & Nesselroade, 1977). The argument that simulation is not new to hology and that any experiment is simulation of real-life events is in order. hology as simulation is its emphasis on homology distinctive feature of microgenesis as simulation is its emphasis on homology he phenomena under study, an aspect that has been more evaporated than orated in experimental design as "external validity." Besides other merits,

3

Microgenesis as a Model for Comparative Developmental Psychology

Otto M. Ewert
University of Mainz, Federal Republic of Germany

I first became acquainted with *Aktualgenese* as a useful technique for analyzing perceptgenesis and the tip-of-the-tongue phenomena of memory processes. The scope of this technique and its theoretical implications have now broadened to cover the whole range from comparing the genesis of percepts in children and adults to the study of psychopathological phenomena like the genesis of misperceptions under threatening cues or the perceptual styles of neurotics and psychotics. In the course of reaching out for new facets of psychological research and the spreading of research groups through Europe and both Americas, the meaning of the term *microgenesis* (i.e., *Aktualgenese*) has undergone some oscillations.

From my point of view as a developmentalist, terms like *sequence, phase, stage, self-regulation, growth,* and *adaptation* sound familiar but at the same time prompt uncertainty about some surplus, or rather sur-minus, meanings they may have in the language code of micro–Aktualgeneticists. Some sharpening of terms seems necessary if microgenesis is to draw closer to the mainstream of developmental psychology or vice versa.

HOMOLOGY, ANALOGY, OR CHANCE?

Microgenesis can be viewed as an extension of a comparative-developmental approach to the study of human behavior, which is how Werner (1948) and his colleagues at Clark University (cf. Langer, 1970) used the term. Speaking of micro-genesis in this sense refers to lines of evolutionary change in phylogenesis, onto-genesis, pathogenesis, ethnogenesis, or short-term individual development. "The final procedure of a comparative developmental psychology is . . . to derive devel-opmental laws generally applicable to mental life as a whole" (Werner, 1948, p. 5). Despite specific material differences, there exist certain parallels between these lines of evolutionary change that takes place through an ordered sequence follow-ing the orthogenetic principle.

In the study of perceptgenesis, the analysis of sequences of change is central for comparing, for example, percepts, afterimages, spiral aftereffects of preopera-tional children and normal adults, or neurotics and psychotics, respectively. The main question in drawing inferences from sequences of events is: what are the guiding rules in finding and stating parallels and equivalences between such lines of short-term development? Any statement concerning such parallels makes implicit or explicit assumptions regarding the sameness or similarity of adaptive behaviors in organisms that differ in their ontogenetic level and developmental history. It is obvious that the primordial question of the identity of two adaptive behaviors cannot be answered by reference to an experimental gadget that triggers a sequence of responses from a subject, as by increasing stepwise the exposure time of a projector slide. Sameness of experimental conditions and identity of nominal stimuli (as compared with effective stimuli) is no guarantee of identity of the elicited responses even in single-subject designs. In other words, in comparing sequences of adaptive behavior on different lines of "genesis," it is necessary to formulate a *tertium comparationis*. Interferences from intra- or interorganismic changes of behavior are possible only insofar as the precursory acts and intermediate and final stages of a given class of behavior are known.

There is no easy solution to this problem of equivalence, but recourse to the concepts of *homology* and *analogy* seems quite promising for making the necessary distinctions. According to Cranach (1976), Remane (1952), and Wickler (1963), behaviors are homologues if they fulfill the following conditions:

> 1. *The criterion of location.* Elements in two separate systems are identified by their links with other elements. Since behavior patterns are structures in time, the placing of their elements must also be defined in relation to a temporal structure.
> 2. *The criterion of the specific quality of structures with respective elements.* This criterion is fulfilled when the structures share a maximum number of peculiar characteristics.
> 3. *The criterion of relatedness through intermediate forms.* . . . Two distinct structures can be regarded as homologous if they are linked by sufficient intermediate forms satisfying the above criteria. (Cranach, 1976, p. 373)

For example, the waxing and waning percept of a bright spot brought into the visual field of an adult observer for a short time and some infants' percepts that have not yet reached object constancy are apparently very similar, but they are controlled by different mechanisms and have different links with other elements. These two percepts are but functional analogies. They are produced by different information-processing systems in adaptation to incoming stimuli and lack an inherent linkage that would allow their explanation in terms of the same necessary conditions.

Another example could be the perception of twigs in a breath of wind, seen by a child in the animistic stage of mental development or seen by a pious worshiper of a tree goddess. Both perceptions, though very similar, do not fulfill the criteria of homology; they too are functional analogies. The similarity results from the adaptation of a child's preoperational cognitive structure to environmental events and from the adaptation of a mature cognitive structure under the influence of deeply rooted belief systems of a peculiar culture, respectively. Now, by contrast, the apparently very dissimilar activities of an infant pulling a string to get a cracker attached to it and an adolescent adjusting a weight to a string to solve some tasks concerning pendulum oscillation are linked to one another by a series of intermediate developmental steps. In respect to the fundamental processes of assimilation and accommodation, they are homologues; and they are, on different levels of cognitive development, functionally equivalent realizations of equilibrated cognitive structures.

The distinction of homologies from mere analogies to a definition of the proper domain of microgenetic re

MICROGENETIC STAGE
AND EXPERIMENTAL ST

To convince a developmentalist that the terms *st* used, it is not enough to present clusters of self-report ing to stimulus exposure times or some other stepwise An unfriendly reviewer of microgenetic work could c in general there are as many "stages" as there are differe Perhaps this overstates the case, but a taxonomy of p helpful not only in reporting empirical findings but in experimental condition to another. Obviously, distin *gefühlsganzheitlich–gefühlseinzelheitlich* (affective holist posed by Krueger and Sander in the beginning of *Akt* cannot adequately describe the host of phenomena stu tinctions have their roots in an application to psycholog pitulation. Renan already in 1890 introduced the term to a general and confused view of the whole followed b parts and finally by the stage of synthesis. Nearly a ce ceptual development proved this assumption too one-si some well-documented facts.

I propose taking the concept of *stage* seriously and taxonomy could be an ordered sequence of adaptive beh or ontogenetic line of developmental change. The searcl nomic stages has to include the eliciting stimuli as well as responding organism, for example, the development of s quantitative deviation from size constancy can be caused dition of the infant eye, which is much shallower than impaired handling information overload by adult schiz should therefore state the organismic preconditions for adaptive behaviors in order to exclude equal-appearing in very different physiopsychological or cognitive processes.

There are, on the other hand, seemingly dissimilar respo and the same characteristic, for example, the rigidity of pe the infant. Contrary to the older view of a holistic phase whole or to the parts, both responses being equivalent in ter opment. The older child can change the frame of reference set of stimuli in different ways. This leads to joint interpre greater plasticity of perceptual structures, that is, a higher

Apart from the promising beginnings of Werner (1948), s adaptive responses have yet to be specified. Developmen would have to function as points of interindividual com formulation of stages of microgenesis should follow from a of microgenetic development and should thus be extraneous of the experimental procedure with its sometimes very spe experimental apparatus.

microgenesis can offer a time-saving, powerful research strategy for the study of long-term changes in structures and functions of human development.

REFERENCES

Baltes, P., Reese, H. W., & Nesselroade, J. R. *Life-span developmental psychology: Introduction to research methods.* Belmont, Calif.: Wadsworth, 1977.

Bertalanffy, L. von. *General system theory.* New York: Braziller, 1968.

Cranach, M. von (Ed.). *Methods of inference from animal to human behaviour.* The Hague: Mouton, 1976.

Langer, J. Werner's comparative organismic theory. In P. H. Mussen (Ed.), *Carmichael's manual of child psychology.* New York: Wiley, 1970.

Palermo, D. S., & Howe, H. E. An experimental analogy to the learning of past tense inflection rules. *Journal of Verbal Learning and Verbal Behavior, 1970, 9,* 410–416.

Parrish, M., Lundy, D. M., & Leibowitz, H. W. Hypnotic age-regression and magnitudes of the Ponzo and Poggendorf illusions. *Science, 1968, 159,* 1375–1376.

Remane, A. *Die Grundlagen des natürlichen Systems der vergleichenden Anatomie und der Phylogenetik.* Leipzig: Geest & Portig, 1952.

Renan, E. *L'avenir de la science.* Paris, 1890.

Sander, F. Experimentelle Ergebnisse der Gestaltpsychologie. In *Bericht über den 10. Kongress für experimentelle Psychologie.* Jena, 1928.

Sjostrom, K. P., & Pollack, R. H. The effect of simulated receptor aging on two types of visual illusions. *Psychonomic Science, 1971, 23,* 147–148.

Werner, H. *Comparative psychology of mental development* (2nd ed.). New York: International Universities, 1948.

Wickler, W. Ökologie und Stammesgeschichte von Verhaltensweisen. *Fortschritte der Zoologie, 1963, 13,* 303–365.

4

Microgenesis and Process Description

Uwe Hentschel
University of Mainz, Federal Republic of Germany

THE CONCEPT OF PROCESS DESCRIPTION

The term *Aktualgenese* as proposed by Sander (e.g., 1927, 1932) was meant to embrace all developmental processes of gestalt, starting off either with a diffuse whole or incoherent parts leading, via preliminary gestalt, to a stable and completely structured whole. According to Sander's conception, this development might have an actual representation in the mind or else the possibility of becoming at least partially conscious. This is a rather broad definition that covers many different aspects. Although Sander was explicitly opposed to the elementaristic psychology of conscious events as favored by Wundt, he retained the concepts of experience and consciousness as central themes.

This volume includes many experiments that could be defined as "microgenetic" in Sander's original sense. In quite a few studies, however, it is obvious that conceptual difficulties may arise if the central meaning of *Aktualgenese* is not to be unduly broadened. To extend the microgenetic concept from an approach with strongly introspective accents wherein the subjective stages of meaning accomplishment are the central points, to one that allows observations from outside to a higher degree, demands an even broader term with less content-related assumptions. This term should be psychologically relevant and also include microgenetic events. At the same time, it should help eliminate confusion with the concept of *Aktualgenese* as originally proposed by Sander. Because the microgenetic paradigm implies a sequential development leading to a final state of stability, this new term could be *process*. This term, which is also part of Sander's definition of *Aktualgenese*, when taken by itself makes it possible to comprehend all sequential changes in a given sequence of states or events. The use of this term would allow, within the limits of psychologically interesting questions, the inclusion of phenomena from very different origins ranging from completely unconscious to higher mental events as well as the traditional personality variables.

The choice of a certain conceptual frame of reference, as in this case, usually delineates certain areas of application, but these limits are often not made explicit. A naive belief that everyone will understand a term the same way is dangerous because as long as the concept is only implicit, theoretical and applicational problems may remain obscure. To find a good definition of *process*, I scanned some dictionaries and was very puzzled to see that the term *process* with a psychological or somewhat related meaning could be found only in the newest editions (e.g.,

59

Brockhaus Enzyklopädie, 1972; *Meyers Enzyklopädisches Lexikon*, 1977). As of 100 or 200 years ago, at least in German, it was used mainly to describe legal and chemical events (e.g., *Grosses Universallexikon*, 1741; *Pierers Konversationslexikon*, 1892), and this restricted meaning was retained until some decades ago (e.g., *Der grosse Brockhaus*, 1956).

To view something as a process would mean in the most general sense to realize that there is an ongoing event and that time becomes an important background variable for the observation of changes usually not occurring randomly and leading to a final point or different stage. *Process* is often used in contrast to *structure*. It is true that in structures changes may also take place, but the aspects used to characterize structures are more substance related, space and the interrelatedness of the components being the more important background variables. Typical metaphors used for structures are *layers* or *crystallizations*, indicating more or less enduring states of stability. It is difficult to say whether the structure-oriented or the process-oriented trend is prevalent in psychology today (Thomae, 1977), or whether both trends may converge in future; but it seems that the measurement and description of processes has been the more difficult task in the past and probably still is today.

As Fahrenberg (1968) pointed out in his survey of process analysis of psychological data, the 19th-century psychophysicists and psychophysiologists already observed signs of intraindividual variability but interpreted them as methodological and measurement errors. Nevertheless, studies explicitly considering the periodic character of performance were introduced in psychological research at a fairly early date. The paper by Öhrn (1889) in which he presented the results of a study on performance oscillation in simple arithmetic tasks is an example. This subject was taken up by others (for a detailed review see Bartenwerfer, 1964) and finally led to a standardized test edited by Pauli (1938). Seashore and Kent (1905) looked for interindividual differences, periodicity, and progressive change in simple mental work, inter alia sensation, and discrimination tasks. Other studies were conducted within the framework of gestalt psychology, for example, on characteristic changes of imagination with time, as exemplified by the studies by Wulf (1922) on leveling-sharpening.

The description of regular processes of storage and reproduction of memorized contents replaced the concept of fixed and lifeless memories in the field of memory research (Bartlett, 1932). Backed by different sources, the concept of process gradually gained importance in psychological research, as can be seen especially in Sander's terminology. An advantage of Sander's conception and his personality-oriented view is that the usual criticism against Gestalt psychology of neglecting the perceiver in its theory of perception (Klein & Schlesinger, 1949) does not hold for this offshoot.

It is almost impossible to set the limits for a profitable use of the term *process* within the psychological domain. If one includes psychophysiological research, use of the term could range, for example, from the description of biochemical events in neuronal transmitting mechanisms (i.e., on the molecular level) to the description of events in the personality sphere (i.e., on the molar level). One could also ask oneself how the relationships between structures and processes should be conceptualized and whether it would be useful to postulate a hierarchy or different distinct hierarchies of processes or whether processes should all be regarded separately.

3

Microgenesis as a Model for Comparative Developmental Psychology

Otto M. Ewert
University of Mainz, Federal Republic of Germany

I first became acquainted with *Aktualgenese* as a useful technique for analyzing perceptgenesis and the tip-of-the-tongue phenomena of memory processes. The scope of this technique and its theoretical implications have now broadened to cover the whole range from comparing the genesis of percepts in children and adults to the study of psychopathological phenomena like the genesis of misperceptions under threatening cues or the perceptual styles of neurotics and psychotics. In the course of reaching out for new facets of psychological research and the spreading of research groups through Europe and both Americas, the meaning of the term *microgenesis* (i.e., *Aktualgenese*) has undergone some oscillations.

From my point of view as a developmentalist, terms like *sequence, phase, stage, self-regulation, growth,* and *adaptation* sound familiar but at the same time prompt uncertainty about some surplus, or rather sur-minus, meanings they may have in the language code of micro–Aktualgeneticists. Some sharpening of terms seems necessary if microgenesis is to draw closer to the mainstream of developmental psychology or vice versa.

HOMOLOGY, ANALOGY, OR CHANCE?

Microgenesis can be viewed as an extension of a comparative-developmental approach to the study of human behavior, which is how Werner (1948) and his colleagues at Clark University (cf. Langer, 1970) used the term. Speaking of microgenesis in this sense refers to lines of evolutionary change in phylogenesis, ontogenesis, pathogenesis, ethnogenesis, or short-term individual development. "The final procedure of a comparative developmental psychology is . . . to derive developmental laws generally applicable to mental life as a whole" (Werner, 1948, p. 5). Despite specific material differences, there exist certain parallels between these lines of evolutionary change that takes place through an ordered sequence following the orthogenetic principle.

In the study of perceptgenesis, the analysis of sequences of change is central for comparing, for example, percepts, afterimages, spiral aftereffects of preoperational children and normal adults, or neurotics and psychotics, respectively. The main question in drawing inferences from sequences of events is: what are the guiding rules in finding and stating parallels and equivalences between such lines of short-term development? Any statement concerning such parallels makes implicit or explicit assumptions regarding the sameness or similarity of adaptive behaviors in organisms that differ in their ontogenetic level and developmental history. It is obvious that the primordial question of the identity of two adaptive behaviors cannot be answered by reference to an experimental gadget that triggers a sequence of responses from a subject, as by increasing stepwise the exposure time of a projector slide. Sameness of experimental conditions and identity of nominal stimuli (as compared with effective stimuli) is no guarantee of identity of the elicited responses even in single-subject designs. In other words, in comparing sequences of adaptive behavior on different lines of "genesis," it is necessary to formulate a *tertium comparationis*. Interferences from intra- or interorganismic changes of behavior are possible only insofar as the precursory acts and intermediate and final stages of a given class of behavior are known.

There is no easy solution to this problem of equivalence, but recourse to the concepts of *homology* and *analogy* seems quite promising for making the necessary distinctions. According to Cranach (1976), Remane (1952), and Wickler (1963), behaviors are homologues if they fulfill the following conditions:

> 1. *The criterion of location.* Elements in two separate systems are identified by their links with other elements. Since behavior patterns are structures in time, the placing of their elements must also be defined in relation to a temporal structure.
> 2. *The criterion of the specific quality of structures with respective elements.* This criterion is fulfilled when the structures share a maximum number of peculiar characteristics.
> 3. *The criterion of relatedness through intermediate forms....* Two distinct structures can be regarded as homologous if they are linked by sufficient intermediate forms satisfying the above criteria. (Cranach, 1976, p. 373)

For example, the waxing and waning percept of a bright spot brought into the visual field of an adult observer for a short time and some infants' percepts that have not yet reached object constancy are apparently very similar, but they are controlled by different mechanisms and have different links with other elements. These two percepts are but functional analogies. They are produced by different information-processing systems in adaptation to incoming stimuli and lack an inherent linkage that would allow their explanation in terms of the same necessary conditions.

Another example could be the perception of twigs in a breath of wind, seen by a child in the animistic stage of mental development or seen by a pious worshiper of a tree goddess. Both perceptions, though very similar, do not fulfill the criteria of homology; they too are functional analogies. The similarity results from the adaptation of a child's preoperational cognitive structure to environmental events and from the adaptation of a mature cognitive structure under the influence of deeply rooted belief systems of a peculiar culture, respectively. Now, by contrast, the apparently very dissimilar activities of an infant pulling a string to get a cracker attached to it and an adolescent adjusting a weight to a string to solve some tasks concerning pendulum oscillation are linked to one another by a series of intermediate developmental steps. In respect to the fundamental processes of assimilation and accommodation, they are homologues; and they are, on different levels of cognitive development, functionally equivalent realizations of equilibrated cognitive structures.

The distinction of homologies from mere analogies or chance effects is necessary to a definition of the proper domain of microgenetic research.

MICROGENETIC STAGES
AND EXPERIMENTAL STEPS

To convince a developmentalist that the terms *stage* and *phase* are properly used, it is not enough to present clusters of self-reports varying in content according to stimulus exposure times or some other stepwise experimental intervention. An unfriendly reviewer of microgenetic work could come to the conclusion that in general there are as many "stages" as there are different exposures of a stimulus. Perhaps this overstates the case, but a taxonomy of phases and stages would be helpful not only in reporting empirical findings but in comparing results from one experimental condition to another. Obviously, distinctions like *Vorgestalt* or *gefühlsganzheitlich-gefühlseinzelheitlich* (affective holistic–affective detailed), proposed by Krueger and Sander in the beginning of *Aktualgenese* (Sander, 1928), cannot adequately describe the host of phenomena studied since then. These distinctions have their roots in an application to psychology of Häckel's law of recapitulation. Renan already in 1890 introduced the term *syncretism*, which refers to a general and confused view of the whole followed by an analytic view of the parts and finally by the stage of synthesis. Nearly a century of research on perceptual development proved this assumption too one-sided and in conflict with some well-documented facts.

I propose taking the concept of *stage* seriously and define a taxonomy. This taxonomy could be an ordered sequence of adaptive behaviors following a micro- or ontogenetic line of developmental change. The search for definition of taxonomic stages has to include the eliciting stimuli as well as the characteristics of the responding organism, for example, the development of size constancy. The same quantitative deviation from size constancy can be caused by the physiological condition of the infant eye, which is much shallower than the adult eye, or by the impaired handling information overload by adult schizophrenics. A taxonomy should therefore state the organismic preconditions for comparison of certain adaptive behaviors in order to exclude equal-appearing responses that originate in very different physiopsychological or cognitive processes.

There are, on the other hand, seemingly dissimilar responses that stem from one and the same characteristic, for example, the rigidity of perceptual organization in the infant. Contrary to the older view of a holistic phase, infants respond to the whole or to the parts, both responses being equivalent in terms of the level of development. The older child can change the frame of reference and organize the same set of stimuli in different ways. This leads to joint interpretations that stand for a greater plasticity of perceptual structures, that is, a higher level of perceptgenesis.

Apart from the promising beginnings of Werner (1948), scales of "orthogenetic" adaptive responses have yet to be specified. Developmental "knots," or stages, would have to function as points of interindividual comparison. In short, the formulation of stages of microgenesis should follow from a theory on the course of microgenetic development and should thus be extraneous to the arbitrary steps of the experimental procedure with its sometimes very special constraints of the experimental apparatus.

MICROGENETIC STAGES AND THE PROBLEM OF EQUIFINALITY

My last critical remark pertains to the lockstep fashion in which microgenetic stages seem to unfold. In most cases, the last step of a microgenetic sequence is well defined as a full-blown, distinct percept or concept. The question I would pose is: Are all preceding steps (or phases, or stages) in such a sequence ordered according to a definite relation? In other words, is only Step N the necessary and sufficient condition for the occurrence of Step $N + 1$? A statistical solution to this kind of problem could be found by using an appropriate model of Mokken analysis.

There is reason to suspect that in microgenesis, like in developmental processes in general, there is some branching off. The final stage in perceptgenesis can probably be reached on more than one path on partly convergent or divergent lines. Bertalanffy (1968) discussed this problem of developing systems under the heading of *equifinality*; several steps in a developmental sequence can be equivalent for the purpose of reaching a final stage of development. I admit that the concept of equifinality is not foreign to microgenesis under other headings, but I think more research on this topic would be extremely helpful in defining and comparing seemingly adaptive behaviors originating at the same level of microgenesis. Microgenesis, in my opinion, could be a typical case for combining a general model of subordinated stages with an analysis of coordinated equivalent "substages" and knots of convergent and divergent lines of microgenesis in the individual.

MICROGENESIS AS A PARADIGM OF AN EXPERIMENTAL DEVELOPMENTAL PSYCHOLOGY

Historically, microgenesis has been among the first and most powerful research strategies in the experimental analysis of developmental processes. In contrast to the traditional descriptive approach to an understanding of development, microgenesis tries to single out the relevant structures and functions of developmental change. The analysis of developmental processes through experiments with adults is achieved by a time-compressed experimental modification of age-related functions, for example, exposing objects tachistoscopically or blurring them. As just a few examples of this approach, lenses have been used to reduce the magnitude of some types of optical illusions, leaving unaltered other types not dependent on changes of percepts (Sjostrom & Pollack, 1971); the same result has been produced by hypnotic age regression (Parrish, Lundy, & Leibowitz, 1968); and the generalization of regular past-tense endings to irregular verbs has been simulated in the learning of an artificial language by college students (Palermo & Howe, 1970).

Insofar as microgenesis is part of the mainstream of developmental research that aims at an explanation of developmental change, the special research strategy of this approach could be called the "simulation of developmental processes" (Baltes, Reese, & Nesselroade, 1977). The argument that simulation is not new to psychology and that any experiment is simulation of real-life events is in order. The distinctive feature of microgenesis as simulation is its emphasis on homology of the phenomena under study, an aspect that has been more evaporated than elaborated in experimental design as "external validity." Besides other merits, microgenesis can offer a time-saving, powerful research strategy for the study of long-term changes in structures and functions of human development.

REFERENCES

Baltes, P., Reese, H. W., & Nesselroade, J. R. *Life-span developmental psychology: Introduction to research methods.* Belmont, Calif.: Wadsworth, 1977.

Bertalanffy, L. von. *General system theory.* New York: Braziller, 1968.

Cranach, M. von (Ed.). *Methods of inference from animal to human behaviour.* The Hague: Mouton, 1976.

Langer, J. Werner's comparative organismic theory. In P. H. Mussen (Ed.), *Carmichael's manual of child psychology.* New York: Wiley, 1970.

Palermo, D. S., & Howe, H. E. An experimental analogy to the learning of past tense inflection rules. *Journal of Verbal Learning and Verbal Behavior, 1970, 9,* 410–416.

Parrish, M., Lundy, D. M., & Leibowitz, H. W. Hypnotic age-regression and magnitudes of the Ponzo and Poggendorf illusions. *Science,* 1968, *159,* 1375–1376.

Remane, A. *Die Grundlagen des natürlichen Systems der vergleichenden Anatomie und der Phylogenetik.* Leipzig: Geest & Portig, 1952.

Renan, E. *L'avenir de la science.* Paris, 1890.

Sander, F. Experimentelle Ergebnisse der Gestaltpsychologie. In *Bericht über den 10. Kongress für experimentelle Psychologie.* Jena, 1928.

Sjostrom, K. P., & Pollack, R. H. The effect of simulated receptor aging on two types of visual illusions. *Psychonomic Science,* 1971, *23,* 147–148.

Werner, H. *Comparative psychology of mental development* (2nd ed.). New York: International Universities, 1948.

Wickler, W. Ökologie und Stammesgeschichte von Verhaltensweisen. *Fortschritte der Zoologie,* 1963, *13,* 303–365.

4

Microgenesis and Process Description

Uwe Hentschel
University of Mainz, Federal Republic of Germany

THE CONCEPT OF PROCESS DESCRIPTION

The term *Aktualgenese* as proposed by Sander (e.g., 1927, 1932) was meant to embrace all developmental processes of gestalt, starting off either with a diffuse whole or incoherent parts leading, via preliminary gestalt, to a stable and completely structured whole. According to Sander's conception, this development might have an actual representation in the mind or else the possibility of becoming at least partially conscious. This is a rather broad definition that covers many different aspects. Although Sander was explicitly opposed to the elementaristic psychology of conscious events as favored by Wundt, he retained the concepts of experience and consciousness as central themes.

This volume includes many experiments that could be defined as "microgenetic" in Sander's original sense. In quite a few studies, however, it is obvious that conceptual difficulties may arise if the central meaning of *Aktualgenese* is not to be unduly broadened. To extend the microgenetic concept from an approach with strongly introspective accents wherein the subjective stages of meaning accomplishment are the central points, to one that allows observations from outside to a higher degree, demands an even broader term with less content-related assumptions. This term should be psychologically relevant and also include microgenetic events. At the same time, it should help eliminate confusion with the concept of *Aktualgenese* as originally proposed by Sander. Because the microgenetic paradigm implies a sequential development leading to a final state of stability, this new term could be *process*. This term, which is also part of Sander's definition of *Aktualgenese*, when taken by itself makes it possible to comprehend all sequential changes in a given sequence of states or events. The use of this term would allow, within the limits of psychologically interesting questions, the inclusion of phenomena from very different origins ranging from completely unconscious to higher mental events as well as the traditional personality variables.

The choice of a certain conceptual frame of reference, as in this case, usually delineates certain areas of application, but these limits are often not made explicit. A naive belief that everyone will understand a term the same way is dangerous because as long as the concept is only implicit, theoretical and applicational problems may remain obscure. To find a good definition of *process*, I scanned some dictionaries and was very puzzled to see that the term *process* with a psychological or somewhat related meaning could be found only in the newest editions (e.g.,

Brockhaus Enzyklopädie, 1972; *Meyers Enzyklopädisches Lexikon*, 1977). As of 100 or 200 years ago, at least in German, it was used mainly to describe legal and chemical events (e.g., *Grosses Universallexikon*, 1741; *Pierers Konversationslexikon*, 1892), and this restricted meaning was retained until some decades ago (e.g., *Der grosse Brockhaus*, 1956).

To view something as a process would mean in the most general sense to realize that there is an ongoing event and that time becomes an important background variable for the observation of changes usually not occurring randomly and leading to a final point or different stage. *Process* is often used in contrast to *structure*. It is true that in structures changes may also take place, but the aspects used to characterize structures are more substance related, space and the interrelatedness of the components being the more important background variables. Typical metaphors used for structures are *layers* or *crystallizations*, indicating more or less enduring states of stability. It is difficult to say whether the structure-oriented or the process-oriented trend is prevalent in psychology today (Thomae, 1977), or whether both trends may converge in future; but it seems that the measurement and description of processes has been the more difficult task in the past and probably still is today.

As Fahrenberg (1968) pointed out in his survey of process analysis of psychological data, the 19th-century psychophysicists and psychophysiologists already observed signs of intraindividual variability but interpreted them as methodological and measurement errors. Nevertheless, studies explicitly considering the periodic character of performance were introduced in psychological research at a fairly early date. The paper by Öhrn (1889) in which he presented the results of a study on performance oscillation in simple arithmetic tasks is an example. This subject was taken up by others (for a detailed review see Bartenwerfer, 1964) and finally led to a standardized test edited by Pauli (1938). Seashore and Kent (1905) looked for interindividual differences, periodicity, and progressive change in simple mental work, inter alia sensation, and discrimination tasks. Other studies were conducted within the framework of gestalt psychology, for example, on characteristic changes of imagination with time, as exemplified by the studies by Wulf (1922) on leveling–sharpening.

The description of regular processes of storage and reproduction of memorized contents replaced the concept of fixed and lifeless memories in the field of memory research (Bartlett, 1932). Backed by different sources, the concept of process gradually gained importance in psychological research, as can be seen especially in Sander's terminology. An advantage of Sander's conception and his personality-oriented view is that the usual criticism against Gestalt psychology of neglecting the perceiver in its theory of perception (Klein & Schlesinger, 1949) does not hold for this offshoot.

It is almost impossible to set the limits for a profitable use of the term *process* within the psychological domain. If one includes psychophysiological research, use of the term could range, for example, from the description of biochemical events in neuronal transmitting mechanisms (i.e., on the molecular level) to the description of events in the personality sphere (i.e., on the molar level). One could also ask oneself how the relationships between structures and processes should be conceptualized and whether it would be useful to postulate a hierarchy or different distinct hierarchies of processes or whether processes should all be regarded separately.

In psychology as a science with a strong inclination to applied problems, theoretical questions are very often put exclusively in connection with methodological problems, concerning, for example, the usefulness of certain tests or statistical methods. This sometimes makes it difficult to state why and how changes in basic theoretical trends take place. Impetus for a theoretical formulation for process-oriented research comes from very different sources, which are often not easy to detect; but the basic theoretical meaning of the process concept and the aim of using it have been explicitly outlined before. Smith (1962), one of the first to use process-oriented methods, proposed the process concept as a theoretical frame of reference for the study of behavior in order to incorporate psychology into the greater family of biologic sciences. In biology, Bertalanffy (1942) had already worked in this direction, stressing the importance of variability as a basic phenomenon of life.

The proposal to use *process* as a theoretical frame of reference can be considered:

In the context of general philosophic considerations that form the basis—often implicitly—of all research endeavors
Within a broad range of epistemological implications
With respect to the pragmatic application of different test methods and the evaluation of their results

The scope of these three categories is too broad to permit exhaustive discussion. The first two are normally not easily differentiated when one looks at the broad categories of realism versus idealism often used to distinguish basic (mostly implicit) standpoints of scientists (Rychlak, 1968). As Rychlak points out, for a scientist leaning toward a realistic point of view, acquiring knowledge is an act of abstraction. According to the idealistic point of view, knowledge would have to be gained by an act of construction. Fundamentally, process could be tackled from almost any metatheoretical standpoint, but I have chosen here to concentrate on Whitehead's famous metaphysical concept. Even though it refers directly to applied problems, it can help to demonstrate how difficult it is to find a common suitable frame of reference for theoretical and empirical aims. My discussion of the third category, general research strategies, is more detailed, concluding with an applicational example that helps to point out the advantages and difficulties of the process approach.

PHILOSOPHIC BACKGROUND

Looking back at the development of different standpoints and theoretical trends in psychology, it is astonishing to see how Whitehead, in his book *Process and Reality* (1929), preceded modern psychological theorizing in many ways without, as far as I know, directly influencing this theorizing except for Murray's (1938) formulations on personality. Naturally, Whitehead is very extensive and absolute in his propositions. He proposed abandoning the concept of substance as referring to unchanging endurance and instead conceived of the world as being composed of a large number of "actual entities," all of them being organisms that become and perish again. "An actual entity endures but an instant—the instant of its becoming, its active process of self-creation out of the elements of the perishing past—and then it, too, perishes and as objectively immortal becomes dead datum for succeeding generations of actual entities" (Sherburne, 1966, p. 206). To have existence, things have to be actual. "There is no going behind actual entities to find anything more real" (Whitehead, 1929, p. 27). Thus the world, according to Whitehead, can be conceived of as a concatenation of actual entities and the processes constituting them.

Referring to psychology, one can see how process has gradually become a core construct for many different theoretical positions. The introduction of the *state concept* (Cattell, 1966a) and the ever-growing influence of situational theories in psychology (Mischel, 1968)—in contrast to the trait concept—point to the increasing interest in concepts covering change.

Not all the basic constructs of Whitehead's concept can be dealt with here, but one important aspect that should be mentioned is the possibility of viewing the process of self-creation of the actual entities as transmission or reception of information. According to Whitehead's terminology, the subjective side of the selected information is feelings. *Feelings* here imply simple physical feelings that can be combined and formed into a new complex unity at the macrocosmic level.

With Whitehead, *causes*, the main subject matter in metatheoretical considerations, attained an alternative explanation that seems important for psychological concepts as well. Obvious theoretical and philosophic implications can be directly derived, for example, for the interactional view, examples and theoretical aspects of which are already often referred to Russell's but not yet to Whitehead's metatheoretical thoughts (Watzlawick & Weakland, 1977).

Although Whitehead does make explicit statements on how the basic construct of process can be imagined (this holding true especially for the macrocosmic level), it is rather difficult to transpose the terminology directly into psychological theories or even to make it directly applicable to psychological research by operationalizing his process concept. Consistent metaphysical systems cannot be the exclusive theoretical basis for specific theories with different aims. They are more likely to influence other theoretical constructs in an indirect way, for example, by influencing their terminology. It still makes a difference whether one deals with the preconditions or the phenomenological results. If one leaves the closed metaphysical system without confining oneself to a purely subjective view of processes as the predetermined and self-evident "reality-mediating agents" and considers instead the process itself as the central object of research, one is free again to choose among different frames of reference. The investigation of processes can of course be undertaken from an idealistic as well as from a completely positivistic standpoint.

A PROBLEM OF KNOWLEDGE

A philosophic standpoint is one way for a researcher to communicate general aims, but he or she also has to show at what level of explanation he or she is operating. Viewing process as an object of research brings to mind the epistemological division into the triad of "observable phenomena," "essential reality," and "symbolic representations" (Popper, 1963). According to Popper, three scientific strategies can be distinguished that are not completely independent of the level of explanation:

1. To find a theory that describes the "realities" behind the appearances, a theory that gives an ultimate explanation

2. To establish inference rules or computation rules that are identical with pure scientific theories

3. To make highly informative guesses, the truth of which can never be proved but which can be tested in a critical way

Popper supports the third strategy, which in a certain way can also be seen as a compromise between the first two. He also adds the conviction that "science is capable of real discoveries" (Popper, 1963, p. 117) and that observations, like the real discoveries themselves, are, in a direct or indirect way, guided by theories.

If one applies this to the investigation of processes, one must have, as mentioned before, the hypothesis, or at least the idea, that the event in question is processlike in nature and that research endeavors can thus be limited to a more or less purely descriptive level. Certain epidemics (Waltman, 1974) are an example; they can be traced over a certain period of time wherein the influence of the past on present and future developments can be hypothesized. Once it is recognized that the event in question might be a process with a certain periodicity or with regular changes leading to an end stage, the next problem is to find a strategy by which to identify the hypothetical nature of the process or the laws by which it is governed and with the help of which it can be described. These laws can be found in different ways and evoke different conclusions. For many processes, the actual goal of research is accomplished when the descriptive level is reached, the next step being the search for appropriate means of intervention. Examples are easily found in medicine and economics. Although it is important to know the development of a disease, the means of intervention are aimed at its cause, if known, and the cause is often not directly related to development. The seasonal dependency of the sales rates of certain products, too, can be self-evident, requiring interventions only and not far-reaching interpretations.

In psychology, especially in the field of personality theory, an additional step is usually necessary in order to arrive at a meaningful interpretation. The measurements have to be transformed into psychologically comprehensible terms (Fahrenberg, 1968). Many processes can be regarded as representing another phenomenon that might be the really interesting one. This corresponds to the relationship between observable phenomena and symbolic representations in Popper's (1963) terminology. These considerations could already lead to possible conclusions, but the intermediate steps are as yet missing.

EMPIRICAL AND THEORETICAL APPROACHES

Researchers who decline to search for a theory that explains the "realities" because it could never be tested empirically and who decide not to consider all possible combinations of research strategies must, nonetheless, confront two general types of research strategies: empirical and theoretical (Coombs, Raiffa, & Thrall, 1954; Shea, 1974), or in another terminology, data driven and theory driven (Bobrow & Norman, 1975). Figure 4.1 shows an attempt to combine a representation of these strategies with important assumptions of Popper (1963) and Cattell (1966b). Although this typology seems convincing, and even though pure examples

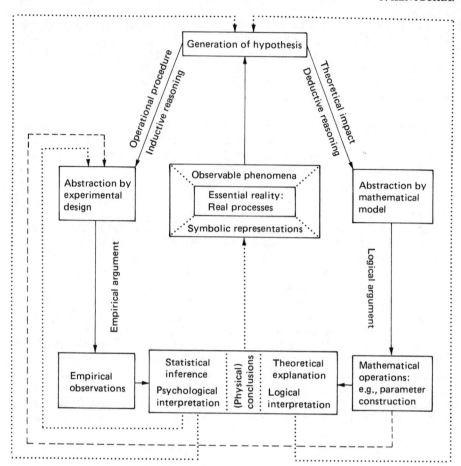

Figure 4.1 Two types of scientific strategies.

could be found in practice, it is difficult to distinguish neatly the empirical and the theoretical strategies because they are rarely used separately. The dotted lines are meant to show possible deviations from the two "pure" strategies. As far as psychology is concerned, theoretical models are also tested empirically, and conclusions derived from an empirical approach are usually not based on single experiments. Results can also influence the original hypotheses and prompt their reformulation. The diagram is useful, nonetheless, for indicating the different main orientations of scientific approaches.

The vaguest point of the diagram is the top, the starting-off point for both approaches, for here one might unexpectedly meet the difficult problem of creative thinking. It is perhaps useful to employ Northrop's term *epistemic correlation,* which he defined as "a relation joining an unobserved component of anything designated by a concept by postulation to its directly inspected component denoted by a concept by intuition" (Northrop, 1947, p. 119). This could be taken as a general statement of the necessity of filling the gap between an observed process and another postulated behavioral characteristic. The procedures to follow to arrive at reasonable conclusions can be either deductive or inductive. Northrop's term *epistemic correlation* was interpreted by Bordin (1965) as an appropriate and necessary rule of simplification in experimental research in general.

As an example of the two approaches shown in Figure 4.1, consider a task using the Picture-Word Test (PWT) (Hentschel, 1973), which was constructed as a parallel version of the Thurstone form (Thurstone, 1944) of the color-word-test (CWT) (Stroop, 1935). The test card has 10 lines like those shown in Figure 4.2. The subject's task is to name the pictures and to ignore the printed words. This task corresponds to the naming of the colors of the incongruously colored color-words in the CWT. The task can be presented as a conventional performance task. The naming time of the 100 items is measured and sometimes compared to the reading of 100 words; the subject is given an interference score. It is possible, like Smith and Klein (1953), to classify naming times as poor or good, perhaps with some steps in between, and also to look for characteristic and meaningful changes that could be registered. According to the two "pure" strategies in Figure 4.1, one could either specify a theoretical measurement model or start doing experiments. In reality, the developments along the two different paths cannot be so neatly separated.

Smith and Klein developed two basic parameters, making it possible, for every presentation of the interference card, to relate the pattern of change (which they arrived at pretty directly by data inspection) to hypothetically meaningful behavioral adaptation patterns and to combine these patterns in a final classification. Smith and Klein called the performance processes "stabilized," "cumulative," "dissociative," and "cumulative-dissociative." Later on, the scoring technique was extended to clinical use, and its relation to clinical criteria at various levels was postulated and empirically investigated (Smith & Nyman, 1959, 1972).

An experimenter might next decide to measure the naming times every second line, producing 5 measurements per card, that is, 25 altogether for each subject. It is also possible to arrive at a simultaneous combination of those 25 measures using computation rules, for example, regression analysis, which is the basis for the scoring model proposed by Sjöberg (1969, 1974) for which Schubö and Hentschel (1977, 1978) more recently formulated an alternative. These approaches, as examples of scoring devices derived from predetermined a priori computation models, have to be placed farther to the right of Figure 4.1.

The descriptive-inductive approach clearly preceded the scoring method using regression analysis. It seems doubtful that the order of introduction could have been reversed without excluding the psychological understanding of the test performance that unquestionably stimulated research and led to a remarkable amount of information coming, above all, from clinic studies with the CWT (Smith & Nyman, 1972).

Within the deductive approach, the data have to be regarded first as functions of the a priori model (Birnbaum, 1974); statements are only possible as to whether

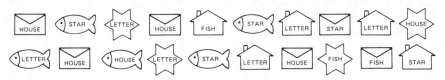

Figure 4.2 Two lines from the Picture–Word Test (PWT).

the conditions of the model are fulfilled or not. If the data and the model fit relatively well, the experimenter could undertake an external validation and a content-related description of the parameters (see the dashed line in Figure 4.1). To operationalize the behavioral adaptation pattern, however, computation rules and measures have to be established for the descriptive-inductive approach as well, and this stresses again the point that, in reality, the clearly separated approaches in Figure 4.1 represent only a relative difference.

PROCESS DIFFERENCES

The choice of a more empirically or more theoretically oriented research strategy is necessarily influenced by the conditions given for a concrete task. The question may be asked whether analyzing a process is a concrete enough task formulation. The qualitative differences among psychologically interesting processes make general application of the process concept and the design of analysis models difficult. The process to be analyzed in the serial CWT or PWT, for example, differs from mere perception processes. In the field of *Aktualgenese*, there is the merogenetic method, as used, for example, by Froehlich and Laux (1969), where, in order to study the perceptgenesis, the amount of information is gradually increased until the complete picture is given, short projection times being used throughout the whole sequence. There also is the hologenetic method (see also Chap. 2 of this volume), as used, for example, in the DMT (Kragh, 1960), where the formation of a stabilized percept is made analyzable by slowly increasing the exposure times. Then there is the metacontrast technique (Smith & Nyman, 1961), which in certain respects is a compromise between the two methods mentioned above because exposure times are increased only together with the addition of another part of the picture.

In addition to being carried out by different research methods, process studies can also be reduced to smaller units or incorporated into larger ones. In a series of experiments, Froehlich (1978) emphasized the contribution of different psychophysiological processes like arousal and attention to an integrated coping process, which brings me back to the problem of a hierarchical organization of processes. It could be helpful to introduce a further descriptive attribute that would allow a division into micro- and macroprocesses. Traditionally, this division is dichotomous, embracing perceptgenesis and ontogenesis, and connected to the hypothesis that in percept-genetic (i.e., microgenetic) reactions, a reflection of ontogenetic events can be found (Flavell & Draguns, 1957; Kragh & Smith, 1970).

There is another, more general formulation in which the range and level of a process contribute to its characterization as a micro- or macroprocess. The different levels can be demonstrated by referring once again to the so-called interference tasks in the CWT and PWT. As Klein (1964) has shown (see also Hintzman, Carre, Eskridge, Owens, Shaff, & Sparks, 1972), the interference is not only an input, but also an output, phenomenon, sensory and motor components being involved.

Hörmann (1960) used Hebb's phase sequences, which should, in order to interpret the phenomenon, be understood as a temporarily fixed pattern of cell-assembly activities. Thus interference can be explained by the involvement of certain groups of neurons in more than one phase sequence. This can be regarded as a hypothetical basic process at the neurophysiological level. The process might be reduced to even more basic events, but for the moment, it is even further away from testability than the phase-sequence hypothesis.

For the subject, the difficulty of the task can become noticeable with each single reaction. The normal reading of color-words or the naming of colors can be described by the *Gestaltkreis* model of perception and motor behavior (Weizsäcker, 1947). The interference task provokes a disturbance of the *Gestaltkreis*, and the intrinsic point of the disturbance, expressing itself in the lack of the usual coherence of the verbal reaction to the perception signal, can already be seen at the phenomenal level in the reactions to single items. Because of technical problems of measurement, a recording of this disturbance does not now seem possible. The process analysis of the CWT, as proposed by Smith and Klein (1953), seems to account more for a general coping process and for the manner in which the subject masters the adaptation to the task as a whole, especially considering the development of the performance. Another process, situated near the macro end of the micro-macro continuum, could be imagined in certain psychodynamic changes of the subject; this, in turn, could influence the course of performance on the CWT or PWT.

To summarize the idea, a hierarchical organization of processes could be conceptualized as a tendency toward increasing integration, the microprocesses standing by themselves at the lower end, while more and more processes are integrated into larger units toward the macro end. Considering the number of ongoing processes in a person, this concept would have an actual aspect, and it could also be viewed as having a historical dimension. With some additional assumptions, it could also cover the traditional micro-macro correspondence and would involve, in the most extreme form stated, as Heiss said in 1948, seeing the whole person as a process or, as Angyal (1965) put it, regarding personality as a "time gestalt."

At the same time, the limit to the application of the term *process* can already clearly be seen here. Personality cannot be conceptualized in a meaningful way without a structural concept that has room also for relatively enduring, stable systems (Sander, 1932) influencing regular behavior organization. On the other hand, the structural concept must not necessarily lead to constructs with a tendency to reification (e.g., Kelly's 1955 term *channelized processes*). Heiss (1949) used the term *stabilized functions* (*funktionale Verfestigungen*) for a description of enduring traits, and Mandler (1962) characterized structures as "temporal and probabilistic linkages of inputs and behavior which are available in functional units" (p. 415). This seems an acceptable compromise for the time being for the purpose of describing different aspects of personality in which the relative importance of situational moments, characteristic processes, and relatively enduring structural units cannot be definitely determined.

CONCLUSIONS

Regarding the different aspects of process presented in this chapter, one can ask if the proposed use of the general term *process* has not been broadened in scope too much. Is it really useful to apply the same term to events that are obviously so different as the two test paradigms mostly referred to, the proper microgenetic phenomena, and the development of performance in the CWT or PWT? Even if no generally acceptable answer seems possible, it can be shown that there is an important common basis in spite of the obvious differences.

To start with the differences, one difference is the duration of the adaptive sequences. Microgenetic processes are very short and analyzable only by using technical aids that allow a fractionalization and artificial prolongation of the sequences. The perceptual-behavioral adaptation process in the interference tasks requires a prolonged exposure of the subject to the task in order to arrive at serial measurements.

Additionally, there are some qualitative differences. In microgenetic tasks, introspection and subjective interpretation are essential elements in the reaction required of the subject; in the interference tests, only serial behavior in the form of verbal reactions without an explicit demand for those subjective elements is studied. There is no doubt, however, that, on the behavioral level, the reaction to the CWT or PWT also includes subjective elements, enough at least to make the tests useful diagnostic instruments.

In spite of the differences, it also seems possible to find common characteristics in the two different tasks I have used as examples for process analysis. In both tasks it is necessary for the subject to adapt, in perceptgenesis to a strategy for overcoming interference in order to reach a stable and good performance according to the subject's potential. In both tasks, the observed performance of adaptation can be hypothetically related to internal structures; and in both tasks, the unfolding over time is the crucial variable for the observation and registration of the phenomena.

Even if it can be argued that process description is a useful umbrella term for the phenomena included in this chapter, it does not seem to be a sufficient characterization. An additional specification of the different phenomena seems unavoidable for all the examples discussed. There is no chance of arriving at a single valid explanation of process analysis. Even with agreement to do process-oriented research, there is ample room for differences in basic theoretical standpoints. There are at least two types of strategies for arriving at certain conclusions, and furthermore, there is the necessity of specifically adapting the test methods to the analytical requirements of the different kinds of processes studied, involving, for example, micro- or macroprocesses or specific qualitative differences in test reactions. Even within either the experimental or the theoretical type of approach (without considering the possible combinations of the two), there is, of course no one explanation. Even for a definite system of a priori computation rules, there is not one, but a whole range, of different possibilities to choose from (see Chap. 5).

All things considered, one can say that the heading *process description* does certainly contribute a very essential but nevertheless only limited amount of information toward a clear demarcation of the frame of reference for an investigation. Deliberately used, it can at least help to clarify the goal of research in an explicit way. The growing interest in the process concept in psychology could also be taken as a sign of what Jaspers (1959) called an "affinity" between a theoretical orientation and a certain field of research. The acceptance of the process concept also implies definite methodological consequences, like the need for parameters comprehending periodicity and the course of behavioral sequences, so that even fluctuations and oscillations become interpretable in a meaningful way. Examples can be taken from different fields and different times. Heiss (1948, 1949), for example, underlined the importance of process characteristics in projective tests and in handwriting. Cattell (1966a) extended the methods of factor analysis in order to cover also the variance owing to situational moments and change. In experimental design and evaluation of test results, the introduction of the process concept has generally led to an increasing interest in the development preceding stable performances in contrast to consideration of final output only. The main advantage of this view is, as Smith emphasizes in Chapter 10, a better understanding of functions.

REFERENCES

Angyal, A. *Neurosis and treatment: A holistic theory.* E. Hanfmann & R. M. Jones, Eds. New York: Wiley, 1965.

Bartenwerfer, H. Allgemeine Leistungstests. In R. Heiss (Ed.), *Handbuch der Psychologie* (Vol. 6), *Psychologische Diagnostik.* Göttingen: Hogrefe, 1964.

Bartlett, F. C. *Remembering.* Cambridge: University Press, 1932.

Bertalanffy, L. von. *Theoretische Biologie* (Vol. 2). Berlin: Borntraeger, 1942.

Birnbaum, M. H. Reply to the devil's advocates: Don't confound model testing and measurement. *Psychological Bulletin,* 1974, *81,* 854–859.

Bobrow, D. G., & Norman, D. A. Some principles of memory schemata. In D. G. Bobrow & A. Collins (Eds.), *Representation and understanding.* New York: Academic, 1975.

Bordin, E. S. Simplification as a strategy for research in psychotherapy. *Journal of Consulting Psychology,* 1965, *29,* 493–503.

Brockhaus Enzyklopädie (Vol. 15). Wiesbaden: Brockhaus, 1972.

Cattell, R. B. Patterns of change: Measurement in relation to state-dimension, trait change, lability and process concepts. In R. B. Cattell (Ed.), *Handbook of multivariate experimental psychology.* Skokie, Ill.: Rand McNally, 1966. (a)

Cattell, R. B. Psychological theory and scientific method. In R. B. Cattell (Ed.), *Handbook of multivariate experimental psychology.* Skokie, Ill.: Rand McNally, 1966. (b)

Coombs, C. H., Raiffa, H., & Thrall, R. M. Some views of mathematical models and measurement theory. In R. M. Thrall, C. H. Coombs, & R. L. Davis (Eds.), *Decision processes.* New York: Wiley, 1954.

Fahrenberg, J. Aufgaben und Methoden der psychologischen Verlaufsanalyse (Zeitreihenanalyse). In K. J. Groffman & K. H. Wewetzer (Eds.), *Person als Prozess: Festschrift zum 65. Geburtstag von Prof. Dr. phil. Robert Heiss.* Bern: Huber, 1968.

Flavell, J. H., & Draguns, J. G. A microgenetic approach to perception and thought. *Psychological Bulletin,* 1957, *54,* 197–217.

Froehlich, W. D. Stress, anxiety, and the control of attention: A psychophysiological approach. In C. D. Spielberger & I. G. Sarason (Eds.), *Stress and anxiety* (Vol. 5). Washington: Hemisphere, 1978.

Froehlich, W. D., & Laux, L. Serielles Wahrnehmen, Aktualgenese, Informationsintegration und Orientierungsreaktion: I. Aktualgenetisches Modell und Orientierungsreaktion. *Zeitschrift für experimentelle und angewandte Psychologie,* 1969, *16,* 250–277.

Der grosse Brockhaus (Vol. 9). Wiesbaden: Brockhaus, 1956.

Grosses Universallexikon aller Wissenschaften und Künste (Vol. 29). Leipzig: Zedler, 1741.

Heiss, R. Person als Prozess. In J. von Allesch, Jacobsen, W., Munsch, G., & Simoneit, M. (Eds.), *Bericht, Kongress des Bundes Deutscher Psychologen.* Hamburg: Nölke, 1948.

Heiss, R. *Die Lehre vom Charakter* (2nd ed.). Berlin: De Gruyter, 1949.

Hentschel, U. Two new interference tests compared to the Stroop color-word test. *Psychological Research Bulletin,* 1973, *13*(6).

Hintzman, D. L., Carre, F. A., Eskridge, V. L., Ownes, A. M., Shaff, S. S., & Sparks, M. E. "Stroop" effect: Input or output phenomenon? *Journal of Experimental Psychology,* 1972, *95,* 458–459.

Hörmann, H. *Konflikt und Entscheidung.* Göttingen: Hogrefe, 1960.

Jaspers, K. *Allgemeine Psychopathologie* (7th ed.). Berlin: Springer, 1959.

Kelly, G. A. *The psychology of personal constructs.* New York: Norton, 1955.

Klein, G. S. Semantic power measured through the interference of words with color-naming. *American Journal of Psychology,* 1964, *77,* 576–588.

Klein, G. S., & Schlesinger, H. Where is the perceiver in perceptual theory? *Journal of Personality,* 1949, *18,* 32–47.

Kragh, U. The Defense Mechanism Test: A new method for diagnosis and personnel selection. *Journal of Applied Psychology*, 1960, *44*, 303–309.

Kragh, U., & Smith, G. J. W. (Eds.). *Percept-genetic analysis*. Lund: Gleerup, 1970.

Mandler, G. From association to structure. *Psychological Review*, 1962, *69*, 415–427.

Meyers Enzyklopädisches Lexikon (Vol. 19). Mannheim: Bibliographisches Institut, 1977.

Mischel, W. *Personality and assessment*. New York: Wiley, 1968.

Murray, H. A. *Exploration in personality*. New York: Oxford University Press, 1938.

Northrop, F. S. C. *The logic of the sciences and the humanities*. New York: Macmillan, 1947.

Öhrn, A. Experimentelle Studien zur Individualpsychologie. In E. Kraeplin (Ed.), *Psychologische Arbeiten*, 1889, *1*, 92–151.

Pauli, R. Die Arbeitskurve als ganzheitlicher Versuch (als Universaltest). *Archiv für die gesamte Psychologie*, 1938, *100*, 401–423.

Pierers Konversationslexikon (Vol. 10) (Ed. J. Kürschner), Stuttgart: Deutsche Verlagsgesellschaft, 1892.

Popper, K. R. *Conjectures and refutations*. London: Routledge, 1963.

Rychlak, J. F. *A philosophy of science for personality theory*. Boston: Houghton Mifflin, 1968.

Sander, F. Über Gestaltqualitäten. In *Bericht 8. Internationaler Kongress der Psychologie*. Groningen, 1927.

Sander, F. Funktionale Struktur, Erlebnisganzheit und Gestalt. *Archiv für die gesamte Psychologie*, 1932, *85*, 237–260.

Schubö, W., & Hentschel, U. Reliability and validity of the serial color-word test: Further results. *Psychological Research Bulletin* (Lund University, Sweden), 1977, *17*(6).

Schubö, W., & Hentschel, U. Improved reliability estimates for the serial color-word test. *Scandinavian Journal of Psychology*, 1978, *19*, 91–95.

Seashore, C. E., & Kent, G. H. Periodicity and progressive change in continuous mental work. *Psychological Review Monographs*, 1905, *(6*, Suppl.), 47–101.

Shea, W. R. The classification of scientific terms as "theoretical" and "observational" in contemporary philosophy of science. In J. A. Wojciechowski (Ed.), *Conceptual basis of the classification of knowledge*. Pullach and München: Dokumentation, 1974.

Sherburne, D. W. *A key to Whitehead's process and reality*. New York: Macmillan, 1966.

Sjöberg, L. On serial scoring of the color-word test. *Acta Psychologica*, 1969, *29*, 150–162.

Sjöberg, L. Psychometric properties of the serial color-word test. *Scandinavian Journal of Psychology*, 1974, *15*, 15–20.

Smith, G. J. W. Process: A biological frame of reference for the study of behavior. *Psychological Research Bulletin* (Lund University, Sweden), 1962, *2*(7).

Smith, G. J. W., & Klein, G. S. Cognitive controls in serial behavior patterns. *Journal of Personality*, 1953, *22*, 188–213.

Smith, G. J. W., & Nyman, G. E. Psychopathologic behavior in a serial experiment: Investigations of neurotic, psychotic, psychopathic and normal subjects. *Lunds Universitets Årsskrift (Lund University Yearbook)*, new series, 2, 1959, *56*(6).

Smith, G. J. W., & Nyman, G. E. A serial tachistoscopic experiment and its clinical application. *Acta Psychologica*, 1961, *18*, 67–84.

Smith, G. J. W., & Nyman, G. E. *Manual till CWT (Serialt Färgordtest)*. Stockholm: Skandinaviska Testförlaget, 1972.

Stroop, J. R. Studies of interference on serial verbal reactions. *Journal of Experimental Psychology*, 1935, *18*, 643–662.

Thomae, H. *Psychologie in der modernen Gesellschaft*. Hamburg: Hoffmann & Campe, 1977.

Thurstone, L. L. *A factorial study of perception*. Chicago: University of Chicago Press, 1944.

Waltman, P. *Deterministic threshold models in the theory of epidemics*. Berlin: Springer, 1974.

Watzlawick, P., & Weakland, J. H. (Eds.). *The interactional view*. New York: Norton, 1977.

Weizsäcker, V. von. *Der Gestaltkreis: Theorie der Einheit von Wahrnehmen und Bewegen*. Stuttgart: Thieme, 1947.

Whitehead, A. N. *Process and reality*. New York: Macmillan, 1929.

Wulf, F. Über die Veränderungen von Vorstellungen. *Psychologische Forschung*, 1922, *1*, 333–373.

5

The Statistical Evaluation
of Processes

Werner Schubö
University of Munich,
Munich, Federal Republic of Germany

As a supplement to Chapter 4 and as an introduction to this chapter, some comments seem necessary on the use of the terms *method* and *model*. If one uses mathematical methods in connection with psychological measures, one certainly assumes that these methods are sensitive to the pertinent aspect of the data, that is, one usually has an explicit or implicit theory about the psychological phenomena that can be represented by the method's mathematical model as applied to the measures. Unfortunately, insensitive mathematical methods are in use (e.g., distances between profiles estimated by means of Pearson's correlation are insensitive to global-level differences) that often lead to unnecessary fuss about the properties of models. In some circles, even the term *method* is taboo. Perhaps as a defensive reaction, other circles avoid the use of the word *model*. I use both of these terms and I hope I do so correctly.

The most familiar statistical methods are connected with group designs, where the group differences within the common distributions of some measures are being investigated. For description of processes one is forced to combine methods of this kind with methods more suited to single-case designs, often summarized by the term *time-series analysis*. A combination of both is necessary because only group statistics allow inferences beyond the sample and only single-case statistics can be used to analyze developments, trends, and intermediate states. A two-step procedure is usually chosen. In the first step, some characteristics are computed for each single case, for example, transition probabilities, regression coefficients, or autocorrelations. These measures are introduced in the second step for group statistical computations, for example, into a chi-square test, an analysis of variance, or a nonparametric analysis. I concentrate here on the first step and demonstrate some possible ways of time-series analysis that are not very sophisticated but still rather unfamiliar. I do not deal with the important features of time series of qualitative variables that could possibly be described as finite Markov chains (Kemeny & Snell, 1960). Here I am concerned with time series of quantitative variables measured on an interval scale, continually keeping in mind that it is often difficult to find adequate interval measures.

To state the case in relatively simple, yet psychologically relevant terms, I use the serial scoring of the CWT as an illustration throughout. The mathematical techniques can easily be transferred to quite different problems in studying long series of measurements on a single case.

The serial scoring of the CWT (Stroop, 1935), as proposed by Smith and Klein (1953) and extended by Smith and Nyman (1959), is based on five presentations of the interference table. This consists of 10 lines, each of 10 color-words, printed in incongruent colors. The subject has to name the color, verbally ignoring the linguistic information. The naming time for every 2 lines is measured, producing five section times for each of the five presentations. A typical example of the sequence of naming times is given in Figure 5.1.

In engineering, business, or economics, the typical question in time-series analysis would be What naming times are to be expected in a sixth presentation of the interference table? This forecasting problem, or the associated problem of control, is important in certain psychological areas, for instance aptitude diagnosis or psychotherapy. But with respect to the statistical evaluation of the process properties of the CWT, it should be more interesting to get some information about the nature of the process. Let me formulate a new question: What type of model is most adequate for the observed data? Because of the unlimited number of possible models, and having the second step in mind, I return to the more modest question, How can we reduce the 25 time values to one or, at most, a few representative and psychologically relevant measures? and consider eight different models.

FIVE MODELS ASSUMING NO CONTINUITY

Smith and Nyman's Combined Linear Regressions

Smith and Nyman chose a two-phase evaluation:

1. A linear regression model within each presentation reduces 5 values to one linear trend and one residual standard deviation. The two quantitative measures are combined into one nominal scale with the possible values *S, C, D,* and *CD.*
2. The five nominal scales from the five presentations are combined into one final classification.

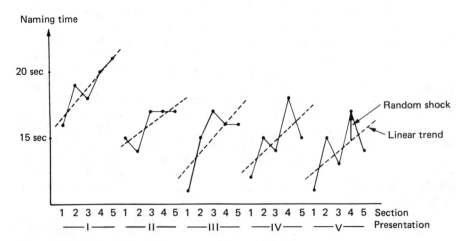

Figure 5.1 Smith and Nyman's linear regression model.

Some additional special measures are disregarded here. Within Phase 1 the regression model is used, presuming that there is basically a linear trend of the naming times. In addition there are random deviations from the linear trend, which can be qualified as random "shocks." This is illustrated in Figure 5.1. Comparing the regression coefficients and the residual standard deviations with norms given in Smith and Nyman (1972) produces in this case the pattern $C S S S S$ and the final classification S.

To provide a complete statement of the regression model, the shocks are assumed to be random drawings from a normal distribution with zero mean and fixed variance. This property of the common regression model must be questioned here; probably some systematic variance owing to learning, fatigue, speech characteristics, or individual reactions to item difficulty is contained in the residual times and could possibly be accounted for by more adequate measures than the lump-sum standard deviation.

Joint Multiple Linear Regression

Whereas Smith and Nyman applied a regression model to each presentation separately, Sjöberg (1969) proposed a joint regression model. Sjöberg's model differs in four major respects from the models used by Smith and Nyman:

1. The parameters that describe the process are quantitative.
2. The parameters are linear functions of the naming times.
3. There are five final parameters instead of one final classification.
4. Given the validity of a set of certain assumptions, reliability estimates for the parameters can be obtained as measures of internal consistency.

In accordance with the shape of the mean times of a group of about 200 subjects, Sjöberg suggests five trend components. Through application of regression algebra, he searches for the linear combination of trends that would provide the best fit for his data. This principle is demonstrated in Figure 5.2. But has he chosen these trend components adequately? Apparently not, because he obtained very low reliability estimates for the parameters, that is, the weights for the five trend components, implying that only a small portion of the total variance is explained by the model.

Deviations from the Mean Naming Times

Schubö and Hentschel (1977) proposed a calibration of the naming times; they subtracted the total means of the consecutive naming times from the naming times of each subject. This procedure eliminates the common variation of naming times, which is possibly due to the fact that the color-word lines are not equally difficult. The residual variance will, in effect, be lower.

Joint Multiple Linear Regression on Orthogonal Trends

Schubö and Hentschel (1977; see also Hentschel & Schubö, 1976; Schubö & Hentschel, 1978) also found that the organization of the trend components in Sjöberg's model was unfortunate. Without changing the set of possible composed

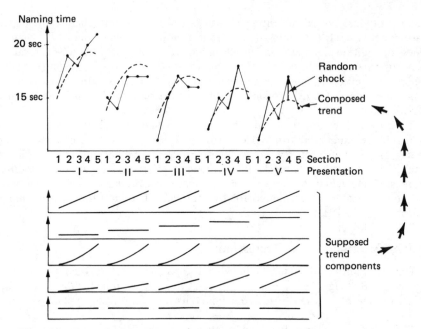

Figure 5.2   Sjöberg's multiple linear regression model

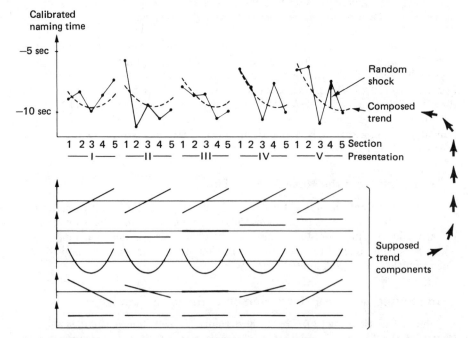

Figure 5.3   Multiple linear regression on orthogonal trend components using calibrated naming times.

trends, through simple orthogonalization of the trend components, they arrived at a new set of parameters with reliability estimates that were .20 higher on average. This result is self-evident, inasmuch as Sjöberg's trend components were highly correlated (see the first, third, and fourth components), whereas the orthogonalized trend components in Figure 5.3 are clearly distinct.

So far I have described models used for the serial evaluation of the serial CWT. From now on I am adding some new, possibly valuable models, that have not yet, as far as I know, been used in this case.

Regression on Different Trend Functions

The use of simple power-function polynomials was common to all treated models. But such polynomials are not good analogues for biologic processes, for they tend in principle to infinity as time tends to infinity. Life processes must take place within certain limits; polynomials are therefore used only as an easy and crude approximation within limited ranges. Trigonometric polynomials, composed of sines and cosines with varying periods, or some kind of exponential polynomials can be used as alternatives.

THREE MODELS ASSUMING DEPENDENCE

The first 5 models assume that the residuals represent independent random shocks. But is there no continuity? Can there not be a progressive determination from one naming time to the following ones? This, indeed, is a basic assumption in much microgenetic theorizing.

If there is a serial dependence of the residuals in linear regression, if the assumed independent random shocks are not really independent, two problems arise. On the one hand, the kind and degree of dependence could lead to psychologically relevant measures, which cannot be disregarded. On the other hand, some results of ordinary least-squares regression analysis will no longer be valid; the estimated variances and standard errors, for instance, understate, perhaps very seriously, the true variances and standard errors (Hibbs, 1974). The *via regia* to the identification of the type of the serial dependence model and to the estimation of the process parameters is the Box-Jenkins approach (Anderson, 1976; Box & Jenkins, 1970).

Trend Elimination through Difference Formation

Before an analysis of such serial correlations can be performed, a stationary time series is necessary; the global trends have to be eliminated. This can be done by replacing the original data by the residuals in a trend analysis; possibly the calibrated naming times could be considered a stationary time series. A very common procedure to reduce global trends is to compute differences between each naming time and the preceding naming time as shown in Figure 5.4, or by higher

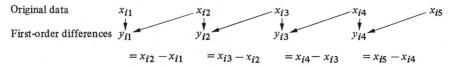

Figure 5.4 Elimination of linear trends within the ith presentation.

order differences. Moreover, periodicity has to be removed, as demonstrated in Figure 5.5. Clearly one loses observations or degrees of freedom through elimination of global trends. Because about 50 observations are needed to achieve reliable parameter estimates, in the case of the CWT, the measurement of naming times should be redefined.

Autocorrelations

The simplest way to describe the remaining serial dependencies is to use autocorrelations or partial autocorrelations. One can take, for instance, the first autocorrelation or the corresponding z-transformed value as a measure for each subject. In the case of my example, the autocorrelation of the naming times is .24; the autocorrelation of the calibrated naming times is $-.19$. This demonstrates the important influence of global-trend removal.

Autoregressive and Moving-average Model

Alternatively, one can introduce an autoregressive model or a moving-average model (Anderson, 1976; Box & Jenkins, 1970) if the series of partial autocorrelations or of autocorrelations, respectively, converges rapidly. A typical second-order autoregressive process is seen in Figure 5.6, where each observed value is a function of the last two observed values plus some random shock. The moving-average model may be demonstrated with the first-order process of Figure 5.7, where each observed value is the average of two successive random shocks. Of course the models, if applied to the serial CWT, have to be adapted to the special situation of interrupted measurement. Both models offer a few regression coefficients, which can be used as possibly relevant measures. In certain instances both models have to be combined to an autoregressive moving-average model (ARIMA). Estimation of the parameters of both models or the combined model is rather troublesome and requires the use of a computer program.

CONCLUSIONS

These models provide a pattern of methods that must usually be checked if an analysis of process data is to be performed. Care has to be taken in choosing the most adequate model in each application. A large amount of work on connections

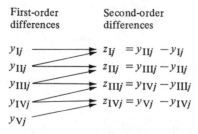

Figure 5.5 Elimination of periodicity (seasonal trend) for the first-order difference times of the jth section.

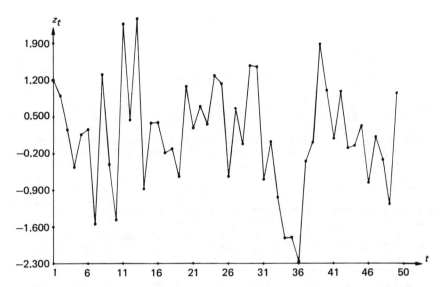

Figure 5.6 Time series of a second-order autoregressive process with the functional equation $z_t = .75\, z_{t-1} - .50\, z_{t-2} + a_t$, where a_t denotes the random shock at time t.

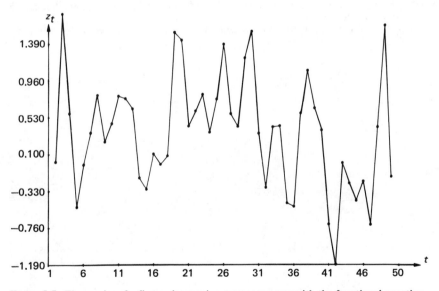

Figure 5.7 Time series of a first-order moving-average process with the functional equation $z_t = .50\, a_t + .50\, a_{t-1}$, where a_t and a_{t-1} denote the random shocks at times t and $t-1$, respectively.

to related variables is necessary because the final criterion is the external validity of the coefficients. Results achieved within one special model cannot immediately be transferred to the psychological process itself.

REFERENCES

Anderson, O. D. *Time series analysis and forecasting.* London: Butterworth, 1976.
Box, G. E. P., & Jenkins, G. M. *Time series analysis forecasting and control.* San Francisco: Holden-Day, 1970.
Hentschel, U., & Schubö, W. Serially scored color-, picture-, and figure-word tests, their intercorrelations and interpretation. *Psychological Research Bulletin* (Lund University, Sweden), 1976, *16*(6).
Hibbs, D. A. Problems of statistical estimation and causal inference in time-series regression model. In H. A. Costner (Ed.), *Sociological methodology 1973-1974.* San Francisco: Jossey-Bass, 1974.
Kemeny, J. G., & Snell, J. L. *Finite Markov chains.* New York: Van Nostrand, 1960.
Schubö, W., & Hentschel, U. Reliability and validity of the serial color-word test: Further results. *Psychological Research Bulletin* (Lund University, Sweden), 1977, *17*(6).
Schubö, W., & Hentschel, U. Improved reliability estimates for the serial color-word test. *Scandinavian Journal of Psychology*, 1978, *19*, 91-95.
Sjöberg, L. On serial scoring of the color-word test. *Acta Psychologica*, 1969, *29*, 150-162.
Smith, G. J. W., & Klein, G. S. Cognitive controls in serial behavior patterns. *Journal of Personality*, 1953, *22*, 188-213.
Smith, G. J. W., & Nyman, G. E. Psychopathologic behavior in a serial experiment: Investigations of neurotic, psychotic, psychopathic and normal subjects. *Lunds Universitets Årsskrift*, new series, 2, 1959, *56*(5).
Smith, G. J. W., & Nyman, G. E. *Manual till CWT (Serialt Färgordtest).* Stockholm: Skandinaviska Testförlaget, 1972.
Stroop, J. R. Studies of interference on serial verbal reactions. *Journal of Experimental Psychology*, 1935, *18*, 643-662.

6

Stimulus Dimensions in Merogenetic Experiments

Ulrich Gilsdorf
University of Basel, Basel, Switzerland

Werner D. Froehlich
University of Mainz,
Mainz, Federal Republic of Germany

The objective of this study is to relate several configurational and informational measures to the merogenetic variety of microgenesis and to the orienting reaction. The usual form of merogenetic picture presentation entails an increase in the pictorial configuration (see Fig. 6.1) under conditions of brief but constant presentation of the stimulus. This series of pictures can be subdivided into phases, for example, as reproduced in part in Figure 6.1, from Phase 1 to Phase 15 of a series. The features of the picture, however, cannot be more exactly specified; in other words, there is no proof that the same increment of information obtains from Step 1 to Step 2 as from Step 2 to Step 3, or between any other two successive steps. To resolve this problem, it is essential to find appropriate measures that can then be transformed into pictorial configurations. Transformation of the pictures can be accomplished by computer program, as shown in our examples. Such a program, written by the first author, is, in fact, available. Following the tenets of information theory (Attneave, 1959), information measures of the pictures in question determine their information value. This, however, could also be elucidated empirically in an exploratory study by presenting computer-generated pictures in pairwise combinations and establishing which of the two pictures in the pair contains more information. Following this operation, subjectively equidistant steps could be selected by means of a Thurstone scale.

An additional advantage of this procedure with a merogenetic picture series standardized on the basis of information theory is the higher degree of precision of the statements about the correlates of information intake by participants, for example, about the succession of their reactions, both physiological and verbal.

Numerous investigations have demonstrated that the orienting reaction, as represented by GSR or by other bioelectric phenomena, is highly dependent on a variety of information-loading factors. These are exemplified above all by the contrast phenomena, by the density and distance measures, and, finally, by all the indicators of geometric configurational properties. In an orientation-reaction experiment, a certain pictorial configuration could conceivably be subjected to analysis retrospectively. Thus, certain physiological reactions related to information

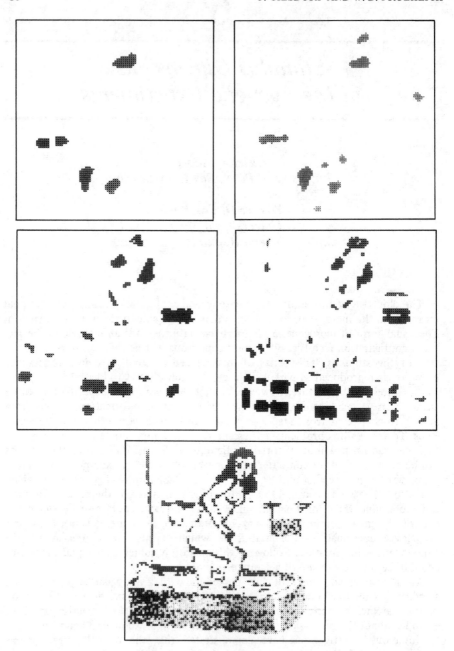

Figure 6.1   Five selected computer-generated pictures from the Smock series.

processing could be analyzed in relation to specific information parameters. This analysis would not necessarily result in capturing the global concept of information processing, but it could conceivably refer to the distance between points, density, brightness, and so forth.

The point of departure for our present undertaking is a study by Froehlich and Laux (1969) in which the relationship between merogenetic microgenesis and orienting reaction was demonstrated. The focus of the present project is on the stimulus-control aspect of merogenetic experiments. Several options for describing increasing complexity and information are provided and supplemented by computational examples. The pictorial referents of these measures are illustrated by several selected pictures from the Smock (1955) series. Finally, an example of applying two informational measures to the prediction of the process of the orienting reaction is provided in the context of the findings by Froehlich and Laux (1969).

GRID PATTERNS AND CONSTRUCTION OF VARIABLES

Before any informational analysis can take place, the materials must be arranged for it. To this end, a grid pattern is constructed by the so-called *rastering procedure.* This pattern consists of a finite set of black or white *grid points* (according to the terminology of Dörner, 1970). Other names for patterns of this kind are *dot pattern, matrix pattern* (Garner, 1962; Klemmer & Frick, 1953; Prinz, 1966), *metric figures* (Fitts, Weinstein, Rappaport, Anderson, & Leonard, 1956), *metric histoforms,* and *cellular polygons* (Zusne, 1970). The resultant grid pattern can be: (a) analyzed for geometric features, (b) treated as a temporal event, and (c) considered as a structural event.

Geometric Aspects

From a geometric point of view, the following variables can be specified:

1. Grid dimensions, that is, number of rows (MROW) and number of columns (MCOL)
2. Number of black grid points (NPNT)
3. Number of connecting lines between any two black grid points (NSIG), which can be computed by means of the following combination formula:

$$NSIG = \binom{NPNT}{2} = \frac{(NPNT - 1)NPNT}{2}$$

(NSIG reappears as the number of "elementary signals")

4. A coefficient of concentration (CONC), which is the mean value of the lengths of the connecting lines between any two black grid points (the distance between two adjacent grid points horizontally and vertically being equal to unity)

Temporal Aspects

A grid pattern can be considered as a temporal event taken from a set of equivalent events. The set (or population) is defined by all the patterns that share the same number of black grid points (NPNT) within a given grid (MROW by MCOL). The number of possible patterns, M, is computed by combinations:

$$M = \binom{MROW*MCOL}{NPNT} = \frac{(MROW*MCOL)!}{(MROW*MCOL - NPNT)! * NPNT!}$$

The magnitude of M can be related to chance probability for any one pattern i to appear. Given that all of these patterns are equally likely to occur, $p_i = 1/M$. Probability is reciprocally related to information content, that is, the smaller the probability, the greater the amount of information (HPOP).

$$HPOP = 1d\left(\frac{1}{p_i}\right) = -1dp_i = 1dM$$

HPOP is a measure of a class of events, dependent only on class magnitude; it tells us nothing about the regularity or complexity of a single pattern.

Pattern information and redundancy regarding sampling problems from patterns are discussed in detail by Corcoran (1971), Fitts et al. (1956), Garner (1962), Prokovnik (1959), and Zusne (1970).

Structural Aspects

In this section we attempt to determine the information content and redundancy of a unique pattern. In this context, Garner (1962, p. 202), in reference to Attneave (1957), Hochberg and Brooks (1960), and Hochberg and McAlister (1953), asked the following question: "[The] measured characteristics are certainly related to the information concepts of constraint or redundancy, but how can we fit measurements of the unique pattern into a paradigm which deals with sets of events and their probabilities?" It may be possible to solve Garner's problem by introducing auxiliary elements, used to synthesize a given pattern. Three devices seem pertinent:

1. The elementary signal approach introduced by Prinz (1966), which was transferred to grids (Prinz himself used dot patterns within a blank square) and extended by the use of "weighted analysis"
2. The information-analytic characteristics (IAC) described by Dörner (1970), who used multivariate information analysis (see Garner, 1962; McGill, 1954) as a means of pattern analysis
3. The esthetic measure (EM) of Bodack (1968), whose definition makes possible the construction of new variables as ratios of other variables

Elementary Signals and Pattern Information

Direct connecting lines between any two black grid points are called *elementary signals*. They can be identified by the following criteria: length or distance; angle with one of the grid base lines; joint occurrence of distance and angle per connecting line (d/a combination). For a grid pattern with NPNT black grid points, the number of possible elementary signals is given by NSIG = NPNT * (NPNT − 1)/2 (cf. Geometric Aspects).

In reference to distances and angles, both an unweighted and a weighted analysis can be undertaken. The unweighted analysis proceeds exclusively from the frequency distribution of elementary signals. The weighted analysis takes into account a priori frequencies in addition to the actual frequency distribution.

As a first step in an unweighted analysis, the NSIG signals of a given pattern are determined; that is, all actually appearing distances are computed, all angles are specified, and all d/a combinations are identified by a specific number. Then all signals are compared with each other, and identical values are eliminated. The resulting three frequency distributions, reflecting how often distinct signals were found, represent the various distances, angles, and d/a combinations. Finally, information content for each distribution is computed by the Shannon entropy formula:

$$ H = - \sum_{i}^{N} (p_i) \mathrm{ld}(p_i) $$

where H = Unweighted information (bits per signal)
p_i = Relative frequency of signal i
N = Number of different signals

$$ p_i = \frac{n_i}{\sum\limits_{i} n_i} = \frac{n_i}{\mathrm{NSIG}} $$

with n_i = Absolute frequency of signal i.

The information measure, H, reflects the average predictability of an elementary signal in a reciprocal way; the greater the H, the less predictable any signal i. H will reach its maximum when all signals are different. Then the above equation can be reduced to $H = \mathrm{ld}(\mathrm{NSIG})$, because $p_i = 1/\mathrm{NSIG}$. H will reach its minimum when only one signal is found; then $n_i = \mathrm{NSIG}$ and $H = 0$.

As already mentioned, in the *weighted analysis* a priori frequencies are taken into account in the Empty Grid 1. The rationale underlying the weighting procedure is that a given signal that is a priori more probable than another signal contributes in the final analysis less information to a pattern.

The number of possible connecting lines is a function of the dimensions of a given grid (MROW, MCOL). Generally, (MCOL*MROW − 1) lines can be drawn from the upper left point to any other grid point. The number in question defines the repertoire of possible signals. Some angles must obviously be identical. Moreover, at least two identical lengths above and below the diagonal from upper left to lower right are bound to appear. Systematic comparisons have shown that usually far more than two distances become equal and that lines of diagonal length can be drawn to off-diagonal grid points (a 100 × 100 grid has the repertoire of 9,999 lines, but only 3,663 distances and 6,009 angles).

The steps of the analysis are:

1. All of the possible connecting lines are drawn and compared, which results in a repertoire frequency distribution of nonidentical distances and angles.

2. The frequency distributions of actually occurring signals are determined (as in the unweighted analysis).

3. The actual signal frequencies are corrected by means of the corresponding repertoire frequencies.

4. Finally, the entropy of weighted actual frequency distribution is computed by the Shannon formula as follows:

$$H^* = -\sum_i^N (p_i^*) \mathrm{ld}(p_i^*)$$

with

$$p_i^* = \frac{n_i l_i}{N^*}$$

and

$$N^* = \sum_i^N n_i l_i$$

where H^* = Weighted information
p_i^* = Relative weighted frequency of signal i
N = Number of actually different signals
n_i = Absolute frequency of signal i
l_i = Absolute repertoire frequency of signal i

Redundancy measures reflect the relative difference between actual and maximal information. *Relative redundancy* is defined as:

$$R = \frac{H_{\max} - H}{H_{\max}} = \frac{\mathrm{ld}\, N - H_{\text{computed}}}{\mathrm{ld}\, N}$$

$$R^* = \frac{\mathrm{ld}\, N^* - H_{\text{computed}}^*}{\mathrm{ld}\, N}$$

For example:

1. The elementary signals are a 3*3 grid.
2. The connecting lines are:

```
1   a   b        The number of possible lines is (MROW*MCOL − 1) = 9, from (.a) to
    c   d   e        (.h).
.   g   h
```

3. The repertoire of distances (squared, to avoid decimals) is:

```
.  1  4
1  2  5
4  5  8
```

Empty grid distribution, 1_i

i	d_i^2	1_i	Lines
1	1	2	.a, .c
2	2	1	.d
3	4	2	.b, .f
4	5	2	.e, .g
5	8	1	.h

4. The repertoire of angles (identified by code numbers) is:

```
.  1  1
2  3  4
2  5  3
```

Empty grid distribution, 1_i

$i = a_i$	1_i	Lines
1	2	.a, .b
2	2	.c, .f
3	2	.d, .h
4	1	.e
5	1	.h

4. The repertoire of d/a signals (code numbers) is:

```
.  2  3
3  4  5
6  7  8
```

Empty grid distribution, 1_i

$i = (d/a)_i$	1_i	Lines
1	1	.a
.	.	.
8	1	.h

6. The computations for the following example are:

```
x  .  .
.  .  y
.  .  z
```

$'.'$: white grid points

Geometric variables:

a. MROW = 3, MCOL = 3
b. NPNT = 3
c. NSIG = $(3 - 1)3/2 = 3$
d. CONC = $(xy + xz + yz)/3 = 2.02$

Set variables:

$$M = \frac{3*3}{3} = 84$$

HPOP = $1d$ 84 = 6.39 (bits per pattern of defined set)

Unweighted and weighted analysis:

Frequency distributions

Signal	i	d_i^2	n_i	1_i	n_i	1_i	$1 = a_i$	n_i	1_i	n_i	1_i	$i = (d/a)_i$	n_i
xy	4	5	1	1		1	4	1	1		1	5	1
xz	5	8	1	1		1	3	1	2		2	8	1
yz	1	1	$\frac{1}{3}$	2		$\frac{2}{4}$	2	$\frac{1}{3}$	2		$\frac{2}{5}$	3	$\frac{1}{3}$

Distances

$$H = 1d\ 3(\text{all } n_i = 1) \qquad H^* = 2(\tfrac{1}{4}\ id\ \tfrac{1}{4}) + \tfrac{1}{2}\ 1d\ \tfrac{1}{2}$$

$$= 1.58 \qquad\qquad\qquad = 1.50$$

$$R = .00 \qquad\qquad\qquad R^* = (2 - 1.5)/2 = .25$$

Angles

$$H = 1d\ 3 \qquad\qquad H^* = \tfrac{1}{5}\ 1d\ \tfrac{1}{5} + 2(\tfrac{2}{5}\ 1d\ \tfrac{2}{5})$$

$$= 1.58 \qquad\qquad\qquad = 1.52$$

$$R = .00 \qquad\qquad\qquad R^* = (2.32 - 1.52)/2.32$$

$$\qquad\qquad\qquad\qquad\qquad = .34$$

d/a signals

$$H = 1d\ 3$$

$$R = .00$$

Information-analytic Characteristics

Dörner (1970) relates multivariate information transmission (cf. Attneave, 1959; Garner, 1962; McGill, 1954) to grid patterns and develops IACs of several orders "to characterize the way in which color is distributed over the grid" (p. 349, trans. by the authors).

The grid pattern can be considered a three-variate space; that is, each grid point can be classified with respect to three variables: vertical position v; horizontal position h; and color c. Garner (1962, p. 145) introduced "the term constraint to refer to the amount of interrelatedness or structure of a system of variables as measured in informational terms." The total constraint of the grid-pattern variable system is divided into the following components by information analysis:

$$U(v{:}h{:}c) = U(v{:}c) + U(h{:}c) + U(\overline{vhc}).$$

$U(v{:}h{:}c)$, total constraint, represents the average mutual predictability, that is, any one variable given the other two.

$U(v{:}c)$, the contingency uncertainty between variables v and c, is a measure of the average color predictability of a grid point, given its vertical position.

$U(h{:}c)$, the contingency uncertainty between h and c, represents the average color predictability of a grid point, given its horizontal position.

$U(\overline{vhc})$, the interaction uncertainty, means the average color predictability, given the vertical and the horizontal positions.

Some systematically varied examples can help to explain what is meant by these measures. Let colors between rows become more and more balanced (for computation formulas, see Garner, 1962, or Attneave, 1959);

```
X  X  X  X     X  X   .  .     X  X   .  .

X  X  X  X     X  X  X  X     X  X   .  .

.  .  .  .     .  .  X  X     .  .  X  X

.  .  .  .     .  .  .  .     .  .  X  X
```

$U(v{:}h{:}c)$	1.0	1.0	1.0
$U(v{:}c)$	1.0	.5	.0
$U(h{:}c)$	.0	.0	.0
$U(\overline{vhc})$	.0	.5	1.0

$U(h{:}c)$: Knowledge of the horizontal position does not help because each column contains two white and two black grid points.

$U(v{:}c)$ and $U(\overline{vhc})$: The more the colors are balanced between the rows, the more knowledge of the vertical and horizontal positions of a grid point is needed to predict its color.

As far as regularity or complexity is concerned, it can be said that the lower the regularity of a given pattern, the higher the value of $U(\overline{vhc})$ and the lower the values of $U(v{:}c)$ and $U(h{:}c)$. High portions of $U(v{:}c)$ and $U(h{:}c)$ would, then, mean imbalance of colors between rows and columns.

Considering the variables of the elementary signal approach, it can be expected that $U(\overline{vhc})$ will be correlated positively with the information measures; $U(v{:}c)$ and $(h{:}c)$, with the redundancy measures.

The Esthetic Measure

The esthetic measure is defined by the ratio

$$\text{EM} = \frac{\text{Structural redundancy}}{\text{Selective information}}$$

According to Bodack (1968, p. 303, trans.), "selective information content . . . is based on the number and frequency of the visual building blocks; i.e., the visual elements . . . , perceived as units . . . Structural information and redundancy are based on the number and frequency of 'connecting elements'; i.e., geometric values that describe the arrangement of the building blocks."

EM can be transferred to grid patterns if white and black grid points are substituted for "building blocks" and elementary signals for "connecting elements." The denominator can be formed by the entropy of the color frequency distribution; the numerator, by the different redundancy measures. The resulting ratios can best be characterized as variables, relating to the perceptual "ease" of processing a given pattern. The greater the value of EM, the more easily a pattern should be processed.

Table 6.1 Values of the measures for the 15 pictures of the Smock series

Picture number	A			B	C^a				D^a				E			
	NPNT	NSIG	CONC	HPOP	$H-D_u$	$H-A_u$	$H-D_w$	$H-A_w$	$R-D_u$	$R-A_u$	$R-D_w$	$R-A_w$	$U(v{:}c)$	$U(h{:}c)$	$U(\overline{vhc})$	$U(v{:}h{:}c)$
1	236	27,730	34.08	1,606.7	9.1	8.6	9.1	4.6	37.8	41.1	44.2	75.6	.047	.037	.076	.161
2	259	33,411	33.17	1,728.6	9.2	8.7	9.1	4.7	38.5	41.7	44.7	75.5	.050	.036	.086	.173
3	276	37,950	39.48	1,816.7	9.8	9.4	9.7	5.1	35.0	37.8	42.0	73.3	.039	.029	.113	.182
4	361	64,980	39.96	2,235.6	10.1	9.7	9.9	5.2	36.5	39.1	43.4	73.9	.045	.039	.138	.224
5	431	92,665	41.89	2,557.6	10.4	10.1	10.1	5.4	36.9	38.5	44.1	73.0	.043	.046	.166	.256
6	516	132,870	41.42	2,925.7	10.4	10.1	10.1	5.4	38.3	40.5	45.7	73.9	.065	.047	.179	.293
7	584	170,236	41.73	3,204.7	10.4	10.2	10.2	5.6	39.7	41.0	46.4	73.2	.055	.050	.215	.321
8	561	157,080	44.07	3,111.7	10.6	10.4	10.3	5.7	38.5	39.7	45.5	72.6	.047	.044	.219	.311
9	683	232,903	43.35	3,589.4	10.6	10.4	10.3	5.9	40.3	41.2	47.0	72.2	.052	.039	.267	.359
10	990	489,555	44.54	4,651.9	10.7	10.5	10.4	6.0	43.1	43.9	49.3	73.1	.066	.065	.333	.465
11	1,067	568,711	46.38	4,892.5	10.8	10.6	10.5	5.9	43.4	44.2	49.5	73.5	.095	.054	.340	.489
12	1,153	664,128	44.54	5,150.6	10.7	10.5	10.4	5.9	44.4	45.4	50.3	73.8	.102	.066	.347	.515
13	1,581	1,248,990	42.89	6,290.9	10.6	10.4	10.3	6.0	47.2	48.3	52.6	74.6	.143	.072	.414	.629
14	2,249	2,527,876	44.84	7,683.4	10.7	10.6	10.4	6.1	49.2	49.9	54.4	75.0	.204	.041	.522	.769
15	2,951	4,352,725	44.21	8,743.5	10.7	10.6	10.4	6.2	51.2	51.6	56.1	75.3	.255	.067	.551	.875

Note. For A, cf. Geometric Aspects in text; for B, cf. Temporal Aspects; for C, cf. Structural Aspects, Unweighted Analysis and Weighted Analysis; for D, cf. Structural Aspects, Redundancy Measures; for E, cf. Information-analytic Characteristics.

[a] D_u = distances, unweighted; A_u = angles, unweighted; D_w = distances, weighted; and A_w = angles, weighted.

Table 6.2 Mean intercorrelations between the variables types

	Geometric measures	H measures	R measures	IAC
Geometric measures	–	.687	.722	.745
H measures		–	.575	.601
R measures			–	.792
IAC				–

APPLICATION TO SMOCK'S SERIES OF PICTURES

In Table 6.1, the measures explained above are applied to the discrete pictures of the Smock series (cf. also the picture examples in Fig. 6.1). As Table 6.2 demonstrates, the measures in question sometimes deviate perceptibly from each other; that is, they cannot be regarded as homogeneous in each instance. This state of affairs suggests the need to consider the use of several measures in empirical investigations as well.

APPLYING TWO MEASURES TO PREDICT
THE ORIENTING–REACTION PROCESS
DURING MICROGENESIS

In Figure 6.2, the predicted process curve is represented by the two predictor variables $H - D_w$ and $H - A_w$ (labeled SCR̂). It closely corresponds to the actual process of the skin-conductance response (labeled SCR) across the 15 pictures

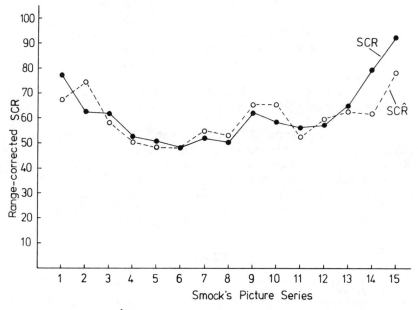

Figure 6.2 SCR and SCR̂ values of range-corrected skin-conductance responses across the 15 pictures of Smock's series.

(R^w = .702). This example illustrates the practical value of these theoretically derived information measures.

CONCLUSIONS

In hologenetic experiments (metacontrast included), the main problem of assessing microgenetic processes consists of relating psychophysical factors of stimulus presentation (e.g., presentation time and luminance) to responses varying in complexity, clarity, and meaningfulness. In merogenetic research, however, the main factors that contribute to the process on the stimulus side are pattern complexity, increase of figural components, density, and so on, leading to the identification and integration of the stimulus in terms of a more or less "realistic" meaning. Thus, meaning develops between the poles of (a) fragments of a pattern of uncertain meaning and (b) a subjectively certain, unambiguous representation.

In most cases, the stimulus scale remains ambiguous. In his famous "farmer's wife" series, Sander (1928) worked with increases of figural components (i.e., lines, triangles, etc.), whereas Smock (1955) used a grid scheme that takes into account the number of "black" spots and their location in terms of logical, geometric, or figural rules, or some combination. In both cases, the "stimulus" can only be evaluated on a nominal or ordinal scale and, therefore, does not provide for a mathematically stringent basis for the use of analysis of variance (ANOVA) or trend analysis for the series. One of the advantages of the computer program developed here is that it is a step toward the definition of the stimulus in terms of increasing information. These various kinds of definitions—based on combinations of measures used—could lead to developing an internal scale of the stimulus.

Sixteen different measures were logically derived and applied to a merogenetic series used by Froehlich and Laux (1969). The proposed method can be used to:

1. Generate pictures consistent with a specific set of characteristics
2. Use these pictures in a Thurstonian scaling procedure to select those pictures showing increases of information (i.e., complexity, density, meaningfulness) in equal-appearing steps
3. Get an estimate of those informational parameters that contribute to the psychological or psychophysiological dependent variables

As demonstrated by the results of the Froehlich and Laux (1969) experiment, a combination of weighted-angle and distance measures leads to a prediction of fit of ORs (phasic GSR components) at several microgenetic "stages." Comparison of these findings with the cubic trend in another experiment (see Froehlich, 1978; p. 127) leads to the conclusion that trend differences might reflect the impact of "cognitive" activities superimposed upon the more "primitive" processing of a mere figural contribution to information entropy in microgenesis.

REFERENCES

Attneave, F. Physical determinants of the judged complexity of shapes. *Journal of Experimental Psychology*, 1957, *53*, 221–227.
Attneave, F. *Applications of information theory to psychology*. New York: Holt, 1959.
Bodack, K. D. Aesthetisches Mass technischer Produkte. *Konstruktion*, 1968, *10*, 391–395.
Corcoran, D. W. J. *Pattern recognition*. Harmondsworth: Penguin, 1971.

Dörner, D. Eine informationstheoretische Methode zur Bestimmung der asthetischen Wirkung von Flächenmustern. *Psychologische Forschung*, 1970, *33*, 345-355.

Fitts, P. M., Weinstein, M., Rappaport, M., Anderson, N. S., & Leonard, J. A. Stimulus correlates of visual pattern recognition. *Journal of Experimental Psychology*, 1956, *51*, 1-11.

Froehlich, W. D. Stress, anxiety, and the control of attention: A psychophysiological approach. In C. D. Spielberger & I. G. Sarason (Eds.), *Stress and anxiety* (Vol. 5). Washington: Hemisphere, 1978.

Froehlich, W. D., & Laux, L. Serielles Wahrnehmen, Aktualgenese, Informationsintegration und Orientierungsreaktion: I. Aktualgenetisches Modell und Orientierungsreaktion. *Zeitschrift für experimentelle und angewandte Psychologie*, 1969, *16*, 250-277.

Garner, W. R. *Uncertainty and structure as psychological concepts*. New York: Wiley, 1962.

Hochberg, J., & Brooks, V. The psychophysics of form: Reversible-perspective drawings of spatial objects. *American Journal of Psychology*, 1960, *73*, 337-354.

Hochberg, J., & McAlister, E. A quantitative approach to figural "goodness." *Journal of Experimental Psychology*, 1953, *46*, 361-364.

Klemmer, E. T., & Frick, F. C. Assimilation of information from dot and matrix patterns. *Journal of Experimental Psychology*, 1953, *45*, 15-19.

Laux, L., & Froehlich, W. D. Serielles Wahrnehmen, Aktualgenese, Informationsintegration und Orientierungsreaktion: II. Dimensionsanalyse von Massen des Hautwiderstandes. *Zeitschrift für experimentelle und angewandte Psychologie*, 1970, *17*, 266-276.

McGill, W. J. Multivariate information transmission. *Psychometrika*, 1954, *19*, 97-116.

Prinz, W. Quantitative Versuche über Prägnanz von Punktmustern. *Psychologische Forschung*, 1966, *29*, 297-359.

Prokovnik, S. J. Pattern variants on a square field. *Psychometrika*, 1959, *24*, 329-341.

Sander, C. F. Experimentelle Ergebnisse der Gestaltpsychologie. In *Bericht über den 10. Kongress für experimentelle Psychologie*. Jena, 1928, pp. 23-88.

Smock, C. D. The influence of psychological stress on the "intolerance of ambiguity." *Journal of Abnormal and Social Psychology*, 1955, *50*, 177-182.

Zusne, L. *Visual perception of form*. New York: Academic, 1970.

II

INDIVIDUAL DIFFERENCES IN PERCEPT-GENETIC ANALYSIS

7

Individual Differences and Microgenesis

Francine A. Lastowski
Tufts New England Medical Center,
Boston, USA

Perception of stimuli presented under suboptimal conditions provides a difficult adaptive challenge. A possible avenue for the study of how personality affects perception presents itself when a person has to go beyond the information given, as in ambiguous stimulus situations. Microgenesis of perception is a potentially valuable research strategy for the study of individual differences within the perceptual process.

Microgenesis is "the sequence of events which are assumed to occur in the temporal period between the presentation of a stimulus and the formation of a single relatively stabilized cognitive response (percept or thought) to this stimulus" (Flavell & Draguns, 1957). One experimental paradigm for the study of microgenesis of perception involves the successive presentation of a stimulus under conditions of increasing clarity. Within this paradigm the most commonly used procedure is that of tachistoscopic presentation of visual stimuli with exposure gradually increasing in duration until veridical perception is attained.

It was the purpose of this study to take a fine-grained look at the processes involved in the development of a percept. Most studies completed within the microgenetic framework rely on verbal reports to infer how the information is processed. Within this framework, however, little attempt has been made to observe how the information is first extracted from the stimulus configurations presented tachistoscopically. Moreover, other than the work carried out by the Lund research group (Kragh & Smith, 1970), the effect of individual differences on this process has been little studied.

To investigate those individual differences that potentially have an effect on the perceptual process, relatively stable, persistent characteristics of behavior that contribute to adaptability were sought; to this end, the concept of temperament was chosen. Work on temperament, however, has mostly been carried out with children. Measures of temperament variables had to be found that would be suitable for use with adults. Chosen were those six factors from Cattell's 16 Personality Factor Questionnaire (Cattell, Eber, & Tatsuoka, 1972) that most closely resembled "temperament" variables and also a checklist devised by the author for assessing temperament variables characteristic of quick adaptors as established by the work of the New York Longitudinal Study group (Chess & Thomas, 1973; Chess, Thomas, & Birch, 1968; Thomas, Birch, Chess, Hertzig, & Korn, 1963). Because the methodological format involved presenting stimuli at decreasing levels of ambiguity, a paper-and-pencil measure for tolerance of ambiguity (MacDonald, 1970) was included along with the measures for specific temperament variables.

Many information theorists believe perception to be a continuous process in which information is obtained in an incremental or "brick-by-brick" fashion (Haber, 1969). Microgenetic theorists (Flavell & Draguns, 1957), however, would describe perception as a process of unfolding, that is, a progression of discrete qualitative jumps or stages. It is the author's belief that *both* processes occur when, under suboptimal conditions, a subject is presented with an ambiguous stimulus configuration.

METHOD

Subjects were 100 undergraduate volunteers from introductory psychology classes at the Pennsylvania State University who were asked to complete the following personality measures: (a) six scales of the Cattell 16PF questionnaire (Factors A, F, G, H, O, L), which appear to correspond to dimensions of temperament (Chess et al., 1968); (b) an adjective checklist of 39 items derived from Chess, Thomas, and Birch's (1968) conception of temperament; and (c) MacDonald's (1970) revision—AT-20—of the Rydell-Rosen (1966) Ambiguity Tolerance Test. Each subject then viewed six stimuli through a two-channel tachistoscope.

The stimuli were six black-and-white rapidograph drawings including a war scene (Stimulus 1), a basketball game (Stimulus 2), a rodeo (Stimulus 3), an automobile accident (Stimulus 4), a park scene (Stimulus 5), and a fire scene (Stimulus 6). For each picture, each of the 37 segments corresponding to the circular location grid was rated for (a) "apparent" (i.e., physical) information and (b) meaning with respect to the whole picture. Additionally the pictures were rated for affective content, using a variation of the semantic differential. Interrater reliability for the ratings of physical information was .89; for the meaning ratings, .85. The 6 stimuli were selected from a pool of 20 so as to make three pairs with each pair matched for the amount of information; that is, matched stimuli contained equivalent amounts of information (physical and in terms of meaning) in scenes of similar location. Each pair contained one affective and one neutral stimulus.

The initial tachistoscopic exposure time for each stimulus was .003 sec, with an increment of .001 sec for each additional trial. Before each trial, a subject had to indicate where he or she intended to focus his or her eyes according to a circular location chart consisting of four concentric circles divided into 37 sectors. After each trial, the subject described what she or he had seen and indicated her or his certainty of response (1 = very sure, 2 = pretty sure, 3 = guess). The subject protocols were randomized within stimuli and rated according to a two-phase scoring system adapted from Friedman's (1952) system for rating Rorschach protocols within a developmental framework. The scoring system resulted in four stages, of which Stage 3 is considered veridical or correct recognition. Interrater reliabilities of .91 and .98 resulted between judges for Phase 1 and Phase 2 respectively.

Because microgenesis, by definition, deals with developmental changes over time, a control condition manipulating intensity with duration held constant was instituted. This methodological control was necessary to rule out the possibility that the observed stage progressions were not a real phenomenon but merely an artifact of an experimental procedure that itself manipulates time, namely, tachistoscopic presentation of stimuli. For the control group, 10 students from graduate programs in psychology were used. These subjects viewed the same six stimuli but, because of the constraints of the apparatus, were administered only 10 trials per stimulus. The stimuli were viewed at increasing levels of intensity (.26, .30, .31, .32, .33, .34, .35, .36, .38, .39 log ft lambert) resulting from a crude system of filters. No personality data were collected for the control group.

RESULTS AND DISCUSSION

Microgenetic Process

It was hypothesized that the development of a percept over time involves a two-stage process: (a) microgenesis and (b) a "brick-by-brick" accumulation of additional detail. This hypothesis was impossible to test formally. Although each stimulus protocol lent itself to the four-stage scoring procedure, there were relatively few Stage 1 ratings. The paucity of Stage 1 ratings was due either to the initial presentations not being brief enough, resulting in only partial ambiguity, or to subjects' need to label their reports in a concrete manner.

Sander (Graumann, 1959) has raised the possibility that in some instances microgenesis starts with discrete detail rather than with a diffuse whole. He does not specify, however, the conditions for this occurrence—whether they be situational, stimulus related, or personal. Although all protocols were readily rated by the stage scoring system, it cannot be ruled out that in certain instances perception may occur in a "brick-by-brick" stepwise fashion. Qualitative jumps are less readily observed when numerous trials with short jumps in exposure time are used. Moreover, many subjects' reporting styles were brief, and one longed for the scattered subjects who gave full reports that allowed their inferential processes to be observed. Thus, it would appear that microgenesis does occur to some extent but that an inferential overlay of brick-by-brick accumulation of information also occurs within the qualitative stage progressions.

A corollary hypothesis was formulated that the microgenetic process can be observed when intensity, rather than time, is manipulated by increasing illumination levels. Although this hypothesis was also impossible to test formally, examination of the protocol data demonstrates the microgenetic progression of stages. In a descriptive sense, the methodological control used in this study demonstrates that, when duration is held constant and intensity is manipulated, the microgenetic stages still occur. Thus there is more evidence that microgenesis is indeed a temporal phenomenon and not limited to a methodology (tachistoscopic presentation of stimuli) that itself manipulates the time factor.

Both the manipulation of intensity and the manipulation of time, however, produce identical cortical processes. On the cortical level, the manipulation of intensity results in an indirect manipulation of time, for below .01 sec the reciprocity law holds true. Perception or neutral activity is dependent on total energy stimulation, that is, on time as well as on intensity. Essentially, less intense stimulation (conditions of ambiguity) takes a longer time to detect (cortical processing) as well as to identify (information processing). Use of the two separate conditions of stimulus presentation adds up to convergent processes, both manipulating time on the cortical level. Both manipulations, however, result in similar stage progressions, or the microgenetic phenomenon being observed.

Individual Differences

The third hypothesis stated that the variations that occur within the microgenetic process would result from individual differences. The statistical procedure
applied to the data was multiple regression analysis. The criterion, or dependent
variable (Variable 1), was the number of trials necessary to achieve a Stage 3, or
veridical, response as determined by the two-phase subject-protocol rating system.
To assess the reliability of the criterion, a correlation matrix was computed for the
various stimulus groupings (Table 7.1). All intercorrelations were significant
($p < .05$) with the exception of Stimulus 4 and Stimulus 6. The emotional and
nonemotional groupings of stimuli were, however, highly correlated ($r = .56$;
$p < .05$). Because reliability across categories is high, the small amount of variance
accounted for in the regression analysis cannot be attributed to the unreliability
of the criterion.

When all eight variables were included in the regression analysis (Table 7.2),
only 9.27% of the variance ($r = .3044$; $df = 9/90$; $F = 1.02$; $p > .05$) was accounted for, and the resulting multiple r was not significant. This is due to the low
correlation of the independent variables with the criterion. The large number of
intercorrelations among the independent variables also accounts in part for the
lack of significance.

Cattell's Factors A (or affectothymia), L (or alaxia), and G (or superego
strength) proved significant ($p < .05$) for the data as a whole ($r = .2762$; $df = 3/96$;
$F = 2.64$). When stimuli were grouped according to emotionality, only Factor G
(superego strength) ($r = .1992$; $df = 1/98$; $F = 4.05$) proved significant ($p < .05$)
for the nonemotional grouping. Factor A (affectothymia) and Factor L (alaxia)
($r = .2509$; $df = 2/97$; $F = 3.26$) proved significant ($p < .05$) for the emotional
grouping.

Because Factors A (affectothymia), L (alaxia), and G (superego strength) capture an identifiable portion of the variance, they merit discussion. Both Factors A
and L are measures of adaptability. The low end of Factor A is characterized by
rigidity. High scorers on Factor L are suspicious and operate on internally oriented
cues. Factor G is a measure of perseverance and planfulness. Only Factor A plays a

Table 7.1 Correlations among variables: All stimuli combined

	1	2	3	4	5	6	7	8	9
1	1.00								
2	.24*	1.00							
3	.05	.30*	1.00						
4	−.06	.17	−.18	1.00					
5	.04	.47*	.55*	−.06	1.00				
6	.07	−.10	.08	−.08	−.06	1.00			
7	.03	−.14	−.05	−.10	−.28*	.24	1.00		
8	.01	.09	−.07	.29*	−.10	.12	.04	1.00	
9	−.04	−.12	−.34*	−.03	−.28*	.21	.32*	−.08	1.00

Note. 1 = criterion (number of trials); 2 = Factor A (affectothymia); 3 = Factor F (sur-
gency); 4 = Factor G (superego strength); 5 = Factor H (parmia); 6 = Factor L (alaxia); 7 =
Factor O (guilt-proneness); 8 = tolerance of ambiguity (AT-20); and 9 = adaptability (adjective
checklist).
*$p < .05$.

Table 7.2 Regression analysis: All stimuli

Variable	F	p(F)	Beta weight	Standard error	Part R^2
Factor A	7.9126	.0061	.3365	1.7264	.0585
Factor L	.9123	.6560	.1034	1.6892	.0095
Factor G	1.0330	.3131	−.1116	2.0273	.0082
Factor H	.5896	.5491	−.1052	2.0264	.0097
Adaptability	.3205	.7313	−.0663	12.5173	.0056
Factor F	.0776	.7779	−.0365	1.8382	.0006
Factor O	.0328	.8509	.0210	1.7465	.0003
AT-20	.0183	.8880	−.0148	6.7632	.0002
Multiple regression	1.0216	.4295			

significant role when the nonemotional stimuli are grouped. This is perhaps due to Factor L having more of an emotional tinge than does Factor A where adaptability is concerned. Factor A is most closely related to adaptability in the cluster of temperament variables identified by the New York Study group. Factor L, although a measure of adaptability, also appears to be related to quality of mood. It can be speculated that Factor G, or perseverance, also plays a nonsignificant role because for nonemotional stimuli it is of less importance to "stick" to the stimuli, forcing cognitive functions to override interference of affective arousal. Perhaps the most surprising finding is the low correlation between tolerance of ambiguity (.01) and the criterion of number of trials necessary to achieve veridical recognition. Tolerance of ambiguity does, however, consistently correlate ($p < .05$) with Factor G, which is a measure of perseverance or planfulness. Tolerance-of-ambiguity measures tend to be high in specificity and measure something different from practical information processing under conditions of uncertainty (Kenny & Ginsberg, 1958).

It cannot be concluded that the personality variables chosen for this investigation are good predictors of how long it takes to come to veridical perception. It also cannot be concluded, however, that temperament or adaptability are not potentially good predictors of variations in the perceptual process. It may be that the variables chosen for the present study do not adequately measure temperament or adaptability per se. Moreover, the results point out the limitations involved in studying temperament variables through the use of self-report measures alone. The New York Longitudinal Study group (Chess et al., 1968) used a multidimensional approach: reports by significant others (parents), behavioral observations, and psychological test results.

Qualitative Analyses

When the data are examined qualitatively, however, individual differences are noted not only in the speed of recognition but in the styles of reporting what was seen. With respect to speed of recognition or number of trials necessary to achieve veridical perception, several groups stood out. First, there were those who very quickly perceived and accurately described the stimuli—many as early as Trial 1. For most of these subjects it was not possible to observe the entire microgenetic sequence. There was the opposite set of subjects, who took a long time to describe the stimuli accurately, many of whom at the end of the maximum number of trials still had not achieved veridical recognition. Patterns of differential responding to emotionally valent versus neutral stimuli were also observed. A small group of subjects appeared to be perceptually vigilant for emotionally valent stimuli. Some of these subjects took a relatively long time to come to grips with nonthreatening stimuli, as if they were less important to figure out than the emotional ones. Other subjects appeared to have no differential responding and took equally long or short times to achieve recognition. The majority of subjects, however, gave the appearance of perceptually defending against emotionally valent stimuli in that it took them proportionately longer to achieve veridical perception of the threatening stimuli. Still other subjects appeared to be vigilant as well as defensive in that very early they had the correct impression of an emotionally valent stimulus but then lost it (some to the extent of describing a totally different scene). Several trials later these subjects went back to their initial impressions.

One indication that memory or set may have a disruptive effect in this type of experimental procedure is the slippage of a concept from one stimulus into the following one. This slippage manifested itself in varying degrees. For example, after perceiving a helicopter in Stimulus 1, some subjects initially saw an airplane cockpit in Stimulus 2. Although both Stimuli 2 and 3 are essentially sporting events, some subjects more directly carried over the concept of a game by initially seeing Stimulus 3 as a skating rink or hockey game. This usually arose from subjects labeling the dangling rope as a "hockey stick." The most dramatic examples of this slippage or carry-over had to do with subjects viewing the injured person in Stimulus 4 as the cowboy who was thrown from the horse in Stimulus 3. This description was apparently generated by subjects seeing the hats on the police and labeling them "cowboy hats."

Often it appeared that a subject would generate an impression of a picture from a specific detail. The examples described in the preceding paragraph are instances of incorrect hypotheses resulting from incorrect labeling of small details. When the specific detail is correctly labeled, however, the subject can quickly describe the picture accurately. For example, if a subject labeled the hats in Stimulus 4 as part of police uniforms or those in Stimulus 6 as part of fire-fighter uniforms, he or she quickly filled in the other details. If a subject initially saw the people in Stimulus 4 as wearing cowboy hats, this error was quickly corrected by correctly noting the police insignia or badge. The data do not lend themselves to sorting out whether expansion of a theme or concept from a specific detail is (a) a common ambiguity-resolving tactic or (b) a specific inferential process related to perceptual activity or (c) an artifact of the experimental procedure that required citing of location of eye fixations. Further empirical investigation is warranted.

Although many of the subjects seemed to be relatively fluid in moving from hypothesis to hypothesis, especially in the early stages, others were not. Those subjects who had the greatest difficulty in abandoning an incorrect hypothesis appeared to operate similarly in that they had nonfluid styles of information intake. For example, a subject may decide that the saddle on the horse rearing up its legs is really a fat man with a hat on and then not be able to ascertain why the other man is falling. Subjects who had the greatest difficulty in switching hypotheses tended to concentrate on the man who was falling but would fail to recheck whether the man with the hat was accurately perceived.

Another frequent observation would appear to be somewhat similar to what is described as the *Vorgestalt* in the German literature. Subjects would give indications of confusion and uncertainty about which of several impressions were accurate. When they would verbalize the correct concept, almost an "ah-ha" experience resulted, and all of the confusing details quickly fell into place. For example, a subject might on Stimulus 3 have the idea that some kind of activity was going on in a ring—that there was a show of sorts that people were watching. The subject might then try out different ideas, from a wrestling match to a circus act, and then locate the label of "rodeo" within her or his construct system. Once the subject had the concept that fit, namely, *rodeo*, the people became cowboys, the animal became a horse, the person became a broncobuster. Early trials, before the concept of rodeo emerged, gave the impression of a searching, a trying out of concepts for fit. With the right conceptual fit, all the details quickly fell into place, and the confusion and vagueness of reports were eliminated.

Interspersed within the protocols are subjects' reports that, though content remains the same, the picture is becoming clearer. One of the control subjects on Trial 9 of Stimulus 2 reported, "I saw the netting of the basket for the first time . . . considering I was very certain [of the basket] on the first trial. But there was no differentiation the first time—there was no detail at all."

Perceptual Defense

It was hypothesized that for all subjects the microgenetic process for emotional, or high-affect, stimuli would be longer than for nonemotional, or low-affect, stimuli. A t test on the difference between means of the emotional and nonemotional stimuli was computed. The emotional stimuli ($\bar{x} = 38.58; SD = 19.50$) took significantly longer ($p < .05$) to recognize than did the nonemotional stimuli ($\bar{x} = 22.93; SD = 15.56$). Thus a perceptual defense process was observed.

It is difficult to explain away the observed "defense" effect by means of the artifact arguments generated by the critics of the traditional perceptual defense studies (Eriksen, 1960; Goldiamond, 1958; Howes & Solomon, 1950). As pictorial stimuli were used in the present study, the problems of controlling for word frequency did not arise. Moreover, response bias is less likely to have played a significant role because the "emotional" stimuli used were not taboo words or even taboo pictures but, unfortunately, common occurrences of everyday modern life: war, car accidents, fires. Expectancy, or set, did, however, play a part for some subjects. Informal perusal of the data indicates that some subjects carried the theme from one stimulus over into their descriptions of the next. For example, some subjects correctly identified the content of the third stimulus as a man falling off a horse at a rodeo. They then "expected" the person on the ground in the fourth stimulus to be the same cowboy. For other subjects, the recognition process was delayed by their having initially adopted a false hypothesis, as Potter (1966) has observed. Still other subjects indicated that they had avoided looking at the potentially anxiety-provoking areas of the stimulus (e.g., the bleeding man in Stimulus 4). This phenomenon is, as Erdelyi (1974) mentions, a special instance of selective attention. For many other subjects, however, there are no direct or simple explanations of why the perceptual recognition process was delayed for emotional stimuli. Erdelyi's (1974) view of the perceptual defense effect as a special instance of selectivity in cognitive processing perhaps best accounts for the data. In this view, selectivity may be brought into play at multiple points along the processing sequence by various mechanisms.

Scanning Strategies

The fifth hypothesis predicted that random scanning would not occur, that is, that fixations during Stages 1, 2, and 3 would be associated with high information and meaning ratings. A chi-square statistic was computed for information and meaning ratings (Tables 7.3 and 7.4). The information ratings were significantly dependent on stage ($\chi^2 = 9.51; df = 1; p < .05$). To examine this relationship in more detail, separate chi-square statistics were calculated for each stimulus and for the nonemotional and emotional stimuli as a group. Only Stimulus 5 (nonemotional) ($\chi^2 = 6.35; df = 1; p < .05$) and the nonemotional grouping ($\chi^2 = 4.83; df = 1; p < .05$) proved significant. If the frequencies are examined, however, there emerges a tendency for proportionally more high-information areas to be fixated on when the stimulus is nonthreatening. An opposite tendency for proportionately more low-information areas to be fixated on emerges for emotionally valent or threatening stimuli.

The meaning ratings were significantly dependent on stage of perception ($\chi^2 = 4.21; df = 1; p < .05$). Separate chi-square statistics were computed for each stimulus and for the nonemotional and emotional stimuli as a group. Stimulus 1 (emotional) ($\chi^2 = 4.02; df = 1; p < .05$), Stimulus 3 (nonemotional) ($\chi^2 = 5.09; df = 1; p < .05$), and Stimulus 6 (emotional) ($\chi^2 = 8.34; df = 1; p < .05$) were significant; Stimulus 4 (emotional) ($\chi^2 = 3.73; df = 1; p < .10$) approached significance. Examination of the frequencies suggests that although high meaning ratings were assigned for both emotional and nonemotional stimuli, there is a tendency for proportionately fewer low-meaning-rated areas to be fixated on for emotional stimuli.

In Stages 1 through 3, the subject attempts to come to grips with the ambiguous stimulus configuration and achieve veridical recognition. During this problem-solving phase of the perceptual process, high-physical-information areas are sought when the stimuli contain nonemotional content. For emotional stimuli, however, the tactic of seeking high-information areas appears to not be operating as effectively. It may be postulated that the emotional content of the stimuli interferes with cognitive functioning so that the strategy of searching for high-information areas breaks down. This is similar to the work of Berlyne (1960), who found that

Table 7.3 Frequency of observations: Information ratings

Stage	Nonemotional stimulus	Information rating High (percentage)	Low (percentage)	Emotional stimulus	Information rating High (percentage)	Low (percentage)
1-3	2 + 3 + 5	792 (72)	313 (28)	1 + 4 + 6	899 (49)	929 (51)
4		605 (76)	188 (24)		318 (47)	365 (53)
1-3	2	105 (78)	30 (22)	1	288 (36)	501 (64)
4		163 (69)	73 (31)		60 (30)	141 (70)
1-3	3	335 (81)	79 (19)	4	407 (63)	235 (37)
4		250 (86)	42 (14)		145 (61)	93 (39)
1-3	5	351 (63)	204 (37)	6	204 (51)	193 (49)
4		192 (72)	73 (28)		113 (46)	131 (54)

Table 7.4 Frequency of observations: Mean ratings

		Information rating			Information rating	
Stage	Nonemotional stimulus	High (percentage)	Low (percentage)	Emotional stimulus	High (percentage)	Low (percentage)
1–3	2 + 3 + 5	1,024 (84)	198 (16)	1 + 4 + 6	1,737 (77)	524 (23)
4		709 (81)	162 (12)		672 (79)	184 (21)
1–3	2	179 (97)	6 (3)	1	516 (52)	475 (48)
4		271 (93)	19 (7)		117 (45)	144 (55)
1–3	3	340 (76)	106 (24)	4	788 (94)	45 (6)
4		211 (69)	97 (31)		281 (91)	27 (9)
1–3	5	505 (85)	86 (15)	6	433 (99)	4 (1)
4		227 (84)	46 (16)		274 (95)	13 (5)

high levels of arousal make it difficult to explore and obtain information, that is, overarousal impairs attention or investigatory strategies. Interference in cognitive functioning has also been suggested by Erdelyi (Erdelyi & Appelbaum, 1973; Erdelyi & Blumenthal, 1973), who hypothesized that the content of information processed early may affect the strategy of analysis for as-yet-unprocessed components of the input.

If the pattern of frequency of search for high-meaning areas is examined, the opposite effect is noted. Although areas rated high in meaning are sought for nonemotional stimuli in both early and late stages of the perceptual process, significantly more high-meaning areas are sought for emotional stimuli in the early stages. If it can be assumed that the meaning rating picks up an affective component of the information, then it would appear that the pull of the affective component of information becomes more prime than the physical component for emotionally valent stimulus configurations.

In nontachistoscopic studies, the emotional valence, or affective meaning, of stimuli has been shown to affect the fixation strategies of subjects (Luborsky, Blinder, & Schimek, 1965; Mackworth & Morandi, 1967; Schröder, 1970; Spence & Feinberg, 1967). Traditionally the perceptual defense effect has been demonstrated in tachistoscopic studies in which, owing to the time factor, the occurrence of multiple fixations is generally impossible. This, however, does not rule out the possibility that the processes of intake or extraction of information may manifest similarities. Thus if at some level the single flash of a stimulus is subjected to serial processing, as would be a constantly present stimulus, then selective strategies for processing the information gained from the next flash may be instituted on the basis of the partial information already obtained (Erdelyi, 1974). One may further speculate that the selectivity involved results from the pull of the affective component of information being stronger than that of the physical component. Thus it may be that cognitive functioning per se is not interfered with under conditions of high arousal but that the same ambiguity-resolving tactics are applied to different aspects or components of the information available. Strategies of extraction of information from a stimulus configuration may thus differ depending on the emotional content and the stage of the perceptual process. If this indeed be true, then the existence of a "preperceiver" or "homunculus" to explain the perceptual defense effect becomes unnecessary. The problem, however, becomes one of determining why emotionally laden information takes longer to process than does neutral, physical information.

An informal perusal of the protocol data suggests that different strategies of scanning are used by different subjects. These strategies deal with the amount of information sought as well as preferences for location of information to be used. Some subjects are "center"-oriented, seldom choosing to examine peripheral areas of information; other subjects give the appearance of randomly scanning the stimulus, irrespective of the information content of areas looked at. Some subjects take in very large sections of information at a time; others take in small areas and in an organized fashion build up to a larger section piece by piece. More study is needed to determine whether these are indeed different strategies of information intake or an artifact of the experimental procedure in that they represent styles of reporting (where a subject says he or she *will* look) rather than styles of "looking" (where a subject *actually* looks).

Certainty Ratings

The sixth hypothesis predicted that high certainty ratings would occur during Stages 3 and 4. A chi-square statistic was calculated for all stimuli. Certainty of response was dependent on stage ($\chi^2 = 500$; $df = 1$; $p < .005$). Proportionately fewer low certainty ratings are observed in Stages 3 and 4 (Table 7.5). Thus as the stimulus configuration increased in clarity with the increase of duration of exposure, subjects reported increasing certainty that their descriptions were accurate.

The uncertainty ratings per se did not help to sort out, to any great extent, the inferential aspects of the perceptual process. Differing patterns of reporting of certainty were observed, however. Some subjects did not report "very sure" until veridical perception was reached. Others, seemingly not willing to risk being wrong, stuck to "pretty sure" throughout the stages. Still others decided that, once they reported "very sure," the stimulus trials would end and were disappointed to discover this not to be true. Thus again the perennial problem of verbal reports enters into the rating of certainty. It is not known when certainty ratings are accurate descriptions of a subject's judgment and when they are an indication of a subject's style of reporting. Although it was not feasible in this study to examine formally the relationship between tolerance of ambiguity and style of reporting, it is possible that a subject's style of reporting may be indicative of an overlearned or generalized response to uncertainty.

It was hoped that the certainty ratings would help alleviate the problem of response in perceptual research. Owing to subjects' confusion concerning the

Table 7.5 Frequency of observations: Certainty ratings for all stimuli

Stage	Certainty ratings	
	High (percentage)	Low (percentage)
1–3	1,545 (57)	1,175 (43)
4	1,787 (87)	262 (13)

use of the certainty ratings, it cannot be conclusively stated that this study indeed investigated perception. It would be more appropriate to conclude that *responses* to perceptual stimuli, not *perception*, were elicited and examined.

IMPLICATIONS FOR FUTURE RESEARCH

Microgenesis, or the process of unfolding of stages in the development of a percept over time, does appear to occur to some extent for some subjects. Bruner's (1957) explanation of perception as an act of categorization perhaps best fits the data of many of the subjects. For what is apparent in many of the verbal descriptions is the occurrence of inferential processes rather than purely "perceptual" ones. A higher degree of initial ambiguity is necessary before the processes involved in Stage 1 can be effectively sorted out.

For stimuli that are emotionally valent, the process of recognition is slowed down. It is not possible at this point to sort out exactly what processes are operative in extending or slowing down the perceptual process. Analysis of the information and meaning ratings, however, lends credence to the possibility of information-extraction processes operating differentially for neutral and emotionally valent stimuli. It is the author's opinion that adoption of an information-processing approach would be the most fruitful empirical avenue for insight into the processes operative in perceptual recognition in general and in the perceptual defense phenomenon in particular.

Although individual differences do appear to be evidenced in the protocol data, the variables chosen for the study account for only a minimal portion of the variance. The potential value of temperament or adaptability variables in the perceptual process cannot be ruled out. More effective measures of temperament must first be developed. Reliance on self-report measures of temperament is contraindicated, whereas the multidimensional approach of the New York Longitudinal Study group (Thomas, Birch, Birch, & Hertzig, 1960; Thomas et al., 1963) is indicated. In light of the apparent high degree of involvement of inferential variables in the perceptual process, it is important for future research to investigate thoroughly the cognitive aspects of individual differences, for example, cognitive styles or individual patterns of decision making. Moreover, to more effectively establish what are universal and what are individual processes operating within the perceptual process, greater attention must be paid to stimulus variables. Thus stimuli must be matched, not only for information and meaning, but for tightness of organization of theme. Attention should also be paid to the number of alternative interpretations of details within stimuli, for the less decisive the physical conditions of a stimulus configuration, the more apparent becomes the influence of organismic variables as a directive factor in the perceptual process.

Subjects in the study varied in speed of recognition, some achieving veridical recognition within one to three trials. There are potentially two sources of individual differences to be investigated, in the development of a percept: (a) the personality variables and (b) sensory and capacity factors. It could prove interesting to determine subjects' absolute threshold sensitivities to light. This would help determine if speed of detection varies proportionately to speed of recognition or identification or if the greater amount of variation is limited to personality or cognitive variables brought to bear by an organism to deal with the adaptive challenge presented by an ambiguous stimulus configuration.

REFERENCES

Berlyne, D. E. *Conflict, arousal, and curiosity.* New York: McGraw-Hill, 1960.

Bruner, J. S. On perceptual readiness. *Psychological Review,* 1957, *64,* 123–152.

Cattell, R. B., Eber, H. W., & Tatsuoka, M. M. *The 16 Personality Factor Questionnaire handbook.* Champaign, Ill.: Institute for Personality and Ability Testing, 1972.

Chess, S., & Thomas, A. Temperament in the normal infant. In J. C. Westman (Ed.), *Individual differences in children.* New York: Wiley, 1973.

Chess, S., Thomas, A., & Birch, H. G. *Temperament and behavior disorders.* New York: Brunner/Mazel, 1968.

Erdelyi, M. H. A new look at the New Look: Perceptual defense and vigilance. *Psychological Review,* 1974, *81,* 1–25.

Erdelyi, M. H., & Appelbaum, G. A. Cognitive masking: The disruptive effect of an emotional stimulus upon the perception of contiguous neutral items. *Bulletin of the Psychonomic Society,* 1973, *1,* 59–61.

Erdelyi, M. H., & Blumenthal, D. G. Cognitive masking in rapid sequential processing: The effect of an emotional picture on preceding and succeeding pictures. *Memory and Cognition,* 1973, *1,* 201–204.

Eriksen, C. W. Discrimination and learning without awareness: A methodological survey and evaluation. *Psychological Review,* 1960, *67,* 279–300.

Flavell, J. H., & Draguns, J. G. A microgenetic approach to perception and thought. *Psychological Bulletin,* 1957, *54,* 197–217.

Friedman, H. Perceptual recognition in schizophrenia: An hypothesis suggested by the use of the Rorschach Test. *Journal of Genetic Psychology,* 1952, *81,* 63–98.

Goldiamond, I. Indications of perception: I. Subliminal perception, subception, unconscious perception: An analysis in terms of psychophysical indicator methodology. *Psychological Bulletin,* 1958, *55,* 373–411.

Graumann, C. F. Aktualgenese: Die deskriptiven Grundlagen und theoretischen Wandlungen des aktualgenetischen Forschungsansatzes. *Zeitschrift für experimentelle und angewandte Psychologie,* 1959, *6,* 410–448.

Haber, R. N. (Ed.). *Information-processing approaches to visual perception.* New York: Holt, 1969.

Howes, D. H., & Solomon, R. L. A note on McGinnies' "Emotionality and perceptual defense." *Psychological Review,* 1950, *57,* 229–234.

Kenny, D. T., & Ginsberg, R. The specificity of intolerance of ambiguity measures. *Journal of Abnormal and Social Psychology,* 1958, *56,* 300–304.

Kragh, U., & Smith, G. J. W. (Eds.). *Percept-genetic analysis.* Lund: Gleerup, 1970.

Luborsky, L., Blinder, B., & Schimek, J. Looking, recalling, and GSR as a function of defense. *Journal of Abnormal Psychology,* 1965, *70,* 270–280.

MacDonald, A. P. Revised scale for ambiguity tolerance: Reliability and validity. *Psychological Reports,* 1970, *26,* 791–795.

Mackworth, N. H., & Morandi, A. J. The gaze selects informative details within pictures. *Perception and Psychophysics,* 1967, *2,* 547–552.

Potter, M. C. On perceptual recognition. In J. S. Bruner, R. R. Olver, & P. M. Greenfield (Eds.), *Studies in cognitive growth.* New York: Wiley, 1966.

Rydell, S. T., & Rosen, E. Measurement and some correlates of need-cognition. *Psychological Reports,* 1966, *19,* 139–165.

Schröder, S. R. Selective eye movements to simultaneously presented stimuli during discrimination. *Perception and Psychophysics,* 1970, *7,* 121–123.

Spence, D. P., & Feinberg, C. Forms of defensive looking: A naturalistic experiment. *Journal of Nervous and Mental Disease,* 1967, *145,* 261–271.

Thomas, A., Birch, H. G., Birch, H. G., & Hertzig, M. E. A longitudinal study of primary reaction patterns in children. *Comprehensive Psychiatry,* 1960, *1,* 103.

Thomas, A., Birch, H. G., Chess, S., Hertzig, M. E., & Korn, S. *Behavioral individuality in early childhood.* New York: New York University Press, 1963.

8

On the Role of Conflict in Microgenesis

John A. Cegalis
Syracuse University, Syracuse, USA

Microgenesis, as elaborated by Flavell and Draguns (1957), refers to changes of percepts and thoughts in microtime, from initially primitive states to more complex states. Although the nature of formal characteristics is currently debated among students of microgenesis, percepts and concepts are described as qualitatively different at different microtime stages or phases in their brief evolution. Not the least of these qualitative differences are affective counterparts to percepts and concepts; microgenetic progressions are viewed as being embedded in affective states. Microgenesis is thus concerned not only with nonimmediate microdevelopmental changes of perception and thinking but with an elaboration of how such changes occur in the context of personality structure and function.

A fundamental question facing proponents of microgenesis is whether microgenesis characterizes the transformations that occur in all percepts in a unitary fashion or whether microgenetic processes are differentially activated. Confusions around this question have led some theorists, notably Haber (1969), to suggest that "basic microgenetic theory can be subsumed under information processing analysis" (p. 3). My research group's orienting hypothesis stipulates that full microgenetic progressions are differently elicited. We consider *disequilibration* a necessary condition for the occurrence of extended microgenetic progressions. Accepting the assumption that microgenesis refers to, and indeed describes, a process of the formation of meaning, we view microgenesis as a process of trace selection occurring within active operational structures that, in consort with affective processes, help to define the broader context of personality. Microgenesis is therefore characterized by constructive and conservational qualities.

Bearing in mind the problem of the unitary nature of microgenesis, we have been both intrigued by and concerned about methodological problems in the study of microgenesis. In the classic stimulus fractionation paradigm, for example, the experimenter's dictum that subjects will respond to a stimulus before its final or full recognition raises several questions: (a) In what sense does continuity of perception obtain after re-presentation of a stimulus, and in what sense does the re-presentation elicit a discontinuous state subject to a unique set of parametric

The studies discussed in this chapter represent research efforts that were generated in the author's research group at Syracuse University, in particular, collaborative efforts with Dr. Patricia Maffeo (1974), Dr. Robert Strickland (1975), and Andrew Ursino. The author is now at Yale Psychiatric Institute, New Haven, USA.

influences? (b) In what sense does cognition (e.g., response strategy, hypothesis testing) contaminate the perceptual process? (c) Of the emerging preformulations, which would attain preconscious or conscious levels in a nonexperimental situation, and in what sense does the experimental manipulation contribute to the availability of particular contents? Kragh's (1970) concern for the overdosage of the stimulus notwithstanding, how do we answer the challenge of critics such as Murphy and Hochberg (1951) who argue that "reduced exposure time probably does little more than reduce the efficacy of the stimulus" (p. 334, n. 3).

A further problem concerns the conceptualization of affectivity and of its role in microgenesis. This problem strikes at the core of differences between Freudian and Piagetian theories and no less at the core of microgenesis. Is perceptual or conceptual structure formed by affectivity in a direct manner as suggested by psychoanalysis, or does affectivity act indirectly via mediating processes such as selective attention as suggested in Piaget's genetic theory?

As suggested, we have assumed that disequilibration is a necessary condition for extended microgenetic development. If this assumption is valid, it might be expected that, in explicitly disequilibrating situations, a better picture of certain characteristics of microgenesis could be obtained. We have further assumed that conflict situations are primary examples of disequilibrating conditions. Conflicts were generated experimentally by: (a) grossly distorting the quality of stimulus organization in perceptual adaptation experiments or (b) juxtaposing stimulus contents that are alien to or consonant with particular processing strategies or personality characteristics. Our research in the former category has suggested that the initial stages of adaptation to distorted sensory input are characterized by dedifferentiated functioning such as increased field dependence and reduced discriminability of signal-noise contours in a concomitant auditory-processing task (Cegalis & Murdza, 1976; Cegalis & Young, 1974). We have also found individual differences in reactions to such conflict, especially among introverts and extroverts, or among repressors and sensitizers (Cegalis & Leen, 1977). I might also mention, parenthetically, that we have frequently observed productions of an autistic, even hallucinogenic, nature during attempts to cope with these conflicts. Given, however, the difficult and complex filiations between ontogenetic and microgenetic developments that are apparent in the perceptual adaptation paradigm, I focus on the latter approach to conflict. In this regard, I discuss experiments on contrasexuality, subliminal perception, and cognitive style.

EXPERIMENT IN CONTRASEXUALITY

Contrasexuality refers to the existence of behavior or emotional characteristics at variance with characteristics typically associated with one's gender identification (e.g., nurturance in males, aggression in females). Several personality theorists have attempted to describe the bifurcation of sexual identification (Freud, 1905/1953; Kohlberg, 1966). On the other hand, few theorists have attempted to formulate an understanding of the integration of contrasexual characteristics in personality. Bakan (1966) described the integration of contrasexuality as the integration of two broad organizing principles, *agency* (male) and *communion* (female). Agency represented tendencies toward self-assertion, mastering, and establishing autonomy or boundaries. Communion represented tendencies toward cooperation, contact, and union. Integration of these shared tendencies was thought to be a developmental task. Limited evidence for Bakan's theory was provided by Block (1973) and Block, Block, and Harrington (1974), who suggested that the integration of contrasexual characteristics occurs during later stages of ego development.

If, as suggested by Werner (1957), perception is a mirror to internal structure, then we might investigate certain characteristics of personality by investigating perceptual processes. To this end, microgenetic theory and methodology may be particularly suitable as a means of conceptualizing and studying internal structure. Approaches developed by Kragh and Smith (1970) are notable in this regard. In fact, Kragh (1970) and Kragh and Kroon (1966) have shed considerable light on the utility of microgenetic (or percept-genetic) techniques for inferring the nature of relationships between deviant behavior and deviant sexual identifications.

Further information concerning the integration of contrasexuality might be gained by investigating the growth of percepts whose stimulus referents are explicitly contrasexual. Recognizing the existence of important individual differences in external as opposed to internal orientations toward perception, we sought to examine microgenetic development of contrasexual percepts in introverts and extroverts.

Methods

Subjects selected were 96 undergraduates with a mean age of 22 years. They were screened for normal visual acuity and classified as introverted or extroverted by means of scores on the Myers-Briggs Psychological Inventory. Tolerance of ambiguity was also assessed according to Budner (1962). Subjects were randomly assigned to four treatment groups, with the restrictions that each group contained equal numbers of introverts and extroverts, men and women ($n = 6$ per cell). The four treatment conditions corresponded to four experimental stimuli: two contrasexual and two noncontrasexual line drawings.

Pilot studies were performed to establish certain of the parameters of the experimental variables. One concern was the comparability of information in similar spatial regions of the four stimuli. To assess comparability, we modified a technique developed by Pollack and Spence (1968). Stimulus drawings were divided into 12 segments and were rated by nonexperimental subjects for the amount of information conveyed by each segment. On the basis of comparisons of these ratings, we concluded that the drawings were sufficiently equivalent in the amount of information conveyed by corresponding segments of the four experimental stimuli. Another concern was the extent to which the drawings could be considered androgenous (containing both masculine and feminine elements). Independent ratings of the four experimental stimuli established that drawings of "man with baby" and "woman with drill" were more androgenous than the remaining stimuli ("woman with baby"; "man with drill").

To facilitate a developmental analysis of percepts containing contrasexual and congruent sexual content, we established a series of microgenetic landmarks a priori: (a) detection of something, (b) global meaning, (c) detailed meaning that is stimulus bound, (d) integrated meaning of a principal figure in conjunction with an activity, (e) first appearance of final correct recognition, and (f) final correct recognition. We assumed this system of landmarks would offer a means of identifying equivalent points in the microgenetic sequence for different subjects.

The presence of affective elements in self-reports was assessed with the scoring system devised by Wiener and Mehrabian (1968) in which emotional distance (nonimmediacy) was assumed to reflect positive or negative affective evaluation implicit in descriptions of percepts. The scoring system was based on subtle denotative differences in word use that indicated spatial separation among the communicator, the object of communication, or the addressee. We hypothesized that subjects who had not attained a contrasexual integration would demonstrate greater emotional distance (nonimmediacy) when communicating about their perceptual experiences of contrasexual stimuli.

After dark adaptation, subjects fixated a central cross (.5 sec) and then reported their perceptions of a briefly presented stimulus. Subjects were first presented a series of 60 practice presentations of a nonexperimental stimulus, in increasing durations of 1 msec, beginning at 1 msec. Practice was provided to familiarize subjects with the need to report all experiences fully, however ambiguous, clear, or trivial. Subjects were then presented experimental stimuli in a preestablished sequence consisting of trials incrementing in 1-, 10-, 100-, 250-, and 1,000-msec increments as determined from pilot studies. All responses were tape-recorded and transcribed.

Results

Protocols were scored by independent raters who were uninformed of the purpose of the experiment and blind to the typing of subjects. Interrater reliabilities were established for ratings of each landmark. The lowest reliability occurred at Landmark 4, where $r = +.89$. Although each landmark was thought to represent a conceptually distinct stage of development, such distinctions were not apparent for all subjects.

Comparisons of the frequency of multiple-landmark criteria in verbal responses (concurrences) indicated that the lack of distinctions between particular landmarks did not result from male–female or introversion–extroversion variables. On the basis of the patterning of concurrences, subsequent analyses were limited to Landmarks 1, 3, 4, and 6.

Table 8.1 summarizes the time-score data for all subjects at all landmarks analyzed. Separate analysis of variance at each landmark indicated that: (a) at Landmark 1, there was a significant interaction between contrasexuality and introversion–extroversion variables, where introverts attained Landmark 1 earlier in the contrasexuality condition than in the congruent situation; (b) there were no significant main effects of interactions between experimental variables at Landmark 3; and (c) at Landmark 4 there was a significant interaction between contrasexual–congruent sexual and introversion–extroversion variables, where introverts reached Landmark 4 earlier than extroverts in the contrasexual condition and extroverts reached Landmark 4 earlier than introverts in the congruent sexual condition.

Scores for emotional distance were obtained from responses at Landmark 6. Results of an analysis of variance of these data yielded a significant interaction between contrasexuality and introversion–extroversion: Extroverts demonstrated greater emotional distance when presented the contrasexual stimulus than did introverts. Extroverts also demonstrated greater emotional distance when presented with contrasexual rather than congruent stimuli.

No significant differences in tolerance of ambiguity were obtained from a comparison of introverts and extroverts. Budner tolerance-of-ambiguity scores were,

Table 8.1 Mean time to attainment of landmarks 1, 3, 4, and 6 in contrasexual and congruent stimulus presentations (in msec)

	Stimulus conditions															
	Contrasexual								Congruent							
	Female[a]				Male[b]				Female[c]				Male[d]			
Subject group	1	3	4	6	1	3	4	6	1	3	4	6	1	3	4	6
Introversion	6.3	10.3	13.3	1,068.8	5.1	9.9	13.8	104.0	6.9	10.6	19.9	24.1	7.0	12.4	17.2	20.3
Extroversion	6.8	11.5	16.3	526.8	6.8	10.2	18.5	645.7	6.2	10.6	14.6	16.5	6.0	9.8	14.3	21.7

[a]Woman with drill.
[b]Man with baby.
[c]Woman with baby.
[d]Man with drill.

however, significantly correlated with time scores at Landmarks 1 and 3 for the contrasexual conditions ($r = +.37$ and $+.29$, respectively). Thus subjects intolerant of ambiguity took significantly longer to attain Landmarks 1 and 3 in the contrasexual conditions.

EXPERIMENTS ON SUBLIMINAL PERCEPTION AND AFFECTIVITY

Dixon (1971) has commented on the common ground between subliminal perception and microgenesis. We have also wondered about interfacing these paradigms and have made an initial attempt in this direction. We were particularly interested in designs in which an emotionally evocative subliminal stimulus was used to modify the neutral emotional characteristics of a supraliminal stimulus (Eagle, 1959; Smith, Spence, & Klein, 1959). In such experiments subjects were first presented a subliminal emotional figure followed by a supraliminal neutral figure, and subjects' responses were scored for emotional content. This experimental design is attractive because it may help to explain essentially autistic responses to affectively neutral situations. Fleeting and ill-perceived feelings, whether evoked by existing stimuli or by memory evocations, may be projected to other stimulus content. We might wonder about the directionality of such effects in the light of current interest in forward and backward masking effects. Is the effect of a subliminal stimulus greater when that stimulus precedes, follows, or is concomitant with a supraliminally perceived stimulus? We might also ask about the effects of subliminal stimuli vis-à-vis a distinct microgenetically evolving percept.

First-study Methods

In a preliminary investigation, 45 undergraduates (15 men, 30 women) were randomly assigned to three conditions: (a) a condition in which subliminal stimuli preceded a supraliminal stimulus; (b) a condition in which subliminal stimuli were presented midway through the presentation of the supraliminal stimulus; and (c) a condition in which subliminal stimuli followed the presentation of the supraliminal stimulus. Stimuli were presented in separate fields of a four-channel tachistoscope. The luminance of each channel was 90 millilamberts.

Separate pilot studies with independent and naïve subjects were conducted to establish certain of the parameters of the experimental variables. In Pilot 1, subjects were asked to compare neutral, angry, and happy faces by ratings on the semantic differential. Both happy and angry faces were judged to be equally and significantly dissimilar to the neutral faces on the evaluative scale. An analysis of composite scores (evaluative, potency, and activity scales combined) indicated the angry face elicited responses of greater magnitude than the happy face. In Pilot 2, thresholds for the detection and full recognition of the neutral face were established in a series of trials in which the temporal duration of the neutral stimulus was increased in 1-msec increments. Neutral stimuli were then repeatedly presented at established thresholds, and subjects rated their emotional reaction to each presentation (response options included positive, negative, or no response). Average threshold for first awareness of stimulation was 20.5 msec, whereas full recognition was 35 msec. These values changed slightly downward over 20 trials, although not significantly so. The duration of the subliminal stimulus (8 msec) was selected as a duration two standard deviations below the lowest average threshold for first awareness of stimulation by the neutral face. None of the subjects was able to report the presence of the subliminal stimulus when presented at this duration. An analysis of subjects' affective ratings of the neutral face indicated the existence of a positive response bias (3:2 over negative responses), and this bias did not differ significantly from the first 10 trials to the second 10.

The juxtapositioning of the subliminal and supraliminal stimuli required by the experimental design raised a question of a form of stimulus interaction known as *masking*. The masking effect of the supraliminal stimulus on the subliminal stimulus was evaluated by measuring the duration of the exposure of an affective face required for the subject to report a noticeable change in any aspect of the neutral face. In this third pilot study, it was determined that none of the subliminal stimuli significantly increased the full-recognition threshold of the neutral face. The masking effect of subliminal stimuli was therefore uniform for all experimental conditions.

In the experiment proper, all 45 subjects were presented 45 trials consisting of random combinations of sub- and supraliminal stimuli with the limitation that angry, happy, and blank subliminal stimuli were each presented 15 times. After each presentation, subjects were instructed to rate the neutral face as positive, negative, or no response. Response latency was also measured.

First-study Results

We determined response bias for each subject by computing correlations between the average affective rating for trials in which a blank subliminal stimulus was presented and the average affective rating of responses to angry and happy subliminal stimuli. No pattern of significant correlations resulted; therefore, we made no attempt to control for individual differences in response bias. We then computed average affective ratings of the neutral face in each of the subliminal stimulus conditions for each of the experimental conditions. These data are presented in Figure 8.1. An analysis of variance of these data indicated that the emotional subliminal stimuli had a significant effect on the magnitude and valence of affective ratings. Affective ratings on trials in which the positive subliminal stimulus was presented were more positive than affective ratings on trials in which a blank or negative subliminal stimulus was presented. The effect of the negative subliminal stimulus was not significant. The analysis also indicated that there were no significant effects attributable to the temporal positioning of the subliminal stimuli. An analysis of response latency yielded no significant differences for any stimulus condition.

Second-study Methods

In a second study, we investigated the influence of an affective subliminal stimulus on the microgenetic development of a complex pictorial stimulus. We randomly assigned 40 subjects (12 men, 28 women) with a mean age of 22.2 years to two experimental and two control groups ($n = 10$ per group). Experimental groups were defined by the temporal position of a subliminal stimulus (the angry face from the first experiment) relative to the complex pictorial stimulus (TAT card 1BM): (a) subliminal stimulus precedes complex stimulus or (b) subliminal stimulus follows complex stimulus. Control groups were defined by the type

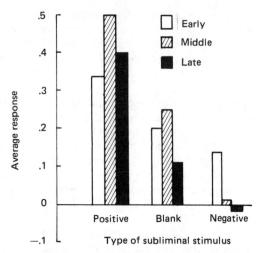

Figure 8.1 Average responses to the neutral supraliminal stimulus for trials using positive,
negative, and blank subliminal stimuli
across early and late experimental conditions.

of subliminal stimulus presented: (a) neutral or (b) blank. Of the 10 subjects in
each control group, half received subliminal stimulation before, half after, the complex stimulus.

The complex line drawing (TAT 1BM) was initially exposed for 20 msec at a
luminance of 30 millilamberts. In each succeeding trial, exposure duration for the
complex stimulus was increased in .10-log steps until all major pictorial elements
were identified. All subliminal stimuli were exposed for 30 msec (a duration two
standard deviations below the first awareness threshold for the complex stimulus as
determined from a pilot study). The dependent measure consisted of the temporal
duration required for recognition of: (a) first awareness of stimulation, (b) first correct identification of a major pictorial element, and (c) final recognition of all
major pictorial elements.

Table 8.2 Modification of microgenetic landmarks: Median of TAT 1BM exposure durations
required for attainment of three landmarks when preceded or followed by
subliminal stimuli (in msec)

Subliminal stimulus and temporal position	Microgenetic landmarks		
	First aware	First element	Full development
Blank			
Early	54	318	1,005
Late	54	216	1,265
Neutral			
Early	50	267	1,688
Late	42	216	845
Affective			
Early	42	318	4,400
Late	52	282	1,005

Second-study Results

The median exposure times required for attaining each recognition level are presented in Table 8.2. We used a Mann-Whitney U test to evaluate differences between treatments. The results of this test indicated that the temporal position of subliminal stimuli did not result in significantly different recognition thresholds for first awareness or first identification of a major pictorial element. A significant temporal position effect was found, however, at the final recognition level when angry and neutral subliminal stimuli were presented. Final recognition required significantly more exposure time when subliminal stimuli preceded, as compared with followed, the exposures of the complex stimulus.

EXPERIMENT ON COGNITIVE STYLES

Cognitive styles may reflect differences in the manner in which information is searched, organized, and transformed in perception, memory, and thought. One of the most thoroughly researched cognitive-style constructs is reflection–impulsivity (Kagan, 1966). The purpose of this study was to determine whether differences in cognitive style would be reflected in the quality and quantity of information available. We used converging methodologies to assess cognitive representations of visual stimuli. The microgenetic technique consisted of repeated tachistoscopic stimulus presentations, beginning at threshold duration and increasing until correct identification of the stimulus was achieved. This method permitted the intermittent scoring of preliminary stages of stimulus identification, an assessment of the quality of the developing percept, and an assessment of temporal durations associated with stages in percept development. A second technique involved a single, brief tachistoscopic exposure of a complex stimulus. We assessed the amount of information available with a signal-detection analysis of responses to positive and negative probe items.

Methods

To permit a developmental analysis of perceptual reports, a series of landmarks in perceptgenesis were identified a priori. The landmarks included: (a) detection of something, (b) global identification, (c) detailed stimulus-bound meaning, and (d) final and integrated recognition. We selected impulsive and reflective subjects from an initial subject pool of 100 undergraduates. First all 100 subjects were pre-screened for visual acuity. All were then administered the Adult Matching Familiar Figures (MFF) Test. Latency of the first response and the number of errors before the correct response were recorded for 12 MFF items. Subjects were then classified as impulsive or reflective according to Kagan's (1966) criteria; 20 impulsive and 20 reflective subjects, divided equally by sex, were selected.

Subjects were administered the Shipley-Institute of Living Scale (an index of intelligence) and the Budner Scale of Tolerance-Intolerance of Ambiguity (an index of tolerance of ambiguity). In the experiment proper, subjects were adapted to the dark for 20 min, and then a detection threshold was determined by five ascending series of stimulus presentations with a complex lithograph. Subjects were then given instructions for responding to the repeated presentation of Escher's "hand with reflecting globe." This stimulus was presented 40 times, beginning at the subject's own detection threshold, with increasing exposure on succeeding trials in $\frac{1}{2}$-log steps, as established from pilot work. The luminance of the stimulus was a constant 90 millilamberts. Responses were tape-recorded and later transcribed. Perceptual reports for each presentation were then scored by independent naïve raters for landmark, distress remarks, major or detail hypotheses, elaborations of stimulus qualities without content, and *Vorgestalt*.

On completion of the microgenetic series, we then tested subjects in the probe task. In this task, subjects were divided arbitrarily into experimental and control groups, with equal numbers of impulsive and reflective subjects per group. Subjects were presented a fixation cross for 1.5 sec, followed by a single 200-msec presentation of a practice, experimental, or control stimulus. A blank gray follow-field was then presented for .5 sec. The practice stimulus was Escher's "three worlds," whereas the experimental stimulus was a print of a farm scene used in previous information-processing research by Haber and Erdelyi (1967). The control stimulus was a reproduction of Escher's "reptiles." After a practice trial, subjects were then presented experimental or control stimuli. After the stimulus presentation, subjects selected, from a list of probe words, those words corresponding to objects seen during the single, brief stimulus presentation.

Of the 28 words on the probe list, half described items to be found in the experimental stimulus. These were the 14 items mentioned most frequently in descriptions of the experimental stimulus by 10 independent raters before the experiment. The remaining 14 probe items were interference items, unrelated to the content of either experimental or control stimuli. Interference items were selected according to the dual criteria of similar word length and comparable frequency in the standard college lexicon (Kučera & Francis, 1970) to stimulus-relevant probe items. Stimulus-relevant and -irrelevant probe items were randomly located on the response sheet. Subjects were instructed to scan the probe list rapidly and consecutively, starting with a word randomly chosen by the experimenter, and to circle with a pen only those items that described what they had seen. A 1-min time limit was imposed. Subjects were not permitted to return to items previously scanned. Subjects in the experimental condition viewed the experimental stimulus only. Control subjects were shown a different stimulus in order to control for a base-rate effect that might account for subjects' selection of stimulus-relevant probe items regardless of the stimulus viewed. The data consisted of the number of stimulus-relevant probe items (hits) and the number of stimulus-irrelevant items (false alarms).

Results

The results of the microgenetic analysis were discouraging. Each subject received a score, in milliseconds, that represented the duration of stimulus presentation at which each of the four perceptual recognition landmarks could be scored. Given the positive skew of these data, scores were submitted to a simple $\log_{10}$ transformation. Transformed data were then subjected to an analysis of variance. There were no significant group or sex differences, and the interaction between groups and sex was not significant. Analysis of qualitative features of response records was also discouraging. An analysis of variance of distress remarks yielded a significant main effect for reflection–impulsivity, with reflective subjects exhibiting distress remarks on more trials than impulsive ones. Yet none of the other qualitative variables yielded significant differences.

Correlational analyses were somewhat more revealing of subject variables in the microgenetic series. Budner tolerance-of-ambiguity scores were positively and significantly correlated with time scores for Landmark 4 ($r = +.34$), indicating that subjects less tolerant of ambiguity required longer intervals before achieving final recognition. MFF error scores correlated significantly with Landmark 4 recognition time ($r = -.56$), indicating that more impulsive subjects required less time to final recognition. Older subjects tended to offer more new detail hypotheses during the microgenetic sequence. The correlation between age and the number of new detail hypotheses was $r = +.43$, $p < .01$. For the overall sample, significant negative correlations emerged between the number of new detail hypotheses offered during the microgenetic sequence and the recognition times scorable at Landmark 2 ($r = -.50$, $p < .001$). Thus for all subjects the tendency to report details was associated with the likelihood of volunteering global recognition hypotheses earlier. The number of new major hypotheses offered during the microgenetic sequence was negatively correlated with Landmark 4 recognition time ($r = -.34$, $p < .05$); thus the general tendency to offer many hypotheses was associated with shorter times to full recognition, whereas fewer hypotheses were associated with longer recognition times.

We assessed differences in availability of stimulus information in the probe task by comparing thresholds for stimulus items retained in memory. Measures of sensitivity were obtained by calculating the area under the *memory operating characteristic* (MOC) *curve* for each subject (Grier, 1971). Area under MOC (A') has been recommended as a suitable nonparametric estimate of sensitivity in situations in which a single hit and false-alarm rate has been obtained. (A' does not require the restrictive assumptions of normal signal-plus-noise and noise distributions and the equality of variance of these distributions required in the use of d'; yet A' has been shown to be highly correlated with d'.) A' measures for each group are presented in Table 8.3. A comparison of these data indicated that impulsive subjects were significantly more sensitive than reflective subjects. Thus availability of stimulus items in memory is greater among impulsive subjects. For comparison, traditional measures of recognition performance are also presented in Table 8.3 as recognition accuracy corrected for chance.

We also obtained measurements of the criteria of likelihood ratios. B'_H has been recommended as a nonparametric estimate of B (Hodos, 1970). Inspection of Table 8.3 indicates that criteria for the impulsive and reflective groups are comparable, and indeed a comparison of these measures yielded no significant difference, $t < 1$. Reflective subjects were not significantly more conservative than impulsive subjects.

We did an analysis of recognition performance of experimental and control

Table 8.3 Probe experiment mean scores

Cognitive style	Dependent variables		
	A'	B'_H	$P_{sn}(s) - P_n(s)$[1]
Reflective subjects	.705*	.488	.239**
Impulsive subjects	.817	.517	.399

[1] Mean recognition scores corrected for chance.
*$p = .05$.
**$p = .02$.

subjects to compare the experimental hit rate to base rate of stimulus-relevant items chosen. This analysis yielded a significant difference. A comparable analysis of differences in the false-alarm rates was not significant. Therefore, experimental groups discriminated stimulus-relevant items significantly better than control subjects, with no appreciable difference in guessing.

CONCLUSIONS

The central and unifying theme of our studies has been the role of conflict in microgenesis. We are as yet unable to provide information on the larger question of whether conflict is a necessary condition for the occurrence of an extended microgenetic sequence. In our view, the methodologies used in the study of microgenesis create conflict conditions to the extent that they create ambiguity. We are, however, able to provide preliminary information on the sufficient effects of externally induced conflict and in particular to comment on the relationship of conflict to affective and personality variables in the context of perceptual microgenesis.

Conflict was induced in our three studies by manipulating stimulus content, by pairing contrary supraliminal and subliminal stimuli, and by creating task demands we thought incompatible with habitual response styles. One of the clearest effects of induced conflict was obtained in the experiment on contrasexuality. The presentation of contrasexual content appeared to affect the rate of percept growth differentially. The effect of conflict was not uniform, however, but appeared to interact with a primary individual-difference variable, introversion–extroversion. Also, the interaction between contrasexual content and individual differences in introversion–extroversion was not uniform at all points in the microgenetic sequence. Generally, however, introverts developed contrasexual percepts more rapidly than extroverts, whereas extroverts developed congruent percepts more rapidly than introverts. This finding was paralleled by the finding that, in the final phase of microgenesis, extroverts were more emotionally distant from contrasexual percepts than introverts.

The results of our second approach were more ambiguous. If all percepts involve microgenesis, then the results of the first of our explorations of subliminal stimulation suggest that temporal positioning of affectively laden subliminal content has little or no appreciable effect on supraliminal neutral content. Neutral contents appear to have been affected by subliminal affective contents when the subliminal content preceded, was concomitant with, or followed supraliminal stimulation. On the other hand, the presence of subliminal content may influence percepts that undergo a protracted microgenetic course of development. In our second subliminal-perception study, neutral and angry subliminal content adversely affected the rate of percept growth toward the latter phases of microgenesis. Unfortunately, we are unable to ascertain whether the negative effect of subliminal content arises simply as a function of spatiotemporal masking or because the ambiguity of the neutral subliminal face is as arousing as the angry subliminal face. Spatiotemporal masking may simply reduce the intensity of the stimulus to be discriminated by decreasing pattern contours (reducing the gradient between signal and noise). In the light of earlier evidence that showed that the effects of neutral and angry subliminal content were similar, we tend toward the interpretation that neutral stimuli contribute toward conflict to the extent that they are ambiguous; they were made all the more ambiguous in the present instance because the temporal duration allowed for their assimilation was curtailed. We also tend toward this interpretation on the grounds of logic. Unassimilated stimulus content, particularly ambiguous or affectively laden content, is likely to produce alterations in arousal level. Unless we are willing to believe that subliminal contents are accurately preperceived or discriminated [a belief apparently held by Silverman (Silverman, Kwawer, Wolitsky, & Coron, 1973)], a more likely assumption is that subliminal content is only partially assimilated. Because it is only partially assimilated, there may be resulting changes in arousal that serve, in turn, to elevate or depress awareness thresholds. Although the final meaning of our subliminal investigations is as yet unclear, we believe that the approach taken in these studies may provide a useful means of assessing the role of affectivity in microgenesis.

Our third approach to conflict was least profitable in immediate implications for microgenesis. Although we expected that reflective subjects would be more conflicted than impulsive subjects at earlier stages of microgenesis, meaningful differences between impulsive and reflective subjects did not emerge. This may mean that the essential difference between these subjects lies less in the qualitative formation of meaning and more in the relationship between availability of information and its expression in overt behavior. It may be that impulsive subjects circumvent fuller microgenetic development in a manner similar to Draguns's (1963) description of the abortion of microgenesis. In the light of the results of our probe experiment and in the light of the ecology of impulsive behavior, the process of abortion may not involve abortion of perceptual development. Rather, the process of constraining behavioral options in macrogenetically advanced operational structures (e.g., reversible decentering) may be aborted. This suggestion follows from the finding that impulsive subjects had greater availability of information than reflective subjects. We suggest, then, that impulsivity is less a process of aborting microgenetic perceptual development and more a process of aborting the microgenetic process of intentionality. Further study of this possibility in the light of Piaget's theory of affectivity may be a useful means of understanding differences between impulsive and reflective subjects. More important, this approach may shed some light on the nature of impulse disorders.

On the positive side, we believe the methodology used in our third approach may be useful in microgenetic research. Use of the sampling methodology outlined in this experiment may allow for a meaningful assessment of quantitative as well as qualitative features of information availability at different points in microgenesis. This approach, used in conjunction with more inferential process-oriented approaches, may contribute to a fuller analysis of personality structure and function.

In addition to the finding that introverts differed from extroverts, we obtained significant correlations between tolerance of ambiguity and durations necessary for the attainment of microgenetic landmarks. Generally, subjects less tolerant of ambiguity required longer exposures to attain particular landmarks. Unfortunately, these correlations were not specific to early or later phases of percept growth. In the contrasexuality experiment, significant correlations were obtained for early landmarks, whereas in the experiment concerned with cognitive style, the final stage of recognition was associated with intolerance of ambiguity. In spite of the uncertainty regarding the temporal locus of the effect of tolerance of ambiguity, we were surprised by the directionality of our findings. We had expected that the rate of percept growth would be faster among subjects least tolerant of ambiguity because such subjects would be motivated by a need for closure. Given the nature of our findings, we would like to investigate the defensive features of tolerance of ambiguity.

In spite of the limited yield from our studies, it seems to us that the study of perceptual and conceptual microgenesis proffers the possibility of greatly contributing to our understanding of personality structure and functioning. In the context of our own limited experience in microgenesis, we remain somewhat skeptical of the limits of analysis when the primary data are limited to verbal self-reports of phenomenological experience. Although such reports provide rich material for inferential synthesis, they suffer from the ambiguity attributed to macrogenetic clinical concentric analyses (e.g., those of Piaget) as elaborated by Smedslund (1969b). It seems to us that indirect approaches, such as the approach to the assessment of affectivity provided by Wiener and Mehrabian (1968), if independently validated, would provide more acceptable means of analysis of subtle microgenetic changes.

Smedslund (1969a) has justifiably chastised contemporary psychologists, particularly experimental psychologists, for their insatiable interest in stimulus characteristics and how they correspond to more obvious changes in behavior. In particular, he has faulted experimental methods that ignore two important regions of uncertainty: a region in which stimuli are given meaning through constructive processes of representation and a region in which subjects actively select responses with regard to formulated intentions. Although it may seem that our use of a priori landmarks reflects our own obsession with stimulus control, we remain interested in, and hope we are guided by, a greater concern with an understanding of preconscious dynamic transformations of stimuli. To this end, we offer a limited speculation on the metatheoretical meaning of our studies.

The existence of conflict logically presupposes a contextual, structural, or functional condition with which some contemporaneous other content, structure, or function is discrepant. Wallach (1949) and others have described this discrepancy as a *trace dissimilarity*. Thus conflict ensues from contemporaneous interaction of subjective (organismic) and objective (stimulus-organization) structure, or between sensory input and memory. Luria (1932) attempted to show that conflict, even experimentally induced conflict, leads to a disorganization of behavior and a destruction of the reactive process. In our view, the resultant of conflict is phenomenal or behavioral discontinuity or both. With regard to the orthogenetic principle, the effect of conflict is probably that of dedifferentiation of perceptions, and we believe we have provided limited evidence. Quantitative evidence of delays in microgenesis and qualitative evidence of momentary regressions may be evidence of dedifferentiation.

REFERENCES

Bakan, D. *The duality of human existence.* Skokie, Ill.: Rand McNally, 1966.

Block, J. Conceptions of sex role: Some cross cultural and longitudinal perspectives. *American Psychologist*, 1973, *28*, 512–526.

Block, J., Block, J. H., & Harrington, D. M. Some misgivings about the matching familiar figures test as a measure of reflection–impulsivity. *Developmental Psychology*, 1974, *10*, 611–632.

Budner, S. Intolerance of ambiguity as a personality variable. *Journal of Personality*, 1962, *30*, 29–50.

Cegalis, J. A., & Leen, D. Individual differences in responses to induced perceptual conflict. *Perceptual and Motor Skills*, 1977, *44*, 991–998.

Cegalis, J. A., & Murdza, S. Changes of auditory word discrimination induced by inversion of the visual field. *Journal of Abnormal Psychology*, 1976, *85*, 318–323.

Cegalis, J. A., & Young, R. The effect of inversion-induced conflict on field-dependence. *Journal of Abnormal Psychology*, 1974, *83*, 373–379.

Dixon, N. F. *Subliminal perception: The nature of a controversy*. London: McGraw-Hill, 1971.

Draguns, J. C. Responses to cognitive and perceptual ambiguity in chronic and acute schizophrenia. *Journal of Abnormal and Social Psychology*, 1963, *66*, 24–30.

Eagle, M. The effects of subliminal stimuli of aggressive content upon conscious cognition. *Journal of Personality*, 1959, *27*, 578–600.

Flavell, J. H., & Draguns, J. G. A microgenetic approach to perception and thought. *Psychological Bulletin*, 1957, *54*, 197–217.

Freud, S. Three essays on the theory of sexuality. *Standard Edition* (Vol. 7). London: Hogarth, 1953. (Originally published, 1905.)

Grier, J. B. Nonparametric indexes for sensitivity and bias: Computing formulas. *Psychological Bulletin*, 1971, *75*, 424–429.

Haber, R. N. *Information-processing approaches to visual perception*. New York: Holt, 1969.

Haber, R. N., & Erdelyi, M. H. Emergence and recovery of initially unavailable material. *Journal of Verbal Learning and Verbal Behavior*, 1967, *6*, 618–628.

Hodos, W. A nonparametric index of response bias for use in detection and recognition experiments. *Psychological Bulletin*, 1970, *74*, 351–354.

Kagan, J. Reflection–impulsivity: The generality and dynamics of conceptual tempo. *Journal of Abnormal Psychology*, 1966, *71*, 17–24.

Kohlberg, L. A cognitive-developmental analysis of children's sex-role concepts and attitudes. In E. Maccoby (Ed.), *The development of sex differences*. Stanford, Calif.: Stanford University Press, 1966.

Kragh, U. A tachistoscopic study of the father relationship in subjects with and without loss of father. In U. Kragh and G. J. W. Smith, (Eds.), *Percept-genetic analysis*. Lund: Gleerup, 1970.

Kragh, U., & Kroon, T. An analysis of aggression and identification in young offenders by the study of perceptual development. *Human Development*, 1966, *9*, 209–210.

Kragh, U., & Smith, G. J. W. (Eds.). *Percept-genetic analysis*. Lund: Gleerup, 1970.

Kučera, H., & Francis, W. N. *Computational analysis of present day American English*. Providence, R.I.: Brown University Press, 1970.

Luria, A. R. *The nature of human conflicts*. New York: Liveright, 1932.

Maffeo, P. A. *A microgenetic approach to the integration of contrasexual characteristics*. Unpublished doctoral dissertation, Syracuse University, 1974.

Murphy, G., & Hochberg, J. Perceptual development: Some tentative hypotheses. *Psychological Review*, 1951, *58*, 332–349.

Pollack, I., & Spence, D. Subjective pictorial information and visual search. *Perception and Psychophysics*, 1968, *3*, 41–44.

Silverman, L. H., Kwawer, J. S., Wolitzky, C., & Coron, M. An experimental study of aspects of the psychoanalytic theory of male homosexuality. *Journal of Abnormal Psychology*, 1973, *82*, 178–188.

Smedslund, J. Meanings, implications, and universals: Toward a psychology of man. *Scandinavian Journal of Psychology*, 1969, *10*, 1–15. (a)

Smedslund, J. Psychological diagnostics. *Psychological Bulletin*, 1969, *3*, 237–248. (b)

Smith, G. J. W., Spence, D. P., & Klein, G. S. Subliminal effects of verbal stimuli. *Journal of Abnormal and Social Psychology*, 1959, *59*, 167–176.

Strickland, R. G. *Microgenesis of subjective meaning in visual perception*. Unpublished doctoral dissertation, Syracuse University, 1975.

Wallach, H. Some considerations concerning the relation between perception and cognition. *Journal of Personality*, 1949, *18*, 6–13.

Werner, H. The concept of development from a comparative and organismic point of view. In D. B. Harris (Ed.), *The concept of development*. Minneapolis: University of Minnesota Press, 1957.

Wiener, M., & Mehrabian, A. *Language within language*. New York: Appleton, 1968.

III

PERCEPTUAL
STABILIZATION
AND DIFFERENTIATION
IN PERCEPTGENESIS

9

Toward a Dialectical Conception of the Percept-Genetic Approach to Perception Personality

Alf L. Andersson
Lund University, Lund, Sweden

There is today a renewed interest in the dialectic as a metatheoretical tool for psychology (e.g., Kosok, 1976; Wozniak, 1975). According to the dialectical position, a basic requirement for a deeper understanding of psychic functioning is the study of consciousness as it unfolds over time. *Consciousness* is viewed as the medium through which a person achieves the integration and coordination of her or his actions.

The developmental unit of the dialectic is a triad consisting of an initial thesis followed in order by an antithesis and a synthesis. The impetus to change is inherent in the triad, which includes factors that are both contradictory and complementary. When one form of synthesis is achieved, it may serve as the thesis for a new and higher developmental unit. My intention here is to show how the dialectical paradigm may be employed in the percept-genetic approach to perception personality, both in its situational (empirical) and conceptual (theoretical) aspects.

TWO PERCEPT-GENETIC TECHNIQUES

For instance, in one trial in the percept-genetic technique usually referred to as the *spiral aftereffect* (SAE) *technique* (see Andersson, Nilsson, Ruuth, & Smith, 1972, for a more detailed presentation), the subject is asked to inspect the center of an inwardly rotating spiral for 45 sec and is thereafter shown a stationary circle onto which his or her aftereffect of an apparent expansion is projected. The subject's task is to determine and report when the spiral aftereffect has terminated, in other words, when he or she experiences the circle as stationary. Thus the SAE trial can be viewed as a developmental unit with dialectical characteristics: first an automatic, more or less unconscious registration of an inward movement (thesis), then the negative aftereffect experience of an outward movement (antithesis), terminated by a judgmental process leading to the conscious conclusion that there is no outward movement—what in the dialectic is referred to as a "negation of the negation" (synthesis).

Concerning the general percept-genetic technique designed to capture the microgenesis or *Aktualgenese* (Flavell & Draguns, 1957) of a percept by means of successively prolonged tachistoscopic exposures, I discuss here the unfolding of the perceptual experience of a motif having a centrally placed, nonthreatening person (a hero figure) and a threatening person located at the periphery. This specific technique is referred to as the *defense mechanism technique* (DMT) and has long maintained a central position in the arsenal of percept-genetic techniques (see Kragh & Smith, 1970, for a detailed presentation). The peripherally placed threat is viewed as instigating anxiety, which is overcome by the subject's set of defenses. According to a dialectical scheme, the process can be described as involving first a subliminal or incidental registration of something threatening, interpreted more or less unconsciously as anxiety (thesis); then nonveridical experiences and reports considered to result from defensive activity (antithesis); terminating in a conscious, veridical report indicating that the subject feels no need for defense ("negation of the negation") because the threatening and other characteristics are pictorial and outside the self (synthesis) (cf. Nilsson, 1977).

DIALECTIC OF COGNITIVE GROWTH

There is thus a formal similarity between the SAE *trial* and the DMT *genesis,* both processes ending with an objectivized percept at the moment of synthesis. According to Werner's (1957) viewpoint, microprocesses like these should have some formal similarity to the macroprocess or ontogenesis found in perceptual development and, more generally, in cognitive growth. In these terms, cognitive growth should follow a dialectical scheme. As it might be instructive to examine a model of this sort, I present one that I and colleagues of mine have used as a tool for understanding cross-sectional SAE results (Andersson, Ruuth, & Ageberg, 1977).

The dialectical scheme of cognitive development is outlined in Figure 9.1.

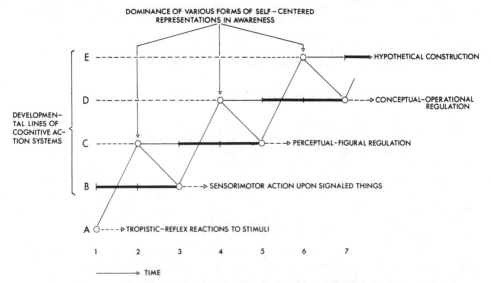

Figure 9.1 Heuristic outline of ontogenetic cognitive development. The small circles represent "nodal points" that are supposed to steer cognitive organization across developmental lines at a given phase (1, 2, 3, etc.) in development. The circles are connected with thin lines to show the dialectical pattern of interaction over time. (From "Patterns of Perceptual Change in the Ages 7 to 15 Years," by A. L. Andersson, E. Ruuth, and G. Ageberg, *Scandinavian Journal of Psychology*, 1977, *18*, 257–265.)

Perceptual-figural regulation (Fig. 9.1C) is assumed to spring from an antithesis to tropistic-reflex reactions to stimuli (Figure 9.1A); conceptual–operational regulation (Fig. 9.1D), from an antithesis to sensorimotor action on signaled things (Fig. 9.1B); and hypothetical construction (Fig. 9.1E), from an antithesis to perceptual-figural regulation (Fig. 9.1C). The antithetical mode of functioning implies that the person's awareness is dominated by her or his new, self-generated cognitive activity. To achieve a synthesis the person must negate her or his over-investment in her or his own self-generated products. A synthesis is achieved within a cognitive action system located on a hierarchical level between those systems providing the person with the thesis and the antithesis. The various syntheses—represented in Figure 9.1 by the end points B3, C5, and D7—equip the person with different tools for distinguishing between self and environment. The sensorimotor end point is achieved when an infant can differentiate between reality and his or her own actions toward reality. The perceptual-figural end point is achieved when a child can distinguish between reality and its appearance; finally, the conceptual-operational end point is attained when an adolescent can differentiate between reality and her or his thoughts about that reality.

SOME EMPIRICAL EVIDENCE

This admittedly abstract scheme may be more intelligible in the light of some SAE data on 4- to 6-year-olds. Some of these children, most typically those who were 5 years old, deviated markedly from their younger and older preschoolmates in reporting very long *initial* SAE durations in a series of five repeated trials. More-over, the initial SAE durations of the 6-year-olds occupied an intermediate range, whereas those of the 4-year-olds were mostly short. Consequently the data were epitomized in the developmental paradigm short-long-intermediate initial SAE duration (Andersson, Johansson, Karlsson, & Ohlsson, 1969).

Considering this developmental paradigm in relation to Figure 9.1, the child reporting the short SAE duration should as yet not have reached period 4, being still dominated by and primarily oriented toward objects in the immediate sur-roundings. The preschool child reporting long SAE duration, who in other words is investing markedly in a self-generated cognitive product like the aftereffect, should be in Period 4. Finally, an intermediate aftereffect duration, representing *decentered perceptual functioning*, to use a term from Piaget, indicates that the child has reached Period 5.

The decentered perceptual mode of Period 5 should facilitate a qualitative shift in cognitive functioning, indicated in the figure by the thick line continuing on the time axis of the conceptual–operational system. In a study of a new group of preschool children, it was also found that children reporting an intermediate SAE could—more often than those with short or long aftereffect durations—distinguish the dream as a phenomenon isolated from the external world. They could also more often counteract the influence of salient attributes of the imme-diate environment and keep quantity invariant in conservation tasks involving substance and liquid; that is, they could employ principles of concrete operational thought in the sense of Piaget (Andersson, Johansson, Karlsson, & Ohlsson, 1969). In another study, it was found that the ability to counteract the influence of the tilted frame when estimating verticality in the rod-and-frame test was most devel-oped among 5- to 6-year-olds reporting an intermediate SAE (Andersson & Ruuth, 1971; cf. Andersson, Ruuth, & Ageberg, 1977). Likewise Lindén (1977) found the intermediate initial SAE duration to be most prevalent among 7- to 8-year-olds who understood that the SAE is a self-generated (apparent) phenomenon. These children also made more correct solutions in the Piaget Landscape Task (on coordination of perspectives) than those with either short or long initial SAE durations.

SENSORIMOTOR–OPERATIONAL VERSUS PERCEPTUAL–CONSTRUCTIVE COGNITION

The scheme presented in Figure 9.1 is partly based on Piaget's ideas on cognitive growth (e.g., Piaget & Inhelder, 1969). The main difference is that my dialectical (multiline) conception aims at capturing the interaction of different cognitive action systems over time. It is no exaggeration to maintain that Piaget was mainly (although not exclusively) interested in the development of sensorimotor actions and in what is here assumed to begin as their antithesis, namely, conceptual–operational thought. Consequently Piaget has studied how humans eventually come to understand objects as independent from their own emotions, feelings, identity, and so on, through coming to use the principles of formal operational thought (D7 in Figure 9.1). There is more to human cognition than that, however. Perceptual-figural regulation, which is closely tied to symbolization (explained further on) and which I assume begins as an antithesis to tropistic-reflex reactions to stimuli, is strongly influenced by the dynamics of the individual person, his or her emotions, affects, feelings, values, and so forth; in other words, by such factors as create a unique relationship between human being and environment. This has been the basic idea of the percept-genetic approach to perception-personality since its start, just as it has been for many other developmental and personality-oriented psychologies, notably those of Werner and Freud.

The cognitive developmental line here referred to as "hypothetical construction" deserves special attention. It is assumed to begin in Period 6 (Fig. 9.1) as an antithesis to decentered perceptual functioning, the person again centering awareness on self-generated cognitive products. Some support for such an idea was obtained in the cross-sectional SAE study that comprised the age span 7 to 15 years (Andersson, Ruuth, & Ageberg, 1977). The prolonged SAE duration previously found to characterize 5-year-olds reappeared among 11-year-olds, although with the notable difference that it showed up in the *final* SAE trials in a series of 10, not initially as with the younger children. This difference was interpreted as indicating an important shift in cognitive functioning from an organization bound to the present phenomenal field to one organized in a temporal sequence "aiming at the potential or hypothetical." In the scheme of Figure 9.1, hypothetical construction is denoted as open ended, the person supposedly having reached the peak line of development in cognitive functioning. In line with Riegel (1973) this mode of functioning can best be described, I think, as being dialectical because the person is now quite free to reconcile objectivizing and subjectivizing devices for the benefit of understanding and planning for the future and for creating unique relationships between self and others on the one hand, self and culture on the other (cf. Turner, 1973).

COGNITIVE GROWTH AND INDIVIDUAL DIFFERENCES

In Figure 9.1 the dialectical principle of cognitive growth is regarded as showing its dominating steering effects on a given action system until the end point (B3, C5, or D7) is reached. This does not mean, of course, that no changes will occur thereafter. As already mentioned, effects on perceptual-figural regulation were observed in Period 6, supposedly owing to the involvement of higher order action systems in the dialectical principle of change. The main changes after an end point is reached are assumed, however, to be related to those steering principles unique to a given person, that is, to such directive schemata or structures as guide the person's cognitive action and belong to her or his *silent mental organization*, to use a term employed by Scheerer (1954). In stressing this aspect the perspective is shifted from one concerned mainly with general principles of development to one taking individual or personality differences into account.

A crucial aspect of any conception of personality must be the unique relationship a person has to his or her environment at a given period of life. I refer to this relationship as his or her *identity*, something not once-and-for-all given but that must be continually achieved and reaffirmed. Because people show different identities, a situation designed to reveal a person's identity must be open ended in the sense that she or he can find and recreate among alternatives that relationship which is preferred by and unique to her or him. Because perceptual growth in microtime unfolds from a subjective to an objective pole of experience, that is, to a pole of veridical experience that normally does not allow for differing interpretations, an analogy between this process and personality growth would not be a happy one. This does not mean that microgenetic material obtained before objectivized perceptual experience is achieved may not contribute to an understanding of the personality of a given person. On the contrary (and this is also shown, for example, by the application of the DMT), such material is essential. For a fuller understanding of it we are compelled, however, to use theoretical conceptions and empirical findings outside the microgenetic situation itself.

REPEATED MEASUREMENT OF SAE DURATION

Consider now repeated measurement of SAE duration where a new inspection of the aftereffect-inducing spiral begins immediately after the subject has reported termination of the aftereffect experiences resulting from the previous inspection. Such repeated measurement usually comprises 10 SAE trials (Andersson, 1971), during which some subjects may show a successive decrease in aftereffect duration, others a successive increase, and some few a pattern characterized by neither a decrease nor an increase over time but, rather, one that reflects a striving to maintain the SAE duration at a given (usually intermediate) level. The arithmetic mean of the last two SAE durations (9th and 10th trials) is taken to indicate the level at which the subject prefers to stabilize the SAE duration, a stabilization that would have been more clear-cut had the trials been extended beyond the 10th. When the technique is used on adults, the individual final or stabilized levels of SAE duration may easily show a value anywhere between 1 and 35 sec.

When SAE duration decreases over trials, the subject obviously prefers an orientation toward object-related, or *nonself*, factors in his or her phenomenal field, factors represented by the stationary circle onto which the aftereffect experiences are projected. Correspondingly, when SAE duration increases, the person shows a preferred orientation toward subject-related, or *self*, factors, the very aftereffect phenomena representing such factors. The whole SAE pattern should be conceived in a dialectical scheme, however. For example, when SAE duration decreases over trials, the person can be assumed to couple, more or less unconsciously, self (after-effect) factors with a negative feeling (thesis), which is then overcome by a positive investment (antithesis) in nonself factors, leading to the successive decrease observed in aftereffect duration. The decrease is finally negated when SAE duration is maintained on a more or less stabilized (unchanging) level (synthesis). This level has previously been referred to as the person's preferred mode of operation (Andersson & Weikert, 1974), a mode that is thus a resolution of the thesis and the antithesis and fits in very well with the definition of identity I have already given.

What tactics can be used to facilitate an understanding of individual differences in final (stabilized) SAE levels? In line with my main idea here, the answer must be that subjects should be ordered in terms of SAE data along a developmental, preferably dialectical, dimension. For that purpose the developmental paradigm I have presented of short-long-intermediate SAE duration can serve, by way of analogy, as a tool. An account of some findings with the SAE technique and the DMT on a group of male army conscripts, aged 20 to 31 years, can make this line of reasoning more comprehensible.

VARIATIONS IN IDENTITY

When the DMT is applied to male subjects, the nonthreatening hero figure is a boy and the peripherally placed threatening figure an elderly man. Conscripts with *short* final SAE duration were found (Andersson & Weikert, 1974) to give microgenetic reports classified as "identification with female or childish roles," both these defense categories being subsumed by Kragh (1969) under the heading "introjection." Identification with a female role is typically scored when the hero figure is denoted as being of the female sex in an extended series of exposures; identification with a childish role is scored when there are two persons in place of the hero or when both hero and peripheral figure are reported as children of about the same age (for details of the scoring relevant in the present context, see Andersson & Weikert, 1974).

A possible interpretation of these findings is that the anxiety caused by the microgenetic situation reactivates primitive representations of security-reassuring people, for example, introjections of a mother figure or of siblings or, somewhat more plausibly perhaps, derivatives of such early introjections. The derivatives can be seen as various forms of identification with the introjections (cf. Sandler & Rosenblatt, 1962), the implication being that the person has adopted a nonautonomous identity related to a basic need for outside support. His sex-adequate or age-adequate role or both (adult male) are easily vulnerable to anxiety, and he defends himself by adopting its negation (the male hero figure is either doubled or of female sex; the male threat is a nonthreatening child).

There was an interesting difference between conscripts reporting *long* final SAE duration and those reporting short or intermediate duration. The former subjects more often characterized the threatening man as a nonthreatening "mother of the hero" or a nonthreatening "child younger than the hero." These microgenetic reports were tentatively referred to as "projected introjections," implying that they in some sense represented an antithesis to introjection.

Defense through projected introjection might be interpreted in the following way. Presuming that a male subject's identification with a female or childish role is easily vulnerable to anxiety (in contrast with anxiety primarily associated with his sex- or age-adequate role), this could lead the subject to defend himself by wishing that representations connected with such a role ("mother," "young child") were not part of himself but rather of another person. In the DMT such "projections" occur with the peripheral figure because that figure, probably more easily than the hero figure, can be taken to represent another person.

When a person is able to negate projected introjections—and she or he should be able to do so when final SAE duration is intermediate—such a negation should not lead to the use of introjection and its derivatives (thesis). Instead, as the study showed, it should involve the experiencing and reporting of more or less *veridical characteristics* regarding sex, age, and number of the DMT figures. Under such conditions a person has probably been able to integrate the nonautonomous and sex- or age-adequate aspects of identity, neither aspect, therefore, being readily vulnerable to anxiety.

The operative modes behind the sequence consisting of introjection or its derivatives (thesis), projected introjection (antithesis), and neither projected introjection nor introjection (synthesis) can thus be expressed as a sequence consisting of (a) negation of the subject's own identity (i.e., negation of his role of adult male), (b) negation of the identity of the other as represented by the peripheral figure (i.e., negation of the characteristics of the threatening male figure), and (c) negation of both the mentioned forms of negation. These operative modes presumably parallel those assumed to characterize relations within a self–nonself (self–other) unit as these are revealed by the final SAE duration. When there is a negation of one's own identity, there should be a high investment in nonself factors (shown by short SAE duration). When there is a negation of the other, there should be a high investment in self factors (shown by long SAE duration). Finally, when there is neither a negation of own identity nor of the other, there should be a balanced investment in self and nonself factors (shown by intermediate SAE duration). This sequence of short-long-intermediate SAE duration has been expressed elsewhere (Andersson, 1971; Andersson, Franzén, & Ruuth, 1971; Andersson & Weikert, 1974) as the following sequence: (a) less sharp differentiation because of the self being experienced as having nonself characteristics, (b) less sharp differentiation because of the nonself being experienced as having self characteristics, and (c) optimal differentiation between self and nonself factors.

VARIATIONS IN STRATEGY USED
TO REESTABLISH IDENTITY

For a more complete understanding of a given person's personality as revealed by his or her SAE pattern, the interpretation of the final SAE duration (identity) should be complemented with an interpretation of his or her strategy used to reach that duration. The dialectical paradigm could be a useful tool for ordering SAE strategies here as well. A short final SAE duration is usually preceded by a successive decrease in aftereffect duration. The antithesis of the decrease is a successive increase. A striving to maintain aftereffect duration at a given level throughout trials usually is obtained when the final SAE duration is of intermediate length. Thus the developmental sequence can be as follows: decrease-increase-maintenance of SAE duration at an intermediate level over trials. In concluding this attempt to use the dialectic as a metatheoretical tool, I present an account of those DMT defenses scored as being most clearly related to these SAE strategies in the group of conscripts (for a full account of the relationships found between defensive organization as measured by the DMT and regulation of SAE duration over trials, see Andersson and Weikert, 1974).

Microgenetic defense reports are disguised representations of anxiety, which, in a psychoanalytic sense (cf. Wolitzky, 1962), can be conceived of as symbolizations of anxiety. These symbolizations carry with them a certain intention or wish on the part of the person (cf. Schafer, 1968). This intention should parallel the one expressed in the SAE strategy. Thus, when SAE duration *decreases* over trials, the person orients herself or himself away from self and toward nonself experiences. The most typical microgenetic defense related to this strategy appeared to be *repression*. Repression was scored when either the hero, the peripheral figure, or both were reported as being an object, an animal, or an inanimate creature. Thus the subject's (unconscious) intention was quite obvious: He attempted to give anxiety as little self reference as possible, if indeed any at all, by denoting the DMT figures as nonhuman.

When SAE duration *increases* over trials, the subject orients himself or herself away from nonself and toward self experiences. The most typical defense related to this strategy was found to be turning against the self (*introaggression*), scored when the hero was explicitly denoted as being hurt or when the DMT situation as a whole involved destruction or chaos. Thus, in sharp contrast to repression, turning against the self implies a strong self reference of anxiety, the hero figure being injured or exposed to injury.

Finally, when the SAE duration is *maintained on an intermediate level* over trials, there is no clear-cut preference for either nonself or self experiences. This strategy was found to be related to a type of *isolation*, scored on the one hand when the peripheral figure was denoted as being a circumscribed surface or an object with a white, light, shining, or empty character and, on the other, when a previous microgenetic report was lost in either one exposure or two consecutive exposures. This might be interpreted as a wish on the part of the subject to negate the self reference of anxiety by making the whole report, or the peripheral figure, devoid of (affective) content. Isolation of this type would seem to be the most "developed" of the three defenses, a form of synthesis of both repression and turning against the self. It could also be seen as the thesis of a higher order dialectical triad where the antithetical microgenetic content refers to dark and often unstructured reports (in contrast to the white and shining characteristics of the isolation report) that usually are interpreted as representing a prevalence of manifest anxiety (Kragh, 1969; Smith, Johnson, Ljunghill-Andersson, & Almgren, 1970). The synthesis of such a higher order triad would be the more or less veridical, nondisguised microgenetic report.

REFERENCES

Andersson, A. L. Personality as reflected in adaptive regulation of visual aftereffect perception: A review of concepts and empirical findings. *Psychological Research Bulletin* (Lund University, Sweden), 1971, *11*(1).

Andersson, A. L., Franzén, G., & Ruuth, E. Discontinuity of spiral aftereffect duration trends in acute schizophrenia. *Psychological Research Bulletin* (Lund University, Sweden), 1971, *11*(14).

Andersson, A. L., Johansson, A., Karlsson, B., & Ohlsson, M. On self–nonself interaction in early childhood as revealed by the spiral aftereffect duration. *Psychological Research Bulletin* (Lund University, Sweden), 1969, *9*(11).

Andersson, A. L., Nilsson, A., Ruuth, E., & Smith, G. J. W. *Visual aftereffects and the individual as an adaptive system.* Lund: Gleerup, 1972.

Andersson, A. L., & Ruuth, E. Relation between spiral aftereffect duration and rod-and-frame test performance in early childhood. *Perceptual Motor Skills,* 1971, *32,* 843–849.

Andersson, A. L., Ruuth, E., & Ageberg, G. Patterns of perceptual change in the ages 7 to 15 years: A cross-sectional study of the rod-and-frame test and the spiral aftereffect technique. *Scandinavian Journal of Psychology,* 1977, *18,* 257–265.

Andersson, A. L., & Weikert, C. Adult defensive organization as related to adaptive regulation of spiral aftereffect duration. *Social Behavior and Personality,* 1974, *2,* 56–75.

Flavell, J. H., & Draguns, J. G. A microgenetic approach to perception and thought. *Psychological Bulletin,* 1957, *54,* 197–217.

Kosok, M. The systematization of dialectical logic for the study of development and change. *Human Development,* 1976, *19,* 325–350.

Kragh, U. *Manual till DMT (Defense Mechanism Test).* Stockholm: Skandinaviska Testförlaget, 1969.

Kragh, U., & Smith, G. J. W. (Eds.). *Percept-genetic analysis.* Lund: Gleerup, 1970.

Lindén, J. Children's understanding of the spiral aftereffect phenomenon as related to aftereffect duration and coordination of perspectives. *Psychological Research Bulletin* (Lund University, Sweden), 1977, *17*(1).

Nilsson, A. Adaptive and defensive aspects of the individual: A systems approach to adaptation in relationship to a psychoanalytic anxiety model. *International Review of Psycho-Analysis,* 1977, *4,* 111–123.

Piaget, J., & Inhelder, B. *The psychology of the child.* London: Routledge, 1969.

Riegel, K. F. Dialectic operations: The final period of cognitive development. *Human Development,* 1973, *16,* 346–370.

Sandler, J., & Rosenblatt, B. The concept of the representational world. *Psychoanalytic Study of the Child,* 1962, *17,* 128–145.

Schafer, R. The mechanisms of defence. *International Journal of Psycho-Analysis,* 1968, *49,* 49–62.

Scheerer, M. Cognitive theory. In G. Lindzey (Ed.), *Handbook of social psychology.* Reading, Mass.: Addison-Wesley, 1954.

Smith, G. J. W., Johnson, G., Ljunghill-Andersson, J., & Almgren, P.-E. *MCT: Metakontrasttekniken.* Stockholm: Skandinaviska Testförlaget, 1970.

Turner, T. Piaget's structuralism. *American Anthropologist,* 1973, *75,* 351–373.

Werner, H. The concept of development from a comparative and organismic point of view. In D. B. Harris (Ed.), *The concept of development.* Minneapolis: University of Minnesota Press, 1957.

Wolitzky, D. L. Research in psychoanalytic theory and perception: Implications for the concept of microgenesis. *Psychological Research Bulletin* (Lund University, Sweden), 1962, *2*(3).

Wozniak, R. H. A dialectical paradigm for psychological research: Implications drawn from the history of psychology in the Soviet Union. *Human Development,* 1975, *18,* 18–34.

10

Stabilization and Automatization of Perceptual Activity Over Time

Gudmund Smith
Lund University, Lund, Sweden

Stabilization and automatization of perceptual activity over time is a basic assumption in the early speculations on *Aktualgenese*. With the history of *Aktualgenese* sketched in other chapters in this volume, I shall not indulge in a retrospective review but just mention the names of Friedrich Sander and Heinz Werner. In a period when perception was most often described as an instantaneous *Abbildung*, these psychologists wanted to direct our attention to perception as a gradual (though often very swift) process, or perhaps even a process of stabilization. It is even more important in the present context that they tried to ascribe certain basic principles to this process. Because they also wanted to define *time* from a double perspective—as macrotime referring to ontogenesis and as microtime referring to the span of the present moment—the principles of stabilization were supposed to apply to ontogenetic development as well as to microgenetic processing.

May it suffice here to remind the readers of Werner's (1948, 1957) well-known attempts to formulate a number of general principles of development. Relating more to thematic material presented with the technique of tachistoscopic fragmentation, Kragh (1955) described microgenetic processes that were particularly suited for inclusion in a dynamic, or psychoanalytic, frame of reference. The general patterns of change he observed did not in any crucial way violate the early *Aktualgenese* tradition. According to Kragh the thematic contents of the microgenesis changed from stages of ambiguity with many condensed meanings to stages characterized by one single, definite meaning, or from stages independent of such categories as time and space to stages closely fitted into the real physical world. Kragh's descriptions were however more closely tied to individual developmental patterns, thus adding a new quality to the mainly general-psychological perspective of Sander and Werner.

Even the developmental principles described by Kragh and his associates can very well be subsumed under the general heading of "stabilization." The event over time, which is called "perceptgenesis" in Lund, obviously leads to increasingly stable perceptions or conceptions of reality; and this stabilization occurs not only in the microgenetic perspective but in the macroperspective of ontogenesis. Concomitant with stabilization in the latter perspective is a growing automatization in the microperspective resulting from repetition of identical or similar microprocesses. Automatization implies that a process is abbreviated, that originally separate preparatory stages are shoved into each other and eventually disappear. With the double time perspective in mind, it is natural for microgeneticists to speculate about the reflection of ontogenesis in the microgenesis. As a result of automatization, however, such a reflection would become increasingly more fragmentary. In other words, the microgenesis gradually loses its personal flavor. At this stage the classical stimulus–response paradigm may reign undisputed.

Stabilization as well as automatization may be viewed as biologic necessities. Through stabilization one creates not only a world recognizable to oneself but a world where one can communicate with others of one's kind with a reasonable amount of mutual understanding. The successive automatization of adaptive microprocesses is the key to an effective energy economy. Energy invested in present enterprises has to be released as soon as possible to meet future demands. Automatization makes this release of energy possible; or to be more concrete and eliminate the dubious energy concept, automatization facilitates the redistribution of attention and intentional effort.

It must be clear by now that the microgenesis cannot lead to a fully stabilized end stage until the ontogenesis has allowed the person to reach a definite conception of reality. Because the microgenesis of a child does not end in such a stable and unambiguous percept as that of a normal adult, it has room for more possibilities. As we have seen in our work with children 4 years of age and older (Smith & Danielsson, 1977), it is typical of many normal children that they tend to retain several alternative meanings close to the end stage of their microprocesses. In adults there is a clearer line of demarcation between the prestages and the concluding end stage. Creative renewal or reconstruction in an adult thus involves much more complicated retrogressive operations than in the child. Because readaptive efforts are thus likely to meet greater resistance in the adult, resort to ingrained, automatized alternatives is a more probable occurrence.

Stabilization and automatization do not necessarily imply that reactions to stimulation from outside have been settled in a fixed pattern once and for all. Various kinds of changes may occur, even in normal adults—sometimes gradual changes, sometimes more abrupt and disruptive ones, changes that imply retreat from outside reality or changes that serve the continued adaptation to it. I can illustrate this specific problem area with our work on visual afterimages (AIs); at the same time, the results highlight the more general aspects of my theme.

SERIAL AFTERIMAGE EXPERIMENTS

Serial experiments with visual AIs began in an early twin study (Smith, 1949), continued in Kragh's *Aktualgenese* monograph (1955), and were resumed again, after more than a decade, in a study of anxiety in the late 1960s (Smith & Kragh, 1967). The bulk of the work reported here stems from the 1970s. Various groups of subjects have been involved, but the basic technique has always been the same. Let me try to describe it very briefly.

The stimulus used for generating AIs was a relatively intense red figure with straight sides and rounded contours at the top and bottom. It had two eyes and a sad mouth schematically drawn in black. (The sad mouth was chosen because a special study—Fries and Smith, 1970—had shown that by using this stimulus we obtained more variation in our scoring dimensions than with a neutral or happy mouth.) The red face was projected from behind on a semitransparent Plexiglas screen where a fixation point coincided with a suitable position for a nose. The width of the projected face was 5.5 cm. When the subject had fixated the initiating stimulus for 20 sec from a distance of 40 cm, the screen was moved to a projection distance of 60 cm. There the subject measured image size by means of two markers that could be moved independently of each other. The subject also described the color and general appearance of the AI. To guide an intensity estimate, a dark and a light field had been exposed on the screen before the red face was shown. With the exception of our youngest children, subjects judged AI brightness on a 10-point scale where the exposed fields represented the end points. The young children were asked for a more crude estimate.

To extinguish the AI, a diffuse red light was exposed for 5 sec after each trial. Usually, 16 trials constitute a series for adult subjects because after 16 trials AIs do not change appreciably, not systematically in any case. In other words, 16 trials seem enough to ensure AI stabilization in most adults. For various reasons, however, 20 trials have been used in some studies, among others, those involving extraneous stimulation reported below. Younger children could hardly be forced to endure such a long and trying session; according, the number of trials for them was cut down to 10. The time required per trial was about 70 sec.

With a stimulus width of 5.5 cm, the so-called Emmert size of the projected image would be 8.3 cm. AIs of 10.5 cm or more were considered large; AIs of 6.5 cm or less, size-constant. The normal negative AI color was blue-green, not clearly green. Reddish, brownish, and similar hues were called positive.

ONTOGENETIC AFTERIMAGE STAGES

Young children, about 4 or 5 years old and at a stage of cognitive development where they could not even comprehend the Piaget Landscape Task (Piaget & Inhelder, 1941), were unable to produce AIs. Consider the peculiar nature of an AI. It appears in the world surrounding the observer but is nevertheless not part of this world because it moves with the observer's eye movements, does not really cover the objects where it is projected, disappears and reappears again, and so forth. Children who cannot comprehend the distinction between their own selves and a "nonself" are obviously incapable of reconciling the contradictions inherent in a phenomenon that, in spite of its subjective origin, materializes in the surrounding world of solid objects.

One or two years later, one finds indications of a better demarcation between what is the child's own private self and what is not. Children at this stage, however, still retain a totally egocentric perspective as evidenced by the Landscape Task, where they prefer the picture representing their own perspective to stand for all possible views of the three mountains. These children are well able to project, measure, and describe AIs; yet they obviously try to simplify the "AI riddle" in their own one-dimensional way by equating the AI phenomenon with other sense impressions. In the words of Piagetian psychology, they show that events emanating from within are still more tightly bound to perception than to cognition. Considered as a quasi-object tied to the projection screen, the AI does not increase relative to the screen when the latter is moved away from the subject but remains more or less size-constant. Its color is still dominated by the stimulus, being positive or neutral (the latter considered a compromise between negative and positive hues).

During the latency period the AI has lost most of its infantile qualities; it is negative and of a size predicted by Emmert's law. Oversaturation of the AI—which will tend to make the blue image look black—is often parried by particular emphasis on the green color element, a reaction also found in compulsive adults (Smith, Fries, Andersson, & Ried, 1971). The microgenetic AI serials are easily stabilized in most of these youngsters; but in an ontogenetic perspective, the stability seems transitory, probably serving a consolidating purpose before the turmoil of the next phase.

Approaching puberty the subjects report more and more large and dark images. From our clinical studies we have learned that these qualities represent anxiety (Smith, Sjöholm, & Nielzén, 1976). Such childish features as, for example, positive hues reappear. Whereas the AIs of latency children were quickly stabilized in the AI serial, stabilization now seems more difficult to attain and, when arrived at, remains precarious. As subjects approach the late teens, however, the stable, retinal AIs become more and more dominant.

As with AIs in children, the stabilized AI products in adults are adapted to the individual conception of the nature of the AI phenomenon. If AIs are conceived as subjective but somehow peripheral (retinal) phenomena, the ordinary textbook image will ensue. If the AI's dependence on outside stimulation is stressed in the instructions, however, the result will be a more childish image, even in normal grown-up people. When a close connection between the retina and the CNS is described by the experimenter, the AI is affected in other ways. Such a "centralistic" AI theory obviously facilitates personal involvement in the AI production, leading to AIs closely resembling early, unstabilized products in a normal AI serial. Color reports, for instance, become more variegated and less tied to the stimulus. This dependence of AI stabilization on the private AI epistemology of the observer was demonstrated in a series of experiments (Smith & Sjöholm, 1974). As I have said, however, because most adults in our culture would agree on a "peripheral" AI theory, their stabilized AIs are apt to be rather standardized, given similar stimulus conditions.

THE MICRODEVELOPMENT OF THE AI

Let me distinguish once again between the concepts of *stabilization* and *automatization*. In naïve subjects, that is, subjects who have not been exposed to systematic AI experimentation before, AIs become more and more stabilized over a series of repeated measurements, a series representing an adaptive process over a relatively brief time span. Just as the final, correct percept is arrived at only by degrees in a tachistoscopic experiment, this percept being preceded by a series of incorrect ones, the stabilized AI is generally preceded in the AI serial by unstabilized products as yet not fully adapted to the stimulus situation. Even in normal grown-ups, for instance, positive or size-constant AIs are not uncommon in early process stages. As the AI serial is repeated, however, these primitive stages are likely to be obliterated and to be replaced by stabilized end products. The AI process has become automatized.

If in the course of an AI process, the stabilization is suddenly broken by reports of primitive AIs—as such AIs have been defined in our experiments with cognitively immature young children—we are obviously confronted with a regression. In a series of AIs reported to be around 8 or 9 cm, that is, of the size expected according to Emmert's law, a subject perhaps reports a size-constant image—and after some subsequent normal size values—another size-constant image. This is a very common occurrence in acutely schizophrenic subjects (Smith, Ruuth, Franzén,

& Sjöholm, 1972) and is correlated with similar discontinuities revealed by other percept-genetic techniques, in our case the metacontrast technique. It would not be enough to talk about a destabilization of the AI process. The term *regression* was just employed because the subject returned to image forms typical of the immature child. It is a rather banal accomplishment to be able to correlate AI results with schizophrenic symptoms. The real accomplishment lies in the definition of schizophrenic functioning made possible through the analysis of the microgenetic processes of these people.

Psychotic regression is only one variant of destabilization, and evidently a rare one. Early German investigators of AIs (Busse, 1920), using such extraneous stimuli as auditory signals, reported color reversals from negative to positive hues in normal, most often rather young observers. It is well known in neuropsychological research that new stimulation may cause an orienting reflex, extinguished by repetitive stimulation, to reappear. Sokolov (1963) has been the classical reference in this kind of work. A more recent example can be found in experiments by Froehlich (1978), who employed distraction pictures in his microgenetic study of attention. To judge from this kind of finding, destabilization as a response to change in the stimulus situation is a normal and common occurrence.

In experiments with visual AIs and the spiral aftereffect, Smith, Sjöholm, and Andersson (1971) administered extraneous auditory stimulation to normal adult subjects. The first signal in the AI serial was given well before the final point of stabilization, on the 8th trial, and was sounded during the last 3 sec of the subject's fixation of the inducing stimulus (the sad face). It was sounded again on the 12th, 16th, and 20th trials. Individual adaptive trends were described from the 1st to the 8th trial in an experimental group and in a control nonsignal group. For this description we used size measurements as well as brightness judgments and calculated consecutive differences between trials. When size and brightness differences had each been classified as increases (growing size, more pronounced darkness), zero change, or decreases, they were considered jointly. The main results showed that the signal caused a disruption of ongoing trends and a repetition of trends characterizing the initial phases of the serial. This led to a prolongation of the adaptive process and, in some cases, to defensive counterreactions. Renewed administration of the signal in later trials gave continually diminishing effects. In a parallel experiment, where the first signal was administered on the 14th trial, little or no destabilization could be detected. Apparently, the process of stabilization had gone too far for the AIs to be affected by extraneous stimulation, at least the kind of stimulation employed in our laboratory.

Using schizophrenic subjects in yet another experiment (Smith & Ruuth, 1973), however, we did not recover this increasing resistance to disruptive stimulation. This study differed from the foregoing one in that four kinds of regressive change (in the dimensions of either size, color, brightness, or meaning) were used to characterize individual adaptive trends from the 1st to the 8th trial. As just said, *regression* was defined as the sudden emergence of a childish AI (e.g., a size-constant one) in one phase when the preceding phase had been typically adult in that respect (not size-constant). Signals were given on Trials 8, 12, 16, and 20. We noted that subjects given a signal tended to repeat the type of regression found in the early part of their serials more often than a nonsignal control group, not only after the first signal but after the third one. In the nonsignal control group, new types of regression were likely to appear at later process stages. A control subject with early size regressions would, for example, switch to color regression as the serial continued, while a signal subject would stick to size regression. The three signals also tended to enhance the pathological AI signs, the third signal most of all. The schizophrenics thus remained vulnerable; their AI processes did not stabilize properly. It is a commonly accepted notion by now that incapacity to habituation is one of the crucial characteristics of schizophrenia.

The schizophrenic subjects demonstrated most dramatically how a person forced to start adaptation all over again seems to have no choice but to follow the same ingrained pattern, however twisted it may seem. In other words, the stabilization of the AI or any other perceptual process does not, as Kragh (1955) also pointed out in his dissertation, imply a change from more to less random variation but, rather, the other way around. The early process instability is typically directed or patterned. This individual process style—to paraphrase the New Look in perception—is reactivated by arousal stimulation (even if the repetition implies an abbreviation). When the typical patterning disappears in the final stage, it is often followed by random variation around the stabilized level. The steering principles behind this microgenetic patterning are most likely to be reflections of the person's ontogenesis and, as shown by twin experiments with AIs (Smith, 1949), of her or his constitutional programming without reference to which the ontogenetic characteristics could hardly be accounted for in full.

DESTABILIZATION AND CREATIVITY

What I have said here about destabilization actualizes a number of related themes, only one of which I take up in this context: *creativity,* or as we prefer to term it, the *generative qualities of perception.* In this recent branch of our research, we do not use AIs but rely on tachistoscopic presentations of single pictures. When reaching the level of correct recognition of the stimulus, however, we proceed backward again by gradually diminishing exposure times. Using placebo pills and "devious" instructions about their effects, one can easily lead the subject either to stick to the correct impression during the backward genesis or to abandon it for more subjective ones, most often those impressions that the subject reported on the way up in the straightforward microgenesis (Smith & Danielsson, 1976). Reactivation of early stages in the inverse part of the experiment was caused by a presentation of the pill as mildly relaxing, making the observer more sensitive to his or her own inner life. The opposite instructions stressed the increased sensitivity to outside stimulation.

The technique has also been exploited—but without placebo and instructions—in a group of humanistic and biologic research workers in Lund. On their way down, these people seemed to combine the tendency to stick to the correct interpretation of the stimulus with a desire for playing with reactivated subjective meanings. The experimenters were often reminded of children who, as I said in the introduction when discussing microgenesis, are reluctant to discard one interpretation for the benefit of a new one but try to retain both meanings as alternatives, sometimes condensed into one complex meaning. The more they were ingenious and creative in their research work, according to independent criteria, the more inclined our subjects seemed to be to reconstruct early microgenetic stages in their backward microgenesis (the G index of agreement reaching a value of $+.67$ and Fisher's two-tailed exact P, based on the fourfold table, a value of

.015). At the same time, even they did not give up the correct meaning of the stimulus picture. These observations may perhaps be related to findings by Knott and Irving (1968) implying that low-anxiety subjects succumb more readily to such regressions than do high-anxiety ones. It should be emphasized, however, that our most creative research workers did not necessarily belong to a low-anxiety category but rather to a category of people with high tolerance for anxiety. The main concern of these people is to free themselves from the bonds of established impressions and to admit, instead, alternative, new, and daring interpretations (cf. also Arieti, 1976). To be creative is, among other things, to be able to destabilize.

CONCLUSIONS

Even if creativity is a relevant theme here, I do not want to stray farther on that subject but rather to conclude with one or two stray thoughts. The study of processes in microgenetic research is very far removed from the preoccupation in conventional academic texts with levels of performance, steady states, attitudes, traits, and the like and has brought microgeneticists close to that part of general biology that concerns itself with issues of growth and adaptation. Even if the starting point for our various enterprises has always been micro- or percept-genetic, we have tried to avoid too narrow and parochial a perspective on psychological problems. The work with perceptgenesis in our laboratory is not meant to stand alone as an isolated theoretical tower but to be associated with broader theoretical perspectives. Among these perspectives, the most obvious is perhaps psychoanalysis as it relates to problems of development, intention, latent determinants, anxiety, defense, and so on. Sandler and Joffe (1967) were among the first outsiders to point out the affinity between a microgenetic model and many basic psychoanalytic assumptions. To be optimally fruitful as a background frame of reference for microgenetic research, however, psychoanalysis should broaden its horizon, leave the 19th-century remnants of Freudian thinking behind, and become more aware of some of the new developments within the behavioral and biologic sciences, for example, those relating to cognitive functioning and development, to subliminal perception, to sleep and activation, to ethological research with the very young infant. In our work with stabilization and automatization of perceptual activity over time, we have found ample reason to relate not only to psychoanalysis but to several of the latter bodies of research as well.

REFERENCES

Arieti, S. *Creativity: The magic synthesis.* New York: Basic Books, 1976.

Busse, P. Über die Gedächtnisstufen und ihre Beziehung zum Aufbau der Wahrnehmungswelt. *Zeitschrift für Psychologie,* 1920, *84,* 1–66.

Fries, I., & Smith, G. J. W. Influence of physiognomic stimulus properties on afterimage adaptation. *Perceptual Motor Skills,* 1970, *31,* 267–271.

Froehlich, W. D. Stress, anxiety, and the control of attention: A psychophysiological approach. In C. D. Spielberger and I. G. Sarason (Eds.), *Stress and anxiety* (Vol. 5). Washington: Hemisphere, 1978.

Knott, J. R., & Irving, D. A. Anxiety, stress and the contingent negative variation (CNV). *Electroencephalography and Clinical Neurophysiology,* 1968, *24,* 286–287.

Kragh, U. *The actual-genetic model of perception-personality.* Lund: Gleerup, 1955.

Piaget, J., & Inhelder, B. *Le développement des quantités chez l'enfant.* Neuchatel: Delacheux & Niestlé, 1941.

Sandler, J., & Joffe, W. G. The tendency to persistence in psychological function and development: With special reference to fixation and regression. *Bulletin of the Menninger Clinic,* 1967, *31,* 257-271.

Smith, G. J. W. *Psychological studies in twin differences.* Lund: Gleerup, 1949.

Smith, G. J. W., & Danielsson, A. A new type of instrument constructed to explore the generative qualities of perception. *Psychological Research Bulletin* (Lund University, Sweden), 1976, *16*(5).

Smith, G. J. W., & Danielsson, A. From open flight to symbolic and perceptual tactics: A study of defense in preschool children. *Scripta Minora Regiae Societatis Humaniorum Litterarum Lundensis,* 1977, No. 3.

Smith, G. J. W., Fries, I., Andersson, A. L., & Ried, J. Diagnostic exploitation of visual aftereffect measures in a moderately depressive patient group. *Scandinavian Journal of Psychology,* 1971, *12,* 67-79.

Smith, G. J. W., & Kragh, U. A serial afterimage experiment in clinical diagnostics. *Scandinavian Journal of Psychology,* 1967, *8,* 52-64.

Smith, G. J. W., & Ruuth, E. Effects of extraneous stimulation on visual afterimage serials produced by young schizophrenics. *Scandinavian Journal of Psychology,* 1973, *14,* 34-38.

Smith, G. J. W., Ruuth, E., Franzén, G., & Sjöholm, L. Intermittent regressions in a serial afterimage experiment as signs of schizophrenia. *Scandinavian Journal of Psychology,* 1972, *13,* 27-33.

Smith, G. J. W., & Sjöholm, L. Can our theory of reality influence our perception of it? *Psychological Research Bulletin* (Lund University, Sweden), 1974, Monogr. 1.

Smith, G. J. W., Sjöholm, L., & Andersson, A. L. Effects of extraneous stimulation on afterimage adaptation. *Acta Psychologica,* 1971, *35,* 138-150.

Smith, G. J. W., Sjöholm, L., & Nielzén, S. Anxiety and defence against anxiety as reflected in percept-genetic formations. *Journal of Personality Assessment,* 1976, *40,* 151-161.

Sokolov, Ye. [E.] N. *Perception and the conditioned reflex.* New York: Pergamon, 1963.

Werner, H. *Comparative psychology of mental development* (Rev. ed.). New York: International Universities, 1948.

Werner, H. The concept of development from a comparative and organismic point of view. In D. B. Harris (Ed.), *The concept of development.* Minneapolis: University of Minnesota Press, 1957.

IV

THE USE
OF PERCEPTGENESIS
IN A PSYCHODYNAMIC
FRAME
OF REFERENCE

11

Perceptgenesis
and the Experimental Study
of Conflict and Defense

Bert Westerlundh
Lund University, Lund, Sweden

In this chapter I provide a short summary of a number of laboratory experiments on conflict and defense (Sjöbäck & Westerlundh, 1975, 1977; Westerlundh, 1976). These experiments have in common the use of the percept-genetic technique to study defenses—in these instances, adaptations of Kragh's original tachistoscopic DMT procedure and scoring system (Kragh, 1969). The psychoanalytic theory of conflict and defense underlies the work. The percept-genetic scoring system relates naturally to such classical presentations of the theory of defense as those of Fenichel (1946) and A. Freud (1946). The experimental operations used are intended to activate warded-off wishes or images of danger and threat; thus they are of a sexual or an aggressive nature. In other respects, their character is quite varied. In two experiments, the operations imply real-life social interactions. In a third experiment, the provocation is contained in a film. Two other experiments use subliminal stimuli as experimental operations. The subjects used in these experiments are normal people; four studies are based on male, one on female, university students. The focus of the experiments is on personality dynamics. The responses— that is, the defensive endeavors of the person as studied by perceptgenesis—are seen as functions both of various aspects of personality organization and of the specific provoking situation to which the person is subjected. This type of research represents a merger of general and differential psychological approaches, with attendant methodological problems.

Certainly, the experimental method has not generally been the method of choice to study psychoanalytic propositions. Kline's (1972) review shows that conflict and defense as studied by academic psychologists have most often been investigated correlationally. Groups of people with differing characteristics—for instance, a specified clinical group and a normal group—have been compared for anxieties, wishes, and defenses. Yet as stressed by Silverman (1976), such studies cannot demonstrate the *causal* relationships posited by psychoanalytic theory. To do this, the wishes and anxieties must be directly manipulated. That is, an experimental paradigm is necessary. The laboratory experiment has, however, been a tool of a psychology that disregards individual differences. Hypotheses are typically presented in a general stimulus–response form, and all subjects are expected to react in the same manner to the experimental operation, a result considered demonstrated if a statistical test of significance allows the rejection of the null hypothesis.

Generally, such a framework is untenable for the study of psychoanalytic propositions. The excellent systematologist Madsen (1966) is certainly right when he claims that the present-day systems that can be designated "general psychologies" are psychoanalysis and behavioristic learning theory. They are not general psychologies in the classical sense of lists of human faculties or passions. Rather, they articulate the general principles of human development or learning that account for differentiated human functioning. In contrast to behaviorism, psychoanalysis is not merely formal. General psychoanalytic theory specifies the basic contents of human development: the dominant modes of libidinal gratification, the central conflicts, the ontogenetic tasks the person has to face. In this way, the general framework of psychoanalysis forms the basis of its differential psychology. No approach has fulfilled the ideographic ideal of psychology as "theoretical biography" better than has psychoanalysis. The experimentalist must come to terms with this orientation toward human differences. Not all people are characterized by the same motives or conflicts. Some people are sexually aroused by female foot apparel; yet were such a shoe presented to an unselected group, the hypothesis of sexual arousal would certainly be disproved.

The problem can be approached in many ways. It is possible to select groups of people who, according to the theory, should be sensitive in a certain conflict area and subject them to experimentation on the conflict in question. It is also possible to select the conflicts to be investigated in such a manner that a great proportion of people can be expected to show defensive reactions when confronted with the experimental provocation. Certain conflicts about sexuality and aggression are to some extent "general," at least in Western society. A conflict epidemiology related to the etiologic constructs of psychoanalysis can suggest investigations that might yield results of a general order owing to the frequency in the population of sensitivity to the conflict in question. The experiments presented here concern such frequently occurring conflicts, thus making it possible to work with unselected subjects. For many of the causal sequences postulated by psychoanalysis, however, experiments on selected groups are necessary. To the general experimental perspective made possible by the frequency of conflicts, there should be added, however, attempts to differentiate within the unselected group, raising the question of what differentiating instrument to choose. I have tried to complement the general experimental picture with a differential one by using further percept-genetic instruments.

It has often been stated (e.g., Hilgard, 1962) that psychoanalytic propositions are of two kinds: etiologic or genetic propositions about the roots of present-day functioning and dynamic concepts about the interplay of motives in the present. Dynamic concepts can be subdivided into (a) structural propositions that articulate intraindividual organization and the relation of person to surroundings and (b) motivational propositions that concern intrapsychic wishes and motives and outer incitements. Obviously, experiments on psychoanalytic hypotheses must be primarily concerned with dynamic interactions in the present. Using the language of analysis of variance, the study of person-by-situation interactions is important here. This type of interaction has recently been stressed in personality psychology (e.g., Endler & Magnusson, 1976), but behaviorists have tended to see such interactions as just another instance of situational specificity. The cognitively oriented researchers primarily represented in the Endler and Magnusson book have hitherto not been able to incorporate their insights into theoretical formulations.

Rather, they persist in considering these phenomena in methodological terms within an ANOVA framework. It seems to me that only a theory like psycho-analysis—a theory of the person's adaptation by means of construction and trans-formation of meanings—can give us hope of reaching those bridge equations (Rapaport, 1960) that would enable us to relate different phenomena within a comprehensive theoretical framework.

Psychoanalytic theory assumes that each person has to command a defense organization consisting of a number of different defensive strategies connected in an intricate hierarchical system (Moser, 1964), the deeper layers of which are rigid and resistant to change (S. Freud, 1937/1964; Rapaport, 1951). The theory further presupposes that different mechanisms in a person's defense organization are activated in different situations and that this selective activation is determined by a number of factors, primarily the intensity of inner and outer incitements, certain general ego functions, and the nature of the incitement. The pattern of interactions is thus set: Certain drive- or anxiety-related experimental operations will activate drive derivatives or images of danger or threat in certain people; depending on their intrapsychic organization, the people will respond with activation of defenses according to the threat-or-danger–anxiety–defense scheme (S. Freud, 1926/1950). It should therefore be possible to approach the problem of what people are sensi-tive to a given conflict by using some independent measure of their defense organi-zations: thus the structure of the following experiments, where the experimental operation is some sort of sexual-aggressive manipulation, the dependent variable is a perceptgenesis, and an attempt is made to study the defense organization of the person by an independent percept-genetic measure.

SOME EXPERIMENTS ON AGGRESSION

A number of my experiments sharing a common design concerned the person as aggressor and as a victim of aggression (Westerlundh, 1976). The DMT, pre-sented at a first session, was used to assess the defense organization of the sub-ject. The second session was the experiment proper. Two father-son pictures were presented in succession, with the experimental operation in between. The father-son pictures, depicting a centrally placed boy and a peripheral older man in neutral in-teraction, were rotated between subjects. The design is thus a pretest-posttest situa-tion in which subjects serve as their own controls. Methodological considerations show this type of design to be reasonable for these experiments; as a matter of fact, it is rather conservative because, among other things, of automatization of percep-tion. In each of three experiments, 40 male university students (different for each experiment) were used as subjects, and each was tested individually. Theoretical considerations made it reasonable to suppose that a number of stimulus-distal re-sponses (interpreted as signs of aggression, anxiety, and defense) to percept-genetic presentations could be activated by anxiety-inducing experimental operations in-volving aggression. These "signs" are disappearance of threat (an instance of isola-tion), denial of aggression, reaction formation against aggression, introaggression, indicators of anxiety (about bodily injury), and reports of aggression (stimulus distal if given in response to the father-son pictures). The main operationalizations of these psychoanalytic concepts are explained in the appendix to this chapter. The following sections give a summary of the main characteristics and some of the main results of these experiments. A brief précis is given in Figure 11.1.

Design
First session, DMT.
Second session, experiment proper with before-after design:

$$\text{Father-son picture } {}^{A}_{B} \text{ —Experimental treatment—Father-son picture } {}^{B}_{A}$$

The father-son pictures are rotated between subjects.

	First experiment	Second experiment	Third experiment
Subjects	$n = 40$ men	$n = 40$ men	$n = 40$ men
Experimental treatment	Double provocation: exposure to failure and punishment	Active aggression: "shock application" by the subject to a "victim"	Aggressively loaded videotape
Hypotheses	Increase in disappearance of threat, denial, introaggression, anxiety, and aggression	Increase in disappearance of threat, denial, reaction formation, introaggression, and aggression	Increase in disappearance of threat, denial, reaction formation, introaggression, anxiety, and aggression

More people are expected to manifest signs of these mechanisms after treatment, i.e., in their reports to the second father-son picture shown.
Results: See Tables 11.1 and 11.2 and Figures 11.2 and 11.3.

Figure 11.1 Summary of the experiments on aggression.

The Subject as Victim

In the first experiment, a specific situation was created wherein the people were subjected to a double threat, failing in a task and being punished for it. The punishment was an electric shock directed by the experimenter at the body of the subject. In conjunction with this situation, a father-son picture was presented tachistoscopically at successively prolonged exposure times. Earlier in the same session, a father-son picture had been presented in an equivalent manner in a nonprovoking situation. At an earlier session, the subject was tested with the DMT. The hypotheses are given in Figure 11.1. Results—before-and-after changes—are presented in Table 11.1. In this first experiment, the hypotheses for introaggression and anxiety received support, but something else happened to the other signs for which predictions were made, as indicated by phase-level distribution data and by correlational analyses. The pattern of before–after change was the same for these signs as for those for which predictions of increase received support. This was not true of the remaining signs for which no predictions had been formulated, that is, reaction formation A and B. Furthermore, a cross-analysis comparing the second father-son genesis in this experiment with the first such genesis in the second and third experiments (Table 11.2) lends support to the predictions. The nonsignificant before–after changes for some of the signs for which predictions were made in this experiment are due to the high frequency of these signs in the first father-son genesis. Their high rate of occurrence seems to have been caused by a situational determinant, an anxious anticipation of the provoking situation in the last part of the experiment. Of course, for ethical reasons, the subjects had to be told that they could be subjected to electric shock in the experiment. This anticipation per se

Table 11.1 Before–after changes in the three experiments on aggression

Signs[a]	Experimental condition[b]		
	1/victim	2/aggressor	3/film
Anxiety	.001	—[c]	<.001
Introaggression A	.020	.011	.002
Introaggression B (DMT Sign 6)	.035	—[c]	.020
Denial A	.194	.172	.109
Denial B (DMT Sign 3)	.194	.172	.109
Reaction formation A	—[c]	<.001	.145
Reaction formation B (DMT Sign 4)	—[c]	<.001	.145
Aggression	.500	.008	.011
Disappearance of threat A	.500	.035	.035
Disappearance of threat B	.500	—[d]	—[d]
All signs	.090	.001	<.001
Barrier reports (of separating isolation)	.032		

Note. All results are in the predicted direction, showing an increase after treatment.

[a]Those signs of defense that were predicted to be reported by an increasing number of subjects after experimental treatment (one-tailed tests). The signs of defense that were predicted would *not* be reported by an increasing number after treatment (two-tailed tests) had no probability values.

[b]Probability values derived by the McNemar test for the significance of changes.

[c]Not predicted to increase in this experiment.

[d]Sign too small to test.

Table 11.2   Cross-analyses comparing results from the first Father-Son genesis in Experiments
2 and 3 and the second Father-Son genesis in Experiment 1

Signs[a]	Experiment 2, first genesis/ Experiment 1, second genesis ($p <$)	Experiment 3, first genesis/ Experiment 1, second genesis ($p <$)
Anxiety	.05	.01
Introaggression A	.01	.01
Introaggression B (DMT)	.05	.05
Denial A	.05	.01
Denial B (DMT)	.05	.01
Aggression	NS	.01
Disappearance of threat A	NS	.05
Disappearance of threat B (DMT)	NS	.05

Note. Predictions were that relatively more subjects would report the signs of defense in
Experiment 1 after treatment. Results supporting these predictions indicate the existence of a
special situational determination in the earlier part of Experiment 1. All results are in the predicted direction.
[a]One-tailed tests.

worked as an effective provocation and raised the frequency of the signs in question
in the first father-son genesis. Another finding, not predicted, but meaningful and
interpretable, was the increase in the number of barrier reports (of separating isolation) in the second father-son genesis.

The Subject as Aggressor

In the second experiment, the subject was given to think that he had to give a
painful electric shock to another human being. The experimenter ordered the
subject to fasten the shock electrodes on the "victim's" wrist and give the shocks.
Of course, the "victim" was an assistant to the experimenter and received no
shocks. After this operation, a father-son picture was presented tachistoscopically
at successively prolonged exposure times. A previous father-son picture was presented in an equivalent manner just before the operation. At an earlier experimental session the subjects were tested with the DMT.

The hypotheses are given in Figure 11.1. The results were expected to be substantially the same as in the first experiment, but indicators of anxiety were not
expected to increase inasmuch as the body of the subject was not threatened.
Instead, reaction formation was expected to increase. This sign should follow after
the (involuntary) aggressive act as a result of superego pressure and have the character of a fantasied reversal of the situation. It was thought that some signs would
change in significance in comparison to the equivalent genesis in the first experiment. Thus, reports of aggression ought, to a higher degree, to become indicators
of aggressive impulses that were evoked.

Results are presented in Table 11.1. The hypotheses received support except
for a variant of disappearance of threat (which was too small to test) and denial.
But, as in the first experiment, correlational analyses showed a pattern of before-
after change for these signs equivalent to that for the other signs about which
predictions were made. That denial does not show a significant increase is due to
the fact that it is frequent in the first father-son series with another meaning; the

DMT series shown earlier creates a set to perceive aggression, and this set is negated: "There is nothing aggressive in the picture." The change of meaning for reports of aggression has received partial support through these findings.

The Videotaped Murder

The basic goal in the third experiment was to obtain results like those in both earlier experiments by using an experimental operation on a different level than those used earlier. In this experiment, the operation consisted of the presentation of an aggressively loaded videotape representing a scene of murder involving two young men. We expected that some subjects would identify with the aggressor and others with the victim and respond accordingly as the real "aggressors" and "victims," respectively, in the two earlier experiments.

A father-son picture was presented at successively prolonged exposure times just after the tape. Another father-son picture was presented in an equivalent manner just before the tape. At an earlier session, subjects had been tested with the DMT. The hypotheses are given in Figure 11.1; results are presented in Table 11.1. The hypotheses received support, except for a variant of disappearance of threat (which was too small to test), denial, and reaction formation. All of these indicators, however, showed change in the predicted direction, although not significant. Moreover, correlational analyses showed that denial in the second father-son genesis had particularly strong positive relationships to some of the significantly increasing signs. Reaction formation had a positive relationship to denial in this genesis but tended to be negatively related to anxiety. These findings seem to indicate a degree of differentiation between the "aggressors" and the "victims" in this experiment; that is, subjects with aggressive impulses that are countered by inhibition of aggression seem to be differentiated from subjects with fear of being attacked.

Taken together, the intercorrelations within the second father-son genesis indicate that a reasonably delimited group of subjects reacted to the threat. This group was characterized by its capacity to react to fictional stimulation. As can be seen when the father-son results are related to those from the DMT, this is a different group from those reacting in the earlier experiments. Reactions to the experimental operation in this experiment may well have had a playful character and may indicate normal, fluid adaptation.

Situational Psychodynamics: Some Final Considerations

There were two purposes underlying this group of experiments. The first was to test psychoanalytic propositions in the laboratory by using specific experimental operations and percept-genetic response measures. This attempt was generally successful, as was especially clear with Experiments 2 and 3. In Experiment 1, special conditions prevailed; the subject's anticipation of the provoking treatment in the latter part of the experiment seems in itself to have been quite an effective threat. We know from these experiments that factors working at quite different levels of psychic functioning can influence percept-genetic reports (see also Forsberg, 1974). In the first experiment, the anticipation effect seems to have resulted in quite a high frequency of aggression and disappearance of threat in the first father-son genesis. A more general effect was found in all three experiments:

a set to perceive aggression in the father-son picture (after presentation of the DMT). The set was negated, and this led to relatively high frequencies of signs of denial in the first father-son genesis in all experiments. Thus, there are some cases in which hypotheses did not find support in the experimental data. Further analyses (cross-analyses between experiments and correlational analyses) provide support for the ideas underlying the hypotheses, however.

The results concerning the before–after change are thus generally as expected. They show that there are a number of percept-genetic signs closely related to aggression and that it is possible to influence these signs experimentally. There are a few results that fall outside of this predicted pattern. In Experiment 1, a significant increase in barrier reports was found after treatment. In response to the threat against their bodies, the subjects perceived the boy and the man in the picture as being separated and isolated from one another by a barrier. This shows the extent to which percept-genetic indicators of defense can be read literally, as actually internalized primitive reaction patterns. Thus it seems that the percept-genetic scoring of defenses represents one of the few cases in which construct validity, predictive validity, and face validity coincide.

The Differential Psychological Perspective

The second purpose of the studies was to introduce a differential psychological perspective and to strengthen the experimental results by correlational analyses. The central analyses are those between the DMT and the second father-son genesis. The DMT was our central measure of personality variables. The main results gained in these analyses for Experiments 1 and 2 are presented in Figures 11.2 and 11.3. These findings can be summarized as follows: In general, the relations found are not very strong. There are few cases of sign-to-sign correspondence (i.e., a specific indicator of defenses in the DMT manifested in the father-son genesis), but there are at the same time the following discrepancies:

1. The definitely dominant group of positive relationships between the instruments is found within the critical group of signs closely related to aggression. In the first experiment, disappearance of threat is the DMT sign showing positive relationships to the critical father-son signs. In the second experiment, the DMT sign showing the most such relationships is reaction formation, followed by disap-

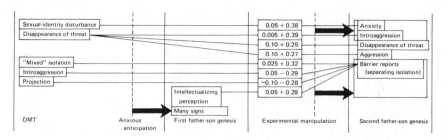

Figure 11.2   The main operative forces and the relationships between the different percept-genetic measures in the first experiment on aggression. The numbers in boxes indicate, first, the level of significance of the relationship; second, the value of D [an index varying from -1 (perfect negative) to $+1$ (perfect positive)].

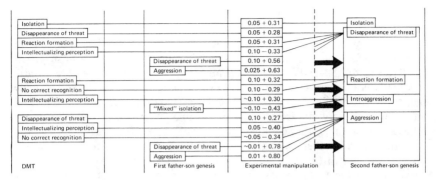

Figure 11.3 The main operative forces and the relationships between the different percept-genetic measures in the second experiment on aggression. The numbers in boxes indicate, first, the level of significance of the relationship; second, the value of D [an index varying from -1 (perfect negative) to $+1$ (perfect positive)].

pearance of threat. Reasonably enough, there is thus a certain differentiation between the experiments.

2. The second-most important group of relationships are the negative ones between the DMT signs of isolation (especially those indicating a characterological compulsive-adaptive style) and the critical group of signs in the second father-son genesis.

3. Furthermore, there exists a small number of relationships that are easily understandable within the framework of the theoretical scheme applied, for example, that the subjects showing an unsuitable defense against increased castration anxiety (signs of female identification) in the DMT react with anxiety representations in the second father-son genesis when they are subjected to bodily maltreatment. To this group of relationships can be added those shown by the significantly increasing barrier responses in the second father-son genesis in the first experiment. Subjects with barrier reports here showed various types of isolation (the sign "mixed isolation") on the DMT, and in the nonthreatening father-son situation they were characterized by intellectualized perception divested of affect. Threats at different levels evoke different defenses within the same general category in a predictable way. Analyses of this kind open a possibility for establishing a strength hierarchy of indicators of defense. Barrier reports in the second father-son genesis also show negative relations to DMT signs of introaggression and projection, probably indicating incompatibility between this strong and rigid sign of isolation and fluid introjective-projective mechanisms.

4. Last, there are a few relationships that are harder to interpret in terms of the theoretical scheme applied, for example, those that concern a general indicator such as no correct recognition.

The DMT-father-son comparisons in Experiments 1 and 2 thus give some differential psychological information that strengthens the experimental results. In accordance with Kragh's (1969) reasoning, DMT reaction formation plays a leading role in conflicts over expression or inhibition of aggression. DMT disappearance of threat seems primarily to indicate ambivalence toward the aggression of objects.

In the third experiment, however, the results are quite different. Here, there are *no* systematic relationships between the DMT and the second father-son genesis. In this experiment, the experimental operation is not a real-life situation but a fictional stimulation. The provoking effect is thus on a much more superficial level. Reports to the DMT are thus related to percept-genetic reports given in intensely threatening real-life situations but unrelated to such reports given under minimal threat. Evidently, percept-genetic instruments can record indicators of defense from very different levels of psychic functioning. The phenomenal manifestations seem to be the same, but the DMT signs reflect basic conflict adaptation, the second father-son genesis in the third experiment reflecting adaptation to a minimal threat. It seems that percept-genetic instruments can be used, for example, in the investigation of defenses on different levels of psychic functioning, and it is not necessary to leave the laboratory to reach a number of such levels.

On the other hand, the lack of relationships in the third experiment is quite reasonable considering the character of the DMT as a technique for clinical diagnosis and selection for high-stress work also and considering the nature of standard experiments in the field of personality. To study human adaptation realistically, an experimental psychology of personality must use a wide spectrum of independent variables, ranging from highly symbolic ones to concrete interactions. In general, the tendency has hitherto been to use highly symbolic operations. Many aspects of personality functioning cannot be uncovered in this way.

TWO EXPERIMENTS USING
SUBLIMINAL STIMULATION

Another line of research has used subliminal stimuli as independent variables. Different opinions have been put forth as to the relative merits of subliminal and supraliminal independent variables in research on psychoanalytic propositions. Silverman (1976), stressing the importance of unconscious motivation and its special role in psychoanalytic theory, stated that "gross behavioral manipulations" are inadvisable because the emerging wish could easily take the form of a conscious impulse. As such, it could be lived out or mastered without being drawn into conflict or leading to "pathological responses." This argument has a sound basis but is a bit forced. Silverman forgets that the motivational states inaugurated by the manipulation will relate to unconscious wishes and thus will easily be repressed. The consequences are conflict activation and defense, as the experiments already presented have demonstrated. Sarnoff (1971), on the other hand, stressed the advisability of establishing independent checks on the effectiveness of the experimental manipulations. Such checks are used to show "whether and to what extent those manipulations have succeeded in creating their intended variations in psychological states" (p. 182); they are more or less impossible to establish when subliminal stimuli are used. Sarnoff's position is that, without such checks, alternative explanations of results cannot be excluded. If results are in accordance with specified predictions based on psychoanalytic theory, however, it seems improbable that the type of construction devised to explain away results from experiments using subliminal perception will have any degree of credibility. Thus, Sarnoff's methodological strictures result in a multiplication of dependent variables, useful per se but not necessary to establish the validity of the experiment. In all, it seems to me that both subliminal and supraliminal experimental operations can be used in research on psychoanalytic propositions.

Method

Two experiments using subliminal presentations as independent variables were performed (Sjöbäck & Westerlundh, 1975, 1977) with the same apparatus and in the same manner. In the first experiment, the subjects were three randomized groups of 40 male university students; in the second, three randomized groups of 40 female university students. The subjects were tested individually. The apparatus presented different stimulus fields to the two eyes. The field for the left eye contained two light diodes, used in the first experiment for measurements of the absolute visual thresholds and in the second one in a time-estimation task. The field for the right eye was equipped for the presentation of pictures. Two stimulus-presentation boxes could be switched so either could be presented to the subject. One of these boxes allowed tachistoscopic presentation of pictures; the other box was for what we have called "amauroscopic" (i.e., protracted low-intensity) presentations (concerning this type of stimulus presentation, see Dixon, 1971). The tachistoscope was used in a perceptgenesis, *ad modum* DMT. The amauroscope had a double function.

The experimental session started with an amauroscopic perceptgenesis. The pictures used depicted a mother-child interaction. Shown in the first experiment was a woman in a reclining position with a small boy in her lap, the boy having one hand on the woman's breast. In the second experiment, the same picture was shown, with the difference that the child was a girl. Presentations (of 5-sec duration) start at 40 volts and proceeded in 10-volt intervals up to 170 (Experiment 1) or 190 (Experiment 2) volts, or until two correct descriptions of the picture were given in sequence. This genesis was intended to elicit responses that would give information about the defense organization of the subject.

The mother-child picture was structurally similar to the pictures presented amauroscopically in the experiment proper. These were the stimuli used as independent variables in the experiment. Threshold data from the amauroscopic genesis, as well as reports from the subjects, indicated that the meaning of these stimuli was in no instance apprehended by the subjects on a conscious level. The stimuli were subliminal in the same sense as tachistoscopically presented pictures below the level of perceptual structuring. At most, some subjects could perceive a diffuse light (corresponding to the tachistoscopic flash; cf. Silverman, 1976). The transformations of meaning seen in response to these stimuli are in accord with the description given by Dixon (1971) of *semiotic nonconscious processing*.

The experiment proper was administered in the second part of the session. A picture showing two persons in neutral interaction was shown tachistoscopically to the right eye; this was the main dependent variable of the experiment. Before each tachistoscopic exposure, absolute visual thresholds (Experiment 1) or time estimations (Experiment 2) were measured by using the diodes in the field for the left eye. At the same time, the amauroscope was used to present subliminally (at a light intensity where no subject could structure any aspect of the stimulus) a picture for 20 sec to the right eye. The three experimental groups were shown different pictures. This was the experimental operation. Each tachistoscopic presentation was thus preceded by a task involving the left-eye diodes and by a subliminal presentation of a picture to the right eye. The characteristics and the main results of the two experiments are summarized in the following sections.

The First Experiment

In the first experiment, using male subjects, the tachistoscopic percept-genetic stimulus was a picture showing two young men standing facing each other in neutral interaction. The subliminal stimuli are described in Figure 11.4; The hypotheses are also included in the figure. "Reaction formation against aggression" refers, for example, to reports of positive interaction between perceived figures; in Table 11.3 this type of report is labeled "reaction formation." "Reaction formation against sexuality" refers to reports of aggressive interactions; in Table 11.3 this type of report is labeled "aggression."

Results supported some of these hypotheses. The general hypotheses concerning the threshold for correct recognition (1) and the number of scored signs (2) in the geneses were confirmed. Signs of isolation (Hypotheses 4 and 6) were significantly more frequent in the aggressive condition than in the control condition. This was especially true for separating isolation, the perception of a barrier between the persons. Outside of the group of isolation signs, only a few types of denial (perceiving the persons as women or as children) were significantly more frequent in the aggressive than in the control condition. Results for the homoerotic condition were more powerful. The types of denial responses just mentioned were also significantly more frequent in the homoerotic than in the control condition. Signs of sexual-identity disturbance (Hypothesis 8) were significantly more frequent in the homoerotic than in the other conditions. The hypotheses polymorphous identifications (9), signs of anxiety (3), and a few variants of separating isolation (4) were significantly more frequent in this than in the control condition. Further, perception of a positive relationship between two male figures (an instance of drive breakthrough) and percepts scored as sexual symbolism were significantly more frequent in the homoerotic condition than in one or both of the other ones.

Presenting these results in table form was not easy. The predictions concern indicators of defense mechanisms such as reaction formation. In this experiment, a number of indicators of varying generality are established for each mechanism. Thus, there is a general class of reaction formation against aggression; a subclass of those reaction formations scored on the basis of reported mood in the picture (in contrast to those scored on the basis of reported activity); subclasses to the subclass depending on reported sex of the perceived figures (e.g., two men in a picture with positive mood, a man and a woman in a picture with positive mood), and so on. Table 11.3 gives total number of tests performed on the indicators of a certain mechanism, number of significances, and the level of these significances. The finer qualitative differentiations had to be excluded. The experimental results do support the main hypotheses (except those concerning reaction formation) but are more complex than anticipated. The types of meaning transformation seen in this experiment are in accord with psychoanalytic theoretical formulations, however, and can hardly be accommodated within any other framework.

Comparisons between the tachistoscopic results and the amauroscopic mother-child genesis gave some interesting information (see Table 11.4). There were no strong relationships between the geneses in the control condition. The aspects of defense organization measured by the two geneses do not overlap. In the aggressive

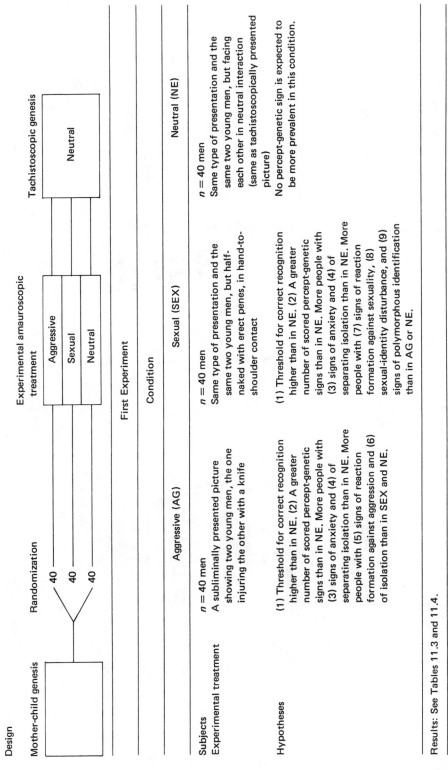

Design

Mother-child genesis	Randomization	Experimental treatment	
		Experimental amauroscopic treatment	Tachistoscopic genesis
	40	Aggressive	Neutral
	40	Sexual	
	40	Neutral	

First Experiment

	Condition		
	Aggressive (AG)	Sexual (SEX)	Neutral (NE)
Subjects	$n = 40$ men	$n = 40$ men	$n = 40$ men
Experimental treatment	A subliminally presented picture showing two young men, the one injuring the other with a knife	Same type of presentation and the same two young men, but half-naked with erect penes, in hand-to-shoulder contact	Same type of presentation and the same two young men, but facing each other in neutral interaction (same as tachistoscopically presented picture)
Hypotheses	(1) Threshold for correct recognition higher than in NE. (2) A greater number of scored percept-genetic signs than in NE. More people with (3) signs of anxiety and (4) of separating isolation than in NE. More people with (5) signs of reaction formation against aggression and (6) of isolation than in SEX and NE.	(1) Threshold for correct recognition higher than in NE. (2) A greater number of scored percept-genetic signs than in NE. More people with (3) signs of anxiety and (4) of separating isolation than in NE. More people with (7) signs of reaction formation against sexuality, (8) sexual-identity disturbance, and (9) signs of polymorphous identification than in AG or NE.	No percept-genetic sign is expected to be more prevalent in this condition.

Results: See Tables 11.3 and 11.4.

Figure 11.4 Summary of the subliminal-stimulation experiments.

| | Second Experiment | | |
| | Condition | | |
	Aggressive (AG)	Sexual (SEX)	Neutral (NE)
Subjects Experimental treatment	*n* = 40 women A subliminally presented picture showing a woman in violent anger with a knife in her hand, approaching a sleeping man with exposed penis	*n* = 40 women Same type of presentation, but showing a woman in copulation with a wolf, *more canino*	*n* = 40 women Same type of presentation, but showing a young woman and a young man facing each other, in neutral interaction (same as tachistoscopically presented picture)
Hypotheses	(1) Threshold for correct recognition higher than in NE. (2) A greater number of scored percept-genetic signs than in NE. More people with (3) signs of anxiety and (4) of separating isolation than in NE. More people with (5) signs of isolation (especially separating isolation) than in NE.	(1) Threshold for correct recognition higher than in NE. (2) A greater number of scored percept-genetic signs than in NE. More people with (3) signs of anxiety and (4) of separating isolation than in NE. More people with (6) signs of repression and (7) of sexual-identity disturbance than in AG or NE.	No percept-genetic sign is expected to be more prevalent in this condition.

Results: See Table 11.5.

Figure 11.4 Summary of the subliminal-stimulation experiments (*Continued*).

Table 11.3 Main results of the first subliminal-stimulation experiment

	Comparisons											
	Aggressive/homoerotic				Aggressive/neutral				Homoerotic/neutral			
	$p<$			Number of testable differences	$p<$			Number of testable differences	$p<$			Number of testable differences
Mechanisms	.001	.01	.05		.001	.01	.05		.001	.01	.05	
Anxiety	0^x	0^x	0^x	3	0	0	0	1	0	1^y	1^y	3
Barrier reports	0^x	0^x	0^x	18	0	6^z	4^z	18	0	1^y	1^y	15
Isolation	0	0	0	4	0	1^z	1^z	4	0^x	0^x	0^x	4
Reaction formation	0	0	1^y	16	0	0	0	14	0	0	1^{xy}	16
Aggression	0	0	0	2	0^x	0^x	0^x	1	0	0	0	2
Introjection (sexual-identity disturbance)	0	0	4^y	17	0^x	0^x	1^{xz}	15	1^y	2^y	2^y	17
Duplication of perceived figures	0	0	0	1	0^x	0^x	0^x	1	0	0	1^y	1
Repression, sexual symbolism	0^x	0^x	1^{xy}	8	0^x	0^x	0^x	2	0^x	0^x	1^{xy}	8
Introaggression	0^x	0^x	0^x	2	0^x	0^x	0^x	2	0^x	0^x	0^x	1
Infantilization of perceived figures	0^x	0^x	0^x	2	0^x	1^{xz}	0^x	2	0^x	1^{xy}	0^x	2

Note. For each mechanism, the number under the significance level indicates the number of significances on that level found in the comparisons in question.
[x]Testing was two tailed.
[y]The significance is due to the fact that more people in the homoerotic (sexual) condition show manifestations of the mechanism in question.
[z]The significance is due to the fact that more people in the aggressive condition show manifestations of the mechanism in question.

159

Table 11.4 Relationships between the experimental and Mother-Child geneses in the first subliminal-stimulation experiment

Experimental condition	Signs in experimental genesis	Signs in mother-child genesis		
		Few signs	Many signs	Sexual-identity disturbance
Aggressive	Variants of barrier reports	.05 −.57 .29		
		.10 −.47 .00		
		~.10 −.41 .00		
		~.10 −.41 .00		
		~.10 −.41 .00		
Homoerotic	Anxiety	.10 −.39 .00		
	Person duplications (polymorphous identifications)	.10 −.36 .00		
	Denial (infantilization)	.10 −.42 .28		
	Variants of sexual-identity disturbance (identifications with opposite sex)		.01 +.79 .50	.05 +.39 .21
			~.10 +.36 .00	.05 +.43 .31
			.05 +.55 .31	
Neutral		No systematic relationships to mother-child genesis		

Note. The three values given for each comparison are, respectively, level of significance (two-tailed tests), value of D [an index varying from −1 (perfect negative) to +1 (perfect positive)], and value of the coefficient of predictive association, λ_B. Concerning the use of these statistics in the present experimental context, see Westerlundh, 1976.

condition, the typical defense "separating isolation" showed a negative relationship to few signs in the mother-child genesis. People with few signs in this genesis tended not to react with defensive operations in the experimental condition. The same type of relationship was seen in comparisons between the reports from the homoerotic condition and the mother-child genesis. Here, anxiety, polymorphous identifications, and a variant of denial tended to be negatively related to few signs in the mother-child genesis. In this condition, there are also some positive relationships. People with many signs, as well as people with signs of sexual-identity disturbance, in the mother-child genesis showed signs of sexual-identity disturbance to a higher degree than others in the experimental genesis. Considering the common erotic theme in the two stimulus conditions, this is a reasonable result. It shows that the introjective signs in the experimental genesis have the character of true introjective defenses and are not simple denials.

The Second Experiment

The subjects, the experimental treatment, and the hypotheses for the different conditions are also presented in Figure 11.4. The hypothesis concerning later correct recognition (1) of the tachistoscopic picture in the experimental conditions was confirmed for the sexual but not for the aggressive condition. The hypothesis concerning increased number of signs (2) received confirmation for both experimental conditions. Further, variants of separating isolation (Hypothesis 4) were significantly more frequent in the experimental groups than in the control group. The result was weak for the aggressive condition, however. The hypothesis concerning anxiety (3) was disproved. Isolation (Hypothesis 5) was not more frequent in the aggressive condition than in the control one; but as mentioned, a variant of separating isolation (barrier reports) was. The hypotheses concerning repression (6) and sexual-identity disturbance (7) were confirmed. Significantly more people showed these signs in the sexual condition than in the control one. The result was stronger for repression than for sexual-identity disturbance. Table 11.5, constructed like Table 11.3, presents these results.

The mother-child genesis indicated that the groups were unequal from the start in a way that could jeopardize the experimental results. More people in both the sexual and the aggressive conditions had signs of repression and many signs in the mother-child genesis compared with people in the control condition. These differences were equalized in an analysis wherein people with these characteristics were removed from the experimental groups, so that the three groups were comparable on the mother-child genesis. Replications of the experimental analyses on the newly created groups gave essentially the same results as the original analyses.

CONCLUSIONS

The results from the two subliminal-stimulation experiments demonstrate that the technique is a promising, sensitive research tool in experiments on psychoanalytic hypotheses. This type of research is important but, as I have tried to indicate, far from simple. Especially in work on unselected subjects, such as the experiments presented here, a number of factors must concatenate to allow a proper test of the hypothesis. In the second subliminal-stimulation experiment, it is remarkable how poorly the aggressive picture performed as a provoking stimulus. This might be due to technical factors concerning stimulus presentation or even to subject selection. Perhaps, in this group of young female university students, the revenge type of the female castration complex is ego-syntonic to such a degree that it is not guilt laden and drawn into conflict. Here, our knowledge of the different factors concerned is not extensive enough to cover the contingencies presented by reality. The experiments together nonetheless give strong support to the general research strategy used.

Comparisons between the tachistoscopic geneses from the different groups and the mother-child genesis in the second experiment gave results at chance level. Results from this type of comparison in the aggression experiments presented earlier in the chapter are meaningful but never very strong. Evidently the meaning of the percept-genetic picture (and added experimental operations) is an important determinant of what aspects of the subjects' defense organization the genesis will reveal. The experimental results certainly support such a view. Thus, the percept-genetic study of conflict and defense reveals the defense organization of the person as a complex, hierarchical, and dynamic system, differentially activated by different outer and inner incitements. Defenses exist on different levels of psychic functioning, and a number of these levels can be reached in the laboratory. This is all to the good for the percept-genetic technique as a tool in experimental research on psychoanalytic propositions. On the other hand, no single perceptgenesis will give a complete picture of a person's defense organization and adaptive possibilities. For such an endeavor, intensive exploration after the manner of Kragh (1960) is indicated. The flexibility found in our studies could, however, be expected to be much smaller in pathological material, where neurotic conflict increases the rigidity of defensive operations.

The material presented here should at least establish the applicability of percept-

Table 11.5 Main results of the second subliminal-stimulation experiment

	Comparisons								
	Aggressive/sexual			Aggressive/neutral			Sexual/neutral		
	$p <$		Number of testable differences	$p <$		Number of testable differences	$p <$		Number of testable differences
Mechanisms	.01	.05		.01	.05		.01	.05	
Barrier reports	0^x	1^{xy}	11	0	1^z	9	2^y	4^y	10
Isolation	0^x	0^x	4	0	0	4	0^x	2^{xy}	3
Anxiety	0^x	0^x	4	0	0	4	0	5^y	3
Repression	0	0	7	0^x	0^x	3	0	5^y	7
Introjection (sexual-identity disturbance)	0	0	15	0^x	1^{xz}	14	0	2^y	15
Reaction formation against aggression	1^{xy}	2^{xy}	24	0^x	0^x	22	0^x	2^{xy}	23
Aggression	0^x	0^x	2	0^x	0^x	2	0^x	0^x	2
Introaggression	0^x	0^x	1	0^x	0^x	0	0^x	0^x	1
Duplication of perceived figures	0^x	0^x	0	0^x	0^x	0	0^x	0^x	0
Infantilization of perceived figures	0^x	0^x	2	0^x	0^x	2	0^x	0^x	2

Note. For each mechanism, the number under the significance level indicates the number of significances on that level found in the comparisons in question. Testing was two tailed.

[x] The significance is due to the fact that more people in the homoerotic (sexual) condition show manifestations of the mechanism in question.

[y] The significance is due to the fact that more people in the aggressive condition show manifestations of the mechanism in question.

genesis in the study of conflict and defense. Generally, the percept-genetic opera-tionalizations adhere closely to psychoanalytic theoretical formulations, perhaps more so than those of any other technique outside of the psychoanalytic situation. Perceptgenesis might well be the method of choice in much laboratory experimen-tation on psychoanalytic propositions.

Concurrently, experimentation is a powerful tool to demonstrate the construct validity of the percept-genetic technique for studying defenses (cf. Sandler & Joffe, 1967). Many forms of extension of the work presented here are possible. The range of possible experimental operations has in no way been fully explored. Technical adaptations can increase the efficiency:cost ratio. An important, still-untried field in inquiry is systematic experimentation on well-defined clinical or characterological groups selected by psychoanalytic criteria. Here, perceptgenesis promises a direct exposition of the working of defenses in experimental situations of great relevance to psychoanalytic theory.

APPENDIX: THE MAJOR PERCEPT–GENETIC OPERATIONALIZATIONS OF DEFENSE

The scoring of defenses in the experiments is based on Kragh's DMT scoring system (Kragh, 1969). Kragh's system is directly related to the aggressively provok-ing DMT pictures, however, so that, for example, a report of a positive relation-ship between perceived figures will not have the DMT significance of reaction formation against aggression if given in a situation where no aggressive provocation exists. Thus, in a sense, every percept-genetic stimulus and experimental situation must have its own scoring scheme reflecting the meaning of the stimulus situation. This must be born in mind when considering the following list of the most impor-tant operationalizations.

Repression. Perceived figures have a quality of rigidity and inanimateness or of being masked, or they are animals.
Isolation. Perceived figures are separated from each other in the field (by barriers), and parts of the configuration are excluded or "whitened"; perception is stripped of affect, and primitive contents are excluded (which are signs of characterological compulsion).
Denial. Existence of aggression is denied or made slight in situations where aggres-sive provocation exists; equivalent operations at other provocations.
Reaction formation. Aggression is turned into its opposite in situations where aggressive provocation exists; equivalent operations at other provocations.
Introaggression. Perceived figures or other structures are hurt, dead, or worthless.
Introjection of the opposite sex (identification with the opposite sex, signs of sexual identity disturbance). Different forms of incorrect and inaccurate attribu-tions of sex are made to perceived figures.
Polymorphous identification. Stimulus-inadequate multiplication of perceived figures occurs.
Anxiety. Perceived figures are described as afraid; the feeling tone in the picture is described as dangerous or unsafe; perceived figures are "blackened" in a stimulus-inadequate way.
Aggression. Aggression is reported between perceived figures.

REFERENCES

Dixon, N. R. *Subliminal perception: The nature of a controversy.* London: McGraw-Hill, 1971.

Endler, N. S., & Magnusson, D. Personality and person by situation interactions. In N. S. Endler & D. Magnusson (Eds.), *Interactional psychology and personality.* Washington: Hemisphere, 1976.

Fenichel, O. *The psychoanalytic theory of neurosis.* London: Routledge, 1946.

Forsberg, C. *Om sambandet mellan perceptuellt försvar och inställningen till dödshjälp* . . . Lund: Department of Behavioral Science, Lund University, 1974. (Mimeo.)

Freud, A. *The ego and the mechanisms of defence.* London: Hogarth, 1946.

Freud, S. Inhibitions, symptoms and anxiety. *Standard Edition (Vol. 20).* London: Hogarth, 1959. (Originally published, 1926.)

Freud, S. Analysis terminable and interminable. *Standard Edition (Vol. 23).* London: Hogarth, 1964. (Originally published, 1937.)

Hilgard, E. The scientific status of psychoanalysis. In E. Nagel, S. Suppes, & A. Tarski (Eds.), *Logic, methodology and philosophy of science: Proceedings of the 1960 International Congress.* Stanford, Calif.: Stanford University Press, 1962.

Kline, P. *Fact and fantasy in Freudian theory.* London: Methuen, 1972.

Kragh, U. Pathogenesis in dipsomania: An illustration of the actual-genetic model of perception-personality. *Acta Psychiatrica Neurologica Scandinavica,* 1960, *35,* 207–222, 261–288, 480–497.

Kragh, U. *Manual till DMT (Defense Mechanism Test).* Stockholm: Skandinaviska Testförlaget, 1969.

Madsen, K. B. *Psykologiens filosofi.* Copenhagen: Royal Danish School of Education, 1966. (Mimeo.)

Moser, U. Zur Abwehrlehre: Das Verhältnis von Verdrängung und Projektion. *Jahrbuch der Psychoanalyse,* 1964, *3,* 56–85.

Rapaport, D. Toward a theory of thinking. In D. Rapaport (Ed.), *Organization and pathology of thought.* New York: Columbia University Press, 1951.

Rapaport, D. The structure of psychoanalytic theory: A systematizing attempt. *Psychological Issues,* 1960, *2,* 6.

Sandler, J., & Joffe, W. G. The tendency to persistence in psychological function and development: With special reference to fixation and regression. *Bulletin of the Menninger Clinic,* 1967, *31,* 257–271.

Sarnoff, I. *Testing psychoanalytic concepts.* New York: Springer, 1971.

Silverman, L. Psychoanalytic theory: "The reports of my death are greatly exaggerated." *American Psychologist,* 1976, *31,* 621–637.

Sjöbäck, H., & Westerlundh, B. *Amauroskopisk subliminal varseblivning: I. Personinteraktioner: Effekter på ljuströskel och perceptgenes.* Lund: Department of Psychology, Lund University, 1975. (Mimeo.)

Sjöbäck, H., & Westerlundh, B. *Amauroskopisk subliminal varseblivning: II. Personinteraktioner: Effekter på tidsskattning och perceptgenes.* Lund: Department of Psychology, Lund University, 1977. (Mimeo.)

Westerlundh, B. *Aggression, anxiety and defence.* Lund: Gleerup, 1976.

12

Defense Mechanisms Manifested in Perceptgenesis

Ulf Kragh
University of Oslo, Oslo, Norway

My purpose in this chapter is to review empirical-experimental research on defense in the percept-genetic framework. In German *Aktualgenese* research, this topic was, to my knowledge, never raised. The Leipzig School did not include psychoanalytic concepts among their own notions. History in itself would not have rendered this impossible. Pötzl had published his experiments as early as 1917, but as yet the relationships between general experimental psychology and the psychology of personality were at a very incomplete stage of conceptual formulation. Krüger's (1924) notions of *Struktur* and of the developmental primacy of emotion could possibly be taken as steps in that direction, but they remained on a very general and abstract level.

In the late 1940s, however, papers on the experimental investigation of defense appeared, for example, by McGinnies (1949). The first preliminary hypotheses concerning a relationship between data obtained in "actual-genetic" experiments on the one hand and processes in terms of defenses on the other, were formulated in connection with the very consistent patterns observed in the "actual-genetic" series of a group of compulsive neurotics (Kragh, 1955). A pattern termed "all-or-none" was typical not only of their tachistoscopic series but of a serial after-image experiment. This serial pattern was linked with the description of compulsives given by, among others, Fenichel (1945). The restriction to this sole clinical group was the principal cause of interest being focused on just one defense, notably *isolation.* It was not until the subsequent analysis of the father-son (actual-genetic) series (AKTs) of a group of young men who had lost their fathers (Kragh, 1955, pp. 198, 333, 337) that I also used the concept of *introjection* as represented by specific changes in the hero (the central person in the stimulus picture).

My next occasion for studying defense in actualgenesis was in connection with experiments performed on a small group of anxiety-hysteric (female) subjects (Kragh, 1959) and on one single case of dipsomania (Kragh, 1960). In the former group TAT cards 6GF and 10 were used. These acts differed from the previous ones in the unusual number of reports of busts, masks, and statues in the place of the man, the peripheral person, particularly in the TAT 6GF. This formed the starting point for a more extensive classification of visual organization in actual-genesis in terms of defense.

Some years later, I initiated a project for the selection of aviation cadets by

The author is now at Lund University, Lund, Sweden.

means of the actual-genetic technique (Kragh, 1961). This made group testing necessary, as well as a few modifications of the original technique. The choice of stimuli was, of course, a matter of prime importance. Using the early findings as well as psychodynamic theorizing, two "parallel" pictures were devised, each of them representing a scene with one central, young, male, "neutral-looking" person (who on the phenomenal level equaled the hero) and one peripheral, threatening, elderly, male, ugly-looking person. The set of underlying assumptions was formulated as follows:

1. The serial, "subliminal" stimulation initiates a process of adaptation to the stimulus in terms of meaningful social reality.

2. The latter may be described as a relationship between a young man and an elderly man (the *reality or adaptive aspect*) or as a relationship between self and father (aspects of *construction* and *reconstruction*, or representation). In more detail, these two alternatives may be spelled out as "elderly man threatening young boy," and "father threatens me," respectively.

3. According to psychodynamic principles, relationships such as those just described would imply the activation of signal anxiety and of defensive processes. The signal anxiety would refer both to castration anxiety and to superego anxiety.

4. The increase in threat in the picture would tend to maximize signal anxiety. This would prove very relevant in selecting people for activities in which rapid and adequate reality testing is of paramount importance. In the initial screening procedure other techniques for estimating the tolerance of stress of these people had also been employed; hence the group to be tested by the actual-genetic method constituted a selected sample.

The first picture constructed to meet these requirements was a combination of TAT card 1 (boy with violin) and the ugly-looking apelike head of a man, which was added to the upper-right corner. The "parallel" picture was a young man sitting on his knees with a gun on his lap, with the upper part of an ugly-looking man placed in the upper-left corner and stretching his hand toward the young boy from behind. The second picture in particular was drawn in a very provocative manner (although this might diminish interserial consistencies to some extent, notably in regard to *micro–macro parallelism*). The reasons for including two "parallel" pictures in the testing procedure were the following.

The total amount of information for each subject would increase, particularly the likelihood of interserial correspondences of sequential patterns. Interserial (intrasubject) consistency might to some extent be used as a measure of the reliability of defensive signs (or in other terms, of the relative importance of *trait defense* versus *state defense*). The pictures were drawn so as to form "parallel" motifs while being at the same time as different as possible in configuration (i.e., position, size, and details). While interpicture similarity might promote interserial consistencies, it also increased the risk of the second series becoming a more or less compressed and distorted retest series.

The four assumptions do not necessarily presuppose the hypothesis of a phase-specific parallelism between ontogenesis and perceptgenesis (the micro–macro theory).

CLASSIFICATION OF DEFENSES

A description of eight classes of *precognitive defensive organization*, including many subclasses, was presented in 1958. The arguments for and the principles underlying that classification have been listed in Kragh (1959), and it is unnecessary to repeat them here. A definition of *regressive defense* was later formulated in connection with the study of a case of dipsomania (Kragh, 1960).

A general feature of these studies of defense in contrast to those issued during the 1950s under the heading of "subliminal perception" was that whereas the latter investigations were concerned with the raising of thresholds in connection with critical, subliminal stimuli, the analysis of precognitive defensive organization paid little attention to such thresholds. Thresholds in terms of stimulus values had already been found to be of relatively minor interest in connection with the actual-genetic analysis of compulsive patients (Kragh, 1955). Another distinctive feature of these studies of defense concerns the vantage point chosen for the analysis of contents. Other kinds of analysis, such as the study of the self-image, would have resulted in focusing on, for example, the exterior and position of the hero. It might in fact also have been possible to extract characteristics analogous to those of the Rorschach test, such as movement of the hero or whole versus details.

Another issue is that of the rationale for selecting eight varieties of defensive organization in the experiment. This choice was made to secure the applicability of the data to the "simple" defenses as studied by Freud (1946) and others, which were also those most generally agreed on in psychoanalytic literature.

Until the late 1950s, work on precognitive defensive organization using the tachistoscopic serial presentation of threatening stimuli had been mainly restricted to a group of compulsive patients, a small group of anxiety-hysteric patients, a comparatively large number of aviation cadets, and one intensive study of a case of dipsomania. Comprehensive case studies in collaboration with psychoanalysts were, and still are, lacking. Criteria until then mainly consisted of compulsive behavior and the pass–fail of aviation cadets and of navy divers, together with an unsystematized description of their behavior in flying and in diving made by their teachers (i.e., commanding officers).

Through the late 1950s and the 1960s, Smith, using a technique emanating from his studies in subliminal perception and called MCT (the metacontrast technique), (Smith, Johnson, & Ljunghill-Andersson, 1970), investigated several groups of neurotics and psychotics; and his results underpinned the plausibility of referring specific types of visual organization to specific defenses. In a group of hysteric patients, for instance, repressive organization was found to dominate. In groups of schizophrenics and of depressives, he was able to demarcate other types of defensive organization than those found in neurotics; one of these types was associated with the defense of projection, others with that of regression.

At this point, I should perhaps say something about the relationship between the DMT and the MCT. I restrict myself to discussing the second series in MCT inasmuch as that series has a much greater resemblance to the DMT than the first series. In the MCT the B stimulus, which corresponds to the central person in the DMT, is brought to the threshold of correct recognition (the C_1 phase level) by the initial procedure. This means that throughout the rest of the series there does not follow a uniform perceptgenesis of the whole field but only of a part of it, corresponding to the A stimulus. The situation is in fact the same as in those rather frequent DMT series in which the hero reaches the threshold of correct recognition at some early presentation while the threshold of the threat is not attained until much later. There are no reasons to believe that defensive visual organization would manifest itself in a different way in the series just mentioned; on the other hand, gross distortions of reality, in terms of distortions of the quasi-stabilized hero by the A stimulus, are likely to manifest themselves with particular clarity in the MCT.

Much research on defense in perceptgenesis (the terminology coming into use toward the end of the 1960s) from 1960 on consisted in the application of the DMT as a tool for the analysis of some theoretical and applied problems. To mention one example, in an investigation on the experience of noise, it was found that those subjects in a noisy district who did not complain about noise showed relatively more isolation, whereas those who did complain in a silent district exhibited relatively more repressive defense (Johansson, 1968). Other investigations (e.g., Johnson, 1960) further demonstrated the validity of the DMT as a discriminator for tolerance of stress.

NEW APPROACHES

During the 1960s, modified techniques of the serial afterimage experiment in the manner of an early study by Smith (1949) were also developed for application to the study of defense. The previously employed red-square standard stimulus was made more "provocative" by changing it into a red oval with schematic, "sad," facial traits; and at the same time, the technique of presentation was improved. The new version was applied to a variety of clinical groups; and apart from demonstrating the technique's value as a diagnostic tool, the results also lent themselves to an interpretation in terms of defense. Among the findings was intermittent occurrence of nearly size-constant and positive afterimages in schizophrenic patients, which occurrence was associated with regression. A new level of complexity was also introduced into the serial afterimage test by Smith and co-workers, by the tachistoscopic presentation of a subliminal "threatening" face at the *middle* of the afterimage series (Andersson, Fries, & Smith, 1970). Effects on the part of the series following the presentation of the subliminal stimulus were associated with (state) anxiety reactions (increase of afterimage size, darkness, or both) and with defense (increase of brightness, which was interpreted as a manifestation of isolation). Quite a few experiments of this kind have been performed so far; in particular, Smith's studies of the development of defensive patterns in young children of different ages may add much to our understanding of the developmental stages of defense (Smith & Danielsson, 1977).

Through the 1960s and 1970s much work relevant to the analysis of defense in perceptgenesis has been done by Andersson in his investigations of the spiral aftereffect and other serial methods (Andersson & Weikert, 1974). Westerlundh (1976) has, among other things, dealt with the effects of anticipation of pain (and other induced states) on defense in perceptgenesis; he has also compared the DMT series and father-son geneses with respect to defensive organization. Other experimental work on defense is that done by Zachrisson (1967), who tested the prediction that the perceptgeneses of sexually provocative picture motifs would display correspondences of defense with the DMT series applied to the same subject. This hypothesis was substantiated.

In the late 1960s a project I led was initiated to construct a handy, workable apparatus for the DMT, to optimize the "threat" pictures, and to collect a comparatively large and representative sample of subjects. During this same time, Neuman (1978) has been adapting the DMT to the selection of aviation cadets. His test has been made the final link in the standard procedure of selecting applicants for military aviation service in Sweden; it has also been introduced into the Danish air force and is likely to be introduced into the Norwegian and the British air forces. Neuman's test puts the emphasis on an elaborated system of weights assigned to the various defenses and to variables like phase level and phase breadth of the defenses. His study explores these criteria and includes an extensive analysis of behavioral data.

I have strayed from a strictly scientific standpoint if, following Plato, one maintains that "techne" is not the same as "episteme." For, although much information has been collected on defense in perceptgenesis, there remains the need for supplementary evidence, both experimental in a narrower sense, and by means of case studies. Some work of the latter kind has been done by Sharma (1977). During the last few years I have also collaborated with a psychoanalyst to relate DMT data to the comprehensive information obtainable in a psychoanalysis. We have given particular attention to the mapping out of the sequential pattern of defenses (together with the vicissitudes of the self-image).

CONCLUSIONS

I am certainly aware of having glossed over many important aspects of defense in perceptgenesis in this sketchy review. For instance, I might have tried to clarify the relationships between percept-genetic organization such as "statues," "masks," or "white painting" on the one hand, and the manifestations of repression and of isolation in psychoanalysis on the other, and then proceeded to analyze in detail as many such relationships as possible. Instead, I conclude with a few comments on the conceptual status of defenses in perceptgenesis. As I noted in passing, I consider this status on a par with that of the defenses in the psychoanalytic framework proper. It has been argued that defenses are metaconstructs, that it would be false to ascribe a real existence to them or, worst of all, to reify them in terms of agencies. I agree that fallacies of the latter kind lie close at hand and should be kept in mind. But from many well-known standpoints of epistemology, even a car in the street on the verge of crushing one, or maybe some subatomic processes, may also be conceptualized as such constructs. I do not see the point of ascribing a lower degree of "reality" to, say, a fence seen between the hero and the peripheral figure in one DMT protocol than to the registration of a stream of neutrons. Nor do I find any difference in principle between concept formation based on evidence from these two fields of controlled investigation.

REFERENCES

Andersson, A. L., Fries, I., & Smith, G. J. W. Change in afterimage and spiral aftereffect serials due to anxiety caused by subliminal threat. *Scandinavian Journal of Psychology*, 1970, *11*, 7-16.

Andersson, A. L., & Weikert, C. Adult defensive organization as related to adaptive regulation of spiral aftereffect duration. *Social Behavior and Personality*, 1974, *2*, 56-75.

Fenichel, O. *The psychoanalytic theory of neurosis*. New York: Norton, 1945.

Freud, A. *The ego and the mechanisms of defense.* New York: International Universities, 1946.

Johansson, C. Reactions to noise in a town district. Lund (Mimeo.), 1968.

Johnson, M. Vad konstituerar en god soldat? (What constitutes a good soldier?). *MPI Rapport,* 1960, *44.*

Kragh, U. *The actual-genetic model of perception-personality.* Lund: Gleerup, 1955.

Kragh, U. Types of pre-cognitive defensive organization in a tachistoscopic experiment. *Journal of Projective Techniques,* 1959, *23,* 315–322.

Kragh, U. Pathogenesis in dipsomania: An illustration of the actual-genetic model of perception-personality. *Acta Psychiatrica Neurologica Scandinavica,* 1960, *35,* 207–222, 261–288, 480–497.

Kragh, U. DMT-variabler som prediktorer för flygförarlämplighet. *MPI Rapport,* 1961, *5.*

Krüger, F. Der Strukturbegriff in der Psychologie. *Bericht über den 8 Kongress für experimentelle Psychologie.* Jena: 1924.

McGinnies, E. Emotionality and perceptual defense. *Psychological Review,* 1949, *56,* 244–251.

Neuman, T. *Dimensionering och validering av percept-genesens försvarsmekanismer: En hierarkisk analys mot pilotens stressbeteende* (FOA Rapport, C 55020-H6). Stockholm, 1978.

Pötzl, O. Experimentell erregte Traumbilder in ihren Beziehungen zum indirekten Sehen. *Zeitschrift für die gesamte Neurologie und Psychiatrie,* 1917, *37,* 278–349.

Sharma, V. *Application of a percept-genetic test in a clinical setting* (LUSADG 1018). Unpublished doctoral dissertation, Department of Psychology, Lund University, 1977.

Smith, G. J. W. *Psychological studies in twin differences.* Lund: Gleerup, 1949.

Smith, G. J. W., & Danielsson, A. From open flight to symbolic and perceptual tactics: A study of defense in preschool children. *Scripta Minora Regiae Societatis Humanorum Litterarum Lundensis,* 1977, No. 3.

Smith, G. J. W., Johnson, G., & Ljunghill-Andersson, P.–E. *MCT: Metakontrasttekniken.* Stockholm: Skandinaviska Testförlaget, 1970.

Westerlundh, B. *Aggression, anxiety and defence.* Lund: Gleerup, 1976.

Zachrisson, A. Variation av stimulusmotiv: Anslutning till DM-testets metod och teori. Lund: Lund University, 1967. (Mimeo.)

V

MEANING ASSIGNMENT, RECOGNITION, AND THINKING AS PROCESSES

13

Meaning Assignment in Perception

Shulamith Kreitler and Hans Kreitler
Tel Aviv University, Tel Aviv, Israel

Our purpose in this study was to explore new resolutions to problems characteristic of the domain of perception. These problems were, first, the relations between the two traditionally distinguished phases in perception—primary perception and secondary perception (or, in classical terms, sensation versus perception)—and second, the relations between rival theoretical approaches each of which is supported by sufficient evidence to establish its validity at least to a certain degree. Major among these approaches are enrichment (Bruner) versus differentiation (Gibson), and feature detection versus template watching. Our attempt to contribute toward the resolution of these problems was based mainly on applying to the study of perception the tool of meaning analysis as developed by Kreitler and Kreitler (H. Kreitler & S. Kreitler, 1976, 1979; S. Kreitler & H. Kreitler, 1968). The considerations that have led toward such an application centered on our conception that perception involves a process of *meaning assignment*. To clarify this conception as well as to make it possible to explain our empirical procedure, it is necessary to present, however briefly, the essentials of our meaning system theory.

MEANING SYSTEM BASIS FOR OUR STUDY

Our meaning analysis studies have led us to define *meaning* as a pattern of meaning values along specific meaning dimensions anchored on some referent. The *referent* may be any input whatever, differing in its complexity, reality, and form of presentation, for example, a word, a picture, a concept, a situation, or a lifetime. *Meaning values* are units of contents, expressed through any means (e.g., through words, drawings, movements, presentation or indication of objects, etc.), that may be classified along one or more meaning dimensions. In contrast to meaning values, which are specific contents, *meaning dimensions* are general aspects of contents, or rather, basic types of potentially possible references to inputs of all kinds. For instance, function of the referent is an example of one meaning dimension; temporal qualities of the referent is another. It is evident that when one characterizes a referent such as "conference" by specifying that it serves the purpose of exchanging information and that it may last for several days, one has made use of two meaning values, the first (i.e., "it serves the purpose of exchanging information") along the meaning dimension of function, and the second (i.e., "it may last for several days") along the meaning dimension of temporal qualities.

We have defined the meaning dimensions on the basis of material collected from several hundred subjects of different ages (3 to 90), genders, professions, social classes, levels of education, and cultural backgrounds, in regard to dozens of inputs differing in variables such as complexity, temporal duration, familiarity, form of presentation, and so on. The standard task we use for the evocation of meaning is to request the subject—in a face-to-face interview or in a questionnaire—to communicate the meaning (general, personal, both, or without specification) of some input to someone else, a hypothetical other person who presumably does not know the meaning of the specific stimulus. Any verbal and nonverbal means of communication are encouraged and considered adequate. We elaborate the data by specifying units of response (viz, meaning values) and characterizing each of them in terms of the meaning dimension(s) it reflects. We have defined 21 different meaning dimensions; Appendix 1 presents the full list, both definitions, and illustrations.

Appendix 1 also presents two additional aspects of the meaning system: *forms of relation* and *types of relation* that serve to further characterize the relations between the meaning values and the corresponding referents. Because these aspects do not play a great role in the present study, we mention them only briefly. Forms of relation express the more formal aspects of the relation between meaning value and referent (that may, for example, be positive or negative), whereas types of relation define the nature of the bond between meaning value and referent (that may, for example, be attributive or metaphoric). Types of relation are basic for characterizing two kinds of meaning: the lexical interpersonally shared meaning and the personal-subjective meaning.

Our definition of meaning as a pattern of values along specific meaning dimensions is more comprehensive and systematic than any of the prevalent definitions of meaning, all of which turn out to be special cases subsumed under it. For example, the dimension of the referent's function, purpose, or role forms the core for the definition of meaning offered by Goldstein and Scheerer (1941) and Rapaport (1945, pp. 149, 403); the dimension of feelings and emotions evoked by the referent is focal in Fromm's (1951, pp. 12, 17-18) definition of meaning; whereas emphasis on the referent's manner of occurrence and operation characterizes operational definitions of meaning acclaimed by positivists such as Bridgeman (1927).

Our studies about meaning have revealed several characteristics of meaning as a system; we mention here only those that were important for the present study. First, meaning is a *stimulus-focused system.* This implies that it is a dynamic system whose qualities become manifest when it is set in operation. A necessary condition for this is the existence or establishment of a focus, namely, a referent. Second, meaning is an *open system.* This implies that more meaning values along more and more meaning dimensions may be assigned to any referent. Thus, the meaning of any referent may vary in extent, scope, and complexity along a continuum that ranges from a minimum of one meaning value along one meaning dimension to practically an indefinite number of meaning values along all of the meaning dimensions. Related to this property are the third characteristic, meaning as a *multidimensional system*, and the fourth characteristic, meaning as a *selectional system.* The characteristic of multidimensionality is partly a product of the fact that meaning as an open system is potentially subject to indefinite elaborations. In contrast, the selectional characteristic limits the extent of elaborations that are potentially possible to those in accordance with the demand characteristics of the referent and the situation in which it is embedded and also in accordance with the person's personality features and subjective preferences and tendencies. One product of the selectional property is the two types of meaning, lexical and personal. Selectivity involves not only exclusion of certain aspects of the meaning system but regulation of the sequence in which various parts occur.

In a series of experiments, we have applied this system of meaning to the study of major cognitive processes, such as problem solving, memory, and abstraction, and have shown, for example, that the nature and number of meaning dimensions available to a person are significantly related to the kind of concepts he or she forms, to the ability to think in an analogical manner, and to the capacity to overcome functional fixedness (S. Kreitler, Arnon, & H. Kreitler, 1978; S. Kreitler, Goldstein, & H. Kreitler, 1978; S. Kreitler & H. Kreitler, in press). Moreover, our findings are not merely correlational; we have also shown that changing meaning produces predictable effects in cognitive functioning. For example, increasing the number of meaning dimensions available to a person such as a retarded (imbecile) child or a brain-damaged aphasic patient improves level of comprehension, generalization, memorizing, and problem solving in the domains of contents subsumed under the trained meaning dimensions (H. Kreitler & S. Kreitler, 1977).

These and other studies of the same kind support the conclusion that meaning is a factor of major significance in cognition, so much so that we have defined *cognition* itself as a meaning-processing system (H. Kreitler & S. Kreitler, 1976, p. 39). Perception is an integral part of cognition. Hence, our definition of the system of cognition requires a renewed clarification of the role of perception within it: *Perception* is that part or stage or subsystem of cognition that deals with the elaboration of inputs. As we have shown (H. Kreitler & S. Kreitler, 1976, Chap. 3), elaboration of inputs involves the assignment of meaning to them. Because meaning assignment may recur at any stage of coping with cognitive contents (for example, in the course of problem solving, meaning transformations, etc.), perception could be considered as a process of dealing with the first stages of meaning assignment to external or internal inputs; and this was the general hypothesis underlying our study. In view of the above-mentioned characteristics of the system of meaning, we expected meaning assignment that occurs within the framework of perception to be a sequential process (viz, meaning as an open system), to consist in the sequential specification of several meaning dimensions to the referent, and to be subject to selectivity. We designed the study to clarify these and other particular features of meaning assignment in and through perception.

METHOD

Subjects

Study participants were 50 normal subjects and 25 schizophrenics. They were of both genders, 16 to 32 years old, with a minimum of 10 years of schooling. They were partly (42 of the normal subjects, 21 of the schizophrenics) of Western (European or American) and partly of Middle-Eastern or North African cultural background. In addition, there were 10 more normal subjects, of the same age and background as the other subjects, to whom only certain stimuli [i.e., the Smock (1955) series] were administered.

Apparatus and Stimuli

For projecting the stimuli to the subjects, we used a 35-mm slide projector with a lens of 100-mm focal length and an aperture of 2.8. In front of the lens we placed an ILEX Number 3 Universal Shutter. To be able to study the microgenetic process, it was necessary to produce a sequence of exposure values (EVs) that would form at least an approximate interval scale. We created such a sequence by manipulating the exposure time and the aperture of the lens; and as Table 13.1 shows, each degree of EV is defined in terms of these two factors, exposure time being either 50, 75, or 100 msec and aperture of the lens being 1 of the 12 degrees of aperture. Pretests showed that some stimuli are more easily identified than others, however, thus reducing the number of differentiable EVs we could produce by manipulating only exposure time and aperture. To keep the number of EVs constant at 10 even for stimuli that were relatively easily identifiable (i.e., mainly words and drawings of objects), we added a third factor, focal sharpness—either full sharpness (produced by adjusting the lens at maximum sharpness of the image), partly reduced sharpness (produced by bringing the lens 6 mm nearer to the slide through $1\frac{1}{4}$ turns inward), and greatly reduced sharpness (produced by bringing the lens 9 mm nearer to the slide through $2\frac{1}{2}$ turns inward).

Manipulating exposure time, aperture size, and focal sharpness, we were able to produce three different EV interval scales: the scale of Series 1, the scale of Series 2, and the scale of Series 3. In each of the three scales, we defined *sequential steps* as intervals reflecting half the amount of light between one degree of EV and the preceding degree of EV. We used the EV scale of Series 1 for the least easily identified stimuli, the EV scale of Series 2 for stimuli of medium difficulty, and the EV scale of Series 3 for the most easily identified stimuli (i.e., only words). For the sake of orientation, it should be mentioned that the EV characteristic of threshold perception was around 10.16 for Series 1; 12.16 for Series 2 and 3 (Table 13.1). Thus in each series we had five EV steps below threshold and four EV steps above. In the experiment proper, each stimulus was projected under conditions of one single EV scale, as determined before the experiment on the basis of pretests.

For each subject we used a set of 20 stimuli, of which there were two parallel sets used interchangeably to increase the range of generalization of the findings. For the same reason we chose stimuli that were highly heterogeneous in contents (objects, humans, or geometric figures), in color (absent, present; in single color or in many colors), style (depiction of movement or complexity), and form of presentation (drawings, photographs, etc.). Appendix 2 gives the stimuli along with their characterization in terms of several binary features, as determined by a consensus of 20 independent judges.

The 40 stimuli actually used in the study were selected from an original set of 120 on the basis of two criteria: (a) great variation in contents and structure (so as to increase the range of generalization of the findings) and (b) intermediate difficulty in identification (so as to enable the microgenetic study by projecting the stimuli under conditions of 10 increasing EVs). Criterion a was attained by selecting stimuli that differed from each other in color, movement, presentation of common objects, depiction of human beings, complexity (as determined by the number of items and their organization), origin of the stimulus (a photograph out of a magazine, a painting, etc.), form (drawing or photograph), and function (words, objects, or forms). Criterion b was attained by selecting, on the basis of

Table 13.1 Degree and description of exposure values in the three series of stimuli

Number of exposures	Series 1: full focal sharpness			Series 2: partly reduced sharpness			Series 3: greatly reduced sharpness		
	Aperture (mm)	Exposure time (msec)	EV	Aperture (mm)	Exposure time (msec)	EV	Aperture (mm)	Exposure time (msec)	EV
1	Minimum	100	15.66	Minimum	100	15.66	Minimum	100	15.66
2	11	100	13.66	16	100	14.66	16	100	14.66
3	8–5.6	100	12.16	11	100	13.66	11	100	13.66
4	5.6–4	100	11.16	11–8	100	13.16	11–8	100	13.16
5	5.6–4	100	10.66	8	100	12.66	8	100	12.66
6	4	75	10.16	8–5.6	100	12.16	8–5.6	100	12.16
7	4–2.8	75	9.66	8–5.6	75	11.66	8–5.6	75	11.66
8	4–2.8	75	9.16	5.6	75	11.16	5.6	75	11.16
9	2.8	50	8.66	5.6–4	50	10.16	5.6–4	50	10.16
10	2.8–2	50	8.16	4	50	9.66	4	50	9.66

Note. Numbers given as ranges indicate a midposition between these numbers.

pretests with 40 subjects, those stimuli that, when projected under conditions of increasing EVs, elicited correct identification of 2 or 3 items in the fifth, sixth, or seventh projection.

In addition to these stimuli, we also used the five series of stimuli prepared by Smock (1955).

Design and Procedure

Each subject was presented 20 stimuli. Each stimulus was projected wholly, 10 times, in an increasing scale of EVs. Hence, the microgenetic procedure we used in this main part of the experiment was hologenic.

The experiment was conducted in individual sessions held in a dark room, the stimuli projected on a white screen. The projector was placed on a low table 1.20 m high. The distance between the subject and the screen was 2.50 m; between the lens and the screen, 2.00 m. The size of the projected image on the screen was 50 by 80 cm. A bar on the screen indicated the upper boundary of the image. In front of the subject, there were a microphone and an undisguised tape recorder. Before each projection there was a warning signal—a click. The interval between successive exposures varied somewhat because of differences in the duration of the subjects' responses but was, on the average, 4 sec. The subject's task was to report verbally as completely and as early as possible anything she or he perceived. The atmosphere was highly permissive and also encouraged guessing, free associations, and the expression of mere hunches.

For the sake of increasing the range of generalization of the findings, we used three experimental conditions: neutral, reward, and punishment. In the neutral condition, only the standard instructions described above were given to the subjects. In the reward condition, the standard instructions were administered plus the promise of a reward (i.e., a ticket for a full-length scientific film, or a guided tour of the psychology laboratories) for subjects who described a greater number of perceived items earlier in the sequence, relative to our presumed "norms." In the punishment condition, the standard instructions were administered plus the threat of a punishment for subjects who did not describe a sufficient number of perceived items early enough in the sequence, again relative to our presumed "norms." The threatened punishment was the requirement to participate later in the second part of the experiment, which was described as particularly long, complicated, and highly unpleasant.

As we have mentioned, there were 10 additional subjects, to whom the Smock stimuli were administered. The administration of these stimuli was nonhologenic (i.e., the sequentially projected stimuli included increasingly more items) and followed strictly the procedures described by Smock (1955). Projection time of each stimulus was .1 sec.

The data were the verbal responses of the subjects, which we elaborated essentially in terms of our meaning system; that is, we noted the meaning dimensions and the forms and types of relation that characterized each unit of response given by a subject.

In addition to participating in the microgenetic session, each subject received— either two months earlier or two months later—a standard meaning questionnaire administered in written form and including as stimuli 11 words (denoting abstract conceptions, concrete objects, verbs, nouns, adjectives, adverbs, and prepositions), three sentences, two paragraphs, and two drawings. Elaborating the responses of the subjects to the questionnaire provided information about the meaning dimensions and the forms and types of relation used regularly by each subject in communicating meaning. The questionnaire was pretested for reliability (test-retest = .98, interjudge = .99) on a sample of 350 subjects.

RESULTS

We present here only that part of the analyses of the data that contributes directly to clarification of the process of meaning assignment in perception. Furthermore, we concentrate on those aspects of the findings that *do not* vary across the three experimental conditions, different groups of subjects, kinds of stimuli, and microgenetic procedures. (The various differences we found in the analyses—as, for example, between normal subjects and schizophrenics in regard to the stage in which a referent is formulated, or between subjects who used the exemplifying-illustrative type of relation frequently and those who used it rarely in regard to the amount of meaning elaboration—are dealt with in another framework, i.e., S. Kreitler & H. Kreitler, in press.) For the sake of clarity, the findings are presented in terms of phases.

First Phase

The most remarkable feature of the first phase of microgenetic perception is the homogeneity of the reported meaning values. All subjects (100%) perceived, in the first or the second or—at the latest—in the third projection, meaning values along at least two of the following three meaning dimensions: the sensory-qualities subdimension brightness (e.g., bright, dark, black, white, or gray), locational qualities (e.g., up, down, or to the right), and quantity (e.g., one or two parts). Some subjects reported these meaning values immediately; others delayed the report for one or two projections. Some subjects reported only one of these meaning values; others, two or three. Some subjects also reported several meaning values along any one or more of these dimensions; others reported only a single meaning value. But by the third projection all subjects had reported meaning values along at least two of these three meaning dimensions. Moreover, only in 6% of the cases (in 14 projections out of the total of 225, i.e., 75 subjects times 3 projections each) did subjects report in the first three projections meaning values along dimensions other than these.

In addition to reporting meaning values in the first phase, subjects also stated a referent. At this stage, the referent was mostly (in 87% of the reports) general, such as a picture, a thing, something, a form, or a blob (all formulations that seem to be stylistic variations denoting the same thing). By the end of the third projection, 43 subjects (i.e., 86% of the total of 50 normal subjects) had formulated a referent. Some did so in the first projection; others delayed until the second or third. Table 13.2 shows that the projection in which a referent was stated depended on the salience of the meaning dimension of contextual allocation in the subject's meaning questionnaire. Subjects who used this dimension frequently stated a referent in the first projection, whereas subjects who did not use this dimension frequently stated a referent only somewhat later, in the second or third projection.

Thus there are two distinct but probably interdependent major lines of develop-

Table 13.2   Relation of frequency of meaning dimension contextual allocation
to when referent is formulated

Frequency of contextual allocation[a]	Referent formulated by number of normal subjects	
	Projection 1	Projections 2 or 3
High	17	2
Low	4	20

[a]"High" and "low" denote frequencies above or below the group median.
$X^2 = 19.68$.
$p < .001$.

ment: one concerning meaning values, and one concerning the referent. Concerning meaning values, the next step consists mainly in perceiving new meaning values along further meaning dimensions. These are subdimensions of sensory qualities: form (e.g., square or having a round contour) and structure (e.g., having two symmetrical parts). Meaning values along these two dimensions occurred in sequence after the former meaning dimensions in 73% of our cases (in the rest, they occurred either earlier or later). There is also further specification of the previous meaning values, and this occurs by adding to the previous meaning values further meaning values along the same meaning dimensions. For example, if the previous meaning value was "bottom," the more specific meaning value is "bottom somewhat to the right," which results from conjoining one meaning value of location ("bottom") with another meaning value of location ("to the right"). Other examples of further specification are: "Square" becomes "a square with one rounded corner," or "gray" is replaced by "gray with whitish spots."

In the next one or two projections, the same principle is repeated: the subject grasps new meaning values along further meaning dimensions and becomes more specific about previous meaning values. The new meaning dimensions are size (e.g., big, small) and the sensory-qualities subdimension color (e.g., in colors, no colors). Their occurrence in the sequence after form and structure was characteristic of 69% of our cases. Further specification of previous meaning values arises from grasping addition meaning values along the meaning dimensions. For example, the meaning value "two symmetrical parts" along the meaning dimension of structure turns into "two symmetrical parts, but on the right there is something that is not on the left."

In the meantime the referent becomes more particular. Two things are important about this particularization of the referent. One is that the particularization occurs by degrees. For example, here is a series of increasingly particular referents in a sequence of projections: something, a picture, not an animal, a figure, a human figure, a man. It is noteworthy that subjects gradually narrow down the domain of application of the referent until they reach a label that applies to a restricted normally acceptable class of things. In the first five projections, 68% of referent presentations were stepwise and included three steps. Another 15% included two steps, but instead of being carried further, they were abandoned and exchanged for another referent.

This brings us to the second important characteristic of reporting the referent: The successive stages are mostly stated as hypotheses. Let us emphasize: The by-now-famous cycle of hypothesis statement, hypothesis check, and hypothesis confirmation or disconfirmation applies almost exclusively to the referent and not to meaning values. In 87% of all cases of stating a referent in this first phase, there occurred expressions indicating the hypothetical status of the referent (e.g., perhaps, I assume, it could be, it seems to me, I bet that, etc.). Only 2% of the meaning values in this phase were thus qualified.

The first phase ends when the referent has been identified through some label specific enough to qualify as an identification tag (usually, it is a category name) but general enough to require further specification and thus trigger the further perception of meaning values. When a subject finds no adequate label, that is, when his or her hypothesis concerning the referent has been disconfirmed, he or she invariably goes back to the original perceptual activity characteristic of Phase 1: to meaning values along the meaning dimensions of sensory qualities (subdimension brightness), locational qualities, quantity, sensory qualities (subdimension form), and structure.

Incidentally, there are indications, not yet fully elaborated, that abandoning a referent is not an all-or-nothing phenomenon but one that takes place in several steps in a characteristic sequence. To illustrate, when gradually specifying the referent in Phase 1, a subject said: "Something on a background, a kind of drawing, perhaps a plan, a drawing of some machine." From this point on she started to dismantle the referent, indicating characteristically the following steps: "not a drawing for a machine; it could hardly be a plan; it is not even a drawing"; then finally, "I see something, a kind of . . . I don't know what on a background." Cases such as this give rise to the idea that not only is confirmation a gradual process but so is disconfirmation.

Second Phase

In most cases, the subjects decide on some referent. When a subject has settled on a label, a new phase begins. We call it a new phase because the meaning values that are reported from this point on depend to a large extent on the referent label that has just been established. As in the first phase, there is regularity in the reported meaning values; but in this phase, the meaning values differ depending on whether the referent is human or nonhuman. If it is human, then the next meaning values to be reported are, first, along the meaning dimension of state, then along the meaning dimension of action. The occurrence of these meaning values at this point in the perceptual process was characteristic of 85% of our subjects. Moreover, the sequence from state to action is almost perfect; we found it in 94% of the cases. This sequence is particularly interesting because it involves passing from a relatively static description to a more dynamic one, from a relatively objective statement to an interpretation. A subject may for instance say: "A person sitting" and then elaborate along the meaning dimension of action: "He is reading some kind of book." In rare cases we got evidence for the active search for meaning values along these meaning dimensions. One subject said: "There is a man there; I cannot say what he is doing." If, however, the label indicates a nonhuman object, then the stated meaning values differ, concentrating predominantly on structure (as in 48% of our cases).

In the second phase, the referent also undergoes a particularization. Instead of "a human figure" the subject reports "a man," then "a woman and a man." Particularization thus takes the form either of increased characterization of the referent (e.g., a man with a beard) or of increased differentiation in describing it (e.g., a man and a woman). In both cases, particularization occurs when the referent incorporates, as it were, new meaning values. However it may be, at the end of Phase 2 the subject has reported a unit that includes a relatively particularized referent involved in action or having a definite structure.

Third Phase

In the third phase, the elaboration of meaning values and referents continues, but the regularity is of a completely different kind. The subject goes on reporting meaning values, but they differ from one subject to another, because—and this is the main point—in the third phase, subjects report meaning values along individually characteristic meaning dimensions. If a dominant meaning dimension in a subject's meaning communications is antecedents and causes, that subject will report that the perceived human referent is doing something because of this or that reason; if, on the other hand, a dominant meaning dimension is range of inclusion, a subject will say that the perceived object referent has this or that part. For 95% of the subjects, one of their three most frequently used meaning dimensions on the questionnaire showed up in the third phase of their microgenetic elaborations. The biserial correlation between the frequency of the dominant meaning dimensions in a person's meaning questionnaire and the dichotomous variable of occurrence or nonoccurrence of the same meaning dimensions in Phase 3 was .93.

This is the main characteristic of Phase 3. Two further points should be added; one concerns meaning values. It may happen, of course, that the meaning dimensions prominent in a subject's meaning questionnaire are those that have already occurred earlier in the sequence, such as structure, color, location, and size. In these cases, we have observed that the subject again elaborates meaning values along these dimensions but with a difference: The meaning values are, as it were, conceptualized; they occur with a rationale and are more specific and sharply delineated, indeed, are more distinctly separated from other meaning values in the same or other dimensions than those reported earlier in the sequence.

The other point concerns the multiplicity of referents. Because in the course of the microgenetic sequence further referents may have been perceived and elaborated, the meaning values added in the third phase serve not merely to elaborate the original referent but if possible to relate the original referent to the additional referents. Referents are often interrelated by turning one referent into a meaning value, or part of a meaning value, of another referent. For example, if one referent is "a man approaching something," and if the other referent turns out to be "a boy," the subject may combine them into "a man approaching a boy" (the boy is then a meaning value along the dimension range of application).

The result of interrelating referents is often a whole scene or story that functions henceforth as the referent for further meaning elaborations. For example, one subject combined the two referents "a girl walking to the back of the picture" and "an airplane" by saying: "The girl is about to leave in the airplane." To this the subject added: "She is going to see a person she loves. But she is sad because the period of longing is over." Characteristically, the meaning elaborations of the expanded referent have less and less to do with the given perceptual cues.

CONCLUSIONS

The general hypothesis that perception involves meaning assignment led us to this analysis of meaning processes in microgenetic sequences. Our analysis has provided several insights into the nature of meaning assignment in the framework of perception:

1. Meaning values and referent are distinct entities in the process of perception, a conclusion based on two types of findings: the course of their development and the manner in which they undergo their different developments. We saw that meaning values develop by following each other in a constant sequence of meaning dimensions. This leads to a *rule-determined accumulation* of meaning values. We also saw that along the same dimension, meaning values undergo further specification through the addition of further meaning values and their conjoining to the same referent. Finally, we noted that the same meaning dimensions may recur in initial and later phases, but their meaning values differ in level of conceptualization. Incidentally, this latter process of conceptualization is akin to the transition from intuitive concepts to operationalized concepts postulated by Piaget, and it has actually been observed in several contexts. Gelman (1972), for example, showed that, developmentally, estimators precede number concepts. In sum, meaning values are accumulated by evocation in a specific dimensional sequence, further specified by conjoining, and conceptualized by rationalizing.

In contrast, a referent is subjected to two processes; it undergoes a particularization and then it undergoes an increase in scope or complexity. The particularization leads from an indefinite title to the label of a commonly acceptable category. This occurs by integrating meaning values under a kind of pressure akin or identical to the pressure that presumably underlies the formation of gestalts. The gestaltlike integration follows the famous cycle of hypothesis testing. Then, the increase in scope or complexity occurs through adding to the referent one or more meaning values that turn into an integral part of the referent.

The distinctness of referent and meaning values especially in the first phases of the perceptual process may have important but hitherto unexplored implications for the theory of perception. For instance, it is plausible to assume that, if the OR (orienting response) appears, its occurrence is affected not by further meaning values but by the development in grasping or constructing the referent. Accordingly, inasmuch as the OR is a kind of "what-is-it?" reaction (H. Kreitler & S. Kreitler, 1976, Chap 3), the referent forms the adequate type of answer to it. Hence, the OR may be expected to occur whenever the referent is not at all, or only tentatively, established and to be extinguished when the referent is firmly established for the perceiver.

2. The cycle of hypothesis testing (which includes in Bruner's terms "primitive categorization," i.e., statement of a hypothesis, "cue search," "confirmation check," and "confirmation completion") is not a general process in perception as claimed by Bruner (1957; Bruner & Klein, 1960) and so many others (Neisser, 1976; Vernon, 1955). It applies mainly to the establishment of the referent but does not apply to the meaning values, at least not in the first and second phases.

3. Perception appears to be the product of a dialectical interaction between meaning values and the referent. The dialectical process consists of meaning values and referent codetermining and coactivating each other's development. As noted, the perception of meaning values precedes or coincides with the emergence of a

referent. The referent, in its turn, is an anchor point that, owing to its function, stands in need of further elaboration and thus acts like a force that stimulates the perception of further meaning values. The addition of meaning values along specific dimensions enables the gradual particularization of the initially indefinite referent. The more particular the referent becomes, the more specific becomes its function as a force for generating meaning value in the meaning-elaboration process. If initially it acted mainly as a wide-spectrum meaning-expanding force stimulating the accumulation of meaning values, it has now become a vector operating in a more particular region. Thus Bruner (1957) and others who speak of the label as producing a complete inhibition against grasping cues contradicting the label were probably mistaken. Once the referent has been identified by a label, there is no further interest in meaning values confirming or disconfirming the label; rather, there is a shift toward meaning values expanding the referent's meaning. Of course the referent codetermines which meaning values will be grasped. The determination is, however, not in regard to specific meaning values but only in regard to particular meaning dimensions. We call perception a dialectical process because the polarity between referent and meaning values is preserved throughout, although both the meaning values and the referent change in nature, scope, and complexity.

In passing, we may suggest that a similar dialectical process between the referent and meaning values takes place while a person uses language for expression, that is, forms phrases and sentences. But in speech, referents often tend to shift and interact more than in perception, so that the dialectical process may not always evolve quite so fully.

4. Our findings show distinct phases in the processes of meaning assignment and meaning elaboration in perception. The transitions from one phase to the next are predictable and regular; yet they are not automatic but depend on the dynamics of meaning elaboration. Because the phases consist of meaning assignment, the nature and scope of the meanings assigned in one phase determine the passage to the next. For example, if a subject did not succeed in labeling the referent by the name of some category, she or he would invariably switch to the beginning of Phase 1 instead of proceeding to Phase 2. Then again, as long as no satisfactory meaning values of state and action were assigned to a sufficiently particularized human referent, the subject would not proceed to the individually shaped meaning elaboration of Phase 3. This explains why in many cases the subjects did not provide Phase 3 material or why in the case of objects, which are more easily particularized, Phase 2 was very short. In contrast, in the case of letters and words, there is no context for Phase 3 elaboration; and thus in the absence of particular stimulation, it does not occur.

5. Our findings lend support to the two rival theories of perception: *feature detection* and *template matching*. Both theories seem to be correct, but each applies in a different domain. Feature-detection theory applies to meaning values— or attributes, sense impressions, and so forth, as they have variously been named in the field of perception (Gibson, 1950; Wallach, 1949). In contrast, the template-matching theory applies to the referent and describes the process of comparing the referent with referents (or "schemes," "schemata," "things," "objects," etc., as they have been called in perception) that either are stored in memory or are constructed in an ad hoc manner and serve as templates. It is noteworthy that the suggested integration resolves the major difficulties confronting each of the theories. Thus, the feature-detection approach has had to struggle with the issue of "constructing" a referent out of the discrete extracted features, whereas the

template-matching approach has had to devise satisfactory answers to the major criticisms leveled against it, namely, that the potentially available number of templates is too limited to fit all possible sense impressions and that perfect matching is impossible. Ineeed, these criticisms turn into advantages when applied to the referent.

6. Our findings allow the integration of the approaches supported by Bruner (1957) and the New Look, on the one hand, and by Gibson (1950, 1966) and the objectivists, on the other hand. The integration is straightforward. The objectivists are no doubt right about the first two phases of perception; the subjectivists and all those who uphold the impact of personality, motives, and values on perception are probably right about the third phase of perception. (Our use of the term *probably* is intended to convey a certain reservation: They are right insofar as motives, personality traits, and so forth can be shown to have shaped a person's meanings.) If our suggested integration is valid, then it also reconciles the rift between enrichment (Bruner) and differentiation (Gibson) in secondary perception. The enrichment is correct in regard to the referent, the differentiation in regard to meaning values.

7. The view that perception is a process of meaning assignment indicates a new approach to the ubiquitous distinction between primary and secondary perception. Briefly, primary perception—following Anderson (1975), Lindsay and Norman (1977), and others—deals with analyzing features of brightness, color, slope, length, and motion, and it results in a holistic analogue percept (Anderson, 1975, p. 31); secondary perception brings about an increase in the number of percepts, in the complexity and distinctness of each, and in their interrelations by means of interpretation and going beyond the information given (Anderson, 1975, Chap. 3). Our findings indicate that, instead of viewing primary and secondary perception as distinct kinds of perception, they should be regarded as two phases along one and the same continuum. Not surprisingly, primary perception overlaps with Phase 1, and secondary perception with Phases 2 and 3. The difference between primary and secondary perception is reduced, then, to the kind of meaning dimensions that occur in each phase, the kind of referent that plays a role in each, and the nature of meaning values that may occur in one phase or the other. In all three respects, there is a progression in the elaboration of meaning. The progression in all three respects cannot be subsumed under any integrating label other than a progression in meaning. Thus, that which binds together primary and secondary perception is the notion of perception as a process of meaning assignment. Moreover, when further extended, this notion allows also for bridging the gap between so-called perception and *conception.* The differences may now be more precisely analyzed in terms of meaning values, referent, and meaning dimensions.

8. Finally, one further remark concerning the remarkable regularity in the sequence of meaning dimensions in Phases 1 and 2: There is sufficient ontogenetic and phylogenetic evidence to support at least parts of the sequence and hence show that it is not spurious or artifactual. For example, it has been found microgenetically that perception of intensity, size, and location precedes perception of shapes (Freeman, 1929), that perception of brightness precedes pattern perception (Spencer, 1969) and shape perception (Forgus & Malamed, 1976). Physiological studies have shown that brightness, black-and-white color, and slope perception precede perception of color (Minsky, 1970; Murch, 1972). Ontogenetically, too, differences in brightness, size, and location have been shown to be perceived

earlier than form and color (Gibson, 1966). Phylogenetic evidence to the same effect could also be adduced (Anderson, 1975). Therefore, the regularity in sequence that we have described seems worthy of being checked physiologically in terms of the brain structures involved sequentially in perception and, as mentioned, in terms of the impact it may have on evoking the OR. Indeed, it may not be accidental that precisely the study of meaning may furnish long-missing cues for unraveling the elusive links between the psychological and physiological levels.

APPENDIX 1: THE SYSTEM OF MEANING

Meaning Dimensions

1. *Contextual allocation and classification* of the referent: the superordinate concept of system of items or relations to which the referent belongs, or the concept of abstract superordinate structure of which it forms a part, as "God" belongs to religion and "eye" is a part of the body.

2. *Range of inclusion* of the referent: the items or parts that constitute the referent or members of the class it designates, as "art" includes painting, music, dance, and so on and as "body" includes head, shoulders, feet, and so on.

3. *Function, purpose, or role* of the referent: the uses to which the referent may be and is usually put; for example, "eating" functions as an excuse for going on a diet; a "watch" shows the time.

4. *Action(s) and potentialities for action* of the referent: actions that the referent does, could do, or which others do with it or to it, and that are not intended to represent its function or role; for example, "man" moves, breathes, consumes, reproduces, and kills.

5. *Manner of occurrence or operation* of the referent: the stages, processes, acts, instruments, means, organs, and so forth involved in the occurrence or operation of the referent, that is, which make it possible or of which its operation consists; for example, "to walk" entails first lifting one leg, then placing it, and so on.

6. *Antecedents and causes* of the referent's existence, occurrence, or operation: the necessary or sufficient conditions for the referent's existence, occurrence, or operation, or the circumstances under which it occurs, as "anger" is provoked by thinking of one's opponent's success and as "but" reflects the impossibility of avoiding the dispensable reservation.

7. *Consequences and results* of the referent's existence, occurrence, or operation: consequences, results, effects, and so on that derive directly or indirectly from the referent's existence, occurrence, or operation or at least take place after the referent's occurrence but do not imply the referent's function or purpose, as "and" can lead to a long sentence and "love" can end in parting, pregnancy.

8. *Domain of application* of the referent: the items (people, objects, events, and so forth) to which the referent usually is or can be applied, the items with which it interacts in some sense or that are affected through it, as "beautiful" is applied to women and the weather or as "eating" affects meat or fruit.

9. *What the referent consists of:* the material out of which the referent is made, as "sea" consists of oxygen and hydrogen atoms and as "chair" is made of wood.

10. *Structure* of the referent: the interrelations of the subparts, the organization and complexity of the material or the system variables on the molar level or

at any submolar level, as, for example, "personality" reflects the ego on top, the id below, the superego clinging around.

11. *State and possible changes in state* of the referent: the actual, potential, or possible state of the referent at any time, and changes that could occur in this state under specified or unspecified conditions, as "God" exists and as "water" evaporates in heat, freezes in cold, but cannot be broken.

12. *Weight and mass* of the referent, measured units or as an estimate; for example, "this rock" is heavy, weighs 20 lb.

13. *Dimensionality and dimensions* of the referent: indication of the size of the referent, and of the number or measures of its dimensions, and so on, for example, "this cube" is a three-dimensional body, 4 in high.

14. *Quantity* of the referent, expressed in measured units or as an estimate, for instance, "world," one of a kind.

15. *Location* of the referent: the usual place, address, or domain in which the referent exists or occurs, relative to other objects or to a fixed reference system, as a "book" is usually found in libraries.

16. *Temporal qualities* of the referent: the time at which the referent exists or existed; the frequency, duration, timeliness, durability, and so on of its occurrence, its age, and so on, as "sadness" has always existed.

17. *Possession and belongingness* of the referent: indication of the referent's actual or potential possessions, to whom or to what the referent belongs or may belong, as "land" may be owned by a government.

18. *Development* of the referent: the ontogenetic or phylogenetic development of the referent; its historical forerunners, personal history, and origins; and its expected or possible development in the future; for example, a "psychologist" is a person who after graduating from high school studied at a university, and so forth, and "buying" is the modern version of exchange, perhaps to be replaced in the future by just taking what one needs.

19. *Sensations the referent has or evokes:* sensory qualities that characterize the referent (i.e., sensations it evokes) or that it has itself, the sensations may be sub-divided into subdimensions referring to *form and shape, brightness, color, nature of surface* (e.g., transparent, decorated), *sound, taste, odor, tactile-kinesthetic qualities, temperature,* and *internal stimulation* (e.g., pain), as a "dog's nose" is black, cold, and wet.

20. *Feelings and emotions the referent has or evokes:* emotional responses that the referent has or that it evokes in others; a "monster," for example, frightens people and probably enjoys it.

21. *Judgments, opinions, and values the referent has or evokes:* the referent's attitudes and the attitudes it evokes in others, including evaluation and judgments of importance; for example, "law" may evoke the view that most of it is bad or unjust, and the rest is superfluous or unenforced.

Form of Relation between Meaning Value and Referent

1. *Assertion* (i.e., positive), as in the statement "Yoga"—it is an Indian discipline.

2. *Denial* (i.e., negative), as in the statement "Yoga"—it is not a religion.

3. *Conjunctive* (i.e., either of two meaning values or both may be related to the referent) as in "Animal"—it preserves itself and its species.

4. *Disjunctive* (i.e., either of two meaning values but *not* both may be related to the referent), as in "Animal"—it is either alive or dead.

Types of Relation between Meaning Value and Referent

1. *The attributive relation,* which consists in specifying certain attributes that are assigned the role of qualities of the referent. The two main forms of the attributive relation are:

   a. *Substance-quality relation,* which is based on assigning to the referent the role of a substance and to the meaning values the role of properties of the substance (e.g., "man"–beautiful, tall, etc.).

   b. *Actional relation,* which is based on assigning to the referent the role of "doer" that causes, brings about, produces, effects, and so forth certain actions or effects stated in the meaning values (e.g., "man" builds houses, pollutes the atmosphere).

2. *The comparative relation,* which consists in stating meaning values related to the referent through the intermediation of another meaning value or stimulus. The four major forms of the comparative relation are:

   a. *Similarity,* which includes identity of synonymy, equivalence, match, and similarity in some specified or unspecified sense (e.g., "moon" is like the earth; "justice" is similar to truth in that both do not exist).

   b. *Dissimilarity,* which includes difference, mismatch, contradiction, contrast, reversal, inversion, and antonymy (e.g., "day" is the contrast of night).

   c. *Complementariness,* which includes also reciprocity (e.g., "husband" has a wife, "wife" has a husband; "parent" has a child, "child" has a parent).

   d. *Relational* relation, which consists in a comparison with some other meaning value or stimulus that explicitly or implicitly serves as a standard (e.g., "intelligent" signifies wiser than the average person).

3. *The exemplifying-illustrative relation,* which consists in stating meaning values of the most diverse meaning dimensions in the form of examples. The most frequent forms of the exemplifying-illustrative relation are:

   a. *Exemplifying instance,* which presents the meaning value through an object, a phenomenon, an event, an animal, or a person (e.g., "evil" as war).

   b. *Exemplifying situation,* which presents the meaning value through a situation, which is a sort of picture that is richer than an exemplifying instance, may include some activity, and has duration, but lacks dynamism and development (e.g., "motherhood"–a woman with a baby in her arms).

   c. *Exemplifying scene,* which presents the meaning value through an unfolding situation or story, structured in a scenodramatic manner ("e.g., 'despair'–a man wanders in the desert, looking for water. Suddenly it seems to him that the desert ends behind the near hill . . . he hears a human voice, he feels a cool hand . . . he falls down on a shrub of thorns, he is wounded, he is too thirsty to cry") (S. Kreitler & H. Kreitler, 1968, p. 317).

4. *The metaphoric-symbolic relation,* which consists in stating meaning values that do not belong strictly to the referent's conventional spheres of connotatation or denotation but are related to the referent or to one of its aspects in a mediated bond. The three major forms of the metaphoric-symbolic relation are:

   a. *Interpretation,* which consists in presenting a general interpretation of the referent or any one of its aspects, stated in terms of abstractions (e.g., "happiness": that which can never be found in the found).

b. *Metaphor,* which consists in presenting an image illustrating the referent or any one of its aspects whereby the illustrative function is mediated through an interpretation (e.g., "life": a colored handkerchief that blazes for a second and disappears in the hand of a magician).

c. *Symbol,* which consists in presenting a metaphoric image that illustrates at least two contrasting aspects of the referent and resolves this contrast at the level of the image (e.g., "wisdom": a "sunny" eye or an "eyelike" sun—the drawing of an eye with rays issuing from its iris, for wisdom is both absorption from the outside, and irradiation from the inside).

APPENDIX 2: THE STIMULI

Stimulus	Color	Movement	Familiar objects	Humans	Complexity	Art
Series 1						
1. Painting by Kandinsky (line composition)	0	0	0	0	1	1
2. Photograph of a child leaving home	1	1	1	1	1	0
3. Painting by Kandinsky (line composition)	1	0	0	0	1	1
4. Photograph of people sitting and eating	0	1	1	1	1	0
5. Painting by Kandinsky (line composition)	1	0	0	0	1	1
6. Photograph of a woman taking a snapshot of a monkey	1	1	1	1	1	0
7. Painting by Klee	0	1	1	0	1	1
8. Photograph of children running on the seashore	0	1	1	1	1	0
9. Drawing of a guitar	1	0	1	0	0	0
10. Drawing of a candle	1	0	1	0	0	0
11. Drawing of a geometric figure (six-sided polygon)	0	0	0	0	0	0
12. Drawing of an umbrella	0	0	1	0	0	0
13. Drawing of a long object within a circle	1	0	0	0	1	0
14. Drawing of a chick coming out of an egg	0	1	1	0	1	0
15. Drawing of children quarreling	0	1	1	1	1	0
16. Drawing of a revolver	0	0	1	0	0	0
17–20. Hebrew words, each of 4 syllables						

APPENDIX 2: THE STIMULI (Continued)

Stimulus	Color	Movement	Familiar objects	Humans	Complexity	Art
Series 2						
1. Photograph of children in a classroom	0	1	1	1	1	0
2. Painting of forms that resemble a camp of tents	1	0	1	0	1	1
3. Photograph of people on the seashore, with a ship in the background	1	1	1	1	1	0
4. Photograph of a couple dancing on a ship	1	1	1	1	1	0
5. Painting by Klee (aqueducts)	1	1	0	0	1	1
6. Photograph of a couple by a tree	0	1	1	1	1	0
7. Modern painting	1	0	0	0	1	1
8. Painting by Klee (perspectives)	0	0	0	0	1	1
9. Drawing of a fish	1	0	1	0	0	0
10. Drawing of geometric figures	0	0	0	0	1	0
11. Drawing of a chair	0	0	1	0	0	0
12. Drawing of a guitar	0	0	1	0	0	0
13. Drawing of geometric figures	1	0	0	0	1	0
14. Drawing of an umbrella	1	0	1	0	0	0
15. Drawing of colliding cars	0	1	1	0	1	0
16. Drawing of a man lifting a cargo	0	1	1	1	1	0
17-20. Hebrew words, each of 4 syllables						

Note. The cipher 1 indicates the presence of the feature; 0, its absence, by consensus of 20 independent judges.

REFERENCES

Anderson, B. P. Cognitive psychology: The study of knowing, learning, thinking. New York: Academic, 1975.

Bridgeman, P. W. The logic of modern physics. New York: Macmillan, 1927.

Bruner, J. S. On perceptual readiness. Psychological Review, 1957, 64, 123-152.

Bruner, J. S., & Klein, G. S. The functions of perceiving. In B. Kaplan & S. Wapner (Eds.), Perspectives in psychological theory. New York: International Universities, 1960.

Forgus, R. H., & Malamed, L. E. Perception: A cognitive-stage approach (2nd ed.). New York: McGraw-Hill, 1976.

Freeman, G. L. An experimental study of perception of objects. Journal of Experimental Psychology, 1929, 12, 241-258.

Fromm, E. The forgotten language. New York: Grove, 1951.

Gelman, R. The nature and development of early number concepts. In H. W. Reese (Ed.), *Advances in child development and behavior* (Vol. 7). New York: Academic, 1972.

Gibson, J. J. *The perception of the visual world.* Boston: Houghton Mifflin, 1950.

Gibson, J. J. *The senses considered as perceptual systems.* Boston: Houghton Mifflin, 1966.

Goldstein, M., & Scheerer, M. Abstract and concrete behavior: An experimental study with special tests. *Psychological Monographs,* 1941, *53*(2, Whole No. 239).

Kreitler, H., & Kreitler, S. *Cognitive orientation and behavior.* New York: Springer, 1976.

Kreitler, H., & Kreitler, S. *Cognitive habilitation by meaning of aphasic patients and imbecile children.* Invited address, Johannes Gutenberg University, Mainz, June 1977.

Kreitler, S., Arnon, R., & Kreitler, H. *Meaning and functional fixedness in thinking.* Unpublished manuscript, Tel Aviv University, 1978. (Based on a master's thesis by R. Arnon.)

Kreitler, S., Goldstein, M., & Kreitler, H. *The effects of meaning training on creativity and fantasy in preschool children.* Unpublished manuscript, Tel Aviv University, 1978.

Kreitler, S., & Kreitler, H. Dimensions of meaning and their measurement. *Psychological Reports,* 1968, *23,* 1307–1329.

Kreitler, S., & Kreitler, H. *Meaning in thinking and action.* New York: Academic, in press.

Lindsay, P. H., & Norman, D. A. *Human information processing* (2nd ed.). New York: Academic, 1977.

Minsky, M. *Mechanisms and images* (Condon Lecture Series). Portland, Ore.: Portland State University, 1970.

Murch, G.M. Binocular relationships in a size and color orientation specific aftereffect. *Journal of Experimental Psychology,* 1972, *93,* 30–34.

Neisser, U. *Cognition and reality.* San Francisco: W. H. Freeman, 1976.

Rapaport, D. *Diagnostic psychological testing* (Vol. 1). Chicago: Year Book, 1945.

Smock, C. D. The influence of psychological stress on the "intolerance of ambiguity." *Journal of Abnormal and Social Psychology,* 1955, *50,* 177–182.

Spencer, T. J. Some effects of different masking stimuli on iconic storage. *Journal of Experimental Psychology,* 1969, *81,* 132–140.

Vernon, M. D. The functions of schemata in perceiving. *Psychological Review,* 1955, *62,* 180–192.

Wallach, H. Some considerations concerning the relation between perception and cognition. *Journal of Personality,* 1949, *18,* 6–13.

14

Perceptual Identification versus Differentiation

Robert Francès
University of Paris X, Nanterre, France

Most of the research done on perception deals with stimulus conditions of a perceptual response, especially with the manipulation of stimulus variables to get information on the accuracy or the speed of this response. Little has been done about the exact nature of the perceptual tasks in which these same stimuli and responses may be involved. The comparative analysis of some fundamental tasks may, however, shed some light on mechanisms that can be conceived to explain the functioning of perception in a given modality. Studies of this kind have been carried out, using correlational methods, with the objective of looking for the relationships among individual differences in capacities to deal with several different tasks (Thurstone, 1944; Vernon, 1947). It is not certain, however, that consistent interindividual differences exist between perception modalities having separate mechanisms. It is well known that in other fields of psychology—for instance, in intelligence—there is a large general factor that accounts for various capacities, each of them implying a distinct mechanism.

Thus in this chapter I use the microgenetic approach to propose and elaborate some distinct operational features proper to each of two modalities of perception: *identification* and *differentiation.* The reciprocal-transfer method serves only as a supplementary proof of the existence of these features, all of them being linked with hypothetical mechanisms of the two modalities that constitute the theoretical framework. Three experiments published between 1964 and 1970 (Francès, 1964, 1967, 1969/1970) are briefly described; all three deal with visual identification, differentiation, or both. The first two were carried out in the laboratory; the last one was done under classroom conditions.

HYPOTHETICAL MECHANISMS

Definitions

Perceptual identification, also called *recognition* or *categorization,* may be conceived as a four-step process. The first step is *collecting* sensory cues from a complex stimulus. These cues may be very weak, brief, or discontinuous in the so-called reduced situations like tachistoscopic presentations, blurring, or masking conditions. Nevertheless, the second step, the *synthesis* of the cues, is the perceiver's attempt to put these cues into a mutual relationship. The cues synthesized by the subject's activity allow the elicitation of a memory trace of the category of the stimulus object or form, a category stored by the subject from past experience. The third step of the process is the elaboration of the *concordance* of the synthesized cues with the elicited trace. If this concordance is satisfying, the subject makes the *decision* to give a categorial response; this decision process is the fourth step of identification.

The four steps are represented in Figure 14.1, on the left side. The whole process is conceived as successive, and this conception is the general case under ordinary conditions. But certain retroactive or feedback cases are observed to proceed from one step to the preceding one or to other steps. For instance, if an erroneous response is given, more cues are collected in a further trial; another synthesis is accomplished; a new concordance is looked for with the elicitation of another trace; and so on. In the case of perceiving ambiguous figures, the same cues are synthesized in two alternative ways; the concordance is looked for with two distinct traces; and two successive decisions are made. Perceptual identification is certainly the most extensively studied of all perception modalities; it is also the most spontaneous one in everyday life.

Differentiation, also called *differential distinction,* may be defined as a post-identification behavior in which the response looked for is a partial aspect or a peculiarity of the already-identified stimulus. Whereas reading a word is an example of identification, looking for a typing error in that word is an example of differentiation. This kind of behavior may be conceived as being linked with the synthesis step of the identification process. A mechanism of *analysis* of the collected cues is at work after the identification response has been given. This analysis occurs only about intrastimulus properties in the simple cases when one is concerned with the details or imperfections of the present object. Interstimulus properties are analyzed when two or more stimuli of the same identity are confronted in a perceptual comparison.

Like identification, differentiation is conceived as a successive process dealing only with the analysis of the same collected cues previously synthesized. Some kind of retroaction may be needed, however, in cases where more cues are necessary to get the correct differential response. In such cases, a further collection of supplementary cues is performed.

Identification and differentiation may be studied either with nonsense forms or words or with meaningful ones. If nonsense stimuli are used, the elicitation of long-term memory trace is partialed out, and one deals only with laboratory phenomena. This kind of perceptual study may be of some use for an elaboration of

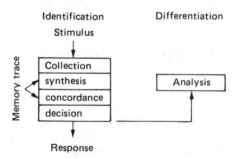

Figure 14.1 The process of perceptual identification and differentiation.

incomplete processes. Only complete categorial identification and differentiation are of interest here, so only meaningful stimuli (digits and words) were used.

Predictions

Some predictions can be deduced from the preceding models of both modalities of perceptual behavior:

1. *Amount of learning.* For an equal number of trials, the amount of learning should be more important for differentiation than for identification. In fact, differentiation is only concerned with one step added to an already-complete identification process: analyzing the cues previously collected, synthesized, confronted with a memory trace, and categorized. In certain cases of differentiation, supplementary cues will be looked for in successive trials of the task. The slope of a learning curve for this kind of behavior must be more rapid than for identification. Even if, in the first few trials, the subject makes more errors, the progress in the task should be greater than in an identification task. These predictions concerning the two kinds of learning can be tested by presenting words in successive trials of perceptual learning, either for identification (reading the words) or for differentiation (detecting an inverted letter in the words).

2. *Identification and accessibility of memory traces.* Identification is easier with familiar stimuli than with unfamiliar ones. This is a well-established fact. Fewer cues should thus be needed for the elicitation of a memory trace in the first case than in the second. This prediction, which is compatible with many results obtained in the psychology of learning processes, can be tested by presenting familiar and unfamiliar words for identification.

3. *Differentiation and the accessibility of traces.* Differentiation is easier with unfamiliar stimuli than with familiar ones. In fact, inasmuch as during the preceding identification process, a larger amount of cues will have been collected for the first case than for the second one, the peculiarity of the stimulus is more likely to be detected with unfamiliar stimuli than with familiar ones. This prediction can be tested by presenting for differentiation words of various levels of familiarity.

4. *Identification and expectedness of the categories.* Identification is easier for expected stimuli than for unexpected ones—another well-established fact—inasmuch as fewer alternatives are in competition for the expected than for the unexpected. Thus the concordance between the synthesized cues and one of the conflicting traces may be found with fewer trials in the first case than in the second one. This prediction can be tested by presenting the same digits for identification, each presentation being announced more or less restrictively, that is, being preceded by an announcement comprising a variable amount of alternatives.

5. *Differentiation and expectedness of the categories.* As differentiation is not concerned with concordance of the synthesized cues with a trace, but with the analysis of the cues, no relationship may be expected between the more or less precise expectation of a stimulus and the precision of the differentiation responses.

6. *Transfer of learning from differentiation to identification.* Positive learning transfer should occur from differentiation to identification. Practice with differentiation consists of detecting a particular cue by analysis from among those collected during a trial. If the given differentiation response is wrong, more cues are collected in further trials. Thus subjects are trained to collect more cues in one trial by the end of the learning process and are then better able to collect a larger amount of

cues in a subsequent identification task, in which the first step is such a collection. This prediction can be tested by giving the subject a learning task in the differentiation of words and, in a second part of the same experiment, by giving her or him a test of identification of other words. The results of this test would have to be compared with those of a control group that had not been submitted to any learning before the test.

7. *Transfer of learning from identification to differentiation.* Negative learning transfer should occur from identification to differentiation. Practice with identification leads to going through the steps of this behavior in a more economical way. It is probable that Steps 1 (collection) and 2 (synthesis) continue to be involved, but the other steps are less certain. For the purpose of prediction, it is sufficient to hypothesize that the learning of identification results in eliciting the memory trace necessary for the response with fewer and less precise cues, which are, nevertheless, synthesized. Thus the intrastimulus peculiarities are less and less noticed in subsequent tasks of differentiation given as a test. Words may be used to test this prediction. While an experimental group is exposed before this test to a learning period of identification with other words, a control group receives only the test.

Some of these predictions were less precisely formulated as hypotheses for the experiments that follow. As a matter of fact, the first two predictions were not yet proposed because the four steps of the identification model had not yet been clearly distinguished and because the true mechanism of differentiation learning had not been so precisely defined in relation to the analysis of the cues alone. This chapter is the first attempt to bring together the results of the previous experiments, and the reflection brought on by this attempt led to the hypothetical models of both mechanisms from which the seven predictions were made.

EXPERIMENTAL RESULTS THAT CORRESPOND
TO THE PREDICTIONS

Amount of Learning

It was established by Francès (1964) that tachistoscopic presentations of digits given in a training session of 30 trials result in a larger amount of learning when the task given to the subject involves differentiation rather than identification. In the first task, the digits (from 0 to 9) printed in black on white had a lacuna on their contours that was randomly distributed through three series of 10 digits. The differentiation task was to give the exact position of the lacunae after one presentation of 37 msec. In the second task, performed by different subjects, the contours of the digits were deleted by blanks randomly distributed. The subject had to identify each digit in one presentation of 37 msec. The errors were corrected after each trial. The subjects were 18 students for each task. The results as divided into three successive blocks of 10 trials were as shown in Table 14.1.

The same result was obtained by Francès (1967) with tachistoscopic presentations of words with 64 trials for each task. The same series of words was given at a constant duration (.05 sec for identification and .15 sec for differentiation) in repeated presentations until the test word was identified or an inverted letter was detected in it, respectively. The subjects were two groups of 14 students. The scores in each trial were measured by the number of presentations necessary to give a correct response. In Figure 14.2 the 64 trials are arranged in eight blocks,

Table 14.1   Correct responses in three successive blocks of 10 trials
of identification and differentiation with digits

	Block 1	Block 2	Block 3
Identification ($n = 18$)	35.5	45.5	54.4
Differentiation ($n = 18$)	23.3	32.2	53.8

and the mean number of presentations is plotted in the corresponding curves (on the left side of the figure). The words in each task were divided into familiar and unfamiliar, a distinction that need not be considered here. The only curves considered for each task are the continuous ones.

Thus in both experiments, using different kinds of materials and techniques, and computing the scores in different ways, the same result was obtained: The range of learning was higher for a differentiation task than for an identification one. This result can be interpreted in relation to the hypothetical mechanisms. The learning of identification involves the four steps and the elicitation of a memory trace, a more complex behavioral adaptation than that demanded by differentiation, which is a postidentification behavior concerned only with the analysis of sensory cues in one presentation or reanalysis using more cues in successive presentations.

Identification versus Differentiation and Accessibility of Traces

The second and third predictions were tested in the words experiment. The material was composed of French words of equal length but divided equally into

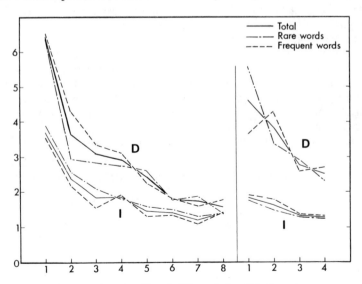

Figure 14.2   Identification (I) and differentiation (D) of words; mean
scores of successive blocks in learning (left) and in tests
(right).

rare and frequent stimuli (mean logarithms of 1.31 and 2.50, respectively, according to the table of Gougenheim et al.). When the scores of both tasks were divided according to the frequency of the stimuli (which was constantly demonstrated to be highly correlated with linguistic frequency), it appeared that identification was easier for frequent words than for infrequent ones, whereas the contrary was true for differentiation. The relationship may be seen in Figure 14.2 by comparing the frequent-words curves to the infrequent-words curves. More presentations are needed for identification of infrequent words than for frequent ones. This difference is observable in most of the eight blocks of the learning curves (on the left side of the figure) and also in the four blocks of a test given to the subjects of the other group, who dealt with differentiation for 64 trials (on the right side of the figure). In contrast, fewer presentations are needed for differentiation of infrequent words than for frequent ones. This difference is less constant, however. It may be observed only in the first four blocks of the learning curves. An analysis of variance was computed on the scores of both groups for the eight blocks of the learning periods. The interaction of groups times frequency was, on the whole, significant.

These results fit well with the corresponding predictions. Moreover it appears that, in the course of a rather long period of differentiation learning, the subjects are trained to collect more and more cues in successive presentations of unfamiliar words, which they have experienced as more misleading than familiar ones.

Identification versus Differentiation and Expectedness of the Categories

The fourth and fifth predictions were tested in the digits experiment. After a training period of 30 trials, either in identification or differentiation, each group received a test of 10 trials in the *same* task in which it had been trained. In the training tasks, expectedness of the stimulus category was manipulated in the following way. Each digit was preceded by an announcement implying three, six, or nine alternatives (e.g., "from 3 to 5," "from 1 to 6," or "from 0 to 8," respectively). The same symbols were presented in the tests in these three conditions of uncertainty. The scores were computed as correct responses given during one presentation. The results for each group are presented in Table 14.2. Percentages of correct responses in each level of uncertainty are given for identification and differentiation either with or without prior learning of the task (the experimental and control groups).

It becomes clear that, in identification, both experimental and control groups

Table 14.2 Effects of expectedness of the categories on identification and differentiation

	Percentage of correct responses		
	Three alternatives	Six alternatives	Nine alternatives
Identification			
Experimental group	76.6	47.3	43.3
Control group	55.0	36.6	30.0
Differentiation			
Experimental group	40.0	36.6	31.6
Control group	20.0	15.0	28.3

gave more or less correct responses according to the levels of uncertainty or to the degree of expectedness of the stimulus categories. In contrast, in differentiation, no relationship is to be found between expectedness of the digits and detection of the lacunae, whether in the experimental or in the control group. The slight tendency noticeable in the experimental group is not statistically significant. These facts may be interpreted according to the hypothetical mechanisms. In identification, the subjects deal with the concordance of the synthesized cues with memory traces that are more or less in conflict because of the number of alternatives given before the presentation. This relationship remains unchanged after a certain period of learning in the same task. In contrast, differentiation is not affected by the expectedness of the symbols because here the task is not concerned with the concordance level. The process involved is the analysis of the cues synthesized for identification before the detection of the lacunae. This analysis becomes more and more accurate with learning but remains unaffected by the degree of uncertainty of the symbols.

Effects of Reciprocal Transfer of Learning in Both Tasks

The last two predictions were tested in the words experiment. Two groups first received a learning session of 64 trials, one of them with identification (Group A) and the other with differentiation (Group B); then they were tested after 24 trials: Group A for differentiation and Group B for identification. The results can be seen in Figure 14.2, where the left side shows the learning curves already discussed (Group A = I; Group B = D), the right side shows the test curves (Group A = D; Group B = I). It appears that Group A performed on the differentiation test at a level comparable to the four first blocks of differentiation learning of Group B, whereas Group B performed on the identification test at a level comparable to the four last blocks of identification learning of Group A. Thus Group A does not seem to have made any progress as a result of previous practice with another task, whereas Group B did. Transfer ratios were computed for each group in the following manner. The four first blocks of learning of Groups A and B were considered as a control-group measure in one task, and the four blocks of the tests of Groups B and A, respectively, were taken as experimental-group measures. Transfer from differentiation to identification (Group B) is 47.2%; transfer from identification to differentiation (Group A) is 10.8%. In the control measures, however, the first blocks may be considered as preliminary trials largely dependent on an adaptation to the tachistoscopic vision. One can consider Blocks 2 to 5 as more reliable measures of control for each task. Computed with these blocks, transfer ratios become 25.5% and 9.05%, respectively.

Thus it may be concluded that reciprocal transfer of learning in each of the tasks has opposite effects linked to their different hypothetical mechanisms. Training in differentiation makes the subject more and more able to collect a larger amount of sensory cues in a single presentation and to do better in a subsequent task of identification in which the first step consists of such a collection. Inversely, when trained in identification, a subject is more and more able to synthesize a lesser amount of cues to get the correct response with the help of long-term memory traces. He or she thus becomes less able to detect any peculiarity in the cues when tested with a task in which the critical step is an analysis of these cues.

Supplementary Evidence from a Classroom Experiment

The words experiment suggested a kind of field experiment dealing with reading and spelling in children. These behaviors have been analyzed for many years by educational psychologists, some of them stressing the affective factors (namely, the attitudes toward the school and the teachers), others stressing the cognitive factors (namely, the ontogenetic acquisition of language), still others stressing the perceptual factors, as for example Diack (1965). In short, reading and spelling appeared to sustain the same relationship as identifying words and differentiating letters in words. While reading, children are supposed to collect some visual cues in order to give as quickly as possible the verbal response that is required for the understanding of a sentence. Inversely, the spelling behavior is linked to a precise analysis of the word and the distinction of the letters in it. In the educational process, reading precedes writing and is generally more extended over time. One may compare this situation with a preponderance of identification over differentiation.

Thus the hypothesis was conceived that training in differentiating words may have an influence on spelling progress in children. An experiment was undertaken (Francès, 1969/1970) according to the following plan: Experimental subjects were presented with texts adapted to their school levels in which some words contained an inverted letter. While reading these texts the children were asked to look attentively at the words and to detect the critical letters. Control subjects were merely required to copy the same texts during sessions equal in length to those of the experimental subjects. The experiment used 62 control and 69 experimental subjects. They were divided according to three school levels and ranged in age from 7 to 10. Control and experimental subjects were taken from the same classes and randomly assigned to one kind of task or the other. During the same school year, eight sessions were arranged for each educational level. All 131 subjects received spelling tests before and after the sessions. One of these tests was particularly sensitive and pertinent to all kinds of spelling mistakes.

The first results indicated that, among all the experimental groups, the test scores were highly correlated with the scores on the initial task of differentiation. The pretest–posttest comparisons of the scores on the test for experimental and control groups were always in the experimental group's favor. An analysis of covariance performed on each of the school-level groups indicated that, taking into account the initial levels of the groups, the experimental group made significantly more progress than the control group in two levels out of the three considered. The differences between the groups were not high but constant. This fact demonstrated that perceptual factors play a role in spelling acquisition and that even a small amount of practice (eight sessions in 8 months, each of them lasting from 30 to 40 min) may develop in children an analytic set toward word perception. This set is operant between the sessions and leads the subject to a more distinct reading of words. The progress in spelling may be conceived as depending on this different way of perceiving words as the result of a generalization process.

CONCLUSIONS

One may consider the experimental results reported here as merely momentary sets induced in the subjects by the devices and instructions given them. It seems first evident that tachistoscopic perception is not very representative of functional perception in general, for the former concerns microgenetic observation; the latter, macrogenetic observation of the behavior.

It is worthy of note, however, that the words experiment (Francès, 1967), performed under laboratory conditions, with brief exposures of single words given to the subject after definite instructions linked with a short tachistoscopic task, provided a good confirmation of the field experiment, a long-term study concerned with macrogenetic observations. This validation of the first system of facts by the second one permits one to consider the duality of identification and differentiation and their mutual relationship through learning as more than a laboratory phenomenon.

The four-step model for identification is a more delicate question. Some models of this kind have been conceived for subliminal versus supraliminal perception by Dixon (1971, p. 38), for perceptual defense by Dixon (1971, pp. 197, 256), and by Erdelyi (1974) for the same phenomenon. My own conception puts aside all affective factors, not because I underestimate their importance, but only for the momentary objective of simplification. It seems of some use to put brackets around motivational factors and to consider the cognitive steps necessary for a complete model of identification, including the intervention of long-term memory traces.

The four-step model is suggested by many kinds of findings dealing with learning, familiarity, or expectedness of the stimuli, and so on. Many experiments are concerned merely with a single aspect of the process, but the model is conceivable only when all the facts are mutually confronted. Another aspect of the model is the duality and antagonism between identification and differentiation. This comparative aspect of the overall study must be stressed because the two modalities of perception are important for the general conception of the function, especially because some steps of identification are proved necessary only through the evidence provided by the comparison. On many occasions a concept is operationally established by converging facts.

The four-step model presented for identification, with the intervention of long-term memory traces, may be used for the assignment of some affective or temperamental influences on perception to a precise step of the perceptual process. We have known for a long time that anxiety, neurosis, and repression impair the identification process. We know that positive valence of the stimuli results in the improvement of this process and that the opposite is true of negative valence. The very nature of these relationships leads one to expect a certain amount of precision through attributing the various effects to one or more steps of identification.

REFERENCES

Diack, H. *Reading and the psychology of perception.* Nottingham: Skinner, 1965.

Dixon, N. F. *Subliminal perception: The nature of a controversy.* London: McGraw-Hill, 1971.

Erdelyi, M. H. A new look at the New Look: Perceptual defense and vigilance. *Psychological Review,* 1974, *81,* 1–25.

Francès, R. Étude comparative de deux conduites perceptives: L'identification de l'espèce et la distinction des différences. *Journal de Psychologie Normale et Pathologique,* 1964, *3,* 281–204.

Francès, R. Identification et distinction différentielle: Deux mécanismes perceptifs et leurs relations réciproques. *Psychologie Française,* 1967, *12*(2), 91–100.

Francès, R. Apprentissage perceptif et apprentissage de l'orthographie. *Bulletin de Psychologie,* 1969/1970, *23,* 6–8, 416–421.

Thurstone, L. L. *A factorial study of perception.* Chicago: University of Chicago Press, 1944.

Vernon, M. D. Different types of perceptual ability. *British Journal of Psychology,* 1947, *38,* 79–89.

15

Language and Logical Structures in Problem Processing

Problems of Thinking about Thinking

Horacio J. A. Rimoldi
*Centro Interdisciplinario de Investigaciones
en Psicología Matemática y Experimental
Buenos Aires, Argentina*

In this chapter, I summarize a few studies on problem solving, thinking, and language that my associates and I have conducted in various countries since 1954. Although most of these studies have appeared in mimeographed form, and some have been printed in journals in various languages, a good portion of the material synthesized here is not easily available. As it is not my aim to summarize bibliography, I avoid citations unless they are directly pertinent to my main purpose as I sketch the theoretical, experimental, and semantic considerations that have emerged as we see them today.

Our main purpose is the study of cognitive performances through the study of problem-solving *processes* rather than problem-solving products (Bloom & Broder, 1950; Rimoldi, 1955, 1960a, 1960b). More specifically we concentrate on: (a) experimental and observational identification of the main cognitive components of problem solving; (b) how problem solving as a dependent variable is affected by independent variables; (c) methodological and technical questions that emerged in characterizing processes; and (d) the invention of appropriate instruments to appraise problem-solving tactics in a variety of situations and across cultural groups. In this chapter I do not necessarily follow the order just presented. My main emphasis is on discovering and describing how processes are generated, how they evolve when subjects solve problems under controlled experimental situations.

GENERAL CONSIDERATIONS, ASSUMPTIONS, AND DEFINITIONS

In trying to avoid unnecessary neologisms, I frequently rely on dictionary meanings. Whenever necessary I provide the needed clarifications.

Problem solving, in our view, occurs at the level of concrete situations that require a solution, at the level of abstract questions proposed for solution, or when both levels are combined. In all cases, subjects search for or move toward a solution (or goal) that is not yet known. This implies that the subject has to recognize that there is a problem to solve. Indeed the thresholds for problem identification and recognition should be systematically explored, not only in relation to age and education, but in relation to logical semantic and biologic components.

The identification of the goal changes as the process of solution advances, as pointed out long ago by Duncker (1945), Köhler (1927), and Wertheimer (1959), among others. It is well known that the goal attained may or may not satisfy previous expectations, hypotheses, hunches, and so on. In this respect, some kind of "intuition" may be of help. It is probably true that a "learned intuition" relates to plain "unlearned" intuition as selective "guessing" relates to chance guessing. But selective guessing may be the result of sophisticated, though beclouded, logical, experimental, or observational performances, or some combination of these.

I assume that problem-solving styles are differentiated by the ways and the means used to reach a solution. Given the same problem, different people, or the same person at different times, may solve it in different ways using different means. This implies searching for and testing information and courses of action to accept or reject various possibilities. In the course of this searching, chains of decisions occur. Decision making is, however, only one of the forms in which problem solving can be studied.

Ways and means can change. Both are basic and may be ordered differently. Consequently, how means and ways are combined and ordered is a fundamental operation in problem solving. Not to have distinguished between ways and means has caused many a misunderstanding. In cognitive processes the function of both logic and language (modality and symbolic system) as well as their interaction should be properly identified. To reduce one to the other leads to dead ends. The manifold interplay of modalities and logic within a goal-directed performance, however, makes of problem solving a dynamic and active pursuit that in some cases is rich in invention and discovery.

Training provides subjects with the information and the operations needed to solve efficiently a limited set of similar problems, for instance, those encountered here and now within a cultural or subcultural milieu. But possessing the information is not enough; it is necessary to operate with it in certain ways. Knowing these ways alone is not enough either, unless the appropriate information is available. The methodological approaches to the problem of training may be summarized into two extremes. One of them refers to the use and practice of operations resulting from the application of abstract axiomatic models that, as such, are little concerned with actual facts. The other considers of foremost importance the acquisition of facts and leaves the logic of the operations that can be performed to chance or to loosely formulated rules of procedure.

These extreme approaches that highlight the differences between ways and means are unnecessarily restrictive. They imply different formulations of science. The first one is a basically deductive approach, and the second one is perhaps more inductive. Our experience in problem-solving research indicates that to ignore the smooth operations that combine appropriate means at the appropriate time is bad for education. It limits the possibility of discovering, inventing, and understanding other fields beyond those in which the subject has been specifically trained; and it is here that a proper balance between education and training seems to be essential. Though training is more rigidly directed toward the attainment of prescribed goals, education transcends specifics and prepares one for the opening up of unexpected ways, for using novel—or old—means in the search for newly defined or redefined goals. Practice in problem solving, then, becomes an effective approach to education and training, depending on the kind of problems used for such purposes.

A problem may be considered "a situation that requires solution" or "a question proposed for solution." This has led many psychologists to concentrate on the study of the final answer, ignoring what goes on before it is reached. The correspondence between the process that precedes the final answer and the final answer itself is not well known. The appropriate rules of inference are only vaguely known and have often been taken for granted. It is our opinion that it is more appropriate to investigate the processes preceding the answers than to rely on final answers exclusively (Bloom & Broder, 1950; Duncker, 1945; Polya, 1954; Rimoldi, 1955, 1960a; Wertheimer, 1959).

Process means a continued forward movement in a space-time field. It is the inner activity that goes on while solving a problem. The overt activity that corresponds to it is the tactic. We assume that tactics map processes and that their correspondence is predominantly one-on-one (Rimoldi, 1967). This assumption makes it possible to infer inner behavior from tactics.

In 1954 we developed an experimental approach that helps to identify the tactics that physicians and medical students follow in diagnosing a clinical case. The sequence of questions they ask to reach a diagnosis defines the tactic. This tactic is experimentally identified by the type of questions asked, their number, and their order in the sequence (Rimoldi, 1955, 1960b). This approach is almost the reverse of what is usually done. The emphasis is on the study of the process through the tactic. Subjects are "free" within the experimental conditions to search actively for the information they want, when they want it. The final solution can then be related to the process that preceded it.

The inclusion of order in characterizing performance is rich in possibilities. H. Poincaré (cited in Bell, 1937) remarked that "a mathematical proof is not a mere juxtaposition of syllogisms, it is syllogisms arranged in a certain order, and the order is more important than the elements themselves" (p. 549). This is also our experience in problem solving.

Using this approach, we do not assume that subjects are basically passive receptors of stimuli. Human behavior includes passive reactions to stimuli as well as such active ones as searching, selecting, ordering, and rejecting. In other words it includes organizing different inputs to reach a goal moving along certain directions and interacting actively with the environment—even organizing or reorganizing an environment. The operations that subjects perform to do this constitute a fascinating field of research.

To solve the same problems, different subjects may ask for and use different amounts of information and combine it in various ways. Discovery results from active searching, and originality includes selecting and organizing in novel and not always logical paths; the same event will therefore play different roles and have different meanings according to where and when it appears in the process. Besides, roles and meanings also anticipate a future in so far as they provide a past for what will follow.

Whitehead (1946) said:

> The doctrine ... is that the whole concept of materialism only applies to very abstract entities, the product of logical discernment. The concrete enduring entities are

organisms, so that the plan of the *whole* influences the very characters of the various subordinate organisms which enter into it. In the case of an animal, the mental states enter into the plans of the total organism and thus modify the plans of the successive subordinate organisms until the ultimate smaller organisms, such as electrons, are reached. Thus an electron within a living body is different from an electron outside it, by reason of the plan of the body . . . and this plan includes the mental state.

In the first place, this formulation implies that a given situation may or may not be perceived as a problem. The state of the organism at a given time will provide a given threshold for problem recognition. This is of great interest in education, in cross-cultural research, and in the study of cognitive processes. In the second place, this changing condition and the consideration that events have a past, a present, and a future introduce a very important and complicating factor: the inclusion of temporal order as an integral part of a process. It implies that the same identifiable event—either "stored" in memory or being used now or laying the groundwork for other events—may have, for each person, an almost endless gamut of meanings. Psychologically speaking, this helps to discriminate between subjects and between their behavioral styles.

BUILDING INSTRUMENTS
AND EVALUATING RESULTS

Research in problem solving has heavily borrowed from the concepts and methodologies developed to study intelligence and thinking. Many of the instruments used in the past were similar to those used to study intelligence. No wonder that a good problem solver was also considered to be "intelligent" and to be a "good thinker." In turn, problem solving has been used to study learning, although I do not discuss here these aspects or those that have to do with the analysis of abstract simulation models (Leontev & Dzhafarov, 1974; Simon & Newell, 1971).

The invention of instruments is an important step in science, but strangely enough the psychology of invention is little known. This activity plays a considerable role in many sciences and has been partly responsible for the great advances that have taken place since the early nineteenth century. Some psychologists have been satisfied, however, to use tightly knit experimental designs and let statistics do the rest. This is of course a generalization and has many exceptions. It is our contention that it is not enough to report significant covariances or complex multivariate findings to validate—or not validate—an instrument. Validity is not primarily a statistical problem. Rather, it has to do with the appropriateness of the instruments used to fulfill the task that they are supposed to perform. When it is not known which variables may be important, it is the duty of the investigator to define—as well as possible at the time—the field of inquiry. Then, instruments considered to be appropriate and discriminating should be invented and tried. This in turn helps to redefine the field and to lay down the rules that should be followed in building more refined instruments. My associates and I have spent much time on this kind of activity (Rimoldi & Fogliatto, 1962; Rimoldi, Fogliatto, Erdmann, & Donnelly, 1964).

The original 1954 presentation of our test of diagnostic skills (Rimoldi, 1955, 1960b) consisted of transcribing medical histories on sets of cards and asking subjects to use these sets and diagnose the case. On the first card a subject was informed about a patient's main complaints. The questions that the subject might wish to ask in order to reach a diagnosis of the case were written on other cards, with matching answers written on the reverse sides. For the subject, the act of picking up a card and reading the information on it amounted to asking a question about the problem. There is no reason why the presentation need be limited to cards; we ourselves have tried many ways, but in all of them the important thing was that the subject be an active searcher and the experimenter be a rather passive component of the experimental situation. The basic technique and conceptualization we enunciated in 1954 was later on used by others (Hubbard, 1963; McGuire, 1967) to prepare some instruments to evaluate medical knowledge. This approach was also used to explore areas other than medical diagnosis, which I do not discuss here (Tabor, 1959; Potkay, 1971; Gunn, 1962; Izcoa, 1964; Creedon, 1971).

The accumulation of a considerable number of experimental protocols convinced us that with this technique it was possible to investigate some of the aspects of problem-solving processes. Besides, the fact that it seemed to work in various content areas gave us hope for future studies. Many approaches not presented here were used to evaluate tactics, and through these approaches the performances of subjects belonging to different kinds of groups could be compared. We finally concluded that the distance between the observed performance and a criterion provided a more satisfactory way of looking at the problem than did calculate statistical averages. This decision was taken early in our work. The criteria were the tactics agreed on by medical "experts" in solving each clinical problem. They represented, we hoped, the goal to be attained by a diagnostician and had little to do with defining norms in terms of averages (Rimoldi, 1960a, 1972, 1973; Rimoldi & Fogliatto, 1962). This manner of evaluating performance is widely discussed today by educators (Block, 1971; Carver, 1974; Glasser & Mitko, 1971). The approach implies a redefinition of the criterion and an interpretation of observed results in terms of that criterion.

The technique I have described constrains subjects to choose only among those questions (i.e., cards) that are presented to them. Instead of using cards subjects may be presented with a geometric drawing and requested to identify an area within it. These areas can have different shapes, colors, or both. Subjects have to identify the area the experimenter has selected. They may ask any questions they desire, for instance, Is it on the right hand side of the figure? Is it blue? Is it in the upper left hand corner? and so on. The experimenter provides the answer and, to identify the tactics, records the order in which the questions are asked. Other procedures have been used, but in all of them, the experimenter obtains the tactics defined by the questions asked, their number, and their sequential position. The testing ends when a subject offers a solution—right or wrong—or when no further questions are asked (Rimoldi & Devane, 1961; Rimoldi, Devane, & Haley, 1961; Rimoldi & Fogliatto, 1962).

To explore mathematical ability, we built problems based on known mathematical formulations presented in concrete, everyday terms. We then administered problems of this type to elementary and high school students. The results suggested that, even when the subjects ignored the mathematical structure of the problem, their tactics implied the understanding of the essential components of that structure. A new method of building problems and of scoring them was then developed (Rimoldi, Haley, Fogliatto, & Erdmann, 1963).

A problem was understood as a language function, or a map, of a logical structure (*structure* here being used to mean a collection of elements with ordered relationships and operations between them). *Language* in our context refers to manner of presentation or to the modality used to realize the relational system of the logical structure. This conceptualization makes it possible to specify logical structures and to dress them in various symbolic systems. Different logical structures can be presented in the same modality, but each structure can also be realized using different symbolic systems. Isomorphic problems have the same relational system and imply the same operations but are presented using different modalities. These isomorphic problems are invariant in terms of logical relations and operations. This concept of invariance is not often explicitly stated. Thurstone (1944), however, spoke of factors as transcending presentation of the material, and the idea behind Spearman's *G* may be understood as a kind of universal neogenetic invariant behind different intellectual performances (Rimoldi, 1951). Logical analysis may serve to determine the inherent logical structure of a concrete problem. We are as of this writing investigating this problem with reference to medical diagnosis.

The structure of a problem fixes its intrinsic difficulty, and all isomorphic problems have the same intrinsic difficulty. Given the same structure, however, the modality used may facilitate or hamper the process of solution. The observed difficulty of the problem results from both the intrinsic and the extrinsic difficulty, the latter depending mostly on the manner of presentation. Different logical structures and different symbolic systems will produce changes in the problem-solving processes and, as a consequence, in the tactics as defined by the ordered sequence of questions.

If the structure is known, it is possible to define ideal tactics. Ideal tactics reduce uncertainty to zero, are the most economical, do not present order reversals, are not redundant, and do not have irrelevant questions. Order reversals occur when specific questions are asked before the more general ones. Redundancy implies asking for the same information more than once. Irrelevancy implies asking for information unrelated to the problem. Each question in the tactics has per se an information value that is a property of that question; but its contribution to the total score will depend on its position in the tactics, inasmuch as, in terms of the previous questions asked, the amount of new information added may be greatly reduced. It may even become zero when the information it provides has already been acquired.

Assume a structure like the one shown in Figure 15.1. Some of the relationships are: $a_1 \in c_2$, $a_1 \in d_2$, and so on, and the operations are $c_2 \cup d_2 = a_1$ and $a_1 \cup b_1 = T_0$, so that b_1 is the complement of a_1 if there is no interaction between a_1 and b_1. However $a_1 \in c_2$, where the order "general to particular" is kept, is logically the same as $c_2 \ni a_1$, but psychologically it may not be so. Besides, asking for $c_2 \to d_2$ and a_1 in that order makes a_1 totally redundant. Knowing a_1 and c_2, d_2 can be inferred. Thus in $c_2 \to d_2 \to a_1$, a_1 contributes with zero value to the tactics, whereas in $a_1 \to c_2 \to d_2$, d_2 is partially redundant because $a_1 - c_2$ gives d_2. Operations of this kind are used to evaluate tactics. Each question has an information value that varies according to its location in the sequence, its redundancy value, and the total number of questions asked. By combining those values according to an established set of rules, an observed score is obtained for each tactic.

As stated, ideal tactics reduce uncertainty to zero (Rimoldi et al., 1964), have no order reversals, are not redundant, and do not have irrelevant questions. In Figure 15.1 the ideal tactics are $a_1 \to e_2$. Any departure from the ideal tactics reduces the score. The scores thus obtained are similar to those developed using the mastery-

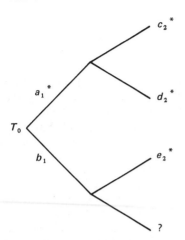

Figure 15.1 Graphic presentation of a problem structure. The question mark corresponds to what the subject has to find out. The ideal tactics is: $a_1 \to e_2$. Asterisks are used to identify the questions presented with the problem. Knowing T_0 and asking for a_1 and e_2 provide all the information needed to solve the problem.

learning concept. Ideal tactics are defined for each problem in terms of logical informational analysis. Isomorphic problems have the same ideal tactics, though the modality used may have a differential effect on the observed tactics. This approach makes it possible to evaluate the contribution of the modality used and to compare how different presentations influence tactics. The fact that a subject does not perform satisfactorily in a given problem is no sure indication that the subject cannot understand the structure implicit in the problem, for he or she may solve without trouble an isomorphic problem. This formulation has implications for developmental psychology of cognition, pathological thinking processes, cross-cultural research, and education. In a restricted sense, it could be hypothesized that thinking may be envisaged as making explicit and communicable to oneself or to others the structure of a problem (Rimoldi, 1967).

DEPENDENCE VERSUS INDEPENDENCE OF LANGUAGE AND LOGICAL STRUCTURES

The operations used to build isomorphic problems imply experimental independence between language and logical structures (Rimoldi, 1976). In other words, a given relational system can be expressed by using different languages or symbolic systems. The following questions remain, however: (a) Are logical structures and languages linearly independent? (b) Are logical structures and languages statistically independent? The second question refers to the interaction between structures and language. If the observed changes in tactics from one symbolic system to another one are similar for various structures, then languages and structures do not interact, in spite of the fact that one symbolic system may give "better" results throughout structures than another. The question, therefore, is one of parallelism or lack of parallelism in the observed changes.

The first question refers to the experimental verification of the linearly independent parameters postulated earlier—languages and logical structures. To explore this problem, a factor analysis was performed on the tactics obtained by administering 16 problems to 150 subjects. (Some of the data reported here correspond partially to some already published in Rimoldi, 1971.) There were four series of problems built around four logical structures named 31, 33, 35, and 60. Structures

31, 33, and 35 are logical trees of progressive complexity; 31 consists of two successive dichotomies, 33 of a trichotomy followed by dichotomies, and 35 of two successive trichotomies. Structure 60 is more complex. The inner symmetry of the structure is not kept, so that of two branches at the same level, one is dichotomized and the other is not. Besides, the final answer requires the union of two branches. Each structure was presented using four symbolic systems: A, usual verbal language; B, an abstract language; C, a negative abstract language; and K, a perceptual language using colored drawings of geometric figures. Each one of the structures therefore generated four isomorphic problems.

For example, in Structure 31 (as shown in Fig. 15.1), the subject had to find out the information corresponding to the branch indicated by the question mark. Problem 31A (Table 15.1) was presented, informing the subject that in a school there are boys and girls preparing a dance. Some of them sell tickets, some sell refreshments, and the question was How many girls sell tickets? In Problem 31K (Table 15.1) the subject was shown drawings corresponding to big and small blue and green squares, and we wanted to know which one of them had been chosen. For instance, what color and size was the selected square? The correspondence between Problems 31A and 31K is as shown in Table 15.1.

In Table 15.2 the results of the factor analysis are presented, and in Table 15.3 are shown the intercorrelations between the corresponding primaries. Table 15.2 shows clearly the existence of a K (perceptual) language factor (Factor VI) that has saturation on all problems presented using drawings regardless of structure. In Factor III all problems with Structure 60 cluster together regardless of language (except Problem 60K, which is loaded only on Factor VI). As expected, the primaries corresponding to these two factors show a low-magnitude intercorrelation. Factor V is defined only by Problem 31A. It is a specific factor and corresponds to the problem administered first.

The tree structures 31, 33, and 35 and the languages A, B, and C are taken into account by Factors I, II, and IV. Languages B and C are common to Factors I and II. Factor I is defined by the tree structures 33 and 35 that, as previously remarked, are more complex than the tree structure 31 that defines Factor II. Because both factors share the same languages, it is not surprising to find a moderately high correlation between them as reported in Table 15.3.

Factor IV includes problems of Series 33 and 35 in Language A. Therefore, it is a verbal language factor and has a substantial correlation with Factor I, probably owing to the fact that both include problems with Structures 33 and 35. Factor II is different from Factor I because of the structure component, and Factor IV is different from Factor I because of the language component. This factorial structure

Table 15.1 Equivalence of two isomorphic problems for structure 31

Elements in structure 31	Language A	Language K
T_0	20 boys and girls	Big and small blue and green squares
a_1	7 refreshments	Big and small blue squares
c_2	5 boys (refreshments)	Big blue squares
d_2	2 girls (refreshments)	Small blue squares
e_2	5 boys (tickets)	Big green squares
?	8 girls (tickets)	Small green squares

Table 15.2 Factor analysis of 16 problems

Variables (problems)	Factors					
	I	II	III	IV	V	VI
33B	.64	–	–	–	–	–
33C	.54	–	–	–	–	–
35B	.48	–	–	–	–	–
35C	.39	–	–	–	–	–
31B	–	.41	–	–	–	–
31C	–	.29	–	–	–	–
60A	–	–	.52	–	–	–
60B	–	–	.73	–	–	–
60C	–	–	.76	–	–	–
33A	–	–	–	.37	–	–
35A	–	–	–	.30	–	–
31A	–	–	–	–	.53	–
31K	–	–	–	–	–	.55
33K	–	–	–	–	–	.67
35K	–	–	–	–	–	.70
60K	–	–	–	–	–	.51

Note. Loadings smaller than ± .25 are not given.

is highly similar to the one obtained by including four extra problems besides the ones reported here. In both cases (Rimoldi, Insua, & Erdmann, in press), the separation of the structure from the language factor is clear.

With reference to the statistical independence of structures and languages, Figure 15.2 shows the main findings. The results are based on the same data used to perform the factor analysis just reported. For instance, in Figure 15.2 the average score for 150 subjects in Problem 31B is approximately .51, while for Problem 35K it is .85, and so on. A three-way analysis of variance with repeated measures in the variable subjects showed that both structures and languages contribute significantly to the variance. In addition, the language-structure interaction is highly significant.

Figure 15.2 shows that the values for perceptual Language K are almost the same as those for verbal Language A in Structures 31, 33, and 35, but in Problem 60K the score is much lower than in Problem 60A. This was expected in terms of the complexity of Structure 60 and the difficulty of handling it using a perceptual-concrete symbolic system. Furthermore, Languages B, C, and A are almost equally effective in handling Structure 60. These and other effects are discussed in greater detail in Rimoldi, Insua, and Erdmann (in press).

Table 15.3 Correlations between primaries

	I	VI	III	V	II	IV
I	1.00					
VI	.23	1.00				
III	.36	.23	1.00			
V	.35	.06	.23	1.00		
II	.39	.17	.14	.07	1.00	
IV	.45	.18	.31	.26	.47	1.00

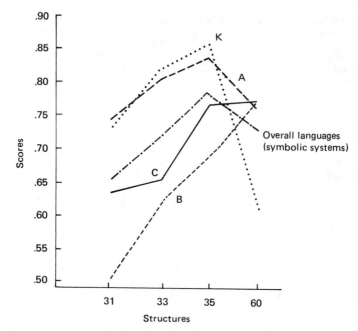

Figure 15.2   Effect of languages (symbolic systems) throughout structures.

Ordinary verbal Language A seems to be consistently good for all problems. Abstract Language B and negative abstract Language C become more effective when the complexity of the structure increases; for instance, they give better results in Structure 60 than in 35, better in 35 than in 33, and so on. This seems to highlight the fact that problem solving is not exclusively a matter of dealing with structures in the abstract but of having the means (i.e., languages) to do so. According to the complexity of these structures, some languages show better results than others. Perceptual Language K is less good than verbal Language A in Structure 60, and abstract Languages B and C give comparatively better results as the complexity of the structure increases. It could be suggested that some languages, like ordinary language, are more universal at the risk of being less precise. Language K is less precise than Language A and breaks down when it is used to express complex structures; the opposite is true of Languages B and C. It therefore seems that finding the symbolic system that best fits the structure of the problem is important.

The properties of the symbolic system used may facilitate solution, understanding, and reformulation or discovery of new problems. It is not only a question of understanding the relational system involved in a problem but of being able to express it using an appropriate symbolic system. Evidence of this is the development and use of mathematical and other symbolic systems that make it possible to express certain structures with less ambiguity than, say, ordinary verbal language.

This does not signify that problem solving and thinking are merely matters of having appropriate symbolic systems. Yet without such symbolic systems, problem solving may be difficult or even impossible, not because the subject is unable to understand the relational system involved in the problem but because she or he has no appropriate ways to express it and to operate with it. To conclude that a subject is not able to deal with a given logical system because he or she cannot solve a problem in which that system is involved may be totally erroneous. The reason may be that the modality used is not easily operated on by the subject. Many examples having to do with the development of science can be interpreted in this manner. The invention of a language may facilitate the solution of old problems and help to envisage new ones. Those in turn may require a new language, and so on in an ever-recurring spiral. The implications for research in psychopathology are straightforward: Either subjects (a) cannot understand relational systems or (b) being potentially able to understand them, cannot operate with them for lack of an appropriate symbolic system or (c) understand the relational system and know the appropriate symbolic system, yet the fit between the two is poor or deficient. In the first case, logical development is seriously curtailed; in the second case, the means of expression are lacking; and in the third case, the connections between logical structures and languages are poorly or badly defined so that they become arbitrary or chaotic. In all cases, thinking and problem solving are affected, but the educational and therapeutic means to be used in each case should be different.

PROBLEM SOLVING AS A DEPENDENT VARIABLE

In this section I report results obtained in problem-solving tasks after controlling certain independent variables. In all cases, problem-solving data refer to the tactics that subjects follow in solving problems.

Problem Solving and Age

In three different studies, we analyzed the effects of age in problem-solving performance. In Study A (Rimoldi & Vander Woude, 1969), 295 subjects between 9 and 78 years of age, classified into 11 age groups, were examined using two isomorphic problems presented both in ordinary and in abstract language. In Study B (Rimoldi, Aghi, & Burger, 1968), 120 subjects at 7, 9, 11, and 13 years of age were administered six problems, three in verbal language and three requiring the manipulation of concrete objects. Among these, two isomorphic problems were built around a simple relational system and presented using the two languages from Study A. Another two isomorphic problems were built using the same two languages around a more complex relational system. In Study C (Rimoldi, Chlapecka, & Aghi, 1970), 710 subjects between 7 and 12 years of age were studied for three successive years using problems built around three structures (31, 33, and 35) of different complexity using three manners of presentation: drawings, verbal language, and abstract symbols.

In all these studies we found that scores tended in all problems to increase with age up to a point. The highest values occur at approximately 25 years of age, remain constant for approximately 15 to 20 years, and then begin to decrease. The two problems used in Study A were isomorphic, and the results showed that scores in the problem presented using verbal language are, at all ages, significantly higher than the scores obtained in the problem presented using abstract language. In Study B we found that the two isomorphic problems based on the less complex structure showed parallel curves through the ages. In the case of the more complex relational system, however, average scores in the two isomorphic problems are about the same up to approximately 10 to 11 years of age. After that age the problem presented in verbal language showed a greater increment in score as age increased than did the problem presented using concrete material. We concluded that, for complex problem structures, languages readily dealt with at lower age levels become paradoxically less easy to handle as age increases. Also, the acquisition, control, and understanding of a given language may act as an inhibitor of previously mastered languages.

These results were confirmed in Study C. The scores in problems of Structures 31, 33, and 35 and presented using drawings separated subjects of 7, 8, and 9 years of age from those of 10, 11, and 12. In problems presented in verbal and in abstract language, however, the separation occurred a year later. Problems presented using drawings also differentiated more sharply at younger than at later ages, whereas the opposite seemed to occur with the verbal and abstract languages. In younger subjects, therefore, maximum discrimination may be obtained using drawings, whereas in older subjects a verbal or abstract presentation is preferable.

The statistical comparisons performed with the results obtained in Study C separated logical Structures 31 and 33 from 35. These two phenomena occur at all the ages that we have studied and verify the factorial and ANOVA results previously reported.

Problem Solving and Academic Level

Some of our results pertaining to academic level are influenced by the age effects just discussed. In two separate studies (Rimoldi & Fogliatto, 1962; Rimoldi et al., 1964), problem-solving performances of high school and college students were compared. In addition, each group was split into two matched subsamples. The experimental group received training in problem solving, while the control group did not. The final results could be briefly summarized as follows: College students showed overall "better" performances than high school students—at the level of the problems as such, at the level of the structures, and at the level of languages. The experimental group performed better than the control group in both college and high school students. This suggest that the college students approached problems more "logically" than the high school students. We also found that the experimental subjects gained more than the control subjects in their average academic grades. Similar results had been reported in an earlier study (Rimoldi & Devane, 1961) in which subjects were given individual training in problem solving plus a chance to review with the experimenter, in a nondirective interview, the tactics they had followed in solving specially prepared problems.

Problem Solving and Perceptual Parameters

Another study (Rimoldi, Insua, & Erdmann, in press) compared the problem-solving scores of subjects who had achieved high, low, and medium scores on several factorially defined perceptual parameters. The subjects were adult college students to whom 16 problems built around four logical structures were administered, each problem being presented in four languages. Of the seven perceptual parameters examined, only three showed clear influence on problem-solving performance. One of these parameters has to do with counting by recognition of group quantity; a subject has to be able to count dots grouped in various patterns. On problems presented in verbal language when the logical structure is complex, subjects high in this factor have significantly higher scores than subjects low in it. This does not occur with other languages and with less complex structures.

The perceptual-closure parameter, represented by the mutilated words test (Thurstone, 1944), also influences problem-solving performance. Subjects low in perceptual closure appear to be better problem solvers when the problems are based on structures of medium-to-high complexity presented in an abstract language. The opposite is also true: high closure ability is not conducive to good problem solving when presentation is in an abstract symbolic system.

Finally, high scores in freedom from *Gestaltbindung* (i.e., freedom to break up Gestalten) (Rimoldi, 1951; Thurstone, 1944), as represented by the Gottschaldt B Test, go together with significantly better performances in problem solving in most languages and structures. This field-independence parameter facilitates problem-solving performance in most situations.

Problem Solving and Sensory Defects

Problem-solving processes of prelingually deaf children were examined using the technique described in this article (Rojo, 1974a, 1974b; Vander Woude, 1970). The results indicated that, in terms of tactics, there is no significant difference between prelingually deaf and normal children in problems presented using colored drawings or concrete objects. As expected, the degree of agreement in normal subjects is higher than in those with auditory deficit if the problems are verbal and require the use of quantity. These results have been verified in our center and will be published.

Miscellaneous Studies and Research in Progress

We hypothesized that, regardless of cultural group, a subject's ability to solve problems will be similar in all subjects provided the structure is presented using a modality that all can understand. Good evidence favoring this hypothesis comes from separate studies performed with American, Argentine, and Swiss children (Erdmann & Buchi, 1968). We thought it appropriate therefore to compare the tactics of 150 Indians of Bolivia and Paraguay with the performance of non-Indian subjects (Rimoldi, 1974; Rimoldi, Braunstein, Gamiz, & Radovanovic, in press). The subjects were administered 10 problems built around Structures 31, 33, and 35. They were presented with a flat board that showed paths among trees in a forest. At the center of the board was a corral, like those used to keep livestock, and the subjects were told that they had to find where the animal was that had escaped from the corral. Subjects were also told that, by lifting up small windows placed on the center of the paths, they could see—by the presence or absence of hoof prints—whether or not the missing animal had traveled along the path. Lifting up a window was therefore equivalent to asking a question.

The Indian groups differed distinctly in how long ago they had become sedentary: the Tobas, over 75 years ago; the Pilaga, over 50 years; the Maka, 40 years ago; and the Ayoreos, only 15 years ago. Comparing the performances of these groups among themselves as well as in relation to the non-Indians, there were 7 out of 76 possible comparisons that showed statistical significance at the .01 level. Some of these differences disappeared, however, after equating groups in terms of subjects' age. Those differences that remained are related to the kind of animal that was missing, inasmuch—we are told by anthropologists—as different animals differentially motivate the Indian groups. For instance, the difference between Tobas and Pilaga, on one side, and Ayoreos, on the other, is apparently due to the fact that the horse (the missing animal) is an important component of the Toba and Pilaga cultures but not of the Ayoreo culture. In short, these results seem to indicate that there are no differences among the Indian groups and between the Indian groups and the non-Indians and that, given an appropriate presentation, subjects' problem-solving tactics are similar regardless of their cultural groups.

We are currently comparing cognitive styles of Canadian and Argentine children. This research has been going on for over 2 years as of this writing, and we are in the process of analyzing the tactics used by both groups. Thus far, we have written a pilot paper (Rimoldi, Bégin, Rechaud de Minzi, & Sacchi, 1982), in which we show how these two nationality groups perform on well-known tests of certain factors. It is interesting to see that the differences appear in those tests that are heavily loaded with presentations that correspond to the type of training emphasized in both countries. For instance, the Canadian children that we studied were much drilled in computational and numerical skills, whereas the Argentine children were drilled in the use of language. Thus it is in tests that appraise these factors that differences are found. On tests that depend on the performance of logical operations involving different types of complex relationships, on the other hand, the two samples are not distinguishable.

CONCLUSIONS

Our studies of cognitive processes in problem solving revealed subjects functioning as active searchers for information, which they then combine in different ways to reach a goal. Ideal tactics, which result from a logical analysis of the problem, provide a point of comparison for evaluating observed tactics. In this evaluation we consider total amount of information, order in which information is requested, redundancy, irrelevancy, and total number of steps in the process.

Isomorphic problems have by necessity the same ideal tactics, but the observed tactics may be different. The comparison of observed tactics in isomorphic problems may then be examined in connection with possible language effects. We do not assume that the best or the more original problem solvers will necessarily follow the ideal tactics. This would be equivalent to assuming that problem solving is a matter of logic and reducing psychology to logic. Psychology may, however, be used to verify logically established concepts.

Our methodology and theoretical assumptions have centered on the subject's activity. In defining psychological stimuli, more than their physical properties should be considered (Yela, 1974). Subjects are more than passive receptors and reactors to "stimuli" over which they have little, if any, control. Subjects ask questions, search, and invent ways and means of solving a problem; they appraise and interpret information and decide when the goal has been reached. This implies that subjects perceive the problem and do something about it and that the important thing is what they do and how they do it.

Knowing the relational system inherent in a problem and the modality in which it is presented facilitates evaluation. If we know the questions that a subject asks and when she or he asks them, the subject's tactics can be referred back to the structure of the problem and to the language used. In other words, tactics are one way of showing how a subject unravels, or "thinks about," a problem. In this context two concepts become important: logical structures and language. The results reported here indicate that they are operationally and linearly independent although they interact statistically. This means that problems built on, or having, a certain logical structure may be better dealt with using one language than another. Problem-solving tactics obtained under various experimental conditions should therefore be interpreted in terms of those parameters that apparently are common to all problems.

Not being able to solve a problem may result from inability to understand the relational system, from lack of understanding of the language used, or from the inability to establish the rules of correspondence between language and structure. Therefore, reducing thinking to language may be as one-sided as reducing it to pure logic. Both are important, and they interact in ways that are experimentally observable.

At various age levels, we found that scores in isomorphic problems show a constant difference. This suggests the possibility of at least rank-ordering languages. Such an effect is clearly observed in isomorphic problems built around the less complex structures. With problems based on more complex relational systems, interactions between languages and structures are present. This has strong educational implications and seems to indicate that the manner of expression used is not at all irrelevant in facilitating or hampering the operations performed with certain relational systems. Evidence coming from various studies indicates that there is also an interaction between age and language.

The evidence coming from subjects with auditory deficit confirms some of the previously discussed findings. If the problems are presented using drawings and concrete objects rather than words, the performance of deaf children shows no difference from normal children matched in terms of age. This does not occur with verbal presentations.

A good problem solver is field independent in the sense of being able to hold a perceptual structure against a disturbing field (i.e., he or she has perceptual flexibility), which permits organizing and reorganizing the perceived patterns in the process of searching for a solution. He or she is not fixated on the immediately given and can express a solution in abstract terms. "This is perhaps the meaning traditionally attached to the concept of intelligence as a capacity to abstract by using operations of the analytic and/or synthetic type" (Rimoldi, Insua, & Erdmann, in press).

In education and training, the question may be asked: Which is the best presentation to be used in introducing concepts in an educational context? Given subjects may profit more from certain types of presentation than from others, depending on their intellectual, perceptual, and personality characteristics. This can lead to the development of psychologically based approaches to individualized education so that mastery of concepts can be more easily obtained. Furthermore, some concepts usually presented in a certain manner may be introduced using other modalities. It is important to remember that a given manner of presentation may not be universally successful and that understanding a concept goes beyond manner of presentation, as I have been stressing. It is safe to assume that verbal language is safer than other modes of presentation after 10 or 11 years of age and perhaps, in most cases, throughout life.

This may explain the success of some modern approaches to teaching, for instance, the abundant use of concrete representations to explain some mathematical concepts, mainly those of set theory. It is not yet known, however, how this language facilitates the acquisition of other mathematical structures if these structures do not lend themselves easily to that language. Other symbolic systems may be necessary to express univocally the structure in question. The invention of a symbolic system is an important step in scientific development; new languages may also facilitate the discovery and explanation of other structures. In short, our results may be used to infer, at the process level, how thinking processes are generated, how they evolve, and how they relate to cognitive styles and to the emergence of a certain response. The relationship between the final response given to a problem and the previous process that led to it does not seem to be well established. Tactics should help in understanding how different people move toward the solution of a problem, which depends on the complexity of the relationships and operations that define the structure of the problem and on the modality used to express them. In this respect many individual differences are found. Some subjects may be able to operate more satisfactorily with one symbolic system than with another. The combination of a subject's preferred symbolic modality with her or his preferred logical relationships and operations define that subject's cognitive style. Variations in these components are observable in a subject's tactics, which result from searching actively for information along her or his own selected path.

APPENDIX: A BRIEF HISTORICAL BACKGROUND

The function of language in communication and learning has been a recurrent theme in history. I append here a few instances that refer directly to the theme of this chapter:

In a famous letter dated July 29, 1654, Pascal wrote to Fermat about "la règle des parties," saying: "Et je vous le dirai en Latin car le Français n'y vaut rien." In Latin and with abstract symbols, he proceeded to develop his subject. About the same time, Boileau, in *L'art poétique*, said: "Ce que l'on conçoit bien s'énonce clairment et les mots pour le dire arrivent aisément."

This was a period in which the discovery of new concepts and the invention of certain symbols to express them contributed to the tremendous advancement in knowledge that then took place. Both Pascal and Boileau seem to have stressed the connection that exists between thought structure and language. Establishing these connections unambiguously helps to explore new structures, which in turn may indicate the need for the invention of new symbolisms. At that time the idea of the first calculator was born in Europe.

In studies on mathematical talent, we found that children asked questions that suggested knowledge of mathematical formulations in which they had not been specifically trained. This was explained by Plato in the dialogue *Meno*. The slave boy, who does not know mathematics, solves some problems. Socrates asks: "He is Greek, and speaks Greek, does he not?" and then continues: "Observe whether he [the slave boy] learns of me or only remembers." The first question, about knowing Greek, has to do with the possibility of operating with a given language. Using the maieutic method, Socrates makes the child bring out what he already has in his mind, which nobody has taught him previously. So the slave boy discovers by himself some mathematical rules.

I am aware that the idea behind this dialogue has been the cause of much controversy. The question raised is philosophic; it has to do with the possibility or impossibility of learning. If I am not mistaken, some biologists are asking similar questions today. Lashley spoke about it in the early 1950s, and the idea that memory processes are dependent on the genetic code seems to be captivating scientists. But this is a far-fetched thought, and I am not able to speak coherently about it (see Blackmore, unpublished). There is, however, the possibility that our human organisms, because of their plan (using the word *plan* in the sense of Whitehead) have the possibility of establishing certain relations and performing certain operations between different kinds of events. Other relations and operations would not be accessible to us. This seems to agree with the evidence that we obtained from our studies, with a very important proviso, that these possibilities seem to transcend specific cultures provided the modality used is the appropriate one and the problem is meaningful. But this is subject for semantics.

In other words, and to bring in an example from another level of inquiry, consider the listeners in Galilee that, coming from different places, could all hear the same message expressed in their own tongue and, in wonderment, asked: "Are they not all Galileans speaking?" Many languages assure that the message will not be missed by anyone; maximum understanding is achieved through modalities that fit each person.

REFERENCES

Bell, E. T. *Men of mathematics: The lives and achievement of the great mathematicians from Zeno to Poincaré.* New York: Simon & Schuster, 1937.

Blackmore, C. *The unsolved marvel of memory.* Unpublished manuscript.

Block, J. H. (Ed.). *Mastery learning: Theory and practice.* New York: Holt, 1971.

Bloom, B. S., & Broder, L. J. *Problem-solving processes of college students: An exploratory investigation.* Chicago: University of Chicago Press, 1950.

Carver, E. P. Two dimensions of test. *American Psychologist,* 1974, *29*(7), 512–518.

Creedon, H. P. *Cognitive processes in educationally disturbed boys.* Unpublished doctoral dissertation, Loyola University, 1971.

Duncker, K. On problem solving. *Psychological Monographs,* 1945, *58*(5, No. 270).

Erdmann, J. B., & Buchi, D. M. *A comparative study of problem solving processes relative to the models developed by Jean Piaget and Horacio J. A. Rimoldi* (Loyola Psychometric Laboratory Publication No. 53). Chicago: Loyola University, 1968.

Glasser, R., & Mitko, A. L. Measurement in learning and instructions. In R. L. Thorndike (Ed.), *Educational measurement.* Washington: American Council of Education, 1971.

Gunn, H. E. *An analysis of thought processes involved in solving clinical problems.* Unpublished doctoral dissertation, Loyola University, 1962.

Hubbard, J. P. Programmed testing in the examination of the national board of medical examiners. *Proceedings of the 1963 Invitational Conference on Testing Problems.* Princeton, N.J.: Educational Testing Service, 1963.

Izcoa, A. E. *A study of schizophrenic thinking in problem solving tasks.* Unpublished doctoral dissertation, Loyola University, 1964.

Köhler, W. *The mentality of apes* (2nd ed.). London: Routledge, 1927.

Leontev, A. N., & Dzhafarov, E. N. Mathematical modeling in psychology. *Soviet Psychology,* 1974, *12*(2), 3–22.

McGuire, C. R. An evaluation model for professional education, medical education. *Proceedings of the 1967 Invitational Conference on Testing Problems.* Princeton, N.J.: Educational Testing Service, 1967.

Polya, G. *Mathematics and plausible reasoning.* Princeton, N.J.: Princeton University Press, 1954.

Potkay, Cl. R. *The Rorschach clinician.* New York: Grune & Stratton, 1971.

Rimoldi, H. J. A. The central intellective factor. *Psychometrika*, 1951, *13*(1), 27–46.

Rimoldi, H. J. A. A technique for the study of problem solving. *Educational and Psychological Measurement*, 1955, *15*(4), 450–461.

Rimoldi, H. J. A. Problem solving as a process. *Educational and Psychological Measurement*, 1960, *20*(3), 249–260. (a)

Rimoldi, H. J. A. The test of diagnostic skills. *Journal of Medical Education*, 1960, *36*(1), 73–79. (b)

Rimoldi, H. J. A. Thinking and language. *Archives of General Psychiatry*, 1967, *17*, 568–576.

Rimoldi, H. J. A. Logical structure and languages in thinking processes. *International Journal of Psychology*, 1971, *6*(1), 65–77.

Rimoldi, H. J. A. Problem solving. In M. A. Fruen & J. W. Steiner (Eds.), *Proceedings of the Fourth Pan American Conference on Medical Education*, Toronto, August 28–30, 1972.

Rimoldi, H. J. A. Artificial and human thinking. In A. Elithorn & D. Jones (Eds.), *Artificial and human thinking*. Amsterdam: Elsevier, 1973.

Rimoldi, H. J. A. *Cognitive aspects of problem solving*. Paper presented at the round table "Problems in the Use of Diagnostic Instruments with Children and Youth of Widely Varied Cultural Backgrounds," American Psychological Association annual meeting, New Orleans, 1974.

Rimoldi, H. J. A. *Cognitive problem solving: Theoretical and experimental issues related to problem processing*. Paper presented at The International Council of Psychologists, 21st International Congress of Psychology, Paris, July 18–25, 1976. (CIIPME Pub. No. 55.)

Rimoldi, H. J. A., Aghi, M., & Burger, G. Some effects of logical structure, language, and age in problem solving in children. *Journal of Genetic Psychology*, 1968, *112*, 127–143.

Rimoldi, H. J. A., Bégin, Y., Richaud de Minzi, M. C., & Sacchi, J. C. Students' psychological characteristics and problem-solving: A cross-cultural study (Argentina-Canada). *Interdisciplinaria Monographs*, 1982, *1*, 1–148.

Rimoldi, H. J. A., Braunstein, J. S., Gamiz, S. M., & Radovanovic, E. G. Problem solving in primitive societies. *Interdisciplinaria Monographs*, in press.

Rimoldi, H. J. A., Chlapecka, T. W., & Aghi, M. *Problem solving processes used by elementary school boys* (Loyola Psychometric Laboratory Pub. No. 58). Chicago: Loyola University, 1970.

Rimoldi, H. J. A., & Devane, J. R. *Training in problem solving* (Loyola Psychometric Laboratory Pub. No. 21). Chicago: Loyola University, 1961.

Rimoldi, H. J. A., Devane, J. R., & Haley, V. V. Characterization of processes. *Educational and Psychological Measurement*, 1961, *21*(2), 383–392.

Rimoldi, H. J. A., & Fogliatto, H. M. *Training in problem solving* (Loyola Psychometric Laboratory Cooperative Research Project No. 1449). Chicago: Loyola University, 1962.

Rimoldi, H. J. A., Fogliatto, H. M., Erdmann, J. B., & Donnelly, M. B. *Problem solving in high school and college students* (Loyola Psychometric Laboratory Cooperative Research Project No. 2199). Chicago: Loyola University, 1964.

Rimoldi, H. J. A., Haley, J. V., Fogliatto, H. M., & Erdmann, J. B. A program for the study of thinking. *Bulletin of the International Assocation of Applied Psychology*, 1963, *12*(2), 23.

Rimoldi, H. J. A., Insua, A. M., & Erdmann, J. B. Personality and perceptual correlates of problem-solving processes. *Interdisciplinaria Monographs*, in press.

Rimoldi, H. J. A., & Vander Woude, K. Aging and problem solving. *Archives of General Psychiatry*, 1969, *20*(Feb.), 215–225.

Rojo, E. A. *Acuerdo en las tácticas de solución de problemas: Sujetos con déficit auditivo y sujetos oyentes*. Buenos Aires: Centro Interdisciplinario de Investigaciones en Psicología Matemática y Experimental, 1974. (CIIPME Pub. No. 33.) (a)

Rojo, E. A. *Tácticas de solución de problemas y respuestas: Sujetos con déficit auditivo y sujetos oyentes*. Buenos Aires: Centro Interdisciplinario de Investigaciones en Psicología Matemática y Experimental, 1974. (CIIPME Pub. No. 34.) (b)

Simon, H. A., & Newell, A. Human problem solving: The state of the theory in 1970. *American Psychologist*, 1971, *26*(2), 145–159.

Tabor, H. B. *Process analysis of Rorschach interpretation*. Unpublished doctoral dissertation, Loyola University, 1959.

Thurstone, L. L. *A factorial study of perception*. Chicago: University of Chicago Press, 1944.

Vander Woude, K. Problem solving and language. *Archives of General Psychiatry*, 1970, *23*(Oct.), 337–342.

Wertheimer, M. *Productive thinking*. New York: Harper, 1959.

Whitehead, A. N. *Science and the modern world: Lowell lectures, 1925*. New York: Macmillan, 1946.

Yela, M. *La estructura de la conducta, estímulo, situación y conciencia*. Madrid: Real Academia de Ciencias Morales y Políticas, 1974.

VI

PSYCHOPHYSIOLOGY IN MICROGENESIS

16

Subliminal Perception and Microgenesis

Norman F. Dixon
University College London, London, Great Britain

There are many points of contact between the data from experiments on subliminal perception and the microgenetic approach to perception (Dixon, 1971). First, research on subliminal perception has demonstrated beyond any reasonable doubt that, in the brief but measurable interval between arrival of a stimulus at the peripheral receptor and its representation in consciousness, the input is subjected to a hierarchy of processing stages: feature analysis, semantic analysis with access to material in long-term memory, emotive classification, and response selection. Second, by using different techniques (e.g., tachistoscopic exposure, low-intensity stimulation, stimulation during sleep, recording on one modality while stimulating on another, dioptic and dichotic stimulation, recording from the exposed cortex, backward masking, binocular rivalry), it has proved possible to examine what is going on at these preconscious stages of perceptual processing. Finally, the sampling of events at these different stages has shown the effects of subliminal stimuli on figural synthesis, on autonomic responses, verbal associations, dreams, brain potentials, drive schemata in memory, reaction times, and sensory thresholds. In short, the phenomena of subliminal perception have been to microgenetic theory as bricks and mortar are to a house. But since 1971 new findings have been added to the edifice.

PRECONSCIOUS INTERSENSORY CONTROL

For many years, evidence has accumulated to suggest that one product of semantic analysis is the controlling of an item's entry into consciousness. This, the phenomenon of perceptual defense, appears (see Dixon 1971, pp. 179-222) to result from the fact that, after cortical discrimination of, say, an emotional word, activation by the ascending reticular system may be modified to reduce or facilitate conscious representation of the material in question. Further evidence (Hardy & Legge, 1968) suggests that this unconscious monitoring and control of stimulus inflow could also occur across modalities. Thus, stimuli threatening to the eye could raise the auditory threshold and vice versa.

In 1972, however, the possibility of yet another dimension to preconscious control processes was suggested by the research of Corteen and Wood. In their study, the subjects shadowed prose presented to one ear while words that had previously been associated with electric shock were presented, along with semantic associates and neutral control words, to the other ear. Three findings emerged of significance for microgenetic theory. First, the subjects were totally unaware of the words on the unattended channel. Second, none of these words interfered with the shadowing task. Third, the shock-associated words *plus* their semantic associates (which had never been presented before) evoked significant GSR. From these data the conclusion may be drawn that, at preconscious stages of perceptual processing, structural and semantic analyses, followed by an emotive–nonemotive classification leading to an autonomic response, may occur without impinging on a concurrent conscious processing task—the shadowing. In other words, to preserve the integrity of a consciously motivated primary task, the brain can carry out parallel processing without interference between inputs.

But what if the secondary subliminal input *could* be used to facilitate the primary task? Under these conditions could the brain make the necessary preconscious judgment to integrate the inflow from two sensory receptors? It seems so. According to a study by Mackay (1973), words, of which the subject is unaware, presented to one ear, may be used to help clarify ambiguous sentences presented to the other ear. For example, interpreting the meaning of a sentence containing the word *bank* presented to one ear depended on whether *river* or *money* was presented to the other ear.

In a comparable study (Henley & Dixon, 1974) the imagery evoked by music, presented subliminally to the left ear, was determined by the meaning of subliminal words presented to the right ear. One may assume that, consciously, subjects were motivated to demonstrate their imaginative interpretations of classical music. Unconsciously, and to this end, their brains made use of cues coming from the right ear. A related experiment with vision has been carried out by Bradshaw (1974). His study showed that the meaning of a centrally fixated homograph (e.g., "palm") may be determined by peripherally placed clarifying words (e.g., tree or hand) even when the subject is unable to report the latter.

Sometimes, of course, and this may be of some significance for the genesis of psychosomatic disorders and for such interference effects as are revealed by the DMT, material of which the subject is unaware because it is on an "unattended" channel may interfere with the primary supraliminal task. Thus in research by Lewis (1970) subliminal synonyms presented to one ear actually interfered with the response to supraliminal words presented to the other ear.

Judging from the Henley and Dixon experiment, which has subsequently been successfully replicated by Mykel and Daves (1979), laterality effects may also play a part in these preconscious stages of processing. Thus it was found that determination of imagery by subliminal words only occurred if the music was routed to the right hemisphere and the words to the left. This makes sense in the light of the known functions of the two hemispheres for processing musical and verbal stimuli, respectively. It would be interesting to discover whether results from applying the DMT would be affected by presenting the hero figure in the left visual field and threat words (as opposed to the ugly male face) in the right visual field. In this context it is interesting to note the recent finding by Sackheim, Packer, and Gur (1977) that subliminal effects are significantly greater in people showing right hemisphericity.

Further evidence of preconscious sensory-control processes has come from the work of one of my students, Walker (1975, 1976), on binocular rivalry. Walker's most important finding was that binocular rivalry can be initiated by the presentation of a subliminal stimulus to the nondominant eye. Besides locating the rivalry mechanism well upstream from the peripheral receptors, Walker's data imply continuous preconscious monitoring of the presence and nature of inputs that are at the time of their arrival denied access to consciousness. Drawing a parallel between these phenomena and the fact that an eye "blinded" by a cortical lesion or functional amblyopia (Ikeda & Wright, 1974) may nevertheless be caused to follow a moving object, Walker has suggested that both sets of data implicate a secondary visual system involving the superior colliculus and the association areas of the cortex. Such a route, from eye to brain to overt behavior, without conscious representation, could well play a major part in those microgenetic stages of the perceptual process that precede the OR.

THE EFFECT OF ANTECEDENT EVENTS ON CONSCIOUS EXPERIENCE

It is a truism that all conscious perceptual experience results from preceding events that may never themselves achieve conscious representation. For example, many researches, reviewed earlier (Dixon, 1971), show how a conscious perceptual experience may be affected by simultaneous presentation of subliminal words, lines, and so on. Since 1971, however, applications of backward masking and MCT in perceptual research (Marcel & Patterson, 1978; Reicher, 1969; Wheeler, 1970) have shown that the response to a consciously perceived word may be profoundly influenced by an immediately preceding, though masked, stimulus.

Thus Marcel and Patterson have shown that, even though a word is pattern-masked such that its presence cannot be detected, its meaning affects subsequent behavior. Evidently pattern masking interferes with access to consciousness, rather than with visual, encoding. Masking studies like this one are important for proponents of the microgenetic approach. First, they achieve total unawareness of the "subliminal" (because masked) stimulus without necessitating those degradations of the stimulus (e.g., very brief or very low-intensity presentations) that have excited so much skepticism regarding the validity of microgenetic and subliminal phenomena. At least one knows in the case of a backward-masked stimulus that something "loud, clear, and measurable" arrived at the peripheral receptors. Second, one knows from the subsequent recovery into consciousness of a masked stimulus, by masking the mask (Dember & Purcell, 1967), that such stimuli do indeed get into the brain and that their effects may remain therein for a measurable if brief period.[1] Third, these experiments provide firsthand evidence of structural and semantic analyses at preconscious stages of perception.

Along with studies by Shevrin (1975) on recording cortically evoked potentials to subliminal pictorial stimuli, and by Riggs and Whittle (1967) on the noncessation of electrocerebral activity during the fading of a stabilized retinal image (see also Lehmann, Beeler, & Fender, 1965), these masking studies should silence any doubts about the ability of the brain to process sensory inflow of which the mind remains unconscious.

THE ROLE OF MICROGENESIS IN PSYCHOSOMATIC DISORDERS

The last point of contact between subliminal perception and microgenesis that I mention here concerns their possible relevance to the genesis of psychosomatic

---

[1] Comparable "recovery" of a tachistoscopically flashed stimulus by poststimulus removal of the background illumination has been shown by Standing and Dodwell (1972).

disorders. In a paper to the 10th European Conference on Psychosomatic Research (Dixon, 1979), I drew attention to the remarkable similarities between a normal person's response to subliminal stimuli and the psychosomatic patient's response to exacerbating stimuli. In both cases, the person converts psychic stimuli into a somatic outlet without awareness of the intervening contingencies.

In psychosomatic disorders, as in perceptual defense, threatening stimuli produce autonomic arousal that eventuates in a somatic response (e.g., peptic ulcer, say, in the one case, and changes in skin conductance in the other). In those psychosomatic disorders that involve hysterical conversion symptoms, the underlying psychic conflict becomes translated into a symbolic outlet. In subliminal perception, symbolic conversion of psychic material must depend on access to unconscious material in long-term memory drive schemata. Finally, both psychosomatic and subliminal phenomena exemplify that stimulus-and-response generalization which follows when sensory inflow escapes what Spence and his colleagues have called "the restricting effects of awareness" (Spence & Holland, 1962).

Considering the almost identical nature of the processes that must underlie the two phenomena, it is remarkable that so few attempts have been made to explore, or to try and remedy, psychosomatic disorders by using subliminal stimuli. Exceptions are:

1. Beech's (1959) study of anorexia nervosa patients. Their prerecognition guesses as to the nature of tachistoscopically presented words supported the hypothesis that the disease involves an unconscious confusion between food and sexual objects.

2. C. Fisher's (1954) use of the Pötzl paradigm to study the psychopathology of a young female patient who had been hospitalized with a severe psychosomatic ileitis. Asked to recall any dreams she might have had on the night after a brief tachistoscopic exposure of a complex picture, the patient described (and drew) a dream that not only incorporated parts of the picture that she had missed the previous day but, in so doing, revealed (albeit unwittingly) a complex of those emotionally charged ideas that had eventuated in her somatic symptoms.

3. S. Fisher (1976a, 1976b) has shown that body boundaries (measured in terms of barrier scores on a projective test) may be disrupted by threatening subliminal auditory stimuli. That this effect of a subliminal stimulus on how a person feels about her or his body's barrier to penetration should (for obvious reasons) be greater for men than for women is just one indication of the great significance of this finding for students of psychosomatic medicine.

CONCLUSIONS

I hope it has emerged from this brief outline that there is much more than mere points of contact between subliminal perception and microgenesis. Data from the numerous studies of subliminal perception constitute incontrovertible evidence for the notion that perception depends on the preconscious processing of information at a hierarchy of levels—a notion that is surely basic to the microgenetic approach.

REFERENCES

Beech, H. R. An experimental investigation of sexual symbolism in anorexia nervosa employing a subliminal stimulation technique: Preliminary report. *Psychosomatic Medicine*, 1959, *21*, 277–280.

Bradshaw, J. L. Peripherally presented and unreported words may bias the perceived meaning of a centrally fixated homograph. *Journal of Experimental Psychology*, 1974, *103*, 1200–1202.

Corteen, R. S., & Wood, B. Autonomic responses to shock-associated words in an unattended channel. *Journal of Experimental Psychology*, 1972, *94*, 308–313.

Dember, W., & Purcell, D. G. Recovery of masked visual targets by inhibition of the masking stimulus. *Science*, 1967, *157*, 1335–1336.

Dixon, N. F. *Subliminal perception: The nature of a controversy*. London: McGraw-Hill, 1971.

Dixon, N. F. Psychosomatic disorder: A special case of subliminal perception? In M. Christie & P. Mellett (Eds.), *Psychosomatic approaches in medicine*. New York: Wiley, 1979.

Fisher, C. Dreams and perception: The role of preconscious and primary modes of perception in dream formation. *Journal of the American Psychoanalytic Association*, 1954, *2*(3), 389–445.

Fisher, S. Conditions affecting boundary response to messages out of awareness. *Journal of Nervous and Mental Disease*, 1976, *162*(5), 313–322. (a)

Fisher, S. Effects of messages reported to be out of awareness upon the body boundary. *Journal of Nervous and Mental Disease*, 1976, *161*(2), 90–99. (b)

Hardy, G. R., & Legge, D. Cross-modal induction of changes in sensory thresholds. *Quarterly Journal of Experimental Psychology*, 1968, *20*(1), 20–29.

Henley, S. H. A., & Dixon, N. F. Laterality differences in the effect of incidental stimuli upon evoked imagery. *British Journal of Psychology*, 1974, *65*(4), 529–536.

Ikeda, H., & Wright, M. J. Is amblyopia due to inappropriate stimulation of the "sustained" pathway during development? *British Journal of Opthalmology*, 1974, *58*, 165–176.

Lehmann, D., Beeler, G. W., Jr., & Fender, D. H. Changes in patterns of the human electroencephalogram during fluctuations of perception of stabilized retinal images. *Encephalography and Clinical Neurophysiology*, 1965, *19*(4), 336–343.

Lewis, J. L. Semantic processing of unattended messages using dichotic listening. *Journal of Experimental Psychology*, 1970, *85*, 225–228.

Mackay, D. G. Aspects of the theory of comprehension, memory and attention. *Quarterly Journal of Experimental Psychology*, 1973, *25*, 22–40.

Marcel, A., & Patterson, K. Word recognition and production: Reciprocity in clinical and normal studies. In J. Requin (Ed.), *Attention and performance* (Vol. 7). Hillsdale, N.J.: Erlbaum, 1978.

Mykel, N., & Daves, W. F. Emergence of unreported stimuli into imagery as a function of laterality of presentation. *British Journal of Psychology*, 1979, *70*, 253–258.

Reicher, G. M. Perceptual recognition as a function of meaningfulness of stimulus material. *Journal of Experimental Psychology*, 1969, *81*, 275–285.

Riggs, L. A., & Whittle, P. Human occipital and retinal potentials evoked by subjectively faded visual stimuli. *Vision Research*, 1967, *7*, 441–451.

Sackheim, H. A., Packer, I. K., & Gur, R. C. Hemisphericity, cognitive set, and susceptibility to subliminal perception. *Journal of Abnormal Psychology*, 1977, *86*, 624–630.

Shevrin, H. Does the averaged evoked response encode subliminal perception? Yes: A reply to Schwartz and Rem. *Psychophysiology*, 1975, *12*(4), 395–398.

Spence, D. P., & Holland, B. The restricting effects of awareness: A paradox and an explanation. *Journal of Abnormal and Social Psychology*, 1962, *64*, 143–174.

Standing, L. G., & Dodwell, P. L. Retroactive contour enhancement: A new visual storage effect. *Quarterly Journal of Experimental Psychology*, 1972, *24*, 21–29.

Walker, P. Stochastic properties of binocular rivalry alternatives. *Perception and Psychophysics*, 1975, *18*(6), 467–473.

Walker, P. The perceptual fragmentation of unstabilized images. *Quarterly Journal of Experimental Psychology*, 1976, *28*(1), 35–45.

Wheeler, D. D. Processes in word recognition. *Cognitive Psychology*, 1970, *1*, 59–85.

17

Brain Potentials, Brain Mechanisms, and Complexity of Visual Information Processing

Donald B. Lindsley
University of California, Los Angeles, USA

Many have tried to understand perceptual information processing by studying brain electrical correlates using average evoked potentials in both humans and animals. There are three kinds of brain electrical activity that we are able to record through the scalp and skull in humans. One is the traditional ongoing *EEG*, first described in 1929 by the neuropsychiatrist Berger. It is comprised of the so-called spontaneous or autonomous alpha rhythm of about 10 waves per sec and the more rapid beta waves and other rhythms.

Sensory stimuli usually block or desynchronize the alpha waves temporarily; but in addition they introduce very small "evoked potentials," which are often masked by the background electrical activity of higher voltage, making them difficult to see or study unless they are *averaged* over a number of trials. Thus, they are called *average evoked potentials* (AEPs). Some of us tried in the late 1940s and early 1950s to extract these stimulus-evoked potentials from the ongoing EEG, or background electrical "noise," without much success; but Dawson (1950, 1954) introduced us to a technique that was workable. With the advent of small special-purpose computers in the 1960s, the recording of AEPs, or *event-related potentials* as some people call them, became almost routine. Briefly, some 50-to-100 stimulus repetitions (light, sound, or touch) are made, and the algebraic sum of these is computed. The evoked potential for each stimulus is assumed to be time-locked to the stimulus, that is, to occur with a constant latency after the stimulus onset. The evoked-potential waveforms, being of similar latency and polarity, will sum and be enhanced; whereas the background EEG activity, because it bears a random relationship to the stimulus onset, will have positive and negative fluctuations that will tend to cancel out, leaving mainly the enhanced AEPs.

The third type of brain electrical activity is the so-called *contingent negative variation*, first described and named by Walter and colleagues (Walter, 1964; Walter, Cooper, Aldridge, McCallum, & Winter, 1964). The paradigm involved in the CNV is usually a warning stimulus followed by an imperative signal to respond or perform some predetermined act. The CNV may be made up of one or more slow negative waves that build up or fill the interval between the warning stimulus and the imperative stimulus, which usually follows in one or more sec. Thus the negative wave(s), or CNV, has been thought to be "contingent" on a relationship between the warning signal and the response signal, a kind of anticipatory or expectancy wave. In recent years, however, this view has lost credence, and other interpretations have been placed on the so-called CNV; for example, see Loveless (1977), Loveless and Sanford (1974), and Rohrbaugh, Syndulko, and Lindsley (1976, 1978, 1979).

Our attempts to study perceptual information processing through AEPs originated when it seemed to me that we should try to find some way to generate patterns comparable to those used in single-cell feature detection by Hubel and Wiesel (1962, 1965) so that we could get AEPs and see whether we could learn from them something about the nature of information processing. Whenever a stimulus is presented and falls upon the retina, it excites receptor rods and cones, bipolar cells, and ganglion cells; these cells send impulses along optic nerve-and-tract fibers to higher nerve centers. The classical, or primary, pathway to the visual striate cortex (Area 17) is via synaptic relays in the lateral geniculate nucleus of the thalamus, the so-called *geniculostriate pathway.* An important recent discovery is that there is also a secondary visual path via the superior colliculus (concerned with eye movements and fixations) to the pulvinar nucleus of the thalamus (which attains maximal size in monkeys and humans, along with increased encephalization) and from there to the extrastriate cortex in visual-association Areas 18 and 19 and in the inferotemporal cortex. In fact there are reciprocal, or two-way, paths between the pulvinar and some of these cortical-projection areas. There are also tertiary pathways by means of which visual impulses reach the reticular formation of the mesencephalon, providing activating and alerting signals to cortex and other higher neural structures. Thus the processing of visual information begins in the retina and continues in each of the structures that pass information on via these primary, secondary, and tertiary pathways of vision. Collectively, there is an integration of information about the nature and location of an image on the retina, about eye movements, orienting and alerting signals, attention, and the meaningfulness and significance of the image pattern. This is what we call *visual pattern perception,* the process that takes place each time the eyes make saccades in scanning the external visual environment searching for stimulus cues that are relevant to one's needs and motivations at the moment and that permit the processing and encoding of relevant information in associated relation to information stored in memory through past experience.

In any of these structures, from retina to visual cortex, a given cell can be shown to have a receptive field, that is, an area on the retina or in visual space from which the initial activation of the visual process begins. As Hubel and Wiesel (1962, 1965) demonstrated, single cells in the visual cortex may be predominantly of the *simple* type in the primary visual cortex, that is, in the striate area (or Brodmann's Area 17) that is responsive to contours, to edges of light and dark, usually moving in one direction at a given angularity and time-limited rate. *Complex* and *hypercomplex* cell types are found in visual-association zones, that is, in Brodmann's Areas 18 and 19; these cells process more complex types of information such as angularity, direction, simple form, and so on. The various types of cells in the retina, lateral geniculate body, superior colliculus, pulvinar, and striate and extrastriate cortexes process visual information with respect to selective properties of the visual stimulus; and some cells, particularly in the visual cortex, are known as *feature detectors.* The original and creative work of Hubel and Wiesel is indeed monumental; but so far as explaining even the simplest of perceptions is concerned, the finding of simple feature-detecting cells is about as far as it goes. Hubel and Wiesel have readily admitted this in an elegantly detailed 60-page article in the

Journal of Neurophysiology (1965). There, in a less-than-1-page section entitled "Implications for Perception," they indicated that there are feature-detecting cells in the visual cortex but that further processing must obviously take place—where in the brain, they do not know—before perception even in its simplest context can be said to occur. This was indeed a factual and honest appraisal at the time that article was written, and although much progress has since been made by those authors and many others, there is *still* no satisfactory explanation of where and how perception comes about. Although processing of information essential to perception may occur in the occipital lobes, there is no absolute assurance that perception occurs there or that visual memories reside there; it now seems likely, in fact, that other areas of the cortex may be involved and perhaps subcortical areas as well.

It is necessary to go beyond simple feature detection to explain the particular stimulus dimensions, where they are brought together in some form of a percept, and how they can eventually form categorizations, concept formations, and so forth. Let me leave these facts and speculations for the moment and turn to our experiments in visual pattern discrimination and information processing in humans and in subhuman primates.

VISUAL PATTERN DISCRIMINATION AND INFORMATION PROCESSING

First, there was a rather simple, but I think very significant, experiment involving AEPs in humans during three levels of complexity of information processing. We wanted to use extremely simple visual-pattern materials approaching in simplicity the stimuli used by Hubel and Wiesel in their search for feature-detecting cells in the visual cortex, stimuli that would display orientation, angularity, and other simple properties. We chose simple three-line patterns with angles and lines of different orientation connected so as not to form a completed figure, patterns that in general could not readily be identified by name. There were six such three-line patterns, five of which were used in all three experiments and in each condition of a given experiment. The sixth pattern, similar to the others, we used in only two of the experiments. These patterns and their code numbers are shown in the two righthand columns of Figure 17.1.

Experiment 1, Conditions A, B, C

Experiment 1 included both our simplest (Condition A) and our most complex (Condition C) levels of information processing. In Condition A the subjects merely observed or looked at the five meaningless and nameless patterns as they appeared every 3-to-5 sec in random sequence, each 20 times, upon the small rectangular oscilloscope screen controlled and programmed by a PDP-12 computer. Subjects were given no task involving the patterns other than to look at them. During the course of the presentation of the 100 stimulus patterns (20 each of five different patterns), the AEPs were obtained. These were averaged across patterns and subjects.

In Condition B exactly the same stimulus-presentation procedure was used, but subjects were told that .5 sec after each brief (9-msec) presentation of a pattern, a code number for identifying the pattern by name would be presented, the duration

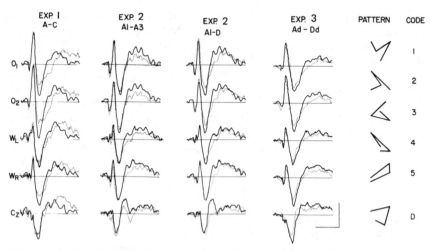

Figure 1   AEPs during information processing under three levels of complexity. AEPs from
left and right visual-association areas (O_1, O_2), left and right Wernicke's areas
(W_L, W_R), and midline motor area at vertex (C_Z) in response to simple, three-
line visual patterns during discrimination tasks before and after pattern-code
learning. Patterns and their code numbers are on the right; the discriminative pattern, D, is at bottom. Exp. 1, A–C: AEPs to visual patterns before (A: solid line)
and after (C: dotted line) pattern-code learning. Exp. 2, A1–A3: AEPs during
habituation tests; first 100 stimulations (A1: solid), third 100 (A3: dotted). Exp.
2, A1–D: AEPs to visual patterns (A1: solid) compared to those during more
complex discrimination task (D: dotted). Exp. 3, Ad–Dd: AEPs during the same
discrimination task before (Ad: solid) and after (D: dotted) learning pattern-code.
Calibrations: 400 msec, 5 μV; negativity upward. (From D. B. Lindsley, D. M.
Seales, and G. F. Wilson, unpublished data.)

of the code-number flash being 1 msec. Subjects were asked to learn to discriminate
the patterns (visual-visual discrimination) and to learn their code numbers—a task
demanding association of visual pattern with visual code. By halfway through
Condition B the subjects generally had learned, according to their reports at the
end of the experiment, to distinguish the patterns and identify them by their re-
spective code numbers.

Condition C was a readout test of this ability. The procedure was exactly the
same as in Condition A except that, about 2 sec after a stimulus disappeared,
subjects were to report its code number verbally. Subjects were asked to delay
this report for 2 sec so as not to have speech effort interfere with the recording
of the AEPs. Thus the simple processing of information (i.e., passive looking or
observing of patterns without any entailed requirements) as in Condition A could
be compared with a more complex level of information processing (visual-visual
discrimination and association) as in Condition C. This task is obviously more
complex than the passive observing of patterns in Condition A. For one thing, it
involves specific goals or requirements. For another, it involves several operations:
discriminating any pattern that appears from each of the four other patterns in the
series; then, once the pattern is identified as a figural entity, associating it with its
correct visually patterned code number, which thereafter gives it meaning and
identity. Given identical stimulus-presentation Conditions A and C and only level of

complexity of information processing differing, we could turn to the AEPs recorded from several brain areas to see whether we could find differences in the brain electrical activity for Conditions A and C and whether such differences varied for different brain regions.

Looking now at the lefthand column of Figure 17.1, labeled "Exp. 1, A–C," one sees that the top two sets of tracings are from the occipital areas O_1 and O_2, left and right visual cortex, or over Brodmann's Area 18 (the visual-association cortex). The next two sets of tracings, labeled W_L and W_R, are from over the region of the left and right supramarginal and angular gyri (Brodmann's Areas 39 and 40), a region often identified on the left as a part of Wernicke's area associated with the symbolic formulation and expression of language. The bottom line, C_Z, is from over a midline central or motor site at the vertex (Brodmann's Areas 4 and 6), a site often used in AEP and CNV studies of psychological functions. A linked-ear reference was used. The solid line is the AEP for Condition A, the passive observance of the patterns, for all six subjects; the dotted line is the AEP for Condition C, the visual-discrimination and visual-association task. As the figure shows, the latter differs from the former in O_1 and O_2 in three principal respects: The second, or large, positive (P_2) wave is markedly reduced in amplitude and considerably broadened in duration, so that its crossing of the base line from positive to negative is delayed; accordingly, the second negative (N_2) wave is delayed and does not return to base line within the epoch duration shown as does the N_2 wave for Condition A. Similar but less marked changes occur over Wernicke's area (W_L and W_R), but no appreciable change occurs over the vertex C_Z, or motor-area, site. In general, the three types of changes observed between simple (Condition A) and complex (Condition C) information processing for both the occipital-area (O_1 and O_2) and Wernicke's-area (W_L and W_R) AEPs were statistically significant, meeting either the .01 or .05 level of significance by the Wilcoxon signed-ranks, two-tailed test. Our detailed computer-analyzed tests of these and other results are not presented here.

Changes are greatest over the visual-association areas (O_1 and O_2) where one might expect visual-visual associations in such a pattern-code formation to take place. Wernicke's area, left and right, shows the same kinds of AEP changes in Condition C, but they are less great, even though statistically significant. The motor region, C_Z, shows nothing of these changes—another indication that the changes associated with complexity of information processing cannot easily be identified with the so-called P_{300} wave thought by some to reflect information processing. P_{300} typically is reported to be enhanced in amplitude with complexity of information processing, to be greater over C_Z than O_1 and O_2 regions, and to be in general a more diffuse type of response, probably associated with arousal and emotional activation to a greater extent than in the case of the P_2 and N_2 response changes noted here, which seem to be important in this type of information-processing context.

Experiment 2, Conditions A1, A2, A3

Experiment 2 was conceived as a habituation control for the results of Experiment 1. In Conditions A through C, there were 300 presentations of the 5 three-line patterns, that is, 60 presentations of each pattern over the three A-through-C conditions. We thought that one possible cause of the reduced amplitude of the

P_2 wave in Condition C of Experiment 1 might be habituation or boredom from sheer repetition rather than the learning of a visual-visual pattern-code task in Condition B and its readout in Condition C. Accordingly, we arranged three repetitions of Condition A (i.e., as A1, A2, and A3) with a new group of seven subjects, of whom we required only passive observance of the patterns, no visual-visual association learning or discrimination.

The second column in Figure 17.1 shows the results for Experiment 2, Conditions A1 through A3. There are literally no changes in the amplitude or the duration of the P_2 wave for any of the recording sites such as there had been for O_1 and O_2 and for W_L and W_R in Experiment 1. There was a reduction in the N_2 wave in A_3, but the N_2 wave returned to base line within the recording epoch. Thus we believe that our AEP results associated with complexity of information processing cannot be attributed to habituation or reduction of attention owing to boredom and repetition of stimuli.

Experiment 2, Conditions A1, A2, A3, D

A second part of Experiment 2 was an attempt to introduce our intermediate level of complexity of information processing into this same experiment. That is, after the "habituation" series A1 through A3, the subjects were shown the sixth, or D, pattern (in the lower righthand corner of Figure 17.1) and told to take note of it and remember it; for it would be included among the other five patterns to be shown again, at which time they would be required to keep silent count of how many times it appeared. In other words, they now had an iconic representation, or memory image, of a given pattern to keep in mind; each time one of the five regular patterns appeared, they had to make a discriminative decision whether it was the memory-image pattern. Thus there were certain operations to be performed, particularly discriminations of the internal memory image of the D pattern from each of the other five patterns, which would be shown in random sequence as before.

The third column of Figure 17.1 shows that, in both the visual (O_1 and O_2) and Wernicke's (WL and W_R) areas, there was evidence of the three changes in the AEPs noted in Experiment 1, that is, reduced amplitude and some broadening of the P_2 wave and some modification of the N_2 wave in the D record (the dotted tracing) as compared to the A_1 (the solid tracing). Because the D pattern was presented only after subjects gained familiarity with the other five patterns during the A1, A2, and A3 series, however, we decided to introduce the D pattern at the beginning of a completely new series with new subjects; hence Experiment 3.

Experiment 3, Conditions Ad, B, C, Dd

There were 11 new subjects in Experiment 3. A different group of subjects was used to avoid the effects of prior experience with patterns. Condition Ad was exactly the same as Condition A of Experiment 1 except that this time, before the start of the experiment, we showed the D pattern in order to provide the subjects an iconic representation, or memory image. The subjects were then informed that they would be exposed to a series of patterns among which the D pattern would be included and that they should keep a count of how many times the D pattern appeared and report the count at the end of the series. After the Ad condition came B and C conditions as in Experiment 1 but these were followed by

Condition Dd, which was exactly the same procedure as Ad except that it occurred *after* the visual pattern-code learning and readout in the B and C conditions. The comparisons here are between Ad and Dd, identical conditions procedurally (but with different antecedents), requiring that subjects simply count the number of D patterns among the other five.

The results of the comparison of the AEPs for the Ad and Dd conditions are shown in column 4 of Figure 17.1. Traces O_1 and O_2, from over the visual-association areas, show in the Ad condition (solid line) a broadening of the P_2 wave, presumably because of the information processing required by this inter-mediate level of task complexity (i.e., distinguishing the D pattern from the five other patterns). Also in the Ad condition for this group of subjects, the P_2 wave appears to be attenuated in amplitude compared to the P_2 wave for different groups of subjects in Experiments 2 and 3. In the Dd condition (dotted tracing) there is a further broadening of the P_2 wave and a reduction in its amplitude. These additional changes in Dd seem to be attributable to the pattern-code learning that preceded the Dd condition but not the Ad condition. Similar but smaller changes occurred in Wernicke's area. Neither the Ad nor Dd AEPs for the C_Z site show broadening the the P_2 wave, nor amplitude reduction, although there is in this sample a differential between Ad and Dd. Other samples in additional replications have not shown a C_Z effect, although the three changes noted in Experiment 1 have repeatedly been found over the O_1–O_2 and W_L–W_R regions.

These results, we believe, demonstrate that AEPs from over visual-association areas of the brain reflect changes, especially in the P_2 and N_2 waves, associated with different degrees of complexity of information processing. In these and other cross-modality studies using visual patterns and auditory code numbers to identify them (to be reported elsewhere in full detail), our attempt is to explain further the relationships we believe to exist between complexity of information processing (i.e., type and level of processing) and the regional differences in electrophysiological changes observed in AEPs. Both in the cortex and in sub-cortical structures of subhuman primates, especially in the primary and secondary visual systems, we have observed, in electrophysiological and lesion studies, evidence of the involvement of certain of these structures in the learning of visual pattern discrimination.

VISUAL-DISCRIMINATION LEARNING

Apparatus

In our cross-modality studies with *Macaca nemstrina* monkeys, we used a simultaneous visual-discrimination apparatus (SVDA) that is somewhat unique and contrasts markedly with the often-used Wisconsin General Test Apparatus. The latter allows a monkey much time to scan around and make a decision about a response under most procedures that have been used. In contrast, our SVDA (see Adkins, Fehmi, and Lindsley, 1969) requires less than 5 sec overall trial time, exclusive of a 15-sec intertrial interval; the actual visual display presenting the pair of patterns to be discriminated is typically 10 msec but may be increased or decreased. With a 10-msec stimulus presentation, a monkey must be trained to be alert and to focus its attention and gaze upon the stimulus area. A 10-msec exposure of the stimulus patterns that the monkey must discriminate and then respond to by pressing one of two adjacent lucite panels upon which the two patterns appear, does not allow the monkey time to make eye-movement saccades or scanning sweeps. Either the monkey must see the two adjacent patterns (which of course are randomly reversed from side to side) as a whole or gestalt and thus learn to discriminate on that basis, or it must learn to detect certain cues that are different in the two patterns and note their absence or presence on one panel or the other. In either case, it is a demanding task, which our monkeys are usually able to learn in about 6 weeks or so to a criterion level of 90% correct or better over 3 successive days. Once they attain this level of performance, their proficiency tends to remain high unless distractions or stimulus variations are introduced.

Procedure

The monkey is seated in a plastic chair with a collar, or bib, that prevents it from reaching wires and electrodes attached to its head but permits it to make arm and hand movements beneath the bib to reach and manipulate the display panels and the "setup" lever on the right, which the monkey must learn to press and release in order to introduce the stimulus patterns on the display panels directly in front of it at eye level. We use either a 300- or a 500-msec delay after release of the lever to allow the monkey time to alert or mobilize its attention and fix its gaze upon the panels. Then 15 sec after a response, whether correct or incorrect, a weak tone signal comes on, indicating that a new trial may begin with the pressing and release of the lever. A trained monkey immediately presses and releases the lever when given the tone signal, maintains a fixed gaze and attentiveness until stimulus panels are illuminated, makes a discrimination and presses a panel with a reaction time from stimulus onset to press of about 800 msec. If the correct panel is pressed (i.e., the panel containing the positive stimulus, which of course is shifted from panel to panel randomly), a banana pellet drops automatically into a small food cup near the setup lever. The monkey automatically reaches for it and eats it during the 15-sec time-out between trials. Incorrect presses are penalized by the 15-sec intertrial wait without reward.

Each of the above steps can be timed and recorded, with correct and incorrect trials automatically registered on counters and appropriate signals introduced on the FM tape-recorded electrophysiological (AEP) responses. The patterns are projected upon the lucite panels by a Kodak Carousel projector adapted for the purpose of shifting the patterns randomly from side to side. The projector lamp is replaced by a Sylvania R1131C glow-modulator tube that can be regulated for intensity and duration of the flash. We often use identical patterns, for example, squares, with one rotated so as to present a *diamond* appearance in contrast; we also have used the letters N and Z drawn symmetrically. In this way we control for stimulus area, brightness, and so on. The article by Adkins, Fehmi, and Lindsley (1969) contains a photo of the entire apparatus, including the projector and the monkey in its chamber. Figure 17.2 shows the monkey in the chamber pressing the correct panel, retrieving the banana pellet reward, and eating it.

Results

Using this apparatus, we (Gould, Chalupa, & Lindsley, 1974) first trained monkeys to discriminate brightnesses of the two panels in order for them to learn

Figure 17.2 Monkey in test chamber of SVDA viewing patterns rear-projected upon lucite display panels that also serve as response panels to be pressed and trigger a microswitch. The monkey presses a setup lever at the right; 300 or 500 msec after release of the lever, the paired stimulus patterns are flashed on the panels for 10 msec. Here the monkey presses the correct panel (the square), receives a banana-pellet reward, and eats it. Normally the patterns disappear before the animal presses the panel because the panel illumination lasts only 10 msec, whereas the trained monkey's reaction time is at least 800 msec; the patterns were left on here for photography. (Photo from "Perceptual Discrimination in Monkeys: Retroactive Visual Masking, by J. W. Adkins, L. G. Fehmi, and D. B. Lindsley, *Physiology and Behavior,* 1969, *4,* 255-259.)

the procedure and programming required in the apparatus. Thereafter, with electrodes implanted in the lateral geniculate nucleus and the striate cortex of the primary (or geniculostriate) visual system, and with electrodes implanted in the prestriate cortex and the pulvinar of the second visual system, as well as in some other subcortical regions, the monkeys were trained in simultaneous pattern discrimination, using the square as a positive stimulus and the diamond as a negative one. During the course of learning the visual discriminations, changes occurred in the patterns of electrical activity (AEPs) in the lateral geniculate and striate cortex of the primary visual system and at the same time in the prestriate cortex and inferior region of the pulvinar nucleus of the second visual system but not in the medial region of that nucleus. These changes began to occur when performance of the monkeys in making the discrimination between the square and diamond patterns attained about the 70% level of proficiency and were enhanced thereafter as performance increased to the criterion level of 90% or above. These changes in the pattern of the AEPs for the striate and prestriate cortex are illustrated in Figures 17.3 and 17.4, respectively. The AEP for the striate cortex, shown in Figure 17.3, reveals a new, sharp wave that appears at a latency of about 33 msec when performance reaches the 71% level. This wave increases in amplitude at 92 and 94% when criterion performance of the discrimination has been attained. A later positive component with a peak latency of about 150 msec appears at 71% and shapes into a narrower, shorter duration wave as performance increases to criterion level.

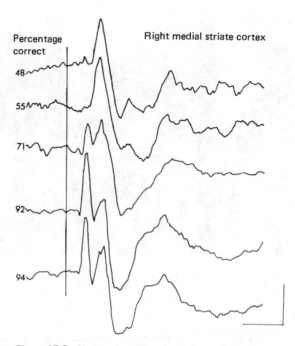

Figure 17.3 Changes in AEPs recorded over the striate cortex (Area 17) of the monkey during learning of a visual pattern discrimination. At performance near chance level (48 and 55%), AEP patterns are very similar. At 71% correct, an early negative wave first becomes prominent, and it increases markedly in amplitude at 92 and 94% correct. Note also that a late positive component becomes organized into a single wave at 71% and is further sharpened and reduced in latency as learning of the discrimination proceeds. The vertical line indicates onset of discriminative stimuli. Calibrations: 100 msec, 40 μV; negativity upward. (From "Modifications of Pulvinar and Geniculo-cortical Evoked Potentials during Visual Discrimination Learning in Monkeys" by J. E. Gould, L. M. Chalupa, and D. B. Lindsley, *Electroencephalography and Clinical Neurophysiology*, 1974, *36*, 639–649.)

In the prestriate area, a region otherwise identified as Brodmann's Area 18, two similar changes in the AEPs occur at the 71% performance level (Fig. 17.4). An early sharp wave, but less sharp and of longer latency than in the striate area, first appears at 71% and continues thereafter at 92 and 94%. Its peak latency is about 60 msec and contrasts with the 33-msec latency of the early sharp wave in the striate cortex. Like the striate cortex, the AEP of the prestriate cortex shows a large, long-duration positive wave first appearing at 71% correct discrimination and continuing to criterion levels at 92 and 94%. Its onset occurs at about 130 msec, and it extends to about 400 msec. It has a peak latency of about 200 msec, which contrasts with the peak latency of a similar late positive wave in the striate-cortex AEP, which is about 150 msec.

The late positive wave of the prestriate area has a long duration and a latency similar to that of the visual-cortex (Area 18) AEPs in humans previously described. Probably not too much should be made of these homologies or loci of recording in human and monkey; but it is interesting, and possibly significant, that late components of the AEPs of both from over Area 18 seem to reflect changes in the AEPs in the course of learning to make visual pattern discriminations where the stimuli are simple linear and angular patterns of different orientations.

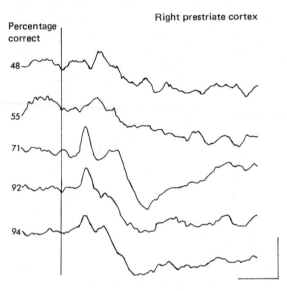

Figure 17.4 Changes in AEPs recorded over the prestriate cortex (Area 18) of the monkey during learning of a visual pattern discrimination. The AEPs are from the same monkey during the same learning of visual pattern discrimination as in Figure 17.3; only a different area of recording is involved. In this visual-association zone, changes in the AEPs occur that are similar to those seen over the striate cortex as shown in Figure 17.3; an early negative component appears at 71% and remains at the same latency but with reduced amplitude at criterion level (92 and 94%). A late positive wave of long duration first appears at 71% and is reduced some in amplitude as learning proceeds. Both of these changes in the AEPs are of distinctly longer latency than those of Figure 17.3. Calibrations: 100 msec, 40 μV; negativity upward. (From "Modifications of Pulvinar and Geniculo-cortical Evoked Potentials during Visual Discrimination Learning in Monkeys" by J. E. Gould, L. M. Chalupa, and D. B. Lindsley, *Electroencephalography and Clinical Neurophysiology*, 1974, *36*, 639–649.)

Although AEPs for the inferior and medial pulvinar-nucleus regions and also for other subcortical regions are not shown here, it has been of considerable interest to us that only the inferior-pulvinar AEPs showed late component changes during the course of visual pattern discrimination. This is a region that receives projections from the deeper layers of the superior colliculus, where individual unit responses appear to be correlated with eye movements that tend to shift a peripheral image to the foveal region of the retina for detailed analysis and information processing. According to Wurtz and Goldberg (1972) and Wurtz and Mohler (1976), the superior colliculus, in addition to its role in the foveation of images, may play a role in the selection of salient images or features of the environment and in this way be involved in visual-attention processes. The transmission of such information to the inferior region of the pulvinar particularly, and perhaps to other regions, combined with the fact that the pulvinar has two-way connections with the prestriate visual cortex and certain regions of the inferotemporal cortex known to be involved in vision, suggests that the pulvinar may well be an important integrative station. It seems to link information influx from the primary visual system (which receives input *from* the striate cortex but apparently does not have reciprocal projections *to* it) to information from the secondary visual (retino-collicular-pulvinar) pathways.

The pulvinar's integrative action may correlate locus of initial stimulation by light or shadow on the peripheral retina with subsequent sharper image formation as eye movements center the image on the fovea for highly detailed analyses. Throughout this process, an initially somewhat amorphous image may gradually become sharpened so that various features are detected and linked in association with other features to form a meaningful percept. This comes about as the image crosses and criss-crosses various receptive fields of neuronal units of the primary visual system located in a variety of structures from the retina to the lateral geniculate and striate cortex and beyond as well as similar receptive fields of the secondary system located in the superior colliculus, pulvinar, and inferotemporal and prestriate occipital cortex. It should be obvious, however, from everyday experience that fixation of gaze upon a visual field, or even upon a specific object or pattern in the visual field, produces no percept unless interest and attention are present. Thus the pulvinar, in addition to its information integrating function, may be part of an arousal, alerting, and attention-controlling system that makes the integrated information conscious and useful for its comparison and identification with memory stores. Thus percepts, concepts, and categorizations may occur, and new memory stores may evolve or old ones become modified.

VISUAL PATTERN DISCRIMINATION AND THE PULVINAR NUCLEUS

The last experiment I describe here has to do with visual pattern discrimination in monkeys (Chalupa, Coyle, & Lindsley, 1976) and the dependence of such a process on the intactness of the inferior region of the pulvinar nucleus. Because the visual pattern discrimination task was the same as in the preceding monkey experiment and involved a brief, tachistoscopic exposure of patterns that required alertness and attention in high degree, this experiment and its results suggest that the inferior pulvinar may indeed be part of an attentional mechanism as well as an integrative center for visual information.

First, 11 *Macaca nemestrina* monkeys were trained in simultaneous brightness discrimination to acquaint them with the apparatus and the procedure. All of them learned this task to criterion level. They were then assigned to one of four groups: three controls without lesions; three with lesions of the medial and lateral pulvinar; four with lesions of the inferior pulvinar; and one with lesions of inferior, medial, and lateral pulvinar. Surgery was then performed, and we produced electrolytic lesions of the designated regions of the pulvinar nucleus. The lesions were verified at the termination of the experiment and found to be subtotal for the regions designated but very satisfactory indeed. Six weeks after surgery all animals, including the controls, which like the experimental animals had no training during this period, were retrained to criterion level on the brightness-discrimination task. This was followed by pattern-discrimination training using N and Z as the discriminative stimuli. After attaining criterion performance on the N–Z discrimination task, two control animals and two with pulvinar lesions (one, inferior; one medial and lateral) were allowed a 6-week interval without training so we could investigate the degree of retention by determining the number of trials required to relearn the discrimination to criterion level.

Our main concern of course was the effect of the pulvinar lesions on the ability of the monkeys to learn a visual pattern discrimination under these conditions requiring a high degree of alertness and attention. The three control monkeys learned the N–Z discrimination to criterion level (3 successive days at 90% or better), and they required from 1,000 to 3,000 trials at 100 trials per day. Similarly, the three monkeys with medial- and lateral-pulvinar lesions reached criterion level within the same range of trials. Of the four monkeys with inferior-pulvinar lesions, two were unable to learn the discrimination and had not advanced beyond chance performance level after 9,000 to 10,000 trials. Two others gradually learned the N–Z discrimination but only after 8,000 to 9,000 trials. The one additional monkey with inferior-, medial-, and lateral-pulvinar lesions was unable to learn the discrimination in 10,000 trials. Thus it is apparent that only inferior-pulvinar lesions prevented or seriously disrupted the learning of visual pattern discriminations.

Furthermore, although the performance of any of the animals who *were* able to learn the discrimination was temporarily disturbed by adding a distraction such as an annulus around the N and the Z stimuli, all quickly recovered to criterion level of performance except the two monkeys with inferior-pulvinar lesions who had learned the task only very slowly after nearly 10,000 trials. With the circles surrounding the letters, one of these could not perform the task at all, after many trials; the other monkey relearned the task but only after more than 2,000 trials. Thus, if adding to the stimulus complex by means of the surrounding circles serves as a distraction to all animals, and if distraction is a deterrent to ability to attend, then it appears that attention is a part of the pattern-discrimination task as we employed it. The intact animals and the animals with medial- and lateral-pulvinar lesions, though initially affected, were soon able to learn to overcome the effects of the distraction and its interference with their ability to attend and to perform the task again. Animals with inferior-pulvinar lesions generally were not able to do so.

Interestingly, of the two pulvinar-lesion animals tested for retention 6 weeks after postoperative pattern-discrimination learning, the one with inferior-pulvinar lesions who had required nearly 10,000 trials to learn the task initially now required 1,400 trials to relearn it after the 6-week period without training or testing.

The other monkey with medial- and lateral-pulvinar lesions had required 3,200 trials to reach criterion level initially but required only 500 trials after the 6-week break. The retention performance of this monkey was similar to that of the two control animals also subjected to this retention test after a 6-week break; one of them required 700 trials and the other 800 trials to reattain criterion performance level. Thus it appears that the animal with inferior-pulvinar lesions was slowed down in retention as well as in acquisition of the pattern discrimination. Such performance deficits are probably attributable to reduced ability to attend.

Finally, it is of interest that in the control monkeys and also in those with lesions that *were* able to learn the pattern discrimination, the day-to-day performance went along at about 50%, or chance level, for several days or more. Then suddenly, as if by "insight" or awareness of a cue to the discrimination, their performance proficiency began to rise and move steadily to criterion level; at the same time, reaction-time measures showed an increase. The increased reaction time appears to be correlated with deliberation and decision time warranted once a cue or clue to the correct solution appeared to have been found. Before cue discovery it appeared that responses were more impulsive and rapid, but with little insight or awareness of cues. After criterion performance was attained, reaction times for responses dropped again, presumably because the cues to the solution had been learned and could quickly and automatically be detected and assessed, thus not requiring as much deliberation and decision time.

CONCLUSIONS

Even the simplest of visual patterns requires a complex network of information-processing mechanisms extending from the retina of the eye over primary, secondary, and possibly tertiary pathways to the cerebral cortex. It is now quite certain that visual pattern discrimination and visual form or pattern perception extends beyond the boundaries of the occipital cortex. It seems clear also that part of the temporal lobe and very possibly also part of the posterior parietal lobe are involved in visual processes. It is with some of these regions, as well as visual-association zones of the occipital lobe, that the pulvinar nucleus of the thalamus has reciprocal connections. As a link in the second visual system, it receives information about the direction of gaze of the eye and its saccadic movements and slow scans, about the position of images in space upon the retina, and about the foveation of images and other items of spatial and temporal importance relative to the eye and visual space. Some of this information it receives via the superior colliculus; and it appears that the pulvinar—by virtue of its connections with the superior colliculus and with extensive regions of visual cortex, especially the prestriate or association cortex but also the striate cortex—may serve an integrative role combining information from both primary and secondary visual systems. In addition, these experiments have shown that it may be part of a mechanism coordinating attention, eye movements, and information flux via primary and secondary visual systems. If so, part of this influence may arise from a tertiary visual pathway via the reticular formation of the lower brainstem whose ascending projections mediate activation, arousal, orienting, alerting, and attention via diencephalic and cortical mechanisms.

An understanding of the processes, both psychological and physiological, underlying perception and other higher cognitive functions is undoubtedly a long way off; but progress is being made, and new channels of illumination are opening up.

There is room for the microapproaches to structure and function, spatially and temporally, but also for the macroapproaches and systems approaches, some of which are represented here.

REFERENCES

Adkins, Y. W., Fehmi, L. G., & Lindsley, D. B. Perceptual discrimination in monkeys: Retroactive visual masking. *Physiology and Behavior,* 1969, *4,* 255–259.

Berger, H. Über das Elektrenkephalogramm des Menschen. *Archiv der Psychiatrie und der Nervenkrankheiten,* 1929, *87,* 527–570.

Chalupa, L. M., Coyle, R. S., & Lindsley, D. B. Effect of lesions on visual pattern discrimination in monkeys. *Journal of Neurophysiology,* 1976, *39,* 354–369.

Dawson, G. D. Cerebral responses to nerve stimulation in man. *British Medical Bulletin,* 1950, *6,* 326–329.

Dawson, G. D. A summation technique for the detection of small evoked potentials. *Electroencephalography and Clinical Neurophysiology,* 1954, *6* (Suppl.), 65–84.

Gould, J. E., Chalupa, L. M., & Lindsley, D. B. Modifications of pulvinar and geniculo-cortical evoked potentials during visual discrimination learning in monkeys. *Electroencephalography and Clinical Neurophysiology,* 1974, *36,* 639–649.

Hubel, D. H., & Wiesel, T. N. Receptive fields, binocular interaction and functional architecture in the cat's visual center. *Journal of Physiology,* 1962, *160,* 106–154.

Hubel, D. H., & Wiesel, T. N. Receptive fields and functional architecture in two non-striate visual areas (18 and 19) of the cat. *Journal of Neurophysiology,* 1965, *28,* 229–289.

Loveless, N. E. Event-related brain potentials in selective response. *Biological Psychology,* 1977, *5,* 135–149.

Loveless, N. E., & Sanford, A. J. Slow potential correlates of preparatory set. *Biological Psychology,* 1974, *1,* 303–314.

Rohrbaugh, J. W., Syndulko, K., & Lindsley, D. B. Brain wave components of the contingent negative variation in humans. *Science,* 1976, *191,* 1055–1057.

Rohrbaugh, J. W., Syndulko, K., & Lindsley, D. B. Cortical slow negative waves following non-paired stimuli: Effects of modality, intensity and rate of stimulation. *Electroencephalography and Clinical Neurophysiology,* 1979, *46,* 416–427.

Rohrbaugh, J. W., Syndulko, K., & Lindsley, D. B. Cortical slow negative waves following non-paired stimuli: Effects of task factors. *Electroencephalography and Clinical Neurophysiology,* 1978, *45,* 551–567.

Walter, W. G. Slow potential waves in the human brain associated with expectancy, attention and decision. *Archiv der Psychiatie und Nervenkrankheiten,* 1964, *206,* 309–322.

Walter, W. G., Cooper, R., Aldridge, V. J., McCallum, W. C., & Winter, A. L. Contingent negative variation: An electrical sign of sensorimotor association and expectancy in the human brain. *Nature,* 1964, *203,* 380–384.

Wurtz, R. H., & Goldberg, M. E. Activity of superior colliculus in behaving monkey: I, II, III, IV. *Journal of Neurophysiology,* 1972, *35,* 542–596.

Wurtz, R. H., & Mohler, C. W. Organization of monkey superior colliculus: Enhanced visual response of superficial layer cells. *Journal of Neurophysiology,* 1976, *39,* 745–765.

18

Visual Evoked Potentials in a Microgenetic Task of Object Recognition

Reiner Beck and Werner D. Froehlich
University of Mainz, Mainz, Federal Republic of Germany

In this chapter our concern is with selected aspects of information processing under the conditions of increasing input distinctness and clarity, when a person's task is to identify a picture's meaning. Our study was designed to contribute to a psychophysiological analysis of visual thinking by virtue of the nature of the dependent variables (i.e., EEG measures and verbal statements); it is relevant to microgenetic research because of the microgenetic mode of task presentation of the independent variables. Our main aims in undertaking the study were (a) to analyze the effects of microgenetic information processing on sensory and cognitive components of *visual evoked potentials* (VEP) and (b) to compare the results from a group of mentally retarded subjects with those from a group of normal subjects to ascertain the cognitive impact and its effect on VEP components.

Microgenesis has to do with visual thinking in general. It is concerned with the serial processing of information and the development and integration in cognitive hypotheses or categories. Especially in those cases where input information is impoverished, cognitive processes come into play only with increasing clarity so that sensory intake overlaps gradually with the more complex processes of checking and comparing. Microgenesis as a process, therefore, is characterized by a sequence of sensory and cognitive events occurring in the period of time between the presentation and investigation of a series of stimulus patterns. It aims at the attainment of a single and relatively stable cognitive response as exemplified by the final, most complete, most distinctive, or subjectively most probable pattern recognition. In other words, between the poles of maximal uncertainty at earlier stages and maximal stability (i.e., redundancy) at the final stages of the series, a kind of guessing procedure takes place, motivated probably by an "effort after meaning" (Froehlich, 1978).

The advantages of microgenetic methods are obvious; through them it can be demonstrated how form perception and form recognition are integrated into visual thinking as unitary cognitive processes that lead to identification.

BACKGROUND

Visual Evoked Potentials

VEPs belong to the so-called event-related potentials. They consist of a fast sequence of positive and negative changes of bioelectric activity in the brain's EEG, and they result from the impact of exteroceptive and interoceptive "stimuli" impinging on the system as a whole. To detect these phasic biosignals of extremely low voltage and low latency, a computerized averaging procedure has to be applied to the EEG pattern. This procedure leads to identification of changes appearing immediately after stimulus onset and lasting about 500 to 600 msec. Concerning their bioelectric genesis, evoked potentials mainly reflect graded changes in synaptic polarization that appear in scalp-recorded EEG in a summed-up way.

The "typical" waveform (see Figure 18.1) should not be taken literally, for the VEP and most other event-related potentials are influenced by various factors stemming from stimulus variables, the functional and psychological state of the system, and—last but not least—the position chosen on the scalp to record the EEG. In the VEP, such variables as stimulus intensity, frequency, hue, patterning, complexity, location in the visual field, task impact (i.e., response to a visual event or response to visually presented warnings or imperative stimuli), together with the recording position, all contribute to variance as well as interindividual and intraindividual differences.

Most probably in *vertex recording,* as in our study, the "visual" response meshes with the activity of modality-independent nonspecific cortical areas, as well as with activities in the nonspecific brainstem's system and in the thalamic reticular-projection system. In general terms, research on the origin of the vertex-evoked potentials has been hampered by the lack of appropriate animal models as well as

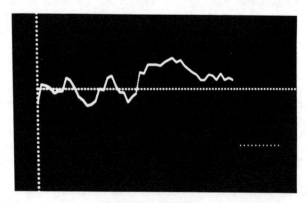

Figure 18.1 An averaged VEP, following a flash of 10-msec duration, of a normal subject recorded from P_Z to the right mastoid process. The average is based on 15 trials. Calibration: 20_mV; 100 msec (the dotted straight line on the right side). Positive and negative voltages appear in succession. The early components vary with stimulus parameters; the later ones are related to decisional processes.

by a significant lack of uniform methodology and lack of choice of paradigms in the human laboratory. Another difficulty is inherent in the fact that, owing to the deficiencies already mentioned, systematic and selective manipulations of specific VEP components have not led to a uniform classification of the psychological meaning of these components. Perry and Childers (1969), for example, concluded that VEPs are primarily of cortical origin but contain yet-unknown, if small, amounts of noncortical activities that are unrelated to visual stimulation or nonneuronal activities. In a more recent summarizing statement (Callaway, Tueting, & Koslow, 1977), however, the nonspecific impact is strengthened with regard to vertex registration.

Although one kind of research activity concentrates on responses to flashes of various intensity and wavelength, our purpose fits in mainly with research dealing with structured stimulus material offering meaningful information to the subject. In studies with increasing stimulus complexity and constant illumination, an increase (in terms of amplitude and latency) in the positive VEP component of about 200 msec after stimulus onset has been interpreted as content sensitive (e.g., Spehlmann, 1965). Unfortunately, eye-movement artifacts mainly appear within 170 and 250 msec too and should therefore be carefully singled out (e.g., Eisengart & Symmes, 1971). Whereas blowing up the size of figures does not have marked effects on this component, geometric changes of stimulus forms evidently do (Sandler & Schwartz, 1971). VEPs to distinct and to blurred pictures also differ with regard to a positivity around 300 msec after onset (Sandler & Schwartz, 1971). John, Herrington, and Sutton (1967) compared the impact on VEPs of flashes, geometric forms, different forms in the same retinal field, and different words in the same retinal field while they controlled pupil size and eye movements. They assume that VEP features are sensitive mainly to the amount of cortical impact; they further conclude that increasing complexity does not lead simply to responses being mediated by an increase of "retinal activity." Lifschitz (1966) demonstrated VEP changes resulting from affective meaning of stimuli, and Gliddon, Busk, and Gary (1971) showed a similar effect in mentally retarded subjects. Studies with colored light or color pictures show some blurred results (cf. Löwenich & Finkenzeller, 1967; Shipley, Jones, & Fry, 1965; White & Eason, 1966), whereas systematic relationships between stimulus intensity and the VEPs' amplitude have been reported by several investigators (cf. Löwenich & Finkenzeller, 1967; Tepas, Guiteras, & Klingman, 1974; White & Eason, 1966). Hence it should be noted that in most studies interindividual and intraindividual contributions to the variance were most prominent. Recently, especially with regard to selective attention, positivity at 300 msec after onset (P_{300}) seems to be of special importance (cf. Courchesne, Hillyard, & Galambos, 1975; Friedman, Simson, & Ritter, 1975; Haider, Spong, & Lindsley, 1964; Hillyard, 1971; Karlin, 1970; Naatanen, 1975; Pribram & McGuinness, 1975; Shelburne, 1972; Sutton, 1971).

Despite the uncertainties about the nature of VEPs, we believe they can contribute a hint of sensory and cognitive components in microgenetic information processing and extraction of meaning, especially in comparisons of mental retardates and normal people. Further, although much work has been invested in solving the technical problems of VEP assessment and classification, there are remarkably few studies dealing with *processes* related to the impact of a cognitive task on a subject.

Microgenetic Technique

Of the two different microgenetic techniques Sander developed—the *meroge-netic*, dealing with collecting and integrating originally unrelated details within the framework of a meaningful hypothesis, and the so-called *hologenetic*, using impoverished forms, as exemplified by tachistoscopic presentation or blurring of edges—our choice was the hologenetic because, for our purposes, the constancies of illumination and time were of primary importance. As the second author has stated elsewhere:

> *Most marked are stages related to pattern detection, and to the attainment of mean-ing, respectively, the latter one nowadays being also labeled perceptual hypothesis. At the end of the process there is either veridical identification or identification based on subjective evidence. Both signify that coping is completed. (Froehlich, 1978, p. 116)*

Brengelmann (1953) and Pinillos and Brengelmann (1953) used the so-called Picture Perception Test that consists of a hologenetic presentation of pictures showing common everyday objects. These authors demonstrated that recognition thresholds and stages differentiate between groups of psychiatric patients and normal people. A similar instrument for general diagnostic purposes was developed by Voigt (1956, 1959). There is, however, a lack of theoretical foundation for picture perception and picture recognition. Goodman (1968) and Hochberg and Brooks (1962) referred to "stored schematic maps"; Gregory (1970) introduced the hypothesis of "stored objects" to explain the process of actualization in reidentifying objects presented on a screen. Referring to the Bruner-Postman approach, Potter (1971) described the process in terms of two stages: (a) the organization of the stimulus and (b) the structural analysis of the visually mediated information with special regard to its complexity (cf. Wiedel, 1974). Gibson (1971, 1973) assumed a "structural equivalence" as the main feature in assessing the resemblance between the picture and the object represented. Hagen (1974) discussed the problem of pictures that cannot represent the object like a copy even though they contain essential information for identification. Our provisional conclusion on the basis of this evidence is quite simple: The process of visual thinking that leads to objective identification in a given visually presented picture is based on a complex interaction pattern between perceptual and cognitive processing.

In a first psychophysiological approach to this problem, Froehlich and Laux (1969) demonstrated that (a) the relation between specific phasic components of the OR (differences between phasic GSR and level of basal resistance) and verbally expressed amounts of pattern integration in a microgenetic task of the merogenetic variety is strong enough to hypothesize a general functional relationship, and (b) the trend in OR over 15 trials shows significantly more curvilinear than linear components, the latter suggesting a *multistage process*. This leads to our further conclusion that the microgenetic paradigm allows one to combine psychological and physiological measures meaningfully. Moreover, the microgenetic paradigm allows control over stimulus features that contribute to changes, and it is also useful for investigations of interindividual differences.

METHOD

Pilot Study

In our pilot study, we selected and standardized the stimulus material. One of our objectives was to construct a series that would differentiate between mental retardates and normal people. There was a pool of 21 pictures showing well-known objects or situations (e.g., a house, a chair, a man on a horse, etc.). From this pool, we selected pictures that were technically suitable in contrast, illumination, and so on. Two additional selection criteria were that no picture be recognized by mental retardates or school children before the fifth presentation and that all pictures be recognized by all subjects, normal or retarded, by the final presentation. The critical variable in all cases was the amount of blurredness, which decreased step-wise from the 1st to the 10th presentation.

With the nine series so selected we checked "subjective distances" with regard to pairwise comparison of blurred pictures. By this procedure, we selected two series of pairs in which blurredness is reduced in equal-appearing steps of clarity and distinctiveness. To control for the equal distribution of the positional value of clues in the pictures (cf. Mackworth & Bruner, 1970), we performed a test of "subjective acquaintance values" (ratings by students, based on four-square fragments of the various pictures). For example, in the series showing a bunch of keys with eight distinct orienting points and the series with a book with three orienting points, the picture of the keys was chosen as the more complex of the two. The keys with their point-of-orientation density were recognized by mental retardates and students later (at presentations 5 to 9) than the book with its three relatively distant reference points (at presentations 4 to 7). Very similar results were obtained upon ascertaining reaction times in normal subjects (students).

Experiment

The main experiment was done under electrooocculographic (EOG) artifact control, selecting only unbiased trials. The subjects were 19 students (mean age, 24.7; *SD* = 3.1; mean IQ = 116; *SD* = 6.9; 13 men, 6 women) compared with 19 mental retardates (mean age, 23.2; *SD* = 2.8; mean IQ = 52.5; *SD* = 15.9; 12 men, 7 women). The mentally retarded did not suffer from any physical illnesses. They had speech ability and spanned the range from "mild" to "severe" retardation. To control for serial effects and to assess standard flash potentials, both groups were divided into two subgroups each: Group 1, which was shown 10 flashes, 10 pictures in the book series, and 10 pictures in the key series; and Group 2, which was shown 10 flashes, the key series, 10 other flashes, and the book series. Room illumination was at 60 lx; keys appearing at 70 lx, the book at 75 lx (mean), and the flashes at 230 lx.

EEG electrodes (Beckman miniature AgAgCl, diameter 10 mm) were affixed to the vertex and right mastoid, with reference at frontal position. The EOG was taken right and left to the temple. Amplification was done using a Princeton 140-113 with a frequency range of .03 to 30 Hz.

Stimuli were presented on a 40-by-40-cm screen. Subjects were placed in a comfortable chair at a distance of 120 cm. Each presentation lasted 500 msec, the interstimulus interval being constantly 3,294 msec. Subjects were instructed not to move or speak and to try to identify the object shown as fast as possible. Shifts from flash to the key or book series were not announced; after the key and book trials, subjects were asked to make verbal statements of the object identified. The instruction was in line with that used by Froehlich and Laux (1969) and Schechter and Buchsbaum (1973), respectively.

RESULTS

Data were analyzed to answer the questions: (a) How do flash responses differ from the key and book responses after them in terms of VEP? (b) How and to what extent do students differ from the mentally retarded in this task? (c) How much does the difference between the key series and the book series contributes to variance? and (d) What signs in VEP correspond to "picture recognition"?

For a more comprehensive graphic representation, the amplitude values are presented relative to maximal amplitude based on an analysis of amplitudes and latencies during the 100 msec after onset. Original data were evaluated by analysis of variance, process factor analyses (Pawlik, 1965), and an interaveraging procedure across subjects' responses.

The P $\times$ Q $\times$ R analysis of variance for repeated measurements on the last two factors showed the following pattern of results. Whereas *early* amplitude changes were mainly related to light-intensity factors between flashes and pictures, *later* amplitude changes (V–VII) seemed to be sensitive to microgenetic impact.

Process factor analysis showed significant results only with regard to flashes. With the first and sixth presentations excluded, all other presentations loaded substantially on the first factor, which, again, has obviously to do with luminance. The sixth presentation, as represented in loadings at the second and third factor, seemed to reflect in both series a "general shift of attention" from more phasic ORs into discrimination (cf. Birbaumer, 1975; Pribram & McGuinness, 1975; Rohracher, 1937). In contrast to some other investigations (cf. Chalke & Ertl, 1965; Repp, 1975), latency data failed to differentiate either between groups or tasks.

The amplitude distribution in flash responses paralleled the abscissa and did not show any significant differences between groups (see Fig. 18.2). Graphic and trend analyses of amplitude changes in the key and book responses, however, showed some interesting features. Whereas among students the identification rate was 100%, among the mentally retarded it was about 30%. In early amplitudes (III–IV) students showed a tendency toward a quadratic trend ($p = .10$) but no detectable trend in the later components (see Fig. 18.3).

Figure 18.3 demonstrates, moreover, that, among students, amplitudes start at a mean value of 68.2%, slow down to 46.0% at Picture 6, then attain again, at the final presentation, a level of 65.2%, which is relatively marked compared to maximal amplitude. Early components in retardates, by contrast, show no significant trend; the later components (V–VI), however, show a tendency toward linearity and a quadratic trend ($p = .10$) in the key series. This result seems to be of differential value, because "identifiers" ($n = 6$) and "nonidentifiers" ($n = 13$) among the retardates differ in an obvious way.

Figure 18.4 demonstrates that, in contrast to identifiers, nonidentifiers show marked amplitudes over the whole series. Moreover, nonidentifiers show later peaks and more latencies in the later components. In mentally retarded subjects

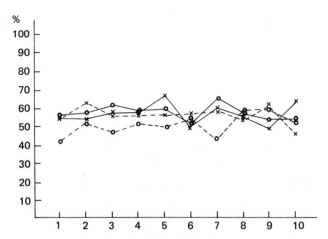

Figure 18.2 The relative amplitude distribution (ordinate) of the two flash series in mental retardates. X line: III–IV amplitude of the first flash series. O line: V–IV amplitude of the second flash series.

(Fig. 18.5) these differences are related to IQ differences between identifiers and nonidentifiers, the cut-off point being about 60.

The EEG in identifiers and nonidentifiers seems to differ especially with regard to early components. Similar results were assessed with the book series, where nonidentifying students also showed a marked decrease in the amplitude distribution of early components.

A quite distinctive feature differing between identifiers and nonidentifiers can

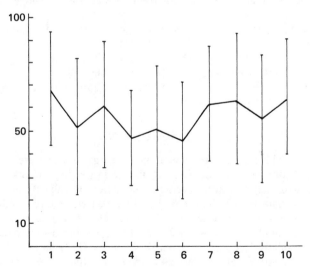

Figure 18.3 The percentage of III–IV amplitude (the vertical axis) of the student group who identified the keys series ($n = 19$) plotted in relation to the microgenetic phases (the horizontal axis).

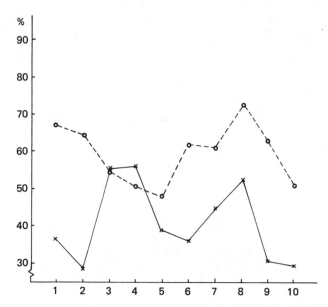

Figure 18.4   The different percentage distributions of III–IV amplitude of the identifiers and nonidentifiers among
the mental retardates. X line: identifiers; O line: nonidentifiers; x axis: microgenetic phases.

be shown with regard to the later components of amplitude changes. Values of nonidentifiers show a general and linear trend down to base line, whereas identifiers
generally exhibit an increase that follows the trend toward clarity in the pictures
presented.

These results suggest that there is no habituation taking place during the microgenetic search for meaning. The results further demonstrate at the EEG level the
multistage process that is reflected mainly in amplitude changes from 123 to 270
msec after stimulus onset. These results are in line with conclusions drawn from
autonomic changes (Froehlich, 1978) and earlier statements about stages identified
from experiential data (verbal reports).

CONCLUSIONS

Descriptive evidence and trend-analytic findings demonstrate a second-order
(quadratic) relation between the blurred picture series (key, book) and the amplitude values. This trend is most pronounced in normal subjects in terms of early
peak-to-peak distances (128-192 msec) and in mentally retarded subjects at later
components with latencies of 180 to 270 msec. This difference also holds for both
identifiers and nonidentifiers. Averaging data across persons leads to a further step.
There are five relatively constant peaks: I, 48 to 92; II, 87 to 121; III, 115 to 164;
IV, 156 to 228; and V, 248 to 330 msec. In general, the students exhibit a marked
wave pattern with amplitudes about 1 to 1.5 μV higher than mentally retarded
subjects. Most obvious are the differences at IV, the so-called vertex potential in
the flash series. This seems to be a sign of differences between the two groups in
attentional or discriminational impact (or both) (see Figs. 18.6 and 18.7).

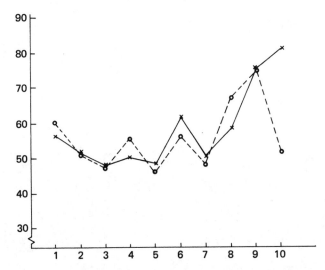

Figure 18.5 The different percentage distributions of V–IV amplitude of the identifiers and nonidentifiers among the mental retardates. X line: identifiers; O line: nonidentifiers; x axis: microgenetic phases.

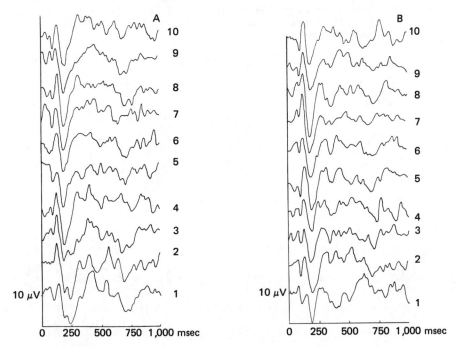

Figure 18.6 The interaveraging VEP series for all students ($n = 7, 19$) with the number of flash presentations increasing (ordinate from 1 to 10). A: first flash series. B: second flash series.

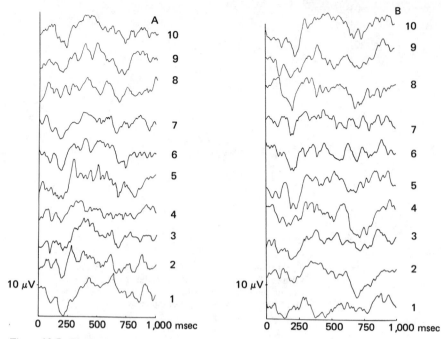

Figure 18.7 The interaveraging VEP series over all mental retardates ($n = 7, 19$) with the number of flash presentations increasing (ordinate from 1–10). A: first flash series. B: second flash series.

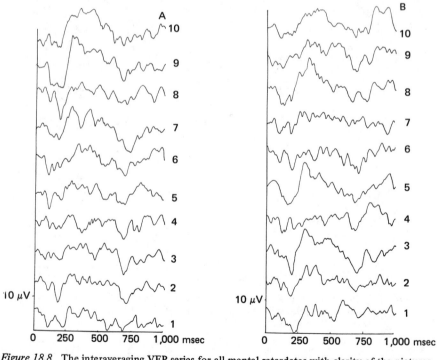

Figure 18.8 The interaveraging VEP series for all mental retardates with clarity of the pictures increasing (from 1–10). A: keys series. B: book series.

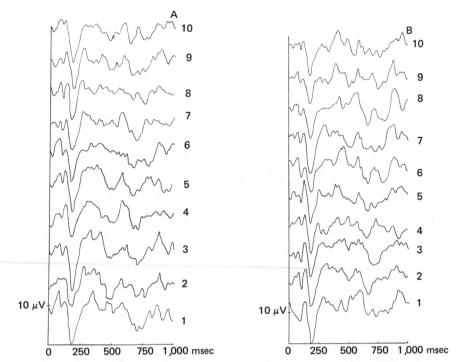

Figure 18.9 The interaveraging VEP series for all students ($n = 7$, 19) with clarity of the pictures increasing (from 1–10). A: keys series. B: book series.

Although a habituation effect in later presentations was observable in retarded subjects, there was an increase of Peak V in the key as well as in book series. This leads to the conclusion that increasing activation also takes place in retarded subjects in the late latency stage (see Fig. 18.8). In contrast to the results in retardates, however, Peaks I, II, and III in normal subjects (48–164 msec) are much more prominent; and all latencies of the five peaks become successively shorter in each of the three series (see Fig. 18.9). With regard to these signs of *response set*, the early peaks especially (I, II, and III) and the *vertex potential* are worth noting.

In summary, we can conclude that the VEP seems to be a valuable instrument for assessing *attentional, discriminational,* or *readiness signs*. The impact of meaning, however, remains a domain of interpretations within the framework of stimulus qualities and the processing of their cognitive experiential representations. In any case, what is most important is that differences between identifiers and nonidentifiers have been established at sensory and information-processing levels.

REFERENCES

Birbaumer, N. *Physiologische Psychologie.* Heidelberg: Springer, 1975.

Brengelmann, J. C. Der visuelle Objekterkennungstest. *Zeitschrift für experimentelle und angewandte Psychologie,* 1953, *1,* 422–452.

Callaway, E., Tueting, P., Koslow, S. H. *Event-related brain potentials in man.* New York: Academic, 1977.

Chalke, F. C., & Ertl, J. Evoked potentials and intelligence. *Life Science,* 1965, *4,* 1319–1322.

Courchesne, E., Hillyard, S. A., & Galambos, R. Stimulus novelty, task relevance and the visual evoked potential in man. *Electroencephalography and Clinical Neurophysiology,* 1975, *39*(2), 131–143.

Eisengart, M. A., & Symmes, D. Effect of eye blink on the visual evoked response in children. *Electroencephalography and Clinical Neurophysiology,* 1971, *31,* 71–75.

Friedman, D., Simson, R., & Ritter, W. The late positive component (P_{300}) and information processing in sentences. *Electroencephalography and Clinical Neurophysiology,* 1975, *38,* 255–262.

Froehlich, W. D. Stress, anxiety, and the control of attention: A psychophysiological approach. In C. D. Spielberger & I. G. Sarason (Eds.), *Stress and anxiety* (Vol. 5). Washington: Hemisphere, 1978.

Froehlich, W. D., & Laux, L. Serielles Wahrnehmen, Aktualgenese Informationsintegration und Orientierungsreaktion: I. Aktualgenisches Modell und Orientierungsreaktion. *Zeitschrift für experimentelle und angewandte Psychologie,* 1969, *16,* 250–277.

Gibson, J. J. The information available in pictures. *Leonardo,* 1971, *4,* 27–35.

Gibson, J. J. *Die Wahrnehmung der visuellen Welt.* Weinheim: Beltz, 1973.

Gliddon, J. B., Busk, J., & Gary, C. G. Visual evoked responses to emotional stimuli in the mentally retarded. *Psychophysiology,* 1971, *8,* 576–580.

Goodman, N. *Languages of art: An approach to a theory of symbols.* Indianapolis: Bobbs-Merrill, 1968.

Gregory, R. L. *The intelligent eye.* New York: McGraw-Hill, 1970.

Hagen, M. A. Picture perception: Toward a theoretical model. *Psychological Bulletin,* 1974, *81,* 471–497.

Haider, M., Spong, P., & Lindsley, D. B. Attention, vigilance, and the cortical evoked potentials in humans. *Science,* 1964, *145,* 180–182.

Hillyard, S. A. The psychological specificity of the contingent negative variation and late evoked potential *(P_{300}).* *Electroencephalography and Clinical Neurophysiology,* 1971, *31,* 302–303.

Hochberg, J. E., & Brooks, V. Pictorial recognition as an unlearned ability: A study of one child's performance. *American Journal of Psychology,* 1962, *75,* 624–628.

John, E. R., Herrington, R. N., & Sutton, S. Effects of visual form on the evoked response. *Science,* 1967, *155,* 1439–1442.

Karlin, L. Cognition, preparation, and sensory-evoked potentials. *Psychological Bulletin,* 1970, *73,* 122–136.

Lifschitz, K. The average evoked cortical response to complex stimuli. *Psychophysiology,* 1966, *3,* 55–68.

Löwenich, V. von, & Finkenzeller, P. Reizstärkenabhängigkeit und Stevenssche Potenzfunktion beim optisch evozierten Potential des Menschen. *Pflügers Archiv,* 1967, *293,* 256–271.

Mackworth, N. H., & Bruner, J. S. How adults and children search and recognize pictures. *Human Development,* 1970, *13,* 149–177.

Naatanen, R. Selective attention and evoked potentials in humans: A critical review. *Biological Psychology,* 1975, *2,* 237–307.

Pawlik, K. Elementarfunktionen ("Faktoren") einfacher Lernvorgänge. In H. Heckhausen (Ed.), *Bericht über den 24. Kongress der Deutschen Gesellschaft für Psychologie.* Göttingen: Hogrefe, 1965.

Perry, N. W., & Childers, D. G. *The human visual evoked response: Method and theory.* Springfield, Ill.: Thomas, 1969.

Pinillos, J. L., & Brengelmann, J. C. Bilderkennung als Persönlichkeitstest. *Zeitschrift für experimentelle und angewandte Psychologie,* 1953, *1,* 480–500.

Potter, M. C. Über perzeptives Erkennen. In J. S. Bruner, R. R. Olver, & P. M. Greenfield (Eds.), *Studien zur kognitiven Entwicklung.* Stuttgart: Klett, 1971.

Pribram, K. H., & McGuinness, D. Arousal, activation, and effort in the control of attention. *Psychological Review,* 1975, *82,* 116–149.

Repp, N. *Zusammenhänge zwischen evozierten Potentialen und der Reaktionszeit mit Intelligenz- und Aufmerksamkeitstests.* Unpublished doctoral dissertation, University of Mainz, Faculty of Biology, 1975.

Rohracher, H. Die gehirnelektrischen Erscheinungen bei Sinnesreizen. *Zeitschrift für Psychologie,* 1937, *140,* 274–308.

Sandler, L., & Schwartz, M. Evoked responses and perception: Stimulus content versus stimulus structure. *Psychophysiology,* 1971, *6,* 727–739.

Schechter, G., & Buchsbaum, M. The effects of attention, stimulus intensity, and individual differences on the average evoked response. *Psychophysiology*, 1973, *10*, 392–400.

Shelburne, S. A. Jr. Visual evoked responses to word and nonsense syllable stimuli. *Electroencephalography and Clinical Neurophysiology*, 1972, *32*, 17–25.

Shipley, T., Jones, R. W., & Fry, A. Evoked visual potentials and human color vision. *Science*, 1965, *150*, 1162–1164.

Spehlmann, R. The averaged electrical response to diffuse and to patterned light in the human. *Electroencephalography and Clinical Neurophysiology*, 1965, *19*, 560–569.

Sutton, S. The sensitivity of the evoked potential to psychological variables. *Electroencephalography and Clinical Neurophysiology*, 1971, *31*, 302.

Tepas, D., Guiteras, V., & Klingman, R. L. Variability of the human average evoked brain response to visual stimulation: A warning. *Electroencephalography and Clinical Neurophysiology*, 1974, *36*, 533–537.

Voigt, H. Die Aktualgenese in der psychologischen Diagnostik. *Psychologische Beiträge*, 1956, *2*, 586–636.

Voigt, H. Die Aktualgenese im Denkprozess. *Zeitschrift für experimentelle und angewandte Psychologie*, 1959, *6*, 496–507.

White, C. T., & Eason, R. G. Evoked cortical potential in relation to certain aspects of visual perception. *Psychological Monographs*, 1966, *80* (24, Whole No. 632).

Wiedel, K. H. *Untersuchungen zur persönlichkeitspsychologischen Fundierung von ästhetischer Praferenz fur visuelle Komplexität*. Unpublished doctoral dissertation, University of Trier, Faculty of Philosophy, 1974.

VII

WHERE SHOULD MICROGENETIC RESEARCH GO FROM HERE?

19

Four Views

Ulf Kragh

In attempting to link the historical impact of *Aktualgenese,* microgenesis, or perceptgenesis with present developments and future possibilities, I am aware of at least two important difficulties: the heterogeneity of the subject matter and the limitation of my own outlook.

Among those who performed the early *Aktualgenese* experiments, only a few were alive after the Second World War. The impact of American psychology, at the same time, grew overwhelming. These may have been two important reasons why *Aktualgenese* did not develop to an extent that matched its potentialities. Other reasons may have been the preference, after the war, for research that promised rapid practical return and the fact that *Aktualgenese* proceeded very little in the direction outlined by Krueger (1953), for example, from general psychology to the psychology of personality.

Werner (1956, 1957), although completely congenial with the genetic approach, never widened his theoretical frame of reference beyond that of general psychology proper. Although he viewed perception in general as a microprocess, he could not understand that it might reflect the historical development of one single person. The microgenetic approach at Clark University almost completely yielded ground to the sensory-tonic field theory. The very promising studies of microgenesis in abnormal subjects (Phillips & Framo, 1954) also seem to have stopped rather abruptly.

Concerning other approaches that are part of the historical background of present-day microgenetic and percept-genetic research, Dixon (1971) and other colleagues (Erdelyi, 1974; Silverman, 1980) have dealt with the themes of subliminal perception and of perceptual defense, and it seems that this field is being cultivated with renewed vigor. The Pötzl experiments, and those of Fischer (1954) and collaborators, seem to have remained restricted to the domain of dream research proper. Schilder (1951), in his paper "On the Development of Thoughts," put forward the idea that one fundamental characteristic of thought processes is recapitulation of ontogeneses, but his suggestions do not seem to have initiated much research.

Why have so many of these beginnings ended in blind alleys? I believe it necessary for a fruitful continuation of microgenetic research that we proceed toward an inclusive theory or model that could subsume manifold phenomena now under consideration. We need a comprehensive theoretical framework to enable us to integrate findings from the fields of general psychology, differential psychology, and the psychology of personality, normal and abnormal. The Lund group has actually tried to outline such a theoretical framework. Even though this framework has not been formulated to integrate all the new empirical findings presented in this volume, it may be helpful to recapitulate some of its basic notions.

1. Reversing the traditional stimulus–response scheme, the Lund group views the stimulus as the *final link* in a process of objectivation. This thinking was inspired by, among others, the neocriticists Natorp (1912) and Cassirer (1929), partly also by Scheerer (1931).

2. Tachistoscopic serial experiments of the late 1940s indicated that the pre-stages of perception might be considered as the equivalents of what is generally termed *associations*. This finding spoke in favor of the just-mentioned reversal of the stimulus–response scheme. It seemed that it might prove advantageous not to think of associations as being triggered by the so-called reproduction motif but as being the antecedents of it; in other words, associations might be defined as reconstructions of a perceptual microprocess.

3. The theoretical elaboration of the last-mentioned finding led to a reconceptualization of memory, including the break with the notions of memory traces (and the like) and of memory as an inert depository of images. Instead, memory might be viewed as an ever-ongoing microprocess. In this connection some efforts were also made to analyze the notion of mental time in the light of microprocesses.

4. In consequence of, and concomitant with, these new notions of memory, a model of personality in terms of the totality of microprocesses at each present moment could also be outlined. But it was not until later that the notion of a hierarchy of condensed meanings made possible some understanding of how the enormous amount of past experiences of one person can possibly be condensed into one single, conscious present.

5. Studying the effects of retesting on perceptgeneses, as well as the effects of using so-called simple stimuli, and frequently using compulsive people as subjects in experiments, the group began to reflect on the possibility that a great many concepts of general psychology were referring exclusively to mental formations of end-stage character. This might explain why marginal phenomena, or phenomena of pre-stage order, had shown up so rarely in general psychology.

6. Early findings of Smith (1949) indicated that the *developmental study* of afterimages could reveal intratwin consistencies in one-egg twins in contradistinction to the computation of *means*, and this inspired the study of serials in which each unit was looked upon as a unique link in a genetic process.

7. Findings of interserial consistencies within one subject, and serial consistencies between percept-genetic series, on the one hand, and the ontogenesis of the same subject, on the other hand, strongly reinforced the theoretical standpoint of a hierarchy of condensed meanings.

Looking to the future, some areas stand out as being particularly important:

1. The experimental study, the operational anchoring, and the possible validation of different concepts of different levels of abstraction in dynamic psychology, like those of structure, dynamics, the preconscious, the unconscious, and defense.

2. The study, in great detail, of a great many features of personality within a genetic and operational framework. Many special fields of personality should be opened to inquiry besides those already investigated to a modest extent, for example, the study of the body image and the self-representation, the vicissitudes of specific object relations, and so forth.

3. The investigation of the relationships between the results obtained in the

study of microprocesses like perceptgenesis, on the one hand, and other process approaches, on the other, in particular within the fields of perception and cognition.

4. The study of memory that discards the use of metaphors like "contiguity" (a spatial metaphor), "likeness" (a metaphor used by Plato), and "memory traces" (a metaphor used by Plato in *Menon* and used also in present-day neurophysiology). This may make possible a reformulation of some classical problems of the psychology of memory.

5. The analysis of the metatheoretical implications of a parallelism between ontogenesis and microgenesis and of the concept of *momentary personality*.

6. Practical applications in many areas already touched on in some of the preceding chapters. I may add, for example, the investigation of leadership by the tachistoscopic presentation of father-son pictures, the study of therapeutic effects, and other applied problems.

Gudmund Smith

I certainly agree with Kragh that we should try to proceed toward an inclusive model under which to subsume the empirical findings of microgenetic research. At the same time, I would like us to keep this model open to influences from other present-day research endeavors in psychology. There is no need to isolate microgenesis as a school of self-generating thinking.

More specifically, let me condense my views of how a microgenetic perspective may be applied to personality description and behavior:

1. To proceed from the present level of microgenetic research, we have to tackle problems concerning (a) the relations among our various types of operations (e.g., merogenetic vs. hologenetic, tachistoscopic vs. serial techniques) and (b) relations between these operations, on the one hand, and the extralaboratory functional reality on the other. This latter kind of inquiry may, above all, imply two things: (a) a continued analysis of the correspondence between the microgeneses unfolded in the laboratory and the alleged ultrashort processes behind everyday perception and (b) a continued attempt to relate microgenetic data to the broad dynamic concept of personality, as suggested by Kragh.

2. These commendable endeavors are not likely to be successful unless we pay more attention to theoretical issues, of which I have three in mind in particular: (a) How are physiological constructs to be exploited in relation to microgenetic formulations? Here I include both physiological variables like blood flow in gray matter and quasi-physiological constructs like *memory trace*. To succeed, we must beware of the naïve use of such constructs so common among psychologists. (b) How should personality be defined to fit the microgenetic approach? A great many constructs within the realm of personality would seem very ill-fitting, for example, trait concepts or concepts derived from personality inventories. (c) What precisely do we mean by the reflection in microgenesis of ontogenesis? Our present theorizing is often vague and seldom leads to testable questions.

Werner D. Froehlich

1. To provide for a better interpretation and understanding of the meaning of microgenesis, perceptgenesis, and visual thinking, I suggest the use of the criteria developed extensively in my Chapter 2: What does the *design represent* (e.g., figural

vs. realistic meaning); what kinds of *parallel processing* are involved; what kinds of *functional equivalents* at what level show their impact; and so on?

2. On the response side, *single-* versus *multiple-reference approaches* should be scrutinized, as Smith (Chap. 10) has also emphasized. I assume that the inclusion of *different levels* (verbal, behavioral, and psychophysiological) leads to a better understanding of the concept of *stages* that characterize the events during *response formation.*

3. With special reference to stages, it seems to be most challenging to compare developments in various paradigms with the *same* subjects.

4. The so-called reversed microgenesis, or disintegration technique, may provide information about the progression from stabilized to unstable conditions in perception and meaning assignment. These progressions, in my view, provide for additional insights on lower and higher level impacts and cognitive or perceptual plasticity under different task conditions. They also contribute to a better understanding of the second step in so-called metacontrast experiments.

5. The psychophysiological approach to investigation now seems to be ready for incorporation into cognitive psychology. This development may (a) open a way toward understanding functional shifts and state controls in the "internal milieu" that are basic to intake and rejection dimensions; (b) because of some identified mechanisms that control *effort* and that are strongly related to emotional feelings, provide a better understanding of the unbalancing arousal or clinical impact in microgenesis and cognitive functioning. What this implies is the need to deal with problems of situational and response stereotypes at both levels, the psychological and the physiological.

6. Special efforts, in my view, are necessary to find an explanatory foundation for the hologenetic kind of tasks. From a heuristic point of view, they open the door to hints about intuitive appraisals and reflexive, defensive, and other kinds of cognitive processing. From a scientific point of view, most obviously there is some surplus of meaning owing to broad analogies (supported by research on subliminal perception, psychophysics, perceptual defense, cognitive control, etc.) as well as to the reliance on self-reports. One of the critical issues is to compare in these paradigms responses to figural, neutral, realistic, and emotionally tuned stimuli in the same subjects in order to provide for some *individual base lines.*

7. Generally, in my view, there is some lack of communality in terms of the *tasks, task conditions, and response analyses* in microgenetic research. I therefore propose to develop in the years to come some standard questions that should be answered before starting new procedures quasi-intuitively. The following framework may perhaps provide for some attention to the problems mentioned:

a. What kinds of theoretical assumptions are made, for example, micro–macro correspondences, recapitulation, and subliminal impacts?
b. What are the theoretical or practical aims of the project, for example, assessment of information-integration mechanisms, diagnostics, and visual acuity?
c. What kinds of experimental techniques are used, for example, long-term presentation of one stimulus and visual thinking tasks, afterimages, serial tasks without or with progressively greater information available, merogenetic or hologenetic tasks, and backward-masking procedures?
d. What levels of measurement are used?

e. What stimuli and procedures are specified in pilot studies that lead to the special choice with regard to representativeness?

f. What level of control is there over situation and motivational impact of instructions, for example, using search- or observation-tuned sets, or ending a procedure either only when veridical perception is given or earlier?

g. What level of control is there over responses? Special problems with verbal reports could eventually be solved by combinations of ratings, use of semantic differentials, or the Kreitler scheme of meaning and cue relationships (see (Chap. 13). The amount of sophistication at this level, however, interferes with the time-frame limitations.

h. What rationale is there for the use of screening variables, for example, questionnaires to assess personality or attitude variables? To what level of response do they relate logically or in terms of models?

i. What kinds of baseline measures are used to define changes and stages?

8. The last and most general issue seems to be that of *information exchange* in microgenetic process research and related issues. I would like to suggest that one place, either Mainz or Lund, become some sort of a repository where one could get information and overviews on microgenesis and related issues.

Juris G. Draguns

The chapters of this volume testify to the vitality of research on microgenesis and to the variety of approaches to its investigation. I have tried to discern some common themes in these heterogeneous approaches and to identify questions and problems that, in light of the evidence presented in this volume, need to be confronted and answered:

1. Is there one model of microgenesis or are there two or more independent ones? Werner's (1948) classic position would appear to favor one prototypic sequence to which all microgenetic progressions conform as special cases of the orthogenetic principle applicable to all kinds of development. In this view, microgenesis proceeds from diffuseness through fragmentation to integration. But we are also aware of what our German colleagues have called *merogenous* microgenesis—one that starts with apprehension of details that are later fused into an integrated whole. Is this simply a case of starting with Stage 2 of microgenesis, or are we dealing with a parallel and different kind of sequence? To what extent are these varieties determined by stimuli, people, contexts, and instructions? Research designs are available to extricate the additive and interactive impacts of these variables, but as yet they have not been applied to the resolution of this problem—one that investigators of microgenesis would do well to tackle individually and collectively.

2. Similarly basic are some questions broached by Hans Kreitler: What is the scope of microgenesis, and what are its outer limits? Does microgenesis encompass all process-oriented approaches to the study of perception, cognition, and related domains of functioning? Does the concept of microgenesis extend to as global a progression as psychoanalysis, in which insights are gradually built and assimilated? My provisional answer is that the term *microgenesis* is properly restricted to fully observable or reportable sequences of events that do not have to be reconstructed. This excludes a great many psychological processes, couched in information theory

or physiological terms, that are inferred. As far as such extended progressions as psychoanalysis are concerned, these processes of gradual self-examination and self-realization cannot be fitted into, or reduced to, a microgenetic sequence. What takes place in the psychoanalytic experience, however, is a succession of a great many microgeneses as the analyzand comes to grips with various bits of her or his experienced and recaptured past. Psychoanalysts agree that this is an uneven and difficult process extended in observable time. Sandler and Joffe (1967) have gone further than anyone else in explicitly integrating these observations with the concept of microgenesis and in providing illustrations of microgenetic events in the psychoanalytic process. Their observations may well serve as a foundation for a more systematic and continuous integration of the microgenetic approach with the psychoanalytic process. Such a merger would benefit both sides. It would contribute toward the systematic observation and documentation of the conduct of psychoanalysis on the one hand, and it would provide valuable instances of microgenesis in a realistic, quasi-naturalistic situation on the other hand. In particular, such observations would contribute information on microgenesis of recollection, a subject that has seen little systematic investigation.

To return to the more general problem of the scope to which the term *microgenesis* legitimately extends, there is nothing to prevent the concurrent and coordinated research on phenomenal and conceptual sequences. Microgenetic observation may provide raw material for theoretical model building on progressions not directly observable; existing models of the information-processing or physiological [e.g., Hebb's (1951) "conceptual nervous system"] variety can be brought to bear on actual microgenetic sequences.

3. A major problem concerns the role of rational-logical processes in microgenesis as well as that of what might be called *organic growth*. Classical microgenetic literature has emphasized development to the neglect of cognition and learning, which enter into and shape the microgenetic act. Among the contributors to this volume, the Kreitlers (Chapter 13) perhaps go furthest in highlighting the rational aspects of microgenesis and in contributing evidence on how the various attributes of meaning are used and integrated in the course of microgenesis. This approach is quite compatible, despite differences in conceptualization and terminology, with the contribution of Francès (Chap. 14), who pointed out the role of differentiation and recognition—differentiation, in his studies, being subordinate and subsequent to recognition, as it logically should be. But what about those instances where differentiation outstrips recognition, where it leads us into blind alleys that delay, prevent, or abort recognition?

Among contemporary investigators, the Lund (and Oslo) group has gone furthest in investigating these states of affairs and in developing methods that bring to the fore the uneven growthlike character of object and meaning attainment. They have worked with the amauroscope (Westerlundh), the DMT (Kragh), and several other techniques (Andersson, Smith, and their collaborators). A general conclusion from this work is that the genesis of percepts is deflected and made uneven, uneconomical, and saltatory as the stimuli become complex, personally relevant, conflict arousing, and threatening.

The results obtained within both of these traditions of microgenetic investigation are equally valid. What they highlight is that two adaptive tasks come into play and acquire differential weight and significance depending on the nature of the microgenetic sequence. The nature of the task and stimulus can be so arranged as to emphasize adaptation to reality or, conversely, coping with one's own wishes and fears. What perhaps limited some of the personality correlates in the study by Lastowski (Chap. 7) was the scientific conscientiousness with which she restricted the scope for individual structuring of microgenetic stimuli. Once one does that and, explicitly or implicitly, communicates this set to the subjects, they become very much attuned to reality, very logical, and perceptive of various kinds of stimulus features. Under these circumstances, they come to approximate optimal information extraction from suboptimally presented stimuli. The Lund group, on the other hand, has, over two decades or more, worked on creating conditions in which optimal information extraction is obstructed or made exceedingly difficult.

These two current trends are, I believe, historically traceable to two fountainheads of microgenetic investigation. Werner was, as is well known, overridingly concerned with the natural growth of stimuli; and to a less extreme degree, so was Sander. The third pioneer of microgenetic investigation, Gemelli (1928), was the first to emphasize rational elements in microgenetic progression, thereby anticipating the more recent development of hypothesis theory by Bruner (1957). What remains to be done is to bring the rational and the *personal*—for lack of a better term—aspects of microgenesis into relation to each other by varying the content of the stimuli (as has been done by Lastowski) as well as the instructions for the task. Once this is done, we will be able to answer the question: Under what circumstances, precisely, is microgenesis optimally directed toward object attainment or toward a variety of self-protective ends?

4. Is microgenesis a continuous process of information acquisition, or is it a succession of several stages? Froehlich (Chap. 2) has stressed the succession of stages as a defining characteristic of microgenesis, and indeed it has been so regarded in traditional microgenetic investigations. There are, however, approaches to studying the continuous growth of information in gradually presented stimuli, exemplified, in particular, by information-processing investigations. In this volume, Rimoldi (Chap. 15) has shown the possibility of studying various kinds of complex conceptual processes in a continuous way. Can his approach be applied to the more traditional study on the genesis of percepts? *Stage* is a concept that is primarily in the eye of the beholder. It is incumbent on us to specify what constitutes a stage and to apply it to the phenomena of various kinds of microgenesis. Ewert has broached this question in his Chapter 3. What is empirically observable is a certain kind of discontinuity; people change their exploration of emerging stimuli in a sudden and saltatory fashion. The application of the notion of stage or phase to this process is a conceptual convenience of varying degrees of utility or cost. We should assess its utility versus its cost and should then make our decision on the advantages and disadvantages of retaining the stage concept. My own preliminary opinion is that the stage concept in microgenesis is a fruitful one and that we have not exhausted its fruitfulness, provided that we keep in mind that the stage is something *we* bring to bear on microgenesis rather than something that naturally and automatically occurs in its course.

5. Individual differences in microgenesis have been alluded to earlier in these remarks and constitute the principal theme of several chapters. The focus of inquiry has been on personality differences; to a lesser extent, age differences have also been investigated through microgenesis. It should be kept in mind, however, that, as the list of authors in this volume amply demonstrates, microgenesis has become an international enterprise. Microgenetic research is pursued on at least

four continents and in numerous countries. Some of the findings will turn out to be specific to the cultures in which they have been obtained, but we do not as yet know which ones. The cross-cultural psychology of perception is an active and expanding undertaking, as the review by Deręgowski (1980) amply demonstrates. Cross-cultural research has not as yet been extended to perceptual or cognitive processes. It is plausible to expect that, just as personality is reflected in various aspects of microgenesis, culturally mediated and shared experience would affect both the style and content of responses during microgenesis. Pursuit of this lead is well worth undertaking not just as an atheoretical shot in the dark, but on the basis of hypotheses derived from perceptual research across cultures or based on the knowledge of cultures involved in the comparison. It is worth noting that Dasen (1977), the foremost Piagetian cross-cultural investigator, has explicitly referred to *Aktualgenese* in attempting to explain the vary rapid acquisition of the principles of conservation in the course of experimental demonstrations by some illiterate non-Western subjects.

6. The applied aspects of microgenesis remain to be discussed. The use of microgenetic techniques in personality assessment has a long history and includes some procedures developed by Sander and recently discussed by Semeonoff (1976). On the contemporary scene it is the Swedish researchers who have contributed the most systematic effort toward this goal, an effort that includes the use of their various techniques in both clinical diagnosis and personnel selection. I wonder, however, about other practical applications of microgenetic techniques and findings. What I have in mind in particular is the use of microgenetic procedures in the training and rehabilitation of learning disabilities and cognitive disorders, whether organically or functionally based. This idea is in part inspired by Hans Kreitler's account (Kreitler & Kreitler, 1977) of the use of the cognitive orientation scheme in the rehabilitation of brain-injured veterans in Israel. Use of microgenetic techniques in such contexts is very much in line with the current emphasis on focused and directed behavior change as opposed to the open-ended techniques exemplified by traditional verbal psychotherapy.

7. The question of fitting microgenetic findings into a comprehensive theoretical framework has assumed urgency. Two such frameworks are prominent in the chapters of this volume: the psychoanalytic one, which constitutes the basic conceptual scheme by which the Lund University investigators abide, and the new formulation of cognitive orientation, as represented by the Kreitlers. Certainly, more work generated by, and fitting into, these explanatory schemes is to be encouraged. In addition to such work, there is room for exploring the usefulness of additional theoretical positions. One candidate for such an examination is social learning theory as formulated by Bandura (1969) and as extended by a number of recent contributors (Mahoney, 1974; Meichenbaum, 1977) to the phenomena of mediation and cognition. Without implying a final judgment on the usefulness of this theoretical framework, I would suggest that there are some points of contact between these newer attempts to account for the planned and future-oriented aspects of our behavior and the phenomena of microgenesis. These remain to be explored and pursued.

8. Finally, there is the question of terminology. In this book, the terms *Aktualgenese, microgenesis,* and *perceptgenesis* have been used as equivalents. Which of them is best and deserves to be universally accepted in English-language usage? Are there subtle shades of meaning expressed by each that would justify its being

preserved? What about English-language equivalents for the German terms *hologen* and *merogen*, which refer to whole- and detail-oriented microgenesis, respectively? Is there a need for these terms? Last, inasmuch as one of the recurring themes of this volume has been that not all process analysis is microgenetic, is there an advantage to coining a new term to signify these other process-oriented approaches in order to differentiate them from the related, yet distinct, phenomenon of microgenesis?

REFERENCES

Bandura, A. *Principles of behavior modification.* New York: Holt, 1969.

Bruner, J. S. On perceptual readiness. *Psychological Review, 1957, 64,* 132–152.

Cassirer, E. *Philosophie der symbolischen Formen (Pt. III), Phänomenologie der Erkenntnis.* Berlin: Springer, 1929.

Dasen, P. R. Cross-cultural cognitive development: The cultural aspects of Piaget's theory. In L. L. Adler (Ed.), Issues in cross-cultural research. *Annals of the New York Academy of Sciences, 1977, 285,* 664–675.

Deręgowski, J. B. Perception. In H. C. Triandis & W. J. Lonner (Eds.), *Handbook of cross-cultural psychology* (Vol. 3), *Basic processes.* Boston: Allyn & Bacon, 1980.

Dixon, N. F. *Subliminal perception: The nature of a controversy.* London: McGraw-Hill, 1971.

Erdelyi, M. H. A new look at the New Look: Perceptual defense and vigilance. *Psychological Review, 1974, 81,* 1–25.

Fischer, C. Dreams and perception. The role of preconscious and primary modes of perception in dream formation. *Journal of the American Psychoanalytic Association, 1954, 2,* 389–445.

Gemelli, A. Contributo allo studio della percezione: IV. Il comparire e lo scomparire delle forme. *Contributi di Laboratorio della Psicologia e Biologia, Università di Sacro Cuore,* 1928, *3,* 385–436.

Hebb, D. O. The role of neurological ideas in psychology. *Journal of Personality, 1951, 20,* 39–55.

Kreitler, H. & Kreitler, S. *Cognitive habilitation by meaning of aphasic patients and imbecile children.* Invited address, Johannes Gutenberg University, Mainz, June 1977.

Krueger, F. *Zür Philosophie und Psychologie der Ganzheit.* Berlin: Springer, 1953.

Mahoney, M. J. *Cognition and behavior modification.* Cambridge, Mass.: Ballinger, 1974.

Meichenbaum, D. *Cognitive behavior modification.* New York: Plenum, 1977.

Natorp, P. *Allgemeine Psychologie nach kritischer Methode (Book 1), Objekt und Methode der Psychologie.* Tübingen: Mohr, 1912.

Phillips, L. & Framo, J. Developmental theory applied to normal and psychopathological perception. *Journal of Personality, 1954, 22,* 464–474.

Sandler, J., & Joffe, W. G. The tendency to persistence in psychological function and development: With special reference to fixation and regression. *Bulletin of the Menninger Clinic,* 1967, *31,* 257–271.

Scheerer, M. *Die Lehre von der Gestalt, ihre Methode und ihr psychologischer Gegenstand.* Leipzig: Barth, 1931.

Schilder, P. On the development of thoughts. In D. Rapaport (Ed.), *Organization and pathology of thought.* New York: Columbia University Press, 1951.

Semeonoff, B. *Projective techniques.* New York: Wiley, 1976.

Silverman, L. H. A comprehensive report of studies using the subliminal psychodynamic activation method. *Psychological Research Bulletin* (Lund University), 1980, *20,* No. 3.

Smith, G. J. W. Psychological studies in twin differences with reference to afterimage and eidetic phenomena as well as more general personality characteristics. *Studia psychologica et paedagogica* (Second series, *Investigationes,* No. 3). Lund: Gleerups, 1949.

Werner, H. *Comparative psychology of mental development* (2nd ed.). New York: International Universities, 1948.

Werner, H. Microgenesis and aphasia. *Journal of Abnormal and Social Psychology, 1956, 52,* 347–353.

Werner, H. The concept of development from a comparative and organismic point of view. In D. B. Harris (Ed.), *The concept of development.* Minneapolis: University of Minnesota Press, 1957.

Author Index

Subject Index